＜＞

FREEDOM AND RELIGION
IN THE NINETEENTH CENTURY

THE MAKING OF MODERN FREEDOM

General Editor: R. W. Davis
Center for the History of Freedom
Washington University in St. Louis

FREEDOM AND RELIGION
IN THE NINETEENTH
CENTURY

≺ ≻

Edited by Richard Helmstadter

STANFORD UNIVERSITY PRESS
STANFORD, CALIFORNIA
1997

Stanford University Press
Stanford, California
© 1997 by the Board of Trustees of the
Leland Stanford Junior University
Printed in the United States of America

CIP data appear at the end of the book

Stanford University Press publications
are distributed exclusively by
Stanford University Press within the
United States, Canada, Mexico, and
Central America; they are distributed
exclusively by Cambridge University
Press throughout the rest
of the world.

<>

Series Foreword

THE STARTLING AND moving events that swept from China to
Eastern Europe to Latin America and South Africa at the end of
the 1980s, followed closely by similar events and the subsequent dissolution of what used to be the Soviet Union, formed one of those
great historic occasions when calls for freedom, rights, and democracy echoed through political upheaval. A clear-eyed look at any of
those conjunctions—in 1776 and 1789, in 1848 and 1918, as well as
in 1989—reminds us that freedom, liberty, rights, and democracy are
words into which many different and conflicting hopes have been
read. The language of freedom—or liberty, which is interchangeable
with freedom most of the time—is inherently difficult. It carried
vastly different meanings in the classical world and in medieval Europe from those of modern understanding, though thinkers in later
ages sometimes eagerly assimilated the older meanings to their own
circumstances and purposes.

A new kind of freedom, which we have here called modern, gradually disentangles itself from old contexts in Europe, beginning first
in England in the early seventeenth century and then, with many
confusions, denials, reversals, and cross-purposes, elsewhere in Europe and the world. A large-scale history of this modern, conceptually distinct, idea of freedom is now beyond the ambition of any
one scholar, however learned. This collaborative enterprise, tenta-
tive though it must be, is an effort to fill the gap.

We could not take into account all the varied meanings that freedom and liberty have carried in the modern world. We have, for example, ruled out extended attention to what some political philosophers have called "positive freedom," in the sense of self-realization
of the individual; nor could we, even in a series as large as this, cope
with the enormous implications of the four freedoms invoked by

Franklin D. Roosevelt in 1941. Freedom of speech and freedom of the press will have their place in the narrative that follows, certainly, but not the boundless calls for freedom from want and freedom from fear.

We use freedom in the traditional and restricted sense of civil and political liberty—freedom of religion, freedom of speech and assembly, freedom of the individual from arbitrary and capricious authority over persons or property, freedom to produce and to exchange goods and services, and the freedom to take part in the political process that shapes people's destiny. In no major part of the world over the past few years have aspirations for those freedoms not been at least powerfully expressed; and in most places where they did not exist, strong measures have been taken—not always successfully—to attain them.

The history we trace was not a steady march toward the present or the fulfillment of some cosmic necessity. Modern freedom had its roots in specific circumstances in early modern Europe, despite the unpromising and even hostile characteristics of the larger society and culture. From these narrow and often selfishly motivated beginnings, modern freedom came to be realized in later times, constrained by old traditions and institutions hard to move, and driven by ambition as well as idealism: everywhere the growth of freedom has been *sui generis*. But to understand these unique developments fully, we must first try to see them against the making of modern freedom as a whole.

The Making of Modern Freedom grows out of a continuing series of conferences and institutes held at the Center for the History of Freedom at Washington University in St. Louis. Professor J. H. Hexter was the founder and, for three years, the resident gadfly of the Center. His contribution is gratefully recalled by all his colleagues.

R.W.D.

Contents

≪ ≫

Acknowledgments

Several foundations have generously supported The Making of Modern Freedom series, and one in particular has supported this volume. Liberty Fund of Indianapolis sponsored the autumn 1995 conference where the volume was widely discussed and put into final shape. We are grateful for all the support we have received, including the strong backing we have always enjoyed from Washington University.

R.W.D.

CONTRIBUTORS

Simon Collier
Vanderbilt University

Jeffrey Cox
University of Iowa

J. P. Ellens
Redeemer College

Raymond Grew
University of Michigan

Nathan O. Hatch
The University of Notre Dame

Richard Helmstadter
University of Toronto

David C. Itzkowitz
Macalaster College

C. T. McIntire
University of Toronto

Ronald J. Ross
University of Wisconsin, Milwaukee

Frank M. Turner
Yale University

R. K. Webb
*University of Maryland,
Baltimore County (Emeritus)*

≺≻

FREEDOM AND RELIGION
IN THE NINETEENTH CENTURY

≺ ≻

Introduction

RICHARD HELMSTADTER

I N HIS INTRODUCTION to *Parliament and Liberty: From the Reign of Elizabeth to the English Civil War*, the first volume in *The Making of Modern Freedom*, J. H. Hexter nails his colors to the mast and tells us that the story of the coming of modern freedom had its formal beginning with the Petition of Right of 1628. Hexter sees the petition, with its declaration of specific rights of Englishmen against imprisonment without just cause and taxation without consent of Parliament, as "the decisive first step in the direction of modern freedom, of liberty as we know it in our world." That first step, he goes on to say, was imperiled by the Protestant Reformation of the sixteenth century, which inaugurated two centuries of religious warfare. The Reformation also, however, opened the door to the emergence of religious liberty, an important component of modern freedom, and in a sense its precursor. Hexter's definition of religious liberty is clear. "Freedom to choose among the religions on offer, or to choose none, or to make up one's own," he writes, "is a liberty common to all the inhabitants of the West today." For Hexter, modern religious liberty has its roots in the Reformation and the religious and political turmoil that followed in the breakup of what we might call the medieval settlement. This places him in a powerful liberal tradition that flows from the seventeenth century, reaches its apogee in the nineteenth century, particularly in the English-speaking world, and continues to have strength in our own day.

Hexter distinguishes sharply between medieval liberties, or privileges, and modern freedom. Medieval liberties were formally defined privileges granted by monarchs to specific individuals or corporations and protected by the law. These liberties, of which there were multitudinous sorts, set the possessors apart from others and gave them privileged positions in society. Modern freedom, on the other hand, he sees as general and democratic. Its ideal is universality. Formal, legal privileges are anathema to modern freedom. Its aspiration and goal is the largest possible degree of individual liberty that is consistent with the public good. This idea of liberty has inspired men and women in Europe and the Americas for many generations, and it continues to do so.

Hexter's definitions of modern freedom and religious liberty, and his sense of their origins, are by no means unusual or idiosyncratic. Attention is drawn to them here because the authors of the chapters that make up this volume take up different positions and give their discussions of religious liberty in the nineteenth-century West a decidedly different coloration. It would be incorrect to suggest that they write off Hexter's vision of liberty as entirely wrong, or advance visions of their own that are comprehensively antagonistic to his. None of the authors in this volume does so. The chapters are pragmatic revisions, not attacks, and each contributor takes seriously that which he revises, even when the revisions are major.

Several of the authors in this volume use the metaphor of the "master narrative" in describing the view of the history of religious liberty that they wish to revise. A master narrative is a version of history that has gained sufficiently broad acceptance that it establishes with some authority the context and general outline of its subject. In the case of religious liberty, there is clearly a dominant master narrative that continues to have power among both scholars and the generally educated public. It is a liberal narrative, using liberal in the sense that would be understood in the time of John Stuart Mill, Gladstone, and Cavour. It is a vision that was fully formed in the nineteenth century when it resonated with major political and cultural issues of that day. During the nineteenth century this historical view captured the imagination of liberals throughout the Western world, in Catholic countries as well as in Protestant.

Put in bare, skeletal terms, without the qualifications, ironies, and subtleties that sophisticated narrators have incorporated, the liberal master narrative of religious liberty runs thusly. In the medieval period the Church oppressed the people. The Church educated only the clergy, and their education was limited. This was a technique for maintaining power. Superstition was widespread. Poverty was the situation of most men and women, while the Church grew rich. The Church used Latin as its language in order to keep the people uninformed. The Bible was not accessible to the general populace. Roman Catholicism constituted a religious monopoly. There was no freedom of religious choice; there was no religious liberty. A few heroes, John Wycliffe chief among them, challenged the corrupt Church, but without lasting success.

Eventually the corruption of the Church became too great for honest men to continue longer in subjection. Martin Luther, in an act of great courage, began the Protestant Reformation. Other Protestant leaders soon appeared to challenge the tottering monopoly of Roman Catholicism. In Protestant lands the Bible was translated into the vernacular and the printing press made wide distribution possible. Liturgies were changed to draw the people more intimately into worship. Facilities for education were improved. Men started to think for themselves and began the long process of throwing off superstition in their quest for knowledge that contained an element of liberty, knowledge that was based on something other than institutional authority.

As part of the process of the Reformation, some men of power were converted to Protestantism and religious wars ensued. For nearly two centuries the framework of European diplomacy was set by the violent opposition of Protestants and Catholics. Protestantism helped define the national identities of progressive northern European countries, especially Holland and England, while the Catholic peoples of the south, especially Spain and Italy, languished in comparative darkness. Spain in the sixteenth century and France in the seventeenth emerged as the leading powers in the Catholic world. The near-miracle of the English defeat of the Spanish Armada, the heroic revolt of the Dutch republic against tyrannical Spain, and Marlborough's victories over absolutist France became celebrated emblems of Protestant nationalism that continued to have power through the nineteenth century and into the twentieth.

Although torn apart by internal conflict, England, in the seventeenth century, emerged as the leader of the Protestant world. In the midst of the great constitutional conflicts of the seventeenth century, a variety of Protestant sects emerged. Modern religious pluralism was prefigured, and the language of religious liberty began to flow. Within England, the Toleration Act of 1689, one of the celebrated milestones on the way to religious liberty, eventually created a situation of relative religious peace.

In France, for centuries the natural enemy of England, a very different history unfolded. There, at the end of the sixteenth century, King Henry IV, forced by political imperatives and supported by a recently developed theory of absolute monarchy, attempted to settle religious division by promulgating the Edict of Nantes in 1598. This edict, which eventually achieved a glorious status in the history of religious liberty, gave to French Protestants the right to practice their own religion in specific Huguenot towns. Nearly a century later, with the administrative machinery of absolutism much better established, Louis XIV, in a position of power much more stable than that of Henry IV, revoked the Edict of Nantes. The revocation has a dark place in the master narrative of religious liberty that overshadows the bright place held by its promulgation. For liberal Protestants the revocation came to sum up and symbolize the tyrannical tendencies of Catholic absolutism.

During the century or so following the Toleration Act of 1689, England enjoyed a period of relative religious peace, at least in comparison with the previous century. Voltaire, focusing on the plurality of religious sects that flourished in a condition of official toleration, professed to see in England the very model of religious freedom, even though Roman Catholics were barely tolerated and Protestant Dissenters suffered under a range of civil disabilities. Nineteenth-century British liberals, and twentieth-century historians of Britain, tend to emphasize the distinction between toleration and liberty and look less favorably than did Voltaire at the level of religious liberty in Hanoverian England. Voltaire's exaggerated respect for English freedoms is instructive, however, for it calls attention to the fact that, generally speaking, issues of religious freedom were addressed in English politics much earlier than they were on the Continent or in Latin America. This is certainly Professor Hexter's conviction. It is a theme that runs through *The Making of Modern Freedom*, and it is supported, directly or indirectly, by most of the contributors to this volume. After the removal of the most burdensome legal disabilities on British Protestant Dissenters and Roman Catholics in 1828 and 1829, European and Latin American liberals, encouraged by progressive British politics and British economic success, considered the British pluralistic religious settlement the way of the future, even though England and Scotland retained their legally established churches and the Anglican Church in Ireland was not disestablished until 1868.

The future arrived even earlier in North America. Before the Toleration Act and after, Protestant Dissenters were among the many peoples who migrated to the New World (Puritans in New England and Quakers in Pennsylvania loom largest in the liberal myth), and there religious liberty flowered even more vigorously than it did in the mother country. The language of religious liberty was woven into the rhetoric of the American Revolution. Religious liberty came to be enshrined as one of the ideals of the new nation, and the separation of church and state was institutionalized in the first amendment to the Constitution: "Congress shall make no law respecting the establishment of religion, or prohibiting the free exercise thereof." The American Revolution helped spur the ambition of Protestant Dissenters in England where they became more aggressive in their campaign for a fuller measure of toleration from the state. Eventually the more radical among them tried to bring the American religious settlement to the United Kingdom through the disestablishment and disendowment of the British state churches.

Eighteenth-century France was a land with very different sorts of religious liberties that, by and large, are not fully recognized in the liberal myth of the history of religious freedom. The Calvinists in the reformed church in the Huguenot country of Bordeaux and the Lutherans in Alsace-Lorraine were not vigorously or systematically persecuted. But they had no security of liberty. The Church of France, the established Catholic Church, enjoyed its Gallican liberties which helped define the Church in its relations with the pope and the French state. These defining and empowering liberties, immensely important though they were for the Church, had little to do with the freedom of individuals to choose and practice the religion they preferred, and it is this freedom of choice that constitutes the core of religious liberty in the liberal myth. The Church of France had a theoretical religious monopoly in the kingdom, even though it could not assert that monopoly in practice; therefore, at least in theory, those who admired the religious settlements in the United States and England saw little religious freedom in eighteenth-century France. The monopoly of the Church of France was broken by the Revolution. In the name of liberty (and equality and fraternity) the Revolution transformed the institutions of the ancien regime. After several radical experiments, a new Church of France was officially recognized by Napoleon with the concurrence of the pope. At almost the same time, Napoleon put the two major Protestant churches, and eventually Judaism as well, on a similar constitutional footing. From the restoration of the monarchy in 1815 until the separation of church and state in 1905, the history of religious liberty was the history of the struggle between the generally progressive state and the Church, a struggle in which the state, increasingly dominated by anticlericals, was ultimately victorious.

In nineteenth-century England another model prevailed. There Protestant Dissenters, allied at times with Catholics and Jews, pressed the case first for greater toleration, and then, after toleration was basically accomplished in 1828 and 1829, the case for equality of privilege with the Church of England. The progress of religious liberty was peaceful, carried on step by step through an increasingly liberal and democratic political apparatus. In England religious freedom was closely associated with emerging democracy, with freedom of trade, with the growth of cities, and, at least by liberals, with modernity, prosperity, and progress.

Even though the modern nation state is to a large degree a liberal creation, liberals throughout the West in the nineteenth century frequently saw liberty as imperiled by the state. In the liberal context, liberty was generally conceived in individualistic terms. Liberty of religion was conceived as the liberty of individuals to choose among faiths, or to choose none. Man versus the state was a binary opposition that resonated among liberals. Established churches, therefore, according to the liberal narrative, were everywhere suspected enemies of freedom of religion. This was the view of voluntarist Protestant Dissenters in England, of anticlericals on the Continent and in Latin America. It became a point of pride among Americans that their constitution enshrined religious liberty, and that the United States was alone among the great nineteenth-century states in having no established church. Religious liberty was equated with the separation of church and state.

The liberal mind of the nineteenth century associated the Catholic Church with the ancien regime, with aristocracy and peasantry and the uninformed, slow-moving world of the countryside. The Catholic Church was also identified as the enemy of modern liberal nation states. The international character of papal authority, the rise of ultramontanism, and the temporal power for the first two thirds of the century made the Church seem the enemy of nationalism. Protestantism, individualism, economic growth, and progressive politics seemed to go hand in hand. The opposition of the Catholic Church to the central features of the modernizing world, and the inevitable decline of the power and influence of such a retrograde force, constituted one of the central elements of the liberal master narrative of the coming of religious liberty. A dark side of this bundle of Protestant ideas, this black legend, about the Catholic Church is the unwitting support it provided for more elemental, more personal, more unthinking antagonism and intolerance that sometimes flared into brutal violence. In Britain, in the United States, in Prussia during the Kulturkampf, the dominant Protestant majority, for a variety of reasons, identified Catholics as the embodiment of the Other, and Catholics were treated in ways that powerfully contradicted the official Protestant vision of religious liberty.

There is a final twist to this master narrative, originating in the nineteenth century and developed in the twentieth. The glorification of Protestantism was stretched by advanced liberals and anticlericals to include secularism and free thought. Indeed, secularization, in the sense of putting the secular aspects of life at the center and marginalizing religion, has been fitted into the master narrative as a kind of extension of Protestantism, progress, and modernization. To see the decline of religion and the secularization of society as inevitable, was, for some in the later nineteenth century, the logical postscript to the narrative in which liberalism and religious freedom are seen as predestined goals in the progress of mankind. Freedom of religion leads to freedom of thought and opinion. Science plays a role here that has not yet been mentioned. Science, of course, is generally seen as on the side of progress. Science is the enemy of superstition. Science is the clear-eyed enemy of the Roman Catholic Church, with its miracles and mummeries of a previous era. The Catholic Church is the enemy of science, with Galileo the great illustration. With only minor adjustments, Protestantism could be substituted for science in the above four sentences. This substitution is in easy harmony with the liberal narrative. It is, however, also possible to substitute the word religion for Catholicism, and to cast religion generally into the narrative as marking a mere stage in the development of civili-

zation, a stage in which faith and credulity played a large role because reason was not yet sufficiently advanced. This vision, associated with Auguste Comte and freethinking liberals of the nineteenth
century, has, in a multitude of formulations, become a commonplace
of our time. Protestantism, in this twist, is a revision of Catholicism,
but only a revision. Secularization is the inevitable next step, and
science carries a flag in the onward march.

This liberal master narrative is the product of a great tradition in
politics and political philosophy and in the writing of history. John
Stuart Mill is among its proponents, as are T. B. Macaulay, S. R.
Gardiner, Francis Parkman, G. M. Trevelyan, and Henry Steele Com-
mager, to name only a few who wrote in English. Underlying this
narrative is a noble dream, liberty for every person, guaranteed by
democratic nation states that promote social progress through not
interfering with those broadly defined areas of life, including religion, that are properly the preserve of free individuals.

At the end of the twentieth century it has become clear that religious liberty requires a more comprehensive definition than it was
accorded in the nineteenth-century liberal vision. The writing of religious history is flourishing, and historians of religion have pushed
back the boundaries of their subject. While politics and theology are
not neglected, they no longer dominate the writing of religious history as they once did. Social and cultural concerns proliferate, and
historians of religion turn their attention to the broad range of human activities that are penetrated and affected by religion.

As the definition of religious liberty becomes broader and more
refined, its history becomes more inclusive, more subtle, and more
complex. In no area is this more evident than in the question of
gender. Among Jews and Christians alike, and across the denominational and factional spectrum from Protestant evangelicalism to
ultramontane Catholicism, the place of religion in home life became more pronounced, and religion played an important part in reshaping popular ideas about gender roles. At the same time that
the churches laid emphasis on the confined domestic sphere as the
ideal context for the lives of girls and women, the increasing participation of women in the lives of the churches opened the door for
women to take part in public life. There was an immense increase
in church organizations of many sorts in the nineteenth century,
and, partly because of the ecclesiastical support for the idea of sepa-

rate spheres for men and women, many new opportunities were opened for women to participate in organized groups of their own. These ranged from popular, sometimes informal, devotional groups, through associations directed toward a wide variety of activities, including charity, the social life of the congregation, training the young, moral reform, and missions at home and abroad. The liturgical revival helped to encourage new religious orders for women among the Catholics and Anglo-Catholics. The churches encouraged women to become professional teachers, missionaries, and nurses. Far removed from the constitutional, legal definition of religious liberty, the changing place of religion in the lives of women in the nineteenth century offers an example relevant to liberty that belongs in the history of religious liberty. While none of the contributors to this volume has chosen to concentrate on this theme, its importance must be acknowledged here.

Several contributors do give attention to the place of religion in the creation and preservation of cultural and ethnic identity. In the past, religion and ethnic identity has been treated as a constitutional question, a matter of minority rights. In this volume, David Itzkowitz shows how the relations of cultural, ethnic, and religious identities created problems for nineteenth-century Jews that ran far beyond the scope of legal toleration. Nathan Hatch argues that the fact of multi-culturalism and ethnic diversity in eighteenth- and nineteenth-century America was the fundamental force that determined the constitutional position on religious liberty, while Thomas McIntire maintains that the constitutional positions of the churches in nineteenth-century France helped maintain multi-culturalism. Questions of ethnic identity, with religion an important signifier, raised a multitude of problems, including practical political problems, in nineteenth-century Europe and North America. Jeffrey Cox demonstrates that for missionaries, particularly the most sensitive and perceptive among them, questions of religion and ethnic identity posed insuperable intellectual and moral dilemmas.

The important distinction between individual and corporate religious liberty is addressed in this volume. In the liberal tradition, individual religious liberty tended to be defined in relation to the supposed tyranny of the Catholic Church. For the Protestant churches, the liberal stress was on the corporate liberty of the denomination or congregation. Individual liberty, of course, was in fact an issue in

every religious organization. Organizations that had achieved toleration, or corporate liberty, from the state might deny religious liberty to their members. This might be done formally or informally.
Churches everywhere imposed standards of belief, practice, and behavior on their clergy and their adherents. They attempted to enforce
these standards through an arsenal of sanctions ranging from legal
action against heretics through excommunication to social disappro-
bation. Pastors, priests, and lay persons frequently found their freedom to do or think as they pleased curtailed by the authority of their
churches. Particular interpretations of the Bible might be mandated
or disallowed; the dress of the clergy, or even the laity, might be regulated; the theater or other areas of cultural life might be declared out
of bounds; various foods and drinks might be forbidden; Sabbath observance might be defined; sexual behavior might be dictated; any
area of life might be touched. It may seem a paradox that it was in
the United States, the land of religious liberty, that personal liberties
were most blatantly violated by sects, such as the Mormons, who
tyrannized their followers.

On the other hand, generally speaking, the cultural values and be-
havioral ideals of the main-line Protestant churches were in harmony
with the dominant values of their times and places. For them, the
vast majority of the conflicts between individual liberty and churchly
authority went unnoticed by more than the persons involved. These
conflicts constitute, nonetheless, evidence for the history of freedom,
and a subject that merits further exploration. In Britain, and a little
later in the United States, a number of cases pitting individual liberty
against corporate authority achieved prominence, particularly in the
area of nascent intellectual freedom where science challenged traditional interpretations of the Bible. The Catholic Church, however,
promoted standards that sometimes conflicted with the dominant
culture in Protestant societies, or with the values of liberal anticlericals in Catholic countries. Judaism was in a similar situation.
These conflicts, at times involving highly sensitive areas of personal
life and deeply held passions, raise complex and ambiguous problems
for religious liberty. When personal passions, church teachings, and
politics intersect, as they did in the case of publicly funded education
for children, the challenges for religious liberty were immense.

For the contributors to this volume, the history of religious liberty is not a narrative of progress ending in celebration. Definitions

of religious liberty, indeed definitions of liberty itself, change with time. As our perspective changes, the convictions of our grandparents meld into ambiguities. The very notions of progress and modernization now meet with skepticism, and so does the associated idea of secularization. In his chapter on science and religion, Frank Turner deals directly with modernization and secularization. Every chapter, moreover, at one level or another, constitutes a critical revision of the ideas of progress, modernization, and secularization.

This volume is not intended as an encyclopedia of nineteenth-century religious liberty. It is, rather, a set of case studies of Britain and the United States, broadened to include the Continent (particularly Catholic Europe), Latin America, and the missionary movement. None of the authors in this volume finds the familiar liberal narrative an adequate interpretive context for understanding his particular subject. Some address this liberal tradition directly and propose modified versions; others approach it implicitly. All revise it, and all revise in ways that echo across the chapters and move, along a variety of paths, in the same general direction.

In the United States, as elsewhere, the ideology of freedom reserves a prominent place for the early symbolic events and founding fathers of religious liberty. Nathan Hatch takes this stand when he writes that the myth of the heroes of religious liberty lies at the heart of American national identity. That "myth of the heroes" is an ideological construction. It glorifies men, like Roger Williams and William Penn, who can be understood as motivated by the grand idea of religious liberty. The idea of religious liberty, once planted, flourished in the New World, and was eventually formalized in the Constitution. In this myth, religious liberty is an ideal that was valued and deliberately forwarded by the forefathers of the nation. Hatch takes issue with this myth.

Hatch downplays the significance of ideology. He argues that the wellspring of American religious freedom ought to be located in the conditions of early American life rather than the ideas of early political leaders. He is skeptical of the view that religious liberty was an aspiration in colonial America. For Hatch there are no heroes. He concentrates instead on the circumstances that he sees as the real causes of formal, legal religious freedom in America. Those circumstances, which set the American experience apart from that of Europe or Latin America, fall into two categories.

The first category stresses the limitations on formal authority that geography and technology impose. Because the American colonies were so distant, Britain was unable to exert ecclesiastical authority there and did not try hard to do so. Episcopalians in America were without a resident bishop until after the Revolution. The Episcopal lay elite were not unhappy with this arrangement, which permitted them to dominate clerical authority. Within the colonies themselves, moreover, Protestant elites in New England, New York, or Virginia were unable to control the religiosity of the people. The upper classes associated with Congregationalism, Presbyterianism, and the Episcopal Church did not have the means at hand to exert discipline over the worship of men and women on the frontiers. Therefore, Hatch argues, there existed in the colonies a de facto condition of religious liberty. Within that circumstance of liberty, popular religious movements, beyond the control of established denominations, swept through the people. Chief among these movements was Methodism, the religious body that eventually placed its stamp on the American national style. Localism, democracy, improvisation, and diversity characterized American religious life.

The second category stresses the ethnic, cultural, and religious pluralism that was the inevitable product of the pattern of European settlement. A bewildering array of groups, with a multiplicity of religious and ethnic definitions, settled in early America. Immigration increased in the late eighteenth and early nineteenth centuries. These immigrant peoples retained much of their European heritage for a very long time, and the resulting plurality of defined religious commitments made it impossible for governments at this time to succeed with any policy other than religious liberty. Religious diversity in early America, along with local independence, nurtured a habit of mind opposed to authority and deeply antagonistic to state control of religion.

While formal religious liberty was never seriously attacked in the nineteenth century, genuine freedom of religion for all groups, let alone individuals, was certainly not secured. Roman Catholics were frequently attacked in speech and print, and sometimes persecuted by the democratic mob. Mormons were persecuted; and so were, at times, abolitionist preachers. The atmosphere of freedom in the United States provided freedom for the tyranny of the majority. The conditions that made for freedom, however, also provided escape routes for the informally persecuted. Mormons moved across the frontier to a land where they became the majority themselves. Catholics were free to establish their own schools and universities. The languages of religious liberty that were used in early America sound very much like the languages that applied in Britain and on the European continent. In America, Hatch contends, the conditions that created religious freedom preceded the language.

The long-held view that science flourishes best in political settings characterized by liberty, and the idea that science itself helps forward liberty, are sub-plots, sometimes awkward sub-plots, within the liberal narrative of modern freedom. Frank Turner locates the foundation of the association of science and liberty, and also the particular connection of science and religious liberty, in the Enlightenment. Voltaire is a key figure. In his *Letters on the English* of 1734, Voltaire praised the religious pluralism of the English, and what he considered was their religious freedom. He associated this freedom, and English liberty more generally, with the success of English science, a success for which Newton, the greatest scientist of his day, was the emblem. For Voltaire, and for many in the succeeding centuries, particularly in the English-speaking world, science has stood for open-mindedness and freedom from the curse of superstition and the trammels of tradition. Solidly on the side of progress, science could be seen to go hand in hand with Protestantism until the middle of the nineteenth century, when Darwin and the geologists and the scientific biblical critics seemed to some to be engaged in warfare with religion generally. As long as the military metaphor applied only to the relations of science and the Catholic Church, as long as Galileo stood as a Protestant symbol of progressive liberty in combat with retrograde, tyrannical, intellectually backward Catholicism, scientific and religious liberty could be identified in the Protestant mind. After Darwin, there were difficulties with this easy association. Even so, accommodations could be made and advanced theology sought support and confirmation from advanced science. In the decades following the publication of *The Origin of Species*, religious liberty, at least in Britain and the United States, became much more a matter of freedom of thought than an issue of freedom of practice, a development well illustrated in Robert Webb's chapter. In the last 25 years or so of the nineteenth century, men of science and men of religion began to drift into separate spheres. In the new narrative

of our own century, which concentrates on the liberating results of
the rise of useful knowledge, religion is marginalized and science,
medicine, and technology become the central themes.

Turner critically revises the central ideas in these governing
frameworks of Protestant and liberal thought. He states his thesis
boldly: "With a few notable exceptional cases the impact of science
upon religious life has been negative unless for some reason it has
been to the tactical advantage of scientists to support religion or to
assume a neutral stance toward it." He points out that recent scholarly work has blurred the sharply etched old accounts of Galileo and
Newton, and, by extension, of Protestantism and Catholicism. Galileo is not so obviously the innocent exponent of scientific truth,
Newton is not so much the model of an open-minded scientist, free
of superstition and buoyed up by English religious freedom. Turner,
indeed, cannot find much correlation in fact between good science
and political or religious liberty. On the contrary, his reading of the
record of the relations of science and liberty impels him to nail a list
of counter-theses to the laboratory door. Scientists, themselves, he
argues at length, were not particularly tolerant in matters of religion.
The limits to their regard for religious liberty seem to have been fixed
at the boundaries set by the moderately liberal mainline spokesmen
of their particular times and places. Scientists were, that is, no more
open-minded than liberal nonscientists, and it is hard to relate their
liberalism to their science.

Science, moreover, has aided the cause of some distinctly non-
liberal movements. Scientific racism, for example, is the product of
scientific anthropology. Science produced eugenics, with its deep disrespect for human individuality and freedom of choice. The cultural
arrogance of the modern West has been in part supported by the scientific study of primitive peoples and has resulted in many acts
of vandalism against the religions of those peoples. For some time
now, led by James Moore's *The Post-Darwinian Controversies*, it has
been the fashion to denounce the warfare between science and religion as a myth of the later nineteenth century. Turner contends here,
pace Moore and his followers, that the military metaphor is appropriate. Scientists in the days of Huxley and Tyndall calculatedly attacked religion and the clergy as part of their campaign to dislodge
old elites and gain professional and social status for themselves, their
colleagues, and science. In the twentieth century the battlefront has

changed, but the war goes on, with science fighting the humanities for the glittering prizes of state support. Turner, in this chapter, effectively undercuts the comfortable assumption that science and liberty go hand in hand and he shows that, in certain circumstances, science poses a threat to religious liberty.

A theme that runs through all the chapters in this volume is that liberty of religion has no clear and simple definition; that it has, instead, a variety of meanings, some ambiguous and some plainly contradictory. Jacob Ellens faces this question head on in his study of what he sees as the two meanings of freedom in early Victorian Britain. Ellens calls "traditional" the meaning of freedom which holds that man is born in sin and finds freedom through redemptive obedience to Christ. Stresses in this traditional conception of freedom fall on discipline of the individual and the good of the whole society whose corporate character is highlighted. This vision of freedom has traditional theological roots, and it is in harmony with the political view of the church, or religion in general, as an important force for the maintenance of public order. That religion and civil discipline go hand in hand is a view, noted in several chapters, that was universally shared by proponents of established churches from Catholic Santiago to Protestant Berlin, a view that was very powerful at the beginning of the nineteenth century and tended to wane as modernizing states developed other means of ordering their citizens. In the first half of the nineteenth century, this understanding of freedom did battle with a newer, liberal vision that focused on the liberty of the autonomous individual. Ellens shows how in England evangelical Dissenters, among others, embraced the liberal, individualistic idea of freedom and supported a range of voluntarist causes that sought liberation from state control, while many Anglicans continued to think in terms of the older, fading ideal of freedom through corporate order.

Ellens describes in detail how the two visions of liberty informed the struggle over subscription to the Thirty-nine Articles in the English universities, and the campaign for the end of compulsory local rates for the support of Anglican parish churches. Both sides used the language of freedom, each with a different meaning. This bold attempt to define two meanings of freedom is different from, but reminiscent of, Hexter's two types of liberty, one modern, the other traditional. Ellens's sympathies, however, lie more with the proponents of discipline and corporate freedom than with the voluntarist supporters of liberal individualism. When politically liberal Protestant Dissenters found their theology in conflict with their politics, he argues, many chose politics.

In his chapter on three English conflicts over theological innovation in the 1860s, Robert Webb points out with neat precision some of the ironies and inadequacies of the language of liberty as it was used by Victorians. He looks first at the prosecution in the courts of Rowland Williams, a clergyman of the Established Church and one of the contributors to *Essays and Reviews*, published in 1860. The essays, generally inspired by recent German work in scientific biblical criticism, caused a furor. The seven contributors, five of them Anglican clergymen, seemed to be undercutting the authority of the Bible. Williams was formally prosecuted for going beyond the limits on theological opinion set by his subscription, as a clergyman, to the Thirty-nine Articles. The ecclesiastical courts which heard the case, and the Judicial Committee of Privy Council which was at the time the final court of appeal in ecclesiastical cases, were established by the authority of the state. Williams and his eminent lawyers, James Patrick Deane and James Fitzjames Stephen, made extensive use of the language of liberty in their case for the defense. Williams went so far as to argue, in Webb's words, that "formularies enforced by ecclesiastical dictation could not possibly carry authority," a statement of commitment to individualistic liberty of conscience that might have been made by a radical Dissenting supporter of the Society for the Liberation of the Church from State Patronage and Control.

In the Williams case, it appears that the door was opened to the language of liberty by the involvement of the state. The conventional language of religious liberty was developed in opposition to the pernicious interference of the state. When law came into a religious conflict in a critically important way, the established language of liberty seemed appropriate. This was so, ironically, even when the state, as in the Williams case, could be asked to defend religious liberty. Appealing to the civil rights enjoyed by all in a liberal kingdom, Stephen called on the JCPC to accord Williams, and all clergy, "that unfettered liberty of conscience which belongs to them as subjects of the Queen of England." The JCPC decided for Williams.

In his authoritative discussion of the battle between the Old School and the New among the Unitarians, which came to a head in 1866, Webb describes another battle in which biblical criticism had a central part. Samuel Bache, minister at Priestley's old chapel in Birmingham, was the leading proponent of the Old School. Bache was alarmed by the New School which had emerged in the 1830s. James Martineau, a leading member, moved away from the cool rationality of the Old School into the uncharted territory being explored by the German biblical critics and the French social scientists. Bache created a storm when he tried in 1866 to push the British and Foreign Unitarian Association into adopting a sort of creed that would set the boundaries of theological toleration beyond which Unitarians must not go. The long-standing Unitarian commitment to freedom made it impossible, even for those who sympathized with Bache, to support formal restriction of their theological liberty. The state was in no way involved, however, and the particular language of religious liberty that was appropriate for the trials of Rowland Williams was not relevant for the Unitarian dispute.

Neither was that language much used by the Quakers in a denominational quarrel over evangelical orthodoxy which began in 1861 with an approving lecture on *Essays and Reviews* by David Duncan, a Manchester Quaker. Duncan continued to attack what he thought was the bibliolatry of the evangelical majority of Quakers who, he claimed, were not faithful to their traditional values of spirit and inner light. The struggle between the liberals and the evangelicals persisted for more than thirty years before the liberals, supported by a new Quaker emphasis on social action, emerged victorious. The long dispute was not couched in terms of religious liberty, even though in broad outline it was similar to the debate that swirled around *Essays and Reviews*. In both the Unitarian and Quaker cases, however, genuine issues of religious liberty were raised within denominations that had long commitments to freedom. But freedom from interference by the state is one thing, and liberty to explore potentially disruptive ideas within closely knit sectarian confines is another. Webb shows that the discipline of conscience, the power of informally organized denominational opinion, and the restraining force of fellowship raised barriers to religious liberty that were just as formidable as the law. He demonstrates, as well, that traditions of liberty, different in each of the three denominations, acted to restrain the imposition of authority.

David Itzkowitz argues that for Jews in nineteenth-century Europe, one of the important meanings of liberty was freedom *from* religion, at least freedom from the rites and disciplines of orthodox Judaism. This, for Itzkowitz, is a much more broadly important matter than the mere freedom of individual Jews to choose whether to throw off some or all of the burdens of orthodoxy. Unlike Christians, European Jews did not think of religious liberty in terms of freedom to worship as they pleased. Itzkowitz maintains that religious liberty, in this formulation, was for Jews a trivial issue because they had this right everywhere that they were permitted to live at all. Over the course of the nineteenth century, at different rates of progress in different places, ghetto walls were breached and the possibility of greater integration with the wider community was opened up for Jews. Itzkowitz argues that it was at this point that questions of religious liberty came into play. Just as the ability of Jewish communities to enforce traditional Judaic obligations was weakened, Jews were forced by circumstance to decide how much of their religious way of life they should give up in order to enter more fully into the life of Christian-dominated society. He shows that as states granted greater freedom to Jews, a process that fits comfortably into the liberal vision of religious liberty, Jews found it increasingly difficult to maintain their Judaism.

Among the various strategies that Jews adopted to deal with this predicament of liberty was increased emphasis on the home as their religious center. This adaptation of separate spheres, supported by the greater attention paid to domestic life in Western society generally, enabled Jewish men to act more freely in the world outside the home. Itzkowitz explores as well the related issue of organized Jewish efforts to persuade states to make changes that would accommodate the fuller participation of Jews in modern European society, an effort that in England drew on the language of religious liberty even when freedom of worship was not involved. The campaign of the Jewish Board of Deputies for legalization of Sunday trading for Jews, in order to put them on an equal footing with Christian competitors, is a case in point. As Jews become increasingly free in nineteenth-century Europe, their Judaism waned and their identity, gradually and imperceptibly, shifted from religion to race. The impacts of increased liberty on the Jews that are discussed in this chapter are not contemplated in the liberal master narrative of religious freedom.

Along with the Jews, Roman Catholics were often treated as a people set apart. They suffered both formal and informal restric-

tions of their liberties. Between 1871 and 1887, Chancellor Otto von
Bismarck carried on an anti-Catholic crusade by mobilizing the law
against the Catholic Church. By the end of the 1870s, when the
Kulturkampf was at its strongest, one half the Prussian Catholic
episcopate was in jail or exile, one quarter of the parishes had no
priests, and 1800 parish clergy were incarcerated or out of the country. Nearly half of the monks and nuns left Prussia, and one third of
the monastic houses were closed. Thousands of Catholic laity were
tried and jailed for assisting priests to evade the punitive new laws.
A wave of popular anti-Catholicism accompanied the Kulturkampf,
with a barrage of anti-Catholic propaganda that drew on the main
themes familiar throughout Europe and the Americas: the Catholic
Church is against progress and for superstition, the Catholic Church
owes its loyalty to Rome and is therefore a danger to the nation state,
the Catholic Church is anti-modern. Liberals were at the forefront
of this denunciation of Catholicism, evincing, Ronald Ross writes,
"outright hatred" for what they saw as an enemy of the modern German nation. The Syllabus of Errors of 1864 and the promulgation of
the doctrine of papal infallibility in 1870 helped liberal nationalists,
in Germany and elsewhere, to find the Church a cause of increased
anxiety. It is no surprise that the Kulturkampf captured sympathy
among liberals in France and England.

Ross lays emphasis on the crucial fact that the Kulturkampf was
not at base a spontaneous popular movement. It was, rather, a matter of reasoned political strategy which aimed at promoting the unity
of the German nation. Because it was official state policy, with the
full backing of the chancellor, the campaign against the Catholic
Church was conducted through the law, with the police and the bureaucracy serving as its principal agents. This very legality helps give
the Kulturkampf a sinister character. Clergy arrested, humiliated,
and marched through the streets by the police; house searches conducted by the police looking for evidence of disloyalty; the Catholic
press suppressed; the civil service cleansed of Catholics; the Army
used to disperse a Catholic crowd gathered to witness the appearance
of the Virgin; nuns and monks and clergy fleeing the country; official
support for popular harassment and intimidation of Catholics. All
this might seem to prefigure the holocaust to come.

Ross, however, clearly demonstrates that in important ways, in
action if not in rhetoric, the Kulturkampf was restrained. No one was

killed, and few were injured. No effort was made to extirpate Catholicism. The state did not try to prohibit Catholic worship, and it did not try to interfere with Catholic dogma. This restraint Ross interprets as consistent with Bismarck's limited aims. Bismarck was concerned with the difficulties of assimilating Polish peasants into the German nation, and this, combined with his more general fear that international Catholicism like international socialism posed a threat to the still fragile German Reich, impelled him to attack the Church and reduce ecclesiastical influence.

The religious liberty issues in the Kulturkampf might seem obvious. Ross, however, shows that the case is not a simple one. The language of liberty that liberals turned against the Church during the Kulturkampf had some basis in fact. The Catholic Church in Germany also turned to the language of religious liberty when it found itself under siege, but the Church was not a solid proponent of such freedom. Some Catholic civil officials who were persecuted in the 1870s had themselves hunted down liberal Protestants in the previous decade. The "Old Catholics," those who refused to accept the doctrine of papal infallibility, were harassed by the main body of Prussian Catholics during the time of the Kulturkampf. Many Catholics were vigorously opposed to Jews and heterodox Christians. A pro-Jesuit crowd sacked the house of a Freemason in Essen in 1872. Most important, the hierarchy of the Church was not agreed that religious liberty, interpreted as liberty for individuals, was safe or desirable. They carefully limited their definition of liberty during the Kulturkampf to liberty from state oppression of the Church as a corporate body. They did not call for freedom of conscience for individuals. It is Ross's balanced conclusion that the Kulturkampf was not different in kind from the movement against the Church in France at the same time. As in France, the religious liberty issue was blurred and complex, not amenable to easy historical judgment.

In the liberal Protestant version of the history of liberty, the Catholic Church, featured heavily as the enemy, is not itself much investigated, and rarely sympathetically. Ross, McIntire, and Simon Collier demonstrate how much our understanding of liberty can be enriched and expanded by closer looks at the Catholic Church in nineteenth-century Germany, France, and Chile. Raymond Grew explores the nineteenth-century history of the Church in Europe generally, and presents a masterly discussion of the variety of Catholic responses to the challenges of modernization. Roman Catholicism, he posits, was an important part of the deepest, most durable, and most politically defining conflict in nineteenth-century European history. The lineup of combatants—religion, Church, authority, and tradition, against secularism, state, freedom, and progress—was as well known throughout the Western world. These conflicts were understood "as part of a larger historical clash, that was at once institutional, ideological, political, and deeply personal." Grew considers the role of the Church in that struggle, concentrating on those points at which developments within the Church intersected with major political and social changes. It is Grew's governing thesis that the Catholic Church was an engaged participant, at many levels, in the evolution of nineteenth-century life. He pictures the Church as an institution of enormous vitality and adaptability, interacting in a myriad of ways with changes in other areas of life. He warns against attempts to simplify this picture, or to argue, simply, that the Church stood for liberty or against it.

Paradox abounds in the nineteenth-century history of the Church. Catholic political parties, formed in opposition to the modern democratic state, became masters of modern democratic politics. The Catholic press, founded to fight against many currents of change in social and political life, became a formidable modern publishing power. While it strongly supported the middle-class glorification of home life and separate spheres, the Church at the same time provided, through its female religious orders, the outstanding contemporary example of women working in careers outside the home. While the Church was committed to an ideal of universality, it played an important role in helping form regional identities. With the liturgical revival of the 1830s and beyond, the number of Catholic orders and congregations proliferated. These religious associations were attacked in the same language used against trade unions. Catholics became defenders of the freedom of association, and contributed to the modern idea of freedom.

Grew describes the Catholic Church at the end of the nineteenth century as more vital and more free than it was at the beginning. Many Catholics felt that they were losing most of their contests with modern political and social life. Grew suggests that they were mistaken, misled, perhaps, by seeing too much importance in ideology, by holding too strongly to the sense of a grand historic clash. He looks, rather, at the many successful adaptations achieved by Catholics. The Church, almost in spite of itself, had become a great modern institution, adept at using the modern keys to power. The language of liberty was one of those keys. Nonetheless, the Church did not accept political liberty as a primary, or even desirable, goal.

The relation of the churches to the modern state is at the center of Thomas McIntire's strikingly organized survey of the alliances of church and state in nineteenth-century France. McIntire emphasizes that the languages of religious liberty in France must be understood within the framework of the distinctive, French context. Even within that context, McIntire, in harmony with his revising colleagues in this book, finds that the received narrative of religious liberty in nineteenth-century France is badly distorted. That story, conceived in terms of the Revolution and spun out by anticlerical liberals in the later nineteenth century, sees the French state engaged in a century-long battle with the Church of France. The progressive state struggles to overcome the reactionary might of a great Catholic stronghold, and, eventually, with disestablishment in 1905, the cause of liberty is triumphant. While this is a different story from the English, in broad outline it can be accommodated within the familiar Protestant plot. Liberty opposes Roman Catholicism; freethinking anticlericals, like English Dissenters, attack state support for the Church; forward-thinking liberals achieve a victory when in 1905 the separation of church and state puts France in the same religious liberty camp as the United States. Convinced that this narrative is fundamentally flawed, McIntire suggests a scheme of revision that creates a different context and follows closely the changes in unstable definitions of religious liberty that arose within an historical framework marked by complexity and diversity.

The language of liberty suffused the relations of the state and the churches in nineteenth-century France, and liberty had a variety of meanings because there was a surprising plurality of religious persuasion. At the beginning of the nineteenth century, there were two major Protestant churches, the Reformed Church, essentially Calvinist, and the Lutheran, as well as a number of very small groups. There were fissures within and among all these organized bodies. In general for the Protestants, and especially for the Calvinists, ideas of liberty focused on the Edict of Nantes of 1598, which gave the Huguenots liberty to practice their religion in certain specified places.

There was a significant Jewish community, split between Orthodox and reforming, who saw the foundation of their liberties in Revolutionary decrees of 1790 and 1791. There were groups, flowing out of the Enlightenment and the Revolution, including the Theophilanthropists, the Freemasons, and the Deists, who discarded much of Christianity; and there were others, including the Cult of Reason and the Cult of Liberty, who functioned as religious sects while claiming to abandon religion. Religious pluralism grew more pronounced through the nineteenth century and fundamentally conditioned the meanings of religious liberty. Within the Catholic Church itself, moreover, religious pluralism among Catholics was critically important to understanding their conceptions of liberty. The newly reunited Church of France, created by Napoleon in concordat with the pope in 1801, contained a multiplicity of factions, sub-organizations, and special interests. Liberty meant different things to all of these diverse religious groups, depending on their particular circumstances at particular times.

The Catholic Church was overwhelmingly the largest religious body, comprehending 97 percent of the population on the eve of the Revolution. During the turmoils of the Revolution, the Church was attacked and, for a time, suppressed. Here in the Revolution is a basis for the anticlerical view of the profound enmity between the Church and the state in the nineteenth century. Even though the Church was reconstituted and its administration modernized under Napoleon, it was far from a monolithic power. The great religious revival in early nineteenth-century France issued in popular religious movements that were hard to control, and in quasi-independent new religious orders and congregations.

McIntire follows the history of the shifting relations of the state with the churches by focusing on the history of state-supported education. Education provided in France, as it did elsewhere, one of the principal battlegrounds on which religious liberty issues were fought. For the first third of the century, the rights of Protestants and Jews to establish schools within the Catholic-dominated state monopoly of education constituted the religious question in education. The Guizot laws of 1833 and 1836 established a state system of primary schools in which religious instruction was mandated. This instruction was, in most schools, Catholic, and most schools were suffused with a Catholic, religious atmosphere. There was room for

Protestant and Jewish influence in the schools in districts where those groups were strong. Under the Guizot system, for the next twenty years or so, the various churches, alarmed by the possibility of a decrease and dilution of the religious element in state-controlled education, were allied in a struggle to press the state toward making room for more religious influence. After the Falloux law of 1850 set up a system of secondary education, in which "moral and religious instruction" was required, the battle shifted, and the religious liberty flag was hoisted by a growing group who supported "l'esprit laïque" in opposition to the influence of the churches. In the decade of the 1880s, religious instruction was attacked in the name of nationalism and citizenship, and the Church itself was besieged, at least in its outskirts. Civil divorce was instituted. The Jesuit order was expelled and other religious orders were suppressed. The Falloux law was replaced piecemeal in the early 1880s, and "moral and religious instruction" became "moral and civic instruction." The religious content of French education moved to generic moral religion, "la morale laïque" and "la foi laïque." McIntire sees the melding together of nationalism, citizenship, and a denatured generalized Christianity, a tendency in state-supported education throughout the Western world towards the end of the nineteenth century, as a religious liberty issue. State support for "la foi laïque" in education continued long after 1905. Therefore, he concludes, the separation of the state and the churches in 1905 cannot be accepted as the end of the religious liberty narrative.

Every contributor to this book sees religion and questions of religious liberty as factors of high importance in nineteenth-century history. This professional, historical judgment helps set the boundaries of their revisionism. Simon Collier comes closer than do the others to expressing skepticism about the role of religious conviction in motivating men of power. In his fascinating account of religious-liberty questions in the political history of nineteenth-century Chile, Collier finds that at several decisive times issues involving the relations of Church and state played a critical, central role in driving political events. Until the formal separation of Church and state in 1925, religious questions remained part of the language of politics. Collier points to the important distinction between religion as a matter of private conscience on the one hand, and ecclesiastical institutions on the other. He cites the possibly apocryphal

line attributed to the early nineteenth-century conservative politician Diego Portales, "You believe in God, while I believe in priests."
In company with Portales, Collier stresses the political importance
of the Church even as he discounts the role of religion. A formidable
armed rebellion in 1859 against President Montt arose out of a conflict between Montt and Archbishop Valdivieso. But the religious issue, Collier maintains, was "a convenient pretext" for rebellion. If it
had not been available, another sort of issue would probably have
been found.

Montt was unpopular for a variety of reasons. Chilean society
ladies took priests and religion seriously; politicians worked with
whatever stuff of politics came to hand. The fact that church and
state questions came frequently to hand does not, for Collier, give
religion a fundamental importance. Collier raises here an interesting
question that, couched in slightly different ways, echoes throughout
this volume. Not one of the authors comes close to suggesting that
the political leaders who dominated states in the nineteenth century
permitted their statecraft to be determined by religious passion. On
the contrary, nineteenth-century men of power are characterized, by
Collier and others, as cool pragmatists moved more by considerations of power than by religious commitment. Religion was a counter
in their game, sometimes a very important counter. In Chile the relations of Church and state provided an enduring set of issues that
was sufficiently important that it helped determine the character of
the political game throughout much of the nineteenth and early
twentieth centuries.

The diversity and freedom from state control that marked religious organizations in the United States was not a feature of Chilean
life. There the overwhelming majority of the population was Roman
Catholic, and the Church was closely associated with the central
state. The principal themes of the debate over Church and state
in Chile reflected the pattern of Catholic Europe. Spokesmen for
the modernizing forces in Chilean society castigated the Catholic
Church as backward looking and a brake on progress. As in France,
anticlerical secularists captured the public education system. As
in Catholic Europe generally, anticlericalism eventually became a
powerful political and cultural force, even as anticlericals, paradoxically, looked to the United States and Protestant Europe for models
of the future. Collier supports the view that the long debate between

the partisans of the Church and the anticlericals served to improve the level of religious liberty, and perhaps promoted, as well, the general level of tolerance in Chilean political discourse.

Questions of cultural tolerance and state power pervade the history of the missionary movement. For English missionaries of the late eighteenth and nineteenth centuries, the ideal of religious liberty was fundamentally important. The theology of the evangelical revival relied on the proposition that men and women were free to choose their religion, free to experience conversion, free to believe in the gospel scheme of salvation through faith. Theology inclined the evangelicals toward voluntarism. Religious freedom at the political level was equally important. Civil and religious liberty, in the contemporary phrase, provided the opportunity for evangelists to do their work. The conjunction of these two sorts of freedom defined for the evangelicals a grand opportunity. As bearers of the truth, and driven by a remarkable optimism, they set out to convert the world, a goal that they believed might be speedily achieved. Jeffrey Cox captures this spirit in his quotation from William Carey, the early Baptist missionary to India, who wrote in 1792 that with "the spread of civil and religious liberty . . . a glorious door is opened, and is likely to be opened wider and wider." The vision of the open door appealed to Anglicans as well as Dissenters, and Anglican missionaries were also attracted to the idea of religious liberty as a necessary condition for their work. Drawn partly by the opportunity to reach huge numbers of people, and partly by the romantic appeal of the exotic, British missionaries went to work in Africa and the East, more often than not in lands under British imperial rule. Cox explores the tensions that arose between the missionary commitment to voluntarism and the pragmatic realities of imperial power.

In India, British rule developed a religious policy that was congenial to the missionaries. With religious plurality in Britain an increasingly evident political fact, and religious division in the subcontinent one of the elements of Indian life with which the Raj had to cope, the British government of India was compelled to take up a position of religious neutrality. This set the standard for the Empire. Neutrality was a form of liberty, and neutrality opened the way for missionaries to save Indian or African souls in their great contest with heathenism. Missionaries were in no formal sense agents of British rule, but they were frequently perceived as such by those whom they tried to convert to Christianity, and Cox indicates that there was good reason for this view. Missionaries had access to British governors, and they cultivated their relations with power. They learned how to use their influence with politicians in London and imperial governments abroad in order to effect humanitarian reforms, such as suppression of the slave trade in Africa or the practice of suttee in India. The more successful were the missionary societies in wielding the instruments of political influence, the more clearly they were associated with political power.

Cox reminds us that missionaries constituted a new profession, with professional as well as religious interests. Missionary bureaucracies, missionary schools and hospitals were costly to maintain. Not funded by the state, missionaries relied on voluntary donations from their supporters in Britain. Consequently, missionaries developed strategies of appeal to these donors. One of those strategies focused on the civilizing benefits which missionaries carried, along with religion, to benighted indigenous peoples. Thus did the imperatives of the marketplace interfere with considerations of liberty.

What conclusions does this volume as a whole suggest? Most obvious is the recognition, supported by all the authors, that the old liberal master narrative of the coming of religious liberty cannot be sustained without major revisions. Religious liberty is shown to have many different meanings that depend on the particular contexts and situations in which the languages of religious liberty were deployed. These different meanings must be appreciated if the history in which they acquired significance is to be properly understood. The idea that religious liberty is a single definable ideal is rejected by all the contributors. The idea that religious liberty can be sufficiently defined so as to have a history that can be cast in narrative form is weakened here, but not entirely discarded. Most of the chapters, though not all, carry the sense that religious freedom, instability of definition notwithstanding, was greater at the end of the nineteenth century than it was at the beginning, just as freedom in general was greater by that time.

This holds for both individuals and churches as corporate bodies. As they moved away from close association with the state, churches became more free to govern themselves and deal with their adherents as they wished. In the second half of the nineteenth century in most of Europe, and a little later in the Americas, churches suffered a decline in political power, social influence, and cultural authority. Freedom, however, is different from power. The sense of the progress of freedom suggested in some of the chapters in this book reflects the durable strength of the nineteenth-century liberal narrative. On the other hand, none of the authors conceives the history of religious freedom in terms of a simple struggle between liberty and oppression. The Catholic Church, to take one striking example, is certainly not subjected to the vilification that has been its fate in the traditional story. Catholicism, instead, is treated here as a vital, adaptable, modern religious form with a set of definitions of liberty that differ in some respects from those of Protestants. Several authors indicate that toward the end of the century both Catholics and Protestants extended their ideas of freedom to include reforming the conditions in which the poorer classes lived and worked. In doing so they faced problems of consistency that missionaries had grappled with a little earlier. The history of religious liberty in this book is a history of complex and tangled conflicts in which no side has a monopoly on the meaning of freedom and no side can claim consistency.

The Whirlwind of Religious Liberty in Early America

NATHAN O. HATCH

C ITIZENS OF THE United States have long considered religious liberty a crowning achievement of the American Revolution and at the heart of national identity. They have also linked liberty of conscience to those legendary heralds who, at the dawn of American history, struggled against all odds to achieve religious freedom. Roger Williams, the founder of Rhode Island, had such an unswerving commitment to religious purity that he established complete religious toleration, arguing that a true picture of commonwealth was a ship at sea with a full complement of Papists, Protestants, Jews, and Turks. William Penn, one of the great idealists of the Anglo-American world, convinced his friend King Charles II to make him the sole proprietor of a tract of land as large as England itself. There he worked to establish a colony with religious freedom, with no military defenses, with the most humane criminal code of his time, and with magnanimous policies toward native Americans.

As the United States won its independence, a strange coalition of humanists and evangelicals joined forces to ensure that religion would not serve as an engine of civil policy. Baptists Isaac Backus and John Leland preached relentlessly that church establishments were a "rotten nest-egg, which is always hatching vipers." Making the same point, with a keen eye for ecclesiastical corruption, Thomas Jefferson and James Madison swore eternal hostility to that "diabolical, hell-conceived principle of persecution."[1]

To focus on such individuals creates a narrative of religious freedom as a heroic enterprise, the achievement of self-conscious and articulated aspiration. Without underestimating the long-term symbolic role of these champions of liberty, it is also instructive to consider whether there was such a close connection between intention and outcome, as Herbert Butterfield would remind us.[2] Sidney Mead and Perry Miller have argued that most Americans were not following the cloud and pillar of high principle, but that they started walking down the road to religious freedom without knowing it.[3]

In retrospect, the evolution of religious freedom in North America seems so natural and uncomplicated—almost foreordained—that it is easy to overlook how unusual, even extravagant, was the hothouse of religious diversity within those colonies that became the United States. By the middle of the eighteenth century, any traditional European churchman would have found the religious environment of America disruptive and disorienting. One Pennsylvania pastor complained that "in religious and church matters, each [person] has the right to do what he pleases. The government has nothing to do with it." Another cleric observed that "here [in New York] the church is like a vineyard without a hedge, like a city without wall, like a house without a door and lock."[4]

Colonial America surged with religious diversity well before any theory could fully explain or justify it. The weakness of the English state and the strength of commercial capitalism conspired to make North America a haven for a variety of British and European dissenters, many of whom had compelling religious or ethnic reasons to flee the Old World. Religion became massively deregulated in the English colonies not by design, but because of governmental and ecclesiastical weakness. The writ of King and Bishop simply could not run in the exotic borderland that England had allowed to develop but could never control. This functional deregulation of religion is in stark contrast to the centralist tradition that characterized both the Spanish and the French experience in America.[5]

English North America was also distinct for the remarkable and unprecedented wave of immigration that mixed English, German, Swiss, Scottish, Scotch-Irish, Dutch, and African. In the twenty years before the American Revolution, as many as 300,000 immigrants poured into English America—a number equivalent to the entire Spanish migration to America during the colonial period. As many as sixteen thousand people were flooding into the English colonies each year, more than the total number of French settlers to Quebec in 150 years.[6] Religious persecution brought more waves of immigrants to the colonies. Huguenots fleeing persecution in France contributed substantially to the building of Charleston, Philadelphia, and New York. In the same vein, the early Jewish communities in Charleston and in New York consisted of Spanish- and Portuguese-speaking Sephardic Jews who had fled the Inquisition in Spain and Brazil.[7]

This chapter will suggest that religious liberty in America, in a legal sense, was premised on the withering of state and ecclesiastical authority and the resulting religious improvisations in the colonial era. At the time of the Revolution, for instance, South Carolina had what Richard Hofstadter has called a "vacant establishment."[8] On paper, the Anglican Church was the official establishment and around Charleston it had some institutional coherence. Yet for commercial reasons, Carolina had always welcomed promising settlers, whatever their religious convictions. In reality, Presbyterians actually outnumbered Anglicans in South Carolina, and its back country simmered with religious and ethnic dissent. In the 1760s, the Anglican missionary Charles Woodmason, accustomed to a disciplined, hierarchically-ruled national church, was scandalized to find enthusiasm and vernacular religion everywhere: "To hear Ignorant Wretches, who can not write—Who never read ten Pages in any Book, and can hardly read the Alphabett discusing such Knotty Points for the Edification of their Auditors, is a Scene so farcical, so highly humoursome as excels any Exhibition of Folly that has ever appear'd in the World, and consequently must give High offence to all Inteligent and rational Minds."[9] With the exception of New England, the British colonies in North America had given up a monopolistic relationship between religion and the state prior to the adoption of the First Amendment.

This chapter will also suggest that the experience of the Revolution and of building a democratic polity undermined the already fragile foundations of church tradition. Episcopalians, Presbyterians, and Congregationalists, closely tied to elite institutions and civil authority, had a difficult time competing in the religious free market of the early Republic. While they commanded a certain high ground of culture and power, they were too weak to restrain upstart vernacular religious movements that blurred the distinction between church and popular religion. Lay-driven, voluntary, participatory, and enthusiastic, these movements became endemic. Methodists, a counter-culture in England, outstripped all other churches in the United States and helped to define its core culture.[10]

Colonial America bequeathed an untidy diversity to the United States, more rampant than any European nation-state or its colonies would tolerate. The early Republic, in turn, profoundly altered the relationship of class and religion in America. The upper classes in America would never control religion; nor would diverse and democratized churches allow the state to control or centralize cultural life. No other Western democracy, not even Canada, would develop a system of higher education so decentralized, independent of state control, and open to the entrepreneurial efforts of religious dissenters.

≺ I ≻

Pluralism and the Withering of State Religion

The most remarkable feature of English colonization was its sheer diversity. After the stability and strength of Queen Elizabeth's reign, seventeenth-century England plunged into decades of chronic infighting between king and Parliament, court and country, bishops and dissenters. The turmoil prodded some people to seek refuge in America and allowed all who pursued their designs there, whether religious or commercial, to do so with little restraint. Widely diverse hybrids of English society took root in America; their most common characteristics were independence and localism. The Chesapeake, New England, and New York and Pennsylvania colonies were extremely diverse societies, each in its own way subversive to religious establishments.[11]

The role of the English Crown and of the Anglican Church was limited in these efforts, in sharp contrast to Spain's conquest of Latin America.[12] The king gave companies and proprietors exclusive rights to initiate settlements, but did not lift his hand to pay for, organize, or directly govern them. Virginia was almost a century old before the missionary arm of the Anglican Church, the Society for the Propagation of the Gospel in Foreign Parts, established a strong presence in the Chesapeake. As late as 1701, three generations after initial settlement, only 25 ordained clergy served Virginia's twenty thousand Anglican church members.[13]

Compounding an inadequate clerical presence was the absence of the traditional parish. The rush to raise tobacco caused settlement to expand into sprawling plantations, hastily arranged into counties, strewn along rivers, with few roads between them; a string of plantations, sometimes 60 miles in length, made up a parish. A clergyman could spend several days simply traveling its length. Thus, the North American environment began to force change in religious patterns and expectations.

The absence of an Anglican bishop in the New World only added to the problem. The Anglican Church in the colonies experienced a truncated hierarchy since the closest bishop resided three thousand miles and three months away in Canterbury or London. No local ordinations took place and few clergy could withstand the power of the laity. The same circumstances that enabled colonial planters to ignore company officers in London allowed local parishes to ignore the home office in Canterbury. Indeed, Anglican planters lobbied against an American bishop until the Revolution.[14]

The institutional void created by the weakness of the Anglican Church caused power to shift in two directions: civil authorities assumed legal functions once exercised by the church, and laymen took on parish duties that once had been the clergy's. In the absence of bishops and ecclesiastical courts, local civil authorities—justices of the peace who together made up the county court—probated wills, prosecuted persons for moral offenses such as adultery or blasphemy, and took care of the indigent and infirm.

Within the local parish, power tended to devolve to local lay trustees or vestries. The office of vestryman was an old one in the Anglican Church and generally involved responsibility for the maintenance of church buildings. On occasion, a vestryman would read prayers and levy taxes for the physical support of the parish. In the New World, vestrymen functioned more as a ruling board of trustees whose authority to tax and to pay clerical salaries left the balance of power tilted in their favor. One Virginia clergyman complained to the bishop of London in 1724 that laymen were keeping him on a short leash. His vestry would not induct him into the parish, a move which in England would have provided tenure and financial security: "I have never been inducted into my living . . . the Parishioners are very defective being . . . adverse from . . . committing themselves solely to the care of one Shepherd . . . They would reserve to themselves this handle of restraint on the Ministry, of not being bound to a Minister . . . lest he should afterwards prove disagreeable to them, in which case they might the more easily cast him off for another more suitable to their humor." [15]

On the eve of the American Revolution, Virginia was beset with anticlerical squires, surging dissenters (Presbyterian, Baptist, and Methodist), and increasingly resentful and assertive Anglican clergymen struggling to replicate the authority and station enjoyed by clergy in England. Parsons in Virginia were clearly dependent upon the goodwill of the gentry, a point underscored in 1749 by passage of the Twopenny Act by the Virginia General Assembly that effectively curtailed clerical salaries. Ten years later the British government, siding with the clergy, overturned the act, infuriating the Virginia gentry. In one of the complicated suits that resulted, the young Patrick Henry first came to prominence as an orator for planters against the clergy. Against this backdrop, Virginia gentry vigorously opposed the naming of an American bishop. Richard Bland, one of their leaders, stated, "I profess myself a sincere son of the established church, but I can embrace her doctrines without approving of her hierarchy." [16]

The Episcopal Church in the South found itself in even worse straits after the American Revolution. In Virginia, no more than 40 of the 107 Episcopal parishes existing in 1784 were able to support ministers from 1802 to 1811. An act of the General Assembly in 1802 declared that the title of the colonial property of the church belonged to the state at large and directed that even the glebe farms, land traditionally set aside for the clergy, be seized for public benefit. The resulting financial collapse of the diocese occurred at the same time that talented young men were seeking to serve the church. In the midst of this dissolution, James Madison, presiding bishop from 1790 to 1812, was able to ordain only one deacon for the entire state in the first decade of the new century. Only three young men were able to train for the priesthood during Madison's tenure. By 1805, Madison was so despondent that he went into seclusion, leaving the church too weak and badly organized to consider expanding with the westward movement.[17]

The irony of American Puritanism is that a persecuted radical minority in England became, through migration, a dominant religious establishment. Beginning in England, the Puritans mounted a wave of dissent that crashed on both sides of the Atlantic. One wave broke upon English society in the English Civil War, the execution of King Charles I in 1649, and the creation of the Interregnum under the Puritan general Oliver Cromwell. The Puritans were intent on cleansing and reforming the corrupt English world. The other surge of dissent was directed toward America and the establishing of a reordered or new English society. Puritan authorities struggled valiantly to bring order and harmony to communities along Massachusetts's rocky coast, but they could never fully escape their history as stubborn dissenters. Independence of mind and local autonomy always simmered just below the surface of New England life.

New England Puritans never made a formal break with the Anglican Church, but they were distinguished from the Anglicans in two ways. First, they were congregationalists, meaning that all authority was contained within each local congregation. The authority to create a new church, to ordain elders, to call or dismiss a minister, and to discipline errant members was all lodged strictly within the local congregation. Puritans often referred to this principle as "non-separating Congregationalism," to show their wish to renew and transform the corrupt Anglican hierarchy in England. One of the great puzzles of New England history is how this common religious system, the "New England Way," persisted for so long despite the autonomy of individual congregations. Towns in New England were free to shape their churches in whatever ways they wished, yet most clung steadfastly and voluntarily to a common mission.[18]

Second, New England churches put particular emphasis on religious experience. Probably the most influential work of theology in early New England was *The Marrow of Theology*. Its Puritan author, William Ames, was trained at Cambridge, exiled to Holland, and intent on coming to America before his untimely death in Rotterdam in 1633. The first sentence of his work defines theology as "living to God," as distinct from knowledge of God. Puritans had no use for religion that did not grip the passions and move the will.[19]

Immigration reinforced this deep commitment to experiential faith. New England churches added an additional requirement for membership beyond orthodox belief and practice: they expected a credible recounting of conversion, or, to say it another way, evidence of a work of grace in the heart. The influential pastor John Cotton, for instance, insisted on faith rather than correct belief as the indispensable quality of a true church. Over several generations, New

Englanders never quite resolved their conflicted understanding of the church: territorially or state supported, yet a gathered and purified communion of visible saints.

New Englanders defended tax-supported ministers chosen by local towns, but theirs was a temperament given to independence rather than compliance and centralization. Politically and religiously, Yankees were staunchly independent, litigious defenders of their liberties. For much of the eighteenth century, their churches bred dissenting offshoots, some Baptist, others independent Calvinist, Anglican, and Unitarian—in belief if not in name. By the time of the Revolution, radical dissent swept throughout New England.[20]

At the same time, the Puritan passion for reading extended the range of independent thought and political engagement. At a time when less than half of the population in England or Virginia was literate, Puritan communities approached universal literacy.[21] The Puritans hoped that reading would inspire piety and orthodoxy—which it did to a remarkable extent for much of the colonial era. As print multiplied, however, mass literacy gave people throughout New England ready access to a diverse range of voices. The remarkable writings of the farmer, foot soldier, and tavern keeper William Manning of Billerica, Massachusetts, attest to the independence of mind and staunch egalitarian convictions fostered in a common citizen by active reading.[22]

New York and Pennsylvania best capture and illustrate the diverse and fragmentary nature of the American experience. In 1647, the four hundred inhabitants of the Dutch settlement on Manhattan Island spoke eighteen different languages. Fifty years later, after the English controlled New York, a leader noted: "Our chiefest unhappyness here is too great a mixture of nations."[23] In the 1750s, Benjamin Franklin complained bitterly about the Germans pouring into Pennsylvania: "Why should the Palatine Boors be suffered to swarm into our Settlements and by herding together establish their Language and Manners to the Exclusion of ours?" Pluralism and diversity have always existed as a fact in North America, but not always in theory.

New York and Pennsylvania were dissimilar in their diversity. New York was probably the most autocratic of the English colonies and its land policies the most feudal of any in America. Manors with thousands of prime acres along the Hudson were granted to a few aristocratic families: the Cortlandts, the Livingstons, the Rensselaers. Hundreds of tenants on these lands, unhappy with their plight, rioted during the 1750s. Hampered by its land policy, New York grew to only a medium-sized colony by the end of the colonial era. No lofty ideals motivated the settlement of New York. From the beginning its mainspring was commercial and pragmatic.

Pennsylvania, by contrast, was the lengthened shadow of one man, William Penn, who as we have seen established a colony without military defenses, with religious freedom, with the most humane criminal code of his time, and with policies toward native Americans that acknowledged their rights and their lands. At the same time, Pennsylvania became an agricultural paradise for middling families. With generous land policies, remarkably fertile soil, and an absence of sharp social distinctions, rural Pennsylvania prospered, in a phrase first used in 1724, as "the best poor man's country in the world." The great migrations of the eighteenth century shunned aristocratic New York and rocky New England and descended upon Pennsylvania, making Philadelphia the hub of a rich agricultural empire and the largest and wealthiest American city.[24]

The middle colonies foreshadowed the ethnic and religious diversity that would become the nation's hallmark. In the colonial era, however, diversity was a troublesome and often destabilizing reality. The settling of North America coincided with a time in Europe when people were ready to die for religious commitments. Traditions clashed far more than they harmonized, and diverse settlers grudgingly tolerated life in a multicultural setting. Few seventeenth-century experiments in diversity functioned harmoniously. While religious commitment could galvanize an entire community, religious diversity injected a strong pattern of turbulence into the already frail social order of colonial life.

The absence of unified control of religion allowed citizens to become religious consumers. A Lutheran minister in New York City, Michael Christian Knoll, complained in 1749 that without ecclesiastical oversight "everyone does what he considers right" in religious affairs. Members were tempted to stray from their faith through "marriage, pride and bread, so that one who is today a Lutheran, he or his child may tomorrow be a Reformed, a Moravian, or a Quaker." Knoll also complained about a long controversy in his congregation over what language to use in worship.[25]

New York's diverse churches, each claiming "to possess the best medicine for the soul and the nearest road to Heaven," were disorienting to lay people. Presbyterian layman William Livingston aptly summarized the frustration of people amid such jarring diversity: "Among which of these Systems shall a candid Inquirer after Truth, look for Christianity? Where shall he find the Religion of Christ amidst all this priestly Fustian [inflated], and ecclesiastical Trumpery?" All of them, he continued, "claim to be orthodox, and yet all differ from one another, and each is ready to damn all the Rest."[26]

In some cases, diverse religious voices moved people to a more individual view of religion, subordinating church affiliation to a larger reality. In subtle ways, the religious market exalted the individual conscience and diminished ecclesiastical authority. Such was the case with Mary Cooper, a deeply religious woman in Oyster Bay, Long Island, who kept a careful diary of her spiritual journey. In her fifties, Mary Cooper attended worship services held at the town's four churches—Quaker, Anglican, Regular Baptist, and New Light Baptist—as well as special meetings by itinerant ministers. She did not always agree with what she heard, but she was prepared to find spiritual nurture in each of the various traditions.[27] By the time of the American Revolution, eleven different Protestant denominations served the area around New York City, making choice a pervasive religious reality.

From the outset, the Pennsylvania colony and its capital city, Philadelphia, were remarkably successful as an economic venture and as a haven for dissenters. In the first two years, some 50 ships brought settlers from England, Wales, Ireland, Holland, and Germany. Land was cheap, religious toleration genuine, and political participation encouraged. By 1700, almost as many Quakers lived in America as in England and the carefully laid out city of Philadelphia rivaled Boston as a commercial center. It was no accident that the shrewd and ambitious Benjamin Franklin abandoned Boston for Philadelphia in 1723. The Delaware valley quickly emerged as the prime breadbasket of the Anglo-American world.[28]

As the eighteenth century progressed, Philadelphia became America's immigration capital. Waves of settlers from Germany, Scotland, and Ireland made the city a center for Lutherans and Presbyterians as well as Quakers. By the 1740s, there were 120,000 Germans in Pennsylvania alone. If they were to keep faith with Lutheran tradition, it could only be done by voluntary means. The evident needs of this German population were addressed by August Hermann Francke and the Pietists at Halle who recruited the young missionary Henry Muhlenberg to go to America in 1742. Muhlenberg, whose congregation was so diverse that he composed sermons in English, Dutch, and German, was a defender of conventicles and hostile to the entrenched orthodoxy of the Hanoverian church. He worked tirelessly to bring clergymen to the colonies and organize an American Lutheranism known for its vibrant piety. From the start these churches had to compete for the attention of the faithful with Zinzendorf and the Moravians and with a host of other sectarian groups.[29] Muhlenberg described in his *Journal* in 1742 how a squabble in a church could confound ecclesiastical authority:

The deacons and elders are unable to do anything about it, for in religious and church matters, each has the right to do what he pleases. The government has nothing to do with it and will not concern itself with such matters. Everything depends on the vote of the majority. A preacher must fight his way through with the sword of the Spirit alone and depend upon faith in the living God and His promises, if he wants to be a preacher and proclaim the truth in America.[30]

Pennsylvania became a magnet for oppressed sects, many communal in nature, alienated from the world and relentless in the pursuit of pure Christianity. Forty-eight Amish and Mennonite settlements flourished in Pennsylvania by 1750. Other religious communities included the Dunkards and Schwenkfelders, and an array of Moravian communities.

One thing was certain: religion in North America would never be closely linked to governmental authority and ecclesiastical institutions. Infused with dissenting zeal and divergent beliefs, and in the absence of any powerful establishment, North American religion veered toward the voluntary and experimental. The vast expanse of land east of the Mississippi also beckoned visionaries to found their own utopias unimpeded by state, church, or society. In the formative years of its settlement, English North America, the site of the first Lutheran Church not created by the state, became a kaleidoscope of religious and ethnic groups, most of them self governing and instinctively resistant to outside interference.

The French experience in Canada underscores the uniqueness of this religious diversity. Only 10,000 French immigrants came to Quebec in the 150 years after 1608. Twenty times that number—from throughout the British Isles and beyond—poured into the port of Philadelphia in the five decades before the American Revolution. The British government was concerned about losing too many of its citizens to America, but it did little to control the exodus. In contrast, the French maintained a highly restrictive immigration policy. Far from an inviting refuge for dissent, French Canada was the closely controlled projection of a highly centralized regime. After 1685, when Protestants were suppressed in France, they were denied access to Quebec. French Huguenots, while settling by the thousands in Charleston, New York, and Boston, were never allowed a foothold among their own countrymen in Canada.

Absolutism was on the rise in seventeenth- and eighteenth-century France and her overseas empire. Ruled by a governor without a representative assembly, Quebec was designed to be authoritarian, royal, feudal, orthodox, and stable. The king's agent controlled access to the fur trade and the seigneurial system of land tenure with settlers owing a series of feudal obligations to the seigneur. To foster a stable agricultural society, the governor even enlisted the Church to threaten farmers with excommunication if they abandoned their farms. An integral part of the state, by 1750 the Roman Catholic Church controlled one-third of Quebec's land.[31]

Like Spain in the sixteenth century, France in the seventeenth did not create environments in the New World conducive to limited government and religious dissent or change. Linking the church tightly to the colonial bureaucracy, both cast a centralist shadow upon the evolution of colonial society. For over a century, the French in Canada did not operate a single printing press—a powerful testimony to the dearth of competing voices.

England was unable to exercise similar control over its colonial ventures. A society deeply divided within itself, England was too preoccupied to make the New World off limits for those out of step with royal intent. On the eve of the American Revolution, as many as 16,000 immigrants per year poured into the British colonies, drawn by differing visions of opportunity—political, economic, and religious. No one designed this experiment in extreme diversity and localism, but neither did any authority prevent it. With distances so vast and institutions so weak, British North America became a grand experiment in the deregulation of religion—fertile soil, indeed, for lively and voluntary religious expression.

≺ II ≻

A Free Market of Religion

In 1776, John Adams posed the question that would preoccupy his generation of American citizens and their children. "It is certain, in theory," he said, "that the only moral foundation of government is, the consent of the people. But to what extent shall we carry this principle?"[32] On the subject of religious liberty, Adams and his generation thought they had carried the principle far enough. Reflecting the religious diversity within the thirteen states, the First Amendment prohibited any governmental establishment of religion and guaranteed free exercise of religious choice.

In his book *The Radicalism of the American Revolution*, Gordon S. Wood recounts the pervasive pessimism that descended upon those Founding Fathers who lived into the early decades of the nineteenth century. A sense of unease and bewilderment courses through their later writings. Benjamin Rush looked back with despair upon his efforts in the Revolution, claiming to feel "like a stranger" in his native land. He decided to burn all his notes for the once-planned memoir of the Revolution. "We are indeed," he said in 1812, "a be-banked, bewhiskied, and a bedollared nation." The dejected John Adams asked in 1813, "When? Where? and How? is the present Chaos to be arranged into Order?" Thomas Jefferson hated the new democratic world he saw emerging in America, a world of rising revivalist and populist modes of faith. The classical republic of the founders' dreams had been transformed by what one of them called "the fiery furnace of democracy." Their own fate now depended upon the opinions and votes of small-souled and largely unreflective ordinary people.[33]

Jefferson's assumption that religious corruption sprang from the privileged status of established churches had motivated his drive for religious liberty. Freedom of religion, according to Jefferson's line of thought, would release churches from ecclesiastical hierarchy and sectarian enthusiasm and set them upon a path of rationality and restraint. What Jefferson actually witnessed, however, was anything but measured decorum. The early Republic was swept off its feet by what Sean Wilentz has deemed "one of the most extraordinary spells of sectarian invention that the nation and world has ever seen."[34] The most powerful social movement of the new nation was that of the Methodist Church, the very embodiment of enthusiasm and authoritative religion.

That the Methodists would come to such a dominant position was a curious and unexpected reality. At the dawn of the American Republic, New England Congregationalists, middle colony Presbyterians, and southern Anglicans cast a dominant shadow in society, politics, and religion. While a few followers of John Wesley had made their way to colonial cities, the Methodists, not yet a separate church from the Anglicans, were an insignificant factor in the American religious economy.

The explosive growth of the Methodist Episcopal Church was the most surprising development in a republic that shunned state-sponsored religion. The American followers of Wesley, with no more than four ministers and 300 lay people in 1771, had been threatened with extinction during the Revolution. All their leaders save Francis Asbury returned to England leaving the Methodist faithful to struggle with the stigma of Toryism throughout the war. Under the tireless direction of Asbury, the Methodists emphasized three themes that Americans found captivating: God's free grace, the liberty of people to accept or reject that grace, and the power and validity of popular religious expression—even among servants, women, and African Americans. Led by unlearned preachers who were committed to sacrifice and travel, the Methodists organized local classes or cells and preaching circuits at a rate that alarmed more respectable denominations. When Asbury died in 1816, the Methodists could claim over 2,000 ministers and 200,000 members.

The miraculous growth, which terrified more established denominations, continued to mid century. Less than 3 percent of all church members in 1776, Methodist ranks swelled to more than 34 percent of all church members by 1850, making them far and away the largest religious body in the nation. Methodists boasted 4,000 itinerants, almost 8,000 local preachers, and over a million members. Nearly one half size larger than any other Protestant body, Methodists could muster more than ten times the preaching force of the Congregationalists, who in 1776 had double the number of clergy of any other church. By 1840, one of every twenty Americans was a member of a Methodist church. By 1850, in a nation where only 25 to 30 percent of the people claimed any religious affiliation, almost one in fifteen Americans belonged to a Methodist church (1.5 million out of 23 million). In Indiana, Methodists outnumbered Presbyterians four to one by mid century and made their political advantage felt. Richard Carwardine has argued convincingly that the internal stresses of Methodism, the largest religious force in the nation at mid century, profoundly influenced the course of the Union as it tumbled toward the carnage of the Civil War.[35]

David Martin has emphasized the contrasting roles of Methodism in British and American culture. However strong Methodism became in Great Britain by the mid-nineteenth century, it remained a dissenting movement and never occupied the high ground of culture and power held by the Church of England. In America, on the other hand, Martin suggests: "Arminian evangelical Protestantism provided the *differentia specifica* of the American religious and cultural ethos." One example of this difference is the American insistence on sincerity and openness rather than on form and privacy. The whole American style became "Methodist" in its emphases, whereas in England the culturally prestigious style remained Anglican. "Enthusiasm of all kinds, religious, cultural and personal, became endemic in America; in England enthusiasm remained intermittent and the object of some mild curiosity. In this respect the two cultures took different paths."[36]

In its message and structure, Methodism embodied a liberal conception of reality that broke decisively with the pre-Revolutionary pursuit of homogeneous community. As a movement of self-conscious outsiders, Methodism embraced the virtue of pluralism, of competition, and of marketing religion in every sphere of life—far beyond the narrow confines of ecclesiastical space. The Methodist itinerant Peter Cartwright recounted how a Presbyterian minister objected to his starting another church within the "bounds of his congregation." Cartwright responded that his were a free people in a free country and they would do as they pleased.[37]

The free religious market that emerged in the early Republic sprang from the withering of both state power with respect to religion and the presumptive authority of traditional churches. Disestablishment in America was not merely a legal entity. Rather, it was the withering of the norms of authority that upheld the established churches. While European churches were shoring up their authority following the convulsions of the French Revolution and Napoleon, America's traditional churches and their college-educated ministers read sermons, and staid liturgies were undergoing tremendous assault. In their book *The Churching of America, 1776–1990*, Roger Finke and Rodney Stark point out that the percentage of Americans belonging to churches dropped precipitously for Congregationalists, Presbyterians, and Episcopalians.[38]

The fundamental account of this period may well be, as Rowland Berthoff suggests, a story of things left out. He argues that it is difficult to write "a coherent account of so disjunctive a history."[39] Churches and religious movements after 1800 operated in a climate of tottering ecclesiastical establishments. The federal government, a "midget institution in a giant land," had almost no internal functions. And a rampant migration of people continued to short circuit old networks of personal authority. American churches did not face the kind of external social and political pressures that in Great Britain often forced Christianity and liberty to march in opposite directions. In America, established religious institutions linked to the upper classes remained too weak to make a whole society accept their language and analysis. In a rapidly expanding society with fluid and inadequate structures of institutional control, there was virtually unlimited social space, without hardened distinctions of social class or religious denominations. In this free religious market, new and dynamic religious movements could take root and thrive.

As Americans rapidly moved into new areas, from New England to the Ohio river valley and to central Tennessee and Kentucky, staid churches could not make the transition. Studies of the New England frontier and hill country by the social historian Alan Taylor have noted the striking incidence of radical religious seers, visionaries, prophets, mystics, and fortune tellers; and how easily traditions of folk magic and mystical insight became intermingled with Christian beliefs for religious seekers, many of whom were unchurched by choice.[40]

During the 1790s, the slow-growing Congregationalists established only five churches in the new towns, compared to the 26 new Baptist and nine new Methodist congregations. By 1800, these dis-

senters outnumbered Congregationalists by three to one. The Standing Order remained largely confined to the more prosperous communities located along the coast. By 1810, only one in eight back
country communities had Congregational churches. Similar conditions prevailed on the frontier in Kentucky and Ohio, with the Methodists easily outstripping the Presbyterians. Referring to the Ohio
territory as this "Land of *Liberty*," Methodist presiding elder John
Sale rejoiced in the decline of deference to religious tradition: "It is
pleasing to me to live in a Country where there is so much of an
Equality and a Man is not thought to be great here because he possesses a little more of this Worlds rubbish than his neighbor."[41]

The explosion and decentralization of religious print early in the
nineteenth century best illustrates how dispersed the American religious market became. Journals appeared as quickly as they van-
ished, creations of common people for a broad popular audience; and
publishing was virtually uncontrolled. Alexander Campbell, for instance, the founder of the Disciples of Christ, sought to transform
American religion from the mountains of western Virginia by two
means: an educational institution, Bethany College, and his own
printing shop. An inveterate journalist, Campbell sought throughout
his career to rise early enough in the morning to write an amount
sufficient to keep his printer setting type for the entire day. In his
study of the popular press in Cincinnati, John Nerone counted over
40 different religious periodicals published before 1848. Of the 133
different periodicals to which citizens of Jacksonville, Illinois, held
subscriptions in 1831 and 1832, nineteen were from Kentucky, nine
from Illinois, eight from New York, six from Ohio, five each from
Washington, D.C., Pennsylvania, and Missouri, four from New England, three from Maryland, two from Tennessee, and one each from
Louisiana and Alabama. Before 1789, all religious journals had issued from either Boston, New York, or Philadelphia. By 1830, religious journals had been published in 195 different cities and towns
and in every existing state but Mississippi. Of the 70 locations with
such publications still active in 1830, over half were west of the
Alleghenies.[42]

The hallmark of religious publishing in this era was a marked
pluralism. Power, influence, and authority were dispersed and most
came by way of democratic means: popular appeal by the printed
word. This climate favored religious insurgents willing to employ

fresh strategies to capture public attention. An excellent case in point is the communications crusade developed by Joshua V. Himes to spread the Adventist message of William Miller. This extraordinary publishing exploit blanketed the nation with an estimated four million pieces of literature within four years, including charts foretelling the end of prophetic times in 1843.[43]

This was a religious culture whose dynamism was at the periphery rather than the center, in sharp contrast to the tightly controlled and centralized traditions of publishing in Quebec and in Latin America. Brazil was not even allowed a printing press until 1808. Elsewhere in Latin America, publishing was limited to tightly knit circles with a strong ecclesiastical and high-society flavor.[44] Even for all its imitation of British sources, popular evangelical literature in the United States maintained a much firmer identification with its intended audience. Many of its authors emerged from the uneducated and less-than-respectable ranks to produce widely accepted popular literature.[45]

≺ III ≻

Religious Liberty and Vernacular Religion

With the onslaught of religious liberty came the rise of vernacular religious movements that blurred the distinctions between church and popular religion. Outbreaks of enthusiasm were a common staple of European and British Christianity in the era of the democratic revolutions. Yet, as David Martin notes, what sets apart the United States is the absence of a revived state church which could, on a local level, hold on to the high ground of culture and power. In the United States, high culture was too weak to inhibit or restrict enthusiastic popular religiosity and the cultural periphery or hinterland remained far more powerful and unobstructed.[46] In this ideal climate for churches growing out of the popular culture, the Methodists and Mormons thrived.[47]

Both Methodism and Mormonism emerged from the crucible of the early Republic, a time of revolutionary change in a republic that turned its back on state-sponsored religion and embraced, for good or ill, the realities of a market economy, the individual pursuit of self-interest, and the legitimation of competing factions. Both move-

ments broke decisively with the kind of churches that had dominated the American colonies. Both succeeded because they were
willing to market religion outside traditional ecclesiastical space and
to cater to the interests of specific market segments—a proliferation
that Adam Smith had predicted would result upon government deregulation of religion.[48] Both empowered ordinary people by taking
their deepest spiritual impulses at face value, by shattering formal
distinctions between lay and clergy, by providing an arena for the entrepreneurial instincts of religious upstarts, and by communicating
the gospel message in the vernacular—in preaching, print, and song.

In two striking ways both the Methodists and the Mormons drew
strength from these folk religious impulses: both focused on the reality of the supernatural in everyday life, and both recruited and organized disciplined bands of young followers who were hungry for
achievement, sacrificial in their zeal, and driven by a sense of providential mission.

In the first two decades of the nineteenth century, Methodist experience brimmed with overt enthusiasm, supernatural impressions,
and reliance on prophetic dreams and visions. Methodist journals
and autobiographies are replete with this kind of supernaturalism.
Freeborn Garrettson believed in the veracity of supernatural impressions, prophetic dreams, and divine healing. In addition to stories
of dreams, shouting, and divine healing, Billy Hibbard's memoir included an account of a woman apparently raised from the dead.
Methodism dignified religious ecstasy; unrestrained emotional release; and preaching by blacks, by women, by anyone who felt the
call. Two African-American women who became successful Methodist exhorters, Jarena Lee and Zilpha Elaw, were dramatically converted through direct revelation and found guidance in prophetic
dreams.[49]

The most celebrated and notorious Methodist itinerant of his day,
"Crazy" Lorenzo Dow, was celebrated as a holy man with unusual
powers. Dow embodied the continuing presence of the supernatural
in daily life. Nicholas Snethen warned British Methodists in 1805
of his presumed prophetic powers: "He has affected a recognizance of
the secrets of men's hearts and lives, and even assumed the awful
prerogative of prescience, and this not occasionally, but as it were
habitually, pretending to foretell, in a great number of instances, the
deaths or calamities of persons, &c."[50] Even Nathan Bangs, who

eventually set his face to rid Methodism of the stigma of enthusiasm, began his itinerant career as a white-hot enthusiast. At the Hay Bay Camp Meeting in Upper Canada in 1805, he was so overtaken by the power of God as he preached and shouted that friends had to support his outstretched arms. Afterwards, he had to be "carried out of the camp into a tent where he lay speechless being overwhelmed for a considerable time with the mighty—Power of God." Assessing this kind of evidence, John Wigger argues that the defining characteristic of American Methodism under Francis Asbury was not a theological abstraction like Arminianism, but a quest for the supernatural in everyday life.[51]

In Great Britain, by contrast, the Methodists sought to put an end to the enthusiasm of the camp meeting to comply with vague government threats against itinerant preaching. In 1807, Lorenzo Dow had been barnstorming through Ireland and northwest England, encouraging large crowds to spend whole days in preaching, praying, exhorting, and singing. Thomas Coke, suspicious of Dow's eccentric appearance, fervent republicanism, and refusal to swear allegiance to George III, threatened to report the American to Lord Castlereagh, chief secretary for Ireland.[52] In the spring of 1807, Dow's preaching in Staffordshire inspired the dissident Methodist Hugh Bourne and his brother James to organize a camp meeting based on the American model. Armed with Dow's pamphlets and songbooks, they convened several day-long meetings during the summer of 1807, the most famous one in May at a place called Mow Cop. Faced with this challenge, the Methodist Conference reacted swiftly and decisively: "It is our judgment, that even supposing such meetings to be allowable in America, they are highly improper in England, and likely to be productive of considerable mischief: and we disclaim all connection with them."[53] For the next five years Methodist authorities worked to destroy the camp meeting. Their nerves were strained by the crescendo of popular activism that threatened the fragile nature of religious toleration for the Methodists.[54]

In America, the rapid expansion of Methodism created conditions that allowed women and African Americans to assume religious leadership. The Methodists gave women extraordinary freedom to speak, encouraging them to share their religious experiences in public. Catherine Brekus has noted at least 21 white and black women who preached or "exhorted" regularly among Methodist congregations.[55] Methodists were also inclined to grant African Americans permission to preach the gospel. By 1810 one leader could list the names of thirteen ordained black ministers and another eleven local preachers.[56] However, an attempt by Methodists to keep black leaders on the fringe of the movement gave rise to a remarkable movement of independent black churches, the first being the African Methodist Episcopal Church founded by Richard Allen in Philadelphia.[57]

By the time Joseph Smith announced his prophetic mission, he was responding to a popular yearning for divine intervention in day-to-day existence. In fact, the clarion call of Smith and his followers was to a militant supernaturalism: a demonstrable revelation from heaven, the reality of miracles and apostolic gifts, and a sure and ongoing channel of prophecy. Arguing that modern churches had a form of godliness but lacked its power, Parley Pratt announced that "the most miraculous displays of the power and majesty of Jehovah" were being revealed in the latter days and that believers could expect "miracles, signs and wonders, revelations, and manifestations of the power of God, even beyond anything that any former generation has witnessed."[58] "I am a God of Miracles," the Lord proclaimed in the *Book of Mormon*, and Latter-day Saints insisted on taking that claim literally.[59] Many such as Sidney Rigdon found the prophetic claims of Joseph Smith compelling; others the reported incidents of divine healing; and others the overt enthusiasm.[60]

Mormons and Methodists shared a common yearning for the miraculous power of the biblical world. They also shared a genius for organizing and consolidating the expansion of the faith. Methodism and Mormonism were, at their core, youth movements with an extraordinary capacity to mobilize people for a cause and to build an organization sustained by obedience and discipline rather than ties of parish, family, and patronage. In both movements a battery of young leaders without elite pedigree constructed fresh religious ideologies around which the movement coalesced. Marvin S. Hill has estimated that of those converted before 1846 whose birth and conversion dates are given, 92 percent (211 of 229) were under 40 at the time of baptism. The median age was between 20 and 25; more than 80 percent (182) were 30 or under.[61] W. R. Ward has noted that Francis Asbury was an entrepreneur in religion, a man who perceived a market to be exploited. The itinerant-based machine he set in motion was less a church in any traditional sense than "a military mission of short term agents" who were not pastorally related to the flock in the traditional European sense.[62]

Mormons and Methodists were driven by a consuming passion to convert the unconverted. They emphasized an urgent missionary purpose as the principal reason for their existence and tailored preaching to warn people of the wrath to come and to "draw in the net." More importantly, they yoked the drive to proselytize to relentless and systematic efforts to deluge the country with preaching. Unlike the young itinerants of the Great Awakening, whose efforts were largely uncoordinated and short lived, the adherents of these movements developed regimented and ongoing schemes for sending out gospel preaching to even the most remote pockets of American civilization. A Baptist clergyman overlooked partisanship to praise the Methodists in 1816: "their complete system of mission circuits is by far the ablest domestic missionary effort ever yet adopted. They send their laborers into every corner of the country."[63]

Equally committed to sending forth a cadre of lay preachers, the Mormons had enlisted a preaching force of 1,900 young men by 1845. The earliest men sent forth on missions included hatters, carpenters, cobblers, glaziers, potters, farmers, school teachers, and former preachers from other denominations. As outlined in Joseph Smith's 1835 work, *Doctrine and Covenants*, Mormon preaching, like Methodist, resisted the Puritan tradition of painstaking study. Preachers were advised against using careful forethought, written notes, and detailed plans. Their overriding focus was to convince the unconvinced of the new restoration. According to an ex-Mormon preacher, the approach was to employ "the most plausible means" available "to get people to unite with them."[64]

The organizational genius of Methodists and Mormons was to embrace and empower common people in a system that was centrally directed in a fixed, even authoritarian way. In their early years, both movements were volatile and unstable, as a variety of fledgling and self-ordained leaders vied for influence, tested the limits of the prescribed authority, and in numerous cases hived off to form their own churches.[65] Yet Mormons and Methodists, unlike Disciples and Baptists, swore by institutional coherence. In the face of clamoring dissent, sometimes fueled by democratic impulses, sometimes by visionary ones, Methodists and Mormons were willing to exercise discipline, even ruthlessly, to preserve a movement in the name of God.

In their authoritarian extreme, the Latter-day Saints represent a striking symbol of the disorienting instability that accompanied a free-market religious economy. The primitive Mormons were an apocalyptic sect, intent on expansion and willing to unsheathe the sword in retaliation for the persecution of their own. What also infuriated their neighbors was their denial of the most basic liberty imaginable, freedom of thought. At its inception, Mormonism throbbed with diversity, multiple revelations, and an array of spiritual gifts. As external threats to the movement increased, the saints closed ranks, demanded the strictest loyalty to the commands of Joseph Smith, and moved toward greater intellectual isolation.[66]

In the most startling revelation of all, in 1843, Joseph Smith announced that all earthly commitments were null and void save the ones sealed by himself: all "covenants, contracts, bonds, obligations, oaths, vows, performances, connections, associations, or expectations."[67] No human obligation—even the solemn vow of marriage—had any meaning unless it flowed from the sealing that only the prophet Joseph had the power to administer for earth and heaven. Smith explained the redemptive power of "celestial marriage" in this way and demanded that his followers submit to it or be damned. As divine prophet, military general, political boss, and even candidate for the presidency of the United States, Smith consolidated power into the hands of a single man and equated compliance to the divine will with loyalty and strict obedience.[68] This demand for absolute control was accompanied by a flurry of striking revelations— the plurality of gods, the tangibility of the divine, and the human potential of becoming a god. In submitting to their prophet and revealer on these matters, Mormon followers were willing to dismiss the architecture of classic Christian theology and practice.[69] Their intentions were far too radical for their neighbors in Missouri and Illinois, yet the lash of persecution, far from disbanding the movement, set in motion a pilgrimage to the Basin Kingdom in which the Mormons could flourish on their own terms for a generation.

≺ IV ≻

Intolerance and Religious Proliferation

This religious marketplace, what one Congregational missionary to Illinois called in 1829 "religious anarchy" and "a sea of sectarian rivalries," could give rise to intolerance and sometimes even persecution. As in the case of Joseph Smith, denials of religious liberty were not generally a function of government but of popular actions, of mobs. It was not the oppression of the powerful that dissenters had to fear in America, Alexis de Tocqueville noted, but the tyranny of the majority: "In America the majority raises formidable barriers around the liberty of opinion; within these barriers an author may write anyway he pleases, but woe to him if he goes beyond them . . . You are free to think differently from me and retain your life, your property, and all that you possess; but you are thenceforth a stranger among your people."[70]

During the 1830s and 1840s, mob action was rampant in America against Catholics in Boston and Philadelphia; against Mormons in Ohio, Missouri, and Illinois; and against abolitionist preachers in a variety of locations.[71] Richard Carwardine has recently shown how the lynching of the Methodist abolitionist Anthony Bewley by a Texas mob in the summer of 1860 inflamed religious and political communities in the North as the crucial presidential election of 1860 approached.[72]

Intolerance and persecution were rarely effective in suppressing religious dissent. Instead, the availability of space in the United States meant that dissent and pluralism generally proceeded apace. The most oppressed group, the Mormons, would certainly have been crushed in Missouri and Illinois had they not been able to trek far beyond the writ of law or mob. The very experience of that pilgrimage solidified the identity of the Latter-day Saints and helped Brigham Young turn a highly fragmented and fragile apocalyptic sect into a major religious community.

Severe popular prejudice against Roman Catholics, particularly with respect to education, emboldened the immigrant church to begin its own effective system of parochial education and, in time, of colleges and universities. To a lesser degree, Methodists in the middle of the nineteenth century often felt discriminated against by Calvinists who exercised effective control of many colleges. They responded by founding 35 colleges between 1840 and 1860. Between the Civil War and 1900, Methodists in the United States founded more than one college or university per year.

In the United States, religious liberty proceeded with almost unrestrained fury, generating a popular culture that Jon Butler has characterized as "awash in a sea of faith."[73] Traditional religious leaders, no less than government officials, lost their authority to mediate the religions that Americans chose. Populist leaders competed for followers in a free market. Immigrant churches formed their own vital communities. Presbyterian, Methodist, and Baptist churches divided over the issues of slavery and race. Utopian and apocalyptic sects sought refuge in the hinterland to work out their own dreams. Lawrence Moore has recently noted that in ante-bellum America, religion came to be hawked as a commodity like other products in the marketplace.[74]

The people of America turned out to be more free to practice religion than their European cousins. This means not that Americans possessed greater foresight or tolerance, but that their institutions were too weak and their communities too diverse to restrain the whirlwind of diversity that descended upon them. At the founding of the Republic, no one wanted or envisioned such a state of religious freedom. It was a frightening and tumultuous era, buffeted by the heavy winds of uncertainty and conflict. It involved not only dismantling the territorial church, but inevitable class warfare over who had the right to speak and organize in the name of God. Several groups, such as the Disciples of Christ, were started as attempts to settle, once and for all, the confusing Babel of religious claims. The deregulation of religion, the popular contagion of the American Revolution, the vast expanse of land, and the continual mixing of peoples—all conspired to make religion a pervasive, if divisive, reality in American life.

On the eve of the Civil War, religious wellsprings had saturated much of popular culture. Almost anyone—from fiery abolitionist to fire-eating defender of slave society—seemed to defend the vision of godly America by an appeal to Holy Writ. The Founding Fathers had dreamed that religious liberty in full flower would bring together a diverse people. Instead, the whirlwind of religious liberty intensified moral crusading and expanded the range of leaders who identified their cause as righteous. The pluralism of a free religious market fired dreams of the kingdom of God in America, but left Americans less capable of realizing them by compromise and consensus.[75]

Science and Religious Freedom

FRANK M. TURNER

TWO EVENTS OF the 1790s suggest the problematic relationship of modern science to both political and religious liberty in the West. During that decade two men of science of transatlantic reputation experienced harsh fates in the wake of the French Revolution. Both Joseph Priestley and Antoine L. Lavoisier had been deeply involved in the discovery of and early theories surrounding oxygen and the debunking of the theory of phlogiston. The questions surrounding the complexities of the relationships of their discoveries and theories are not relevant to this chapter. What is relevant is their clear standing as major natural philosophers in their respective nations and the fact of their international reputations. Yet despite their scientific achievements and fame the decade of the French Revolution brought personal disaster to both men.

On July 14, 1791, a Church and King mob stormed Priestley's home in Birmingham, England. In the turmoil Priestley suffered the destruction of his house, his laboratory, and his personal possessions. Ultimately he left England. He had become the target of the Church and King mob because he was a Unitarian minister who held radical political opinions about, among other things, religious liberty. He and other Unitarian radicals were also known to be sympathetic to the revolutionary groups in France. Such persons had been the object of Edmund Burke's conservative political polemic in *Reflections on the Revolution in France*, published the previous year.

Almost two years later, on May 8, 1794, Lavoisier, having been condemned by a revolutionary tribunal, was executed in Paris. In addition to having been a natural philosopher, he was also a tax farmer under the Old Regime. The personal profit he had made in that position and the discredit into which such activity had fallen more than counterbalanced his scientific achievements and his service on scientific commissions during the earlier months of the Revolution. At the height of the Terror the revolutionaries perceived little need for politically compromised men of science.

The political danger that overwhelmed these two distinguished natural philosophers may suggest some of the complexity surrounding the subject of science and political liberty. The scientific accomplishments of Priestley and Lavoisier could protect neither from political vilification and persecution arising from very different political sources. The counterrevolution in England supporting an established church overturned the life of the one scientist—to use the term anachronistically—while the most radical stage of the French Revolution with its profound anticlericalism and policy of dechristianization killed the other. Both religious establishmentarianism and anticlericalism stood indifferent to scientific achievement. Science as science or men of science as men of science seemed to have little or no independent influence or authority in the face of the larger political forces of the day.

≺ I ≻

The Traditional Argument

The history of the relationship of science and religious freedom must be considered as part of the larger subject of science and liberty in the modern world. The emergence of societies in which ever widening arenas of freedom have been established is one of the key elements in the history of the past several centuries. The liberty of the West has contributed to the expansion of both religious association and theological speculation and to the unprecedented expansion of scientific knowledge and organization. Science has contributed to religious liberty, and the example and character of religious liberty have aided the cause of science. But the relationships between science and religion in regard to liberty have never been simple.

The stories of Priestley and Lavoisier should give pause to any effort to relate science directly with liberty, let alone science with religious liberty. Yet for the last three centuries there has existed in European and American thought a broad belief that in some manner science can and does aid the cause of liberty and that liberty does and can aid the cause of science. This outlook, as will be seen, originated among the writers of the Enlightenment and received new support among scientifically minded Victorian intellectuals such as John Stuart Mill and T. H. Huxley. In this century such an outlook was, for example, fundamental to Karl Popper's influential vision of the philosophy of science. It also informed much of the work of Robert K. Merton, John Herman Randall, Jr., and James B. Conant and others involved in the history of science and intellectual history during and after World War II.[1] Much of the rhetoric of science in the West during the Cold War suggested a similar role for science as the foundation for liberal democracy. The pursuit of science appeared to embody a variety of values including tolerance, honesty, and disinterestedness that meshed with a liberal democratic political ethos.[2] C. P. Snow made the argument even more explicit in his *The Two Cultures* in which he portrayed scientists as operating in a fundamentally democratic culture.[3]

There have existed other important arguments for the connection of science with human freedom. These have included the role of scientific technology in freeing human beings from the traditional limitations imposed by nature and the use of medical science in liberating human beings from the pain of disease and premature death. This ideology of science and freedom began to flourish in the late nineteenth century as medicine became more professionalized and as its spokesmen attempted to set forth a professional ideology at one with middle-class values. This occurred about the same time that technology through the Second Industrial Revolution began to make an ever-expanding impact on everyday life in the West. As a consequence, within and without the scientific community medical science and technology entered the articulated vision of numerous futuristic writers as major liberators of humankind.[4]

Since the early eighteenth century, most especially in the English-speaking world, there has also existed a subplot to this story of science supporting the expansion of freedom. That subplot has contended that science also aids religious liberty. The subplot is somewhat less certain and rarely as noisily voiced, but it has existed nonetheless. Usually the concept of science expanding the realm of religious liberty has been associated with four arguments. The first is that modern, progressive science has flourished in the same political climate which has nurtured religious liberty and toleration. The second argument is that scientific knowledge has informed modern religious and theological thinking and has allowed the proponents of such thought to liberate themselves from earlier obscurantist ideas. Third, there has been a general assumption that religious minorities and natural philosophers at least in Europe had a common goal of liberating themselves from residual feudal structures and illiberal political structures that inhibited liberty both of religion and of thought. Finally, from the 1930s through the end of the Cold War, spokesmen for science pointed out that the liberal society of the Western democracies, supported by science, in contrast to both Nazi and Communist cultures permitted freedom of religion.

If one wished to point to a foundational text linking science to both political freedom and religious liberty, it would be Voltaire's *Lettres Philosophiques* of 1734, which are better known as *Letters on the English*. After running into trouble with aristocratic thugs in France, the young Voltaire had spent a number of years in England. He admired the liberty of early Hanoverian English society. The press functioned with considerable openness and could vocally criticize the government. There was a broad arena of open speech and political debate. There was no fear that opponents of the government would encounter the personal violence Voltaire had met in France. Like other visitors from the Continent, he had never previously witnessed such social phenomena.

English religious liberty also deeply fascinated Voltaire, who associated it with the more general political climate. At one point in the *Letters on the English*, Voltaire exclaimed, "This is the land of sects. An Englishman, as a free man, goes to Heaven by whatever route he likes."[5] He further commented, "If there were only one religion in England there would be danger of despotism, if there were two they would cut each other's throats, but there are thirty and they live in peace and happiness."[6] Such a world of religious liberty existed nowhere on the Continent. For Voltaire and other French philosophes English religious pluralism demonstrated that religious liberty as a good in itself could foster social stability, civility, and more general intellectual freedom. Voltaire would never lose his zeal for religious freedom and toleration, as demonstrated by much of his later writing and his role in the Calas affair.[7]

English science also made a deep impression on Voltaire. By chance his time in England had coincided with Newton's death in 1727 and the scientist's subsequent elaborate burial in Westminster

Abbey. Voltaire would later write a major exposition of Newton's thought that would mark him as one of the major Newtonians of the day. Indeed he spent much energy in the course of his life trying to defeat Cartesianism in the name of Newtonianism. Whereas Voltaire celebrated pluralism in religion, it seems not to have crossed his mind that there should be pluralism in science or that the absence of such pluralism might raise questions of intellectual liberty.

In Voltaire's mind there existed a clear and certain connection between English liberty and English science. Voltaire observed of Newton, "His great good fortune was not only to be born in a free country, but at a time when, scholastic extravagances being banished, reason alone was cultivated and society could only be his pupil and not his enemy."[8] Voltaire did not mention that 1642, the year of Newton's birth and of the outbreak of the Civil War, might or might not have marked an era when England was a free country. Voltaire also portrayed Newtonian thought as having flourished in this climate of freedom to which he, like others of his day, believed the philosophy of Locke had contributed much. In other words, Voltaire extended retrospectively the relatively liberal climate of the early eighteenth century into the seventeenth.

Voltaire, like other philosophes, most particularly D'Alembert in the *Preliminary Discourse* (1751) to the *Encyclopedia*, linked Bacon, Locke, and Newton as the apostles of the overthrow of scholasticism and the awakening of the spirit of Enlightenment, a spirit which he believed encompassed toleration and religious liberty. This Enlightenment view of the scientific revolution and its rejection of scholasticism paralleled the interpretation of the Protestant Reformation as a revolt against the medieval church. In both cases heroic figures had repudiated clerically dominated medieval intellectual outlooks and social structures for a culture in which ultimately a variety of intellectual and religious viewpoints might flourish. A secular intellectual reformation followed a Protestant religious reformation.

The Reformation understood as a movement of heroic individuals seeking religious and theological liberty against an obscurantist, authoritarian church would provide the archetype for seeing the later liberation of scientific thinkers from religious authority and the categories of religious thought. Both movements could and would be portrayed as modes of human liberation. Furthermore, through much of that process until the Victorian turmoil over geology and evolution, scientists and Protestants (often the same people) did not encounter significant tension in this vision of dual liberation. After all Bacon had championed revelation through two books—that of the scripture and that of nature. As both a religious and a cultural Protestant, he had called men of science to study both volumes for an understanding of the divine. Religious and cultural Protestants would call for a priesthood of believers free to interpret each book. Furthermore, the case of Galileo had associated scientific and religious liberty in the minds of Protestants. So long as both Protestants and scientists (who might or might not be religiously observant) could see the Roman Church as a common enemy, there was much space for cooperation.

Throughout the eighteenth century other authors associated science and enlightened thought with modes of religious progress. Joseph Priestley and Richard Price, among the English Unitarians, saw the expansion of knowledge in general and of science in particular working toward a healthy rationality in religious matters that would in turn foster a more liberal political order. They also associated the expansion of scientific knowledge with the second coming of Christ.[9] The Scottish Enlightenment historian William Robertson, who was principal of the University of Edinburgh and moderator of the Scottish Kirk, held a similar outlook without embracing millenialism.[10] For Adam Smith, science served as a prophylactic against superstition and enthusiasm, both of which were dangerous to religious toleration and intellectual progress. He explained, "Science is the great antidote to the poison of enthusiasm and superstition; and where all the superior ranks of people were secured from it, the inferior ranks could not be much exposed to it."[11] Rational, scientific ideas, understood as a broad swath of natural knowledge diffused among the elites, could function as a barrier against religious extremism and the undue influence of clergy and thus provide a substitute for the state attempting to use force against the clergy or religious groups. The influence of science would prevent individual sects from being able to impose their own narrow orthodoxy on the larger society. The open-mindedness of science would combat the close-mindedness of a single religious group. Science in this manner provided the necessary backdrop for a culture of both moderate liberty and moderate religion. In this respect, by contending that the presence of scientific knowledge and understanding would themselves guarantee a multiplicity of religious sects, Smith went well beyond Voltaire.

Ironically, Burke's *Reflections on the Revolution in France* also worked to establish a link, even if one with primarily negative connotations, between science and religious liberty. Burke portrayed the Revolution as having been brought about by rationalistic, skeptical, abstract ideas hatched by French literary cabals. Burke also ridiculed scientific language and associated it with political and social disruption. Furthermore, there were distinguished English men of science, most importantly Priestley, among the politically radical English Nonconformists. By implication Burke's ideas served to associate natural philosophy in Britain and elsewhere with the politics of the Revolution. Burke thus associated science with a vision of too-excessive political liberty and with a radical concept of religious liberty.[12]

The latter association had been rendered quite simple because radical English Nonconformists had already connected their own calls for religious liberty with more general demands for political and intellectual liberty. For example in the 1770s the Unitarian David Williams had declared to his co-religionists:

Your very existence depends on your changing the reason of your dissent, which used to be an opinion of superior orthodoxy and superior purity of faith and worship, for another which is the only rational and justifiable reason of dissent—the inalienable and universal right of private judgment, and the necessity of an unrestrained enquiry and freedom of debate and discussion on all subjects of knowledge, morality, and religion. This may be called Intellectual Liberty. This should be the general reason of dissent.[13]

The attempt to identify and equate religious liberty with the general thrust of intellectual liberty may well have seemed a clever tactic in the 1770s. But by the close of the century the equation left both exposed to the wave of counterrevolution. The more Burke and others associated the French Revolution with the excesses of intellectual liberty which was at least rhetorically associated with science, the more endangered religious minorities became if they had linked their cause with that of the march of mind.

During the 1790s and throughout the first three decades of the nineteenth century the calls to repeal the Test and Corporation Acts, the drive for Catholic Emancipation, and the demand for greater latitude of theology and liturgy in the Church of England were conflated by their opponents with radical politics, rational thought, and the scientific spirit that Burke had portrayed as fostering the upheavals of the French Revolution. Conservatives entertained little doubt that the spirit of science fostered religious liberty and toleration that threatened the status quo. Furthermore, as Adrian Desmond has recently demonstrated, there did exist a good deal of political radicalism and anticlericalism and even downright anti-Christian thought among the science faculty at University College London and more especially in the London medical community.[14] Several of these medical radicals confronted formal or informal censure. Political and religious conservatives could therefore present science as something that must be limited in its ideas and cultural role lest it ignite political and religious upheaval.

In light of these difficulties, other early nineteenth-century English men of science, especially those who founded the British Association for the Advancement of Science, took care to avoid political and religious commentary. As Arnold Thackray and Jack Morrell argued over a decade ago, the spokesmen for the early British Association took every possible precaution to see that science avoided radical or excessively liberal political associations.[15] That policy paradoxically allowed a very significant step toward an expanded religious liberty in Great Britain and was so seen by opponents of religious pluralism such as the early Tractarians. The British Association gathering under the banner of investigating nature established a genuine nondenominational venue where Anglicans and Nonconformists of all stripes gathered in a tolerant atmosphere of mutual cooperation and respect while representatives of the same religious groups did battle with each other in virtually every other area of early Victorian life. The British Association leadership thus established public discourse on science as a realm of civil religious pluralism.[16]

The effort to realize formal religious pluralism in Great Britain as well as on the Continent was an essential element in modern European religious liberty. In this regard Europe differed from the United States. In the latter nation religious pluralism burgeoned forth from the Revolution onward in terms of both denominational divisions and the democratization of the clergy as well.[17] Pluralism, as well as constitutional guarantees of freedom of religion, was the American way of religious life. By contrast in Britain despite the existence of broad toleration, the Church of England retained formal political privileges until the repeal of the Test and Corporation Acts in 1828 and the enactment of Catholic Emancipation in 1829. Thereafter the Church of England continued to enjoy numerous financial, social, and political advantages including the membership of their bishops in the House of Lords. English religious liberty had to go beyond toleration to be genuinely free. If religious liberty meant only the right to worship legally, it was clearly an incomplete form of civic liberty. The achievement of religious pluralism needed to embrace the right to worship freely and to enter civic life on a more or less equal footing. It also required a mutual recognition of the social, if not necessarily the theological, legitimacy of a variety of religious denominations. Such an understanding of religious freedom had become all the more important in the early nineteenth century as a significant itinerant ministry developed among English Dissenters.[18] It was just that recognition of the social legitimacy of various religious groups that the British Association embodied as did no other social or intellectual institution of the second and third quarters of the century.

There was an important reason why the British scientific community could provide a venue for religious pluralism and religious freedom. From the late seventeenth century through the publication of the Bridgewater Treatises in the 1830s, natural theology had provided what Robert Young once termed a "common context" for the discussion of science, religion, and society.[19] The content of natural theology presented a vision of nature and society that validated the culture of northwestern Europe in general and Great Britain in particular. It was an ecumenical theology about which learned practitioners of science from numerous denominations could largely agree. Furthermore, to the extent that natural theology was rooted in the scientific and progressive ideas of the late seventeenth century and the social-political vision associated with those ideas, it implicitly embraced a religiously tolerant world view. The general vision of natural theology was that of a liberal, commercial society with social hierarchy to be sure but also one in which law and a moderate social, intellectual, and religious pluralism prevailed.[20]

From the middle of the nineteenth century onward spokesmen for science managed to tie their cause to a progressive vision of human liberty. Across Europe, America, Latin America, and even China science during the last quarter of the nineteenth century came to be seen as a force that would liberate human beings from traditional society, one of the chief institutions of traditional society being religion.[21] Scientific thought came to be one of the chief weapons of this utopian vision of release from tradition. Both the natural and the social sciences came to be regarded as vehicles for liberating human beings from religion or at least from intellectually or socially obsolete religions. Winwood Reade encapsulated such a vision for popular consumption in *The Martyrdom of Man* of 1872. This book presented a world in which a radically naturalistic enlightenment grounded in science would overturn traditional intellectual and religious darkness and allow humankind to realize its full potential.

It is important to observe that only a few voices from science actually advocated atheism. What was far more prevalent from Herbert Spencer to Henri Bergson was the belief that science would liberate human beings from worn-out religious ideas and lead them to a new modern spiritual awareness. Advocacy of such intellectual or theological liberation could draw support from traditional ideas about religious liberty. The advocates of the new religions or new spiritual awareness based on science should benefit from the same religious liberty as had more traditional religious groups. In that respect, the model of religious liberty could be used to further ideas highly critical of traditional religions.

Normally in the historiography of Victorian intellectual life, historians have emphasized the conflict that ensued within the world of Victorian science as the symbiotic relation of science and religion made possible by natural theology came asunder under the impact of evolutionary thought. That such a conflict took place as Victorian science became more professionalized and separated from distinctly theological concerns is certainly true and well documented. But there was another tendency also at work whereby a certain area of cooperation developed between some scientists and certain advanced theologians. Both sets of thinkers, like the eighteenth-century Unitarian David Williams, associated their causes with intellectual freedom and in doing so they tended to support one another.

Within the Victorian intellectual elite, no doubt John Stuart Mill more than any other writer allowed a doctrine of individual liberty to be connected with scientific thought and religious liberty, each being seen as a version of individual opinion. Mill's philosophy of science, as discussed in his *System of Logic*, clearly presented science as among other things embodying open-mindedness. Such open-mindedness also characterized both toleration of various religious views and the capacity to criticize contemporary religious beliefs. In *On Liberty* (1859) Mill contended for the widest possible freedom of speech and opinion as a force for social and intellectual progress. That the progress he had in mind was intellectual is clear from his emphasis on the flourishing of genius. It would also appear, as recently argued by Joseph Hamburger, that Mill had a religious agenda in *On Liberty*.[22] Wide liberty of thought and discussion would allow for the possibility of extensive religious discussion and experiment. In turn, the latter might lead to the possibility of religions which would be an alternative to Christianity. By the time of Mill, enlightened scientific thought was thus emphasizing either liberty from any form of traditional religion or the liberty to explore new non-Christian religious alternatives that might be discovered rationally or scientifically. Liberty of thought was coming to be as much a part of religious liberty as liberty of practice and association.

Because of Mill's arguments and the more general climate of Victorian liberalism, advanced spokesmen for science and advanced spokesmen for theology could for one last time make a common appeal to the cultural Protestant model of freedom of thought resisting old fashioned, obscurantist religious authority. As James Moore has contended, the spokesmen for science and scientific naturalism urged the existence of a necessary conflict with religion and pressed the military metaphor.[23] The general argument was that religious authority, whether of the Roman Catholic Church, Anglican bishops, or Protestant synods, was halting the advancement of thought and inhibiting intellectual freedom. Some religious voices moved to associate themselves with the liberal, naturalistic assault on dogma.

Despite the ongoing controversies between some scientists and some clergy, there developed during the second half of the century a close but not always comfortable relationship between the ideas and practice of progressive science and those of liberal or progressive religion. Advocates of science and of liberal religious thought shared a general desire to be left alone by existing religious authority. Advanced theological thinkers saw themselves in a cultural and religious situation parallel to that of advanced scientists. This linkage was all the more plausible in the mid-nineteenth century when historical and philological scholarship, regarded at the time as a science, was the major engine of theological change and revision. Indeed one of the earliest references to a conflict between science and religion related not to the physical but to the philological sciences.[24] The fact that the tools of the higher criticism of the Scriptures, including philology, comparative mythology, sociology, and critical history, were regarded and described as "scientific" meant that science came to be associated with the liberty of those scholars to pursue their theological research and publication.

The growing impact of science on the wider culture in turn served as an argument for reassessing and revising theology. Theological liberals tended to believe either in a progressive revelation or in an existing revelation being rethought according to the categories of progressive science. Consequently progressive religion required some theologians to break through older patterns of thought and to demand successfully and unsuccessfully the right to think more freely and more liberally. Protestant liberals commencing with Baden Powell and F. D. Maurice and followed by the authors of *Essays and Reviews* (1860) contended that theology must conform itself to the new knowledge of physical and historical science. Later William Robertson Smith, who pioneered the anthropological study of religion, would make similar claims during his trial for heresy within the Free Church of Scotland. The Anglican high church contributors to *Lux Mundi* would assert a similar position, as would the authors of *Foundations* in 1912. A similar pattern appeared on the Continent. Thus, advanced science ironically became something of a stalking horse for advanced theology. Liberal theologians could demand freedom for new speculation in matters of faith and theology on the basis of the new knowledge achieved by a science liberated from previous intellectual and institutional theological constraints.

The drive for the repeal of the religious tests at Oxford and Cambridge saw a similar combination of concern for science and liberal religion. Advocates of repeal argued that neither liberal theology nor modern science could be pursued so long as the religious tests were required. Again the liberty of science and the liberty of religion enjoyed a symbiotic relationship. In this climate strange bedfellows could and did appear. Even the most aggressive agnostics were capable of suggesting a kind of liberal religion that might constitute an accepted religious establishment. In a remarkable passage of 1871 T. H. Huxley wrote that he could

conceive the existence of an Established Church which should be a blessing to the community. A Church in which, week by week, services should be devoted, not to the iteration of abstract propositions in theology, but to the setting before men's minds of an ideal of true, just, and pure living; a place in which those who are weary of the burden of daily cares, should find a moment's rest in the contemplation of the higher life which is possible for all, though attained by so few; a place in which the man of strife and of business should have time to think how small, after all, are the rewards he covets compared with peace and charity. Depend upon it, if such a Church existed, no one would seek to disestablish it.[25]

Huxley is envisioning a church which would not offend advanced liberal or scientific sensibilities. He is implying that if a Christian church, most especially the Church of England, would allow itself to be informed by the ideas of science and to allow those ideas to work their way through its intellectual and theological structure, that church would be liberated from secular attacks on it and perhaps even from the then current attacks of Protestant Nonconformists. Such a vision of a moderate established religion that would accommodate itself to modern knowledge resonated across a considerable spectrum of Victorian intellectual life as both liberal scientists and liberal clergy sought to establish an intellectual and religious life purged of dogma.

   Nonetheless, despite the several decades of cooperation among a small group of scientists and liberal theologians, the ultimate tendency of the larger contemporary intellectual and social forces was for the dividing of men of science and men of religion into separate cultural spheres. The old religious alliance forged during the Newtonian period between science and religious liberty came apart permanently in the wake of Darwin as the Newton of the biological sciences. The common context between science and religion afforded by natural theology simply collapsed because eventually neither party shored it up. Scientists wanted to establish their own professional liberty and were willing to leave religion out of the picture and let religious groups do as they pleased so long as they left science alone.[26] Within the world of theology, the various religious parties also tended to retreat into exclusive conclaves such as Keble College or Pusey House in Oxford where persons of distinct theological outlooks worked within their own communities and no longer sought to dominate the entire church or university. Within the sorting out process, the liberal theologians tended to dominate university theological faculties, but not individual colleges, religious houses, or grass roots institutions of religious life.[27]

Some scientists, social scientists, and clergy sought to establish new secular or at least non-Christian religions. This was certainly true of Comte's Religion of Humanity, which linked fraternity, altruism, and social elitism with an epistemological program of intellectual advance. Comte's thought had a considerable impact in both Europe and America as well as in Latin America. Bernard Lightman has very persuasively argued that many of the voices associated with British scientific naturalism actually hoped to expound a new natural religion which would be based on nineteenth-century science but stand free from the ecclesiastical links of traditional natural religion.[28] Such efforts, which never were particularly successful in establishing long-lasting institutional bases, were protected by traditional views of freedom of religion.

The basis of thinking about religious freedom had been transformed in the second half of the nineteenth century. Originally in the late eighteenth century the association of religious liberty with intellectual liberty employed the latter as a polemical vehicle to achieve the former. But the situation was reversed at least among the cultural elites in the late nineteenth century. The freedom sought by the advanced religions of science or other secular religions was defended more often than not on the grounds of freedom of thought and expression rather than freedom of worship. This marks an important transition for the concept of religious freedom. It was no longer based on a deep concern for religious congregations themselves. Religious liberty understood as intellectual liberty became located in the conscience of the individual rather than in the corporate rights of the individual religious community functioning within a larger society. Thus conceived, religious liberty became the freedom for the pursuit of polite and learned antinomianism and as such was the culmination of the social demands of both nineteenth-century science and romantic religion, the former having located itself in the genius of the individual scientist and the latter in the subjective experience of the individual.

This broad overview suggests that from the seventeenth century through at least the third quarter of the nineteenth century numerous writers linked science to ideas of liberty. The fundamental framework for this interpretation of the intellectual and political history of the past three centuries has been the emergence of Western society from the confines of a church-directed culture. The second framework has been the rise of useful knowledge to a point dominating all others. In that regard, it has been the usefulness of science, medicine, and technology that has really constituted the point of connection between science and liberal society. Those who advocated the dominance of useful knowledge believed either that the advance of science would produce a purer form of religion than traditional Christianity or that the advance of science would eventually make religion unnecessary. In either case science would be liberating.

≺ II ≻

The Traditional Argument Reconsidered

This traditional narrative of the association of science with freedom in general and religious freedom in particular represents a very selective reading of the history of Western science, social history, and religious life. It ignores the history of the organization of science; chooses only particular cases, notably the British; excludes the social sciences; and takes a narrow view of what human activities constitute science. It also assumes a generally Protestant view of religion; acquiesces in a consistently hostile attitude toward Roman Catholicism, taking little or no account of Jesuit contributions to science; wholly ignores the position of Judaism in the modern Western experience; and pays no attention to the relationship of science to non-Western religions. A counternarrative, well supported by historical evidence and assuming somewhat different perspectives, is possible.

Much conceptual confusion has surrounded the relationship of science to liberty and religious liberty. If the connection of the sciences to various forms of liberty is to have any meaning at all, several conditions would need to prevail:

a. Scientific knowledge should flourish more fully in a climate of political liberty than in alternative climates.

b. Science should in some manner actually contribute to liberty of action and thought in a variety of venues and not inhibit such liberty.

c. Science should, as science, support religious liberty understood in this context as religious pluralism or at the very least not inhibit it.

d. Religion must not prevent science from flourishing.

e. Religious liberty should aid science and not inhibit its advance and the diffusion of scientific knowledge.

f. Science must not lead to state inhibitions on individual liberty.

These conditions would appear to be the minimal framework for a meaningful relationship to be drawn between science and liberty. One could refine them or add additional conditions, such as a maximally comprehensive religious liberty, but these six conditions do appear to be the minimal framework.

At no time during the past three centuries have all of these conditions obtained in any major European nation or in the United States. There is no clear pattern of liberty contributing to science or science to liberty if one breaks out of the ideology of scientism itself. Scientists clearly did seek to associate themselves and their enterprise with the values and institutions of liberal society in parts of the transatlantic world during the nineteenth century, but only for the purpose of achieving an independent role for themselves in that society. The model of earlier religious liberty understood as voluntary associations being able to function free of state interference did, however, provide a model for an independent, autonomous role for science. By contrast, with a few notable exceptional cases the impact of science upon religious life has been negative unless for some reason it has been to the tactical advantage of scientists to support religion or to assume a neutral stance toward it.

The belief or faith that science and liberty are mutually sustaining arises from conceiving science as an exclusively positivistic enterprise. Through this definition of science, the enterprise constitutes sound positivistic knowledge displacing earlier forms of mistaken understanding. Science here, as argued in the earlier portion of this chapter, assumes in the secular sphere the role that Protestantism had historically played in the religious. Such a definition of science is ahistorical and inadequate to the task of describing the variety of human activities that from the sixteenth century forward have been included under the terms science and natural philosophy. Recent research has made quite clear that from the time of the Scientific Revolution through at least the third quarter of the nineteenth century there existed a series of competing definitions of science both as a mode of knowledge and as a social activity.[29]

A more critical examination of science in early modern Europe does not sustain links between the science of that era and the emergence of free political institutions. During the first century following the publication of Copernicus's *De Revolutionibus* (1543) virtually no links existed between the new science and political liberty or religious toleration. Indeed much early modern science flourished under absolutist regimes. This relationship of science and absolutism has not been widely explored. Even Enlightenment supporters of Newton who criticized Descartes's physics nonetheless saw the latter's philosophy and mathematics as enormously important for the new science. Although Descartes often worked and published outside France, his education and thought had been nurtured under early seventeenth-century French absolutism and within Roman Catholic institutions. Galileo, of course, stood as a figure of great Enlightenment and Victorian admiration. He was the intellectual liberator *par excellence*. Whereas most later commentators inevitably saw Galileo as a martyr of the new science to Roman Catholic religious authority, more recent scholars of the Galileo case have presented a much more complicated picture. Pietro Redondi retains the religious dimension of Galileo's condemnation, but relates it to issues of the Eucharist rather than to discrepancies between the new astronomy and the Bible.[30] Mario Biagioli has argued that Galileo's career must be interpreted in the context of the patronage relationships within the courts of Italy. According to this view, the condemnation of Galileo arose as much from his faltering patronage network in the baroque court culture of papal Rome as it did from ecclesiastical disapproval of his natural philosophy.[31] Even if one were not fully to accept these new interpretations, one must still admit that Galileo chose to leave the service of the Venetian Republic for that of the Medici princes and that he carried out his most important experiments and achieved his most important insights within the context of absolutist Italian courts. Finally, the seventeenth-century political philosopher most clearly associated with the new science was Hobbes, whose *Leviathan* (1651) became the byword for absolutist political philosophy and atheism and who personally had little sympathy with religious liberty.

The earliest general case for the association of political and religious liberty with science is that made by Voltaire and other Enlightenment philosophes with regard to England and occasionally in passing to Holland.[32] It was Enlightenment anglophilia combined with the achievements of seventeenth-century English science that made the English case the archetype for the link between science and liberty. There has, of course, been a long debate among historians of science about the relationship of Puritanism to science. But the traditional political case for the association of liberty and science rested not on the Puritan connection, but rather on the careers of Francis Bacon, Isaac Newton, and John Locke. These were the three great intellectual liberators for the Enlightenment. But what is the connection of the thought and life of these men with political and religious liberty? It is problematical at best.

Francis Bacon could appear as an intellectual liberator only in the hindsight of more than a century when Enlightenment philosophes separated his metaphysical and epistemological opinions from the political, legal, and administrative world in which he functioned. Bacon served as lord chancellor of James I. To the extent that he could, James I would have liked to strengthen the power of the monarchy over that of the troublesome Parliament. James had notoriously little sympathy for religious pluralism especially as manifested by the Puritans of his day. Throughout his career Bacon viewed himself not as an independent intellectual but rather as an intellectual who as a lawyer and as a natural philosopher was working toward strengthening the authority of the monarchy and central state. Bacon's thought did attack scholasticism, but his ideas in regard to science would have encouraged the creation of academies and a scientifically educated bureaucracy. He sought to reform both the law and natural philosophy for the purpose of increasing the power of knowledge as it would be manifested in a society administered by a strong, well-informed monarchy. All of the evidence about Bacon's political and scientific opinions would indicate that he would have strongly opposed the later seventeenth-century political and religious groups who demanded religious liberty and challenged monarchical authority. One of the most recent scholars of Bacon's view of science has gone so far as to contend, "Francis Bacon's natural philosophy, after all, was a natural philosophy appropriate to a centralizing and imperial state."[33] It is not surprising that Louis XIV's minister Colbert had no difficulty in pointing to the thought of Bacon when establishing the French academies in a monarchy that eschewed both political liberty and religious pluralism.

The situation of Newton is even more interesting. To be sure Newton sat in the Convention Parliament after the revolution of 1688 and served in later parliaments. He was also for many years the warden of the mint under the post-1688 monarchy. Margaret Jacob, James R. Jacob, and Larry Stewart have emphasized the connection between later Newtonians, the realization of the revolutionary settlement, and Whig patronage.[34] Yet what were the political conditions under which Newton carried out his research and wrote the *Principia*? Newton, as a man of science, was a natural philosopher of the English Restoration under which there existed little religious liberty and during which both Protestant Nonconformists and Roman Catholics encountered considerable persecution.[35] Furthermore, he actually wrote the *Principia* during the early 1680s, which were certainly the years of the most intense efforts of Charles II to rule in an absolutist manner. Newton published the book in the very year in which James II was turning the English political scene topsy turvy by an opportunistic, and what is generally regarded as insincere, policy of toleration gauged to strengthen the monarchy. Quite simply, Voltaire's previously quoted comment to the contrary, Newton achieved and published his most important insights under a generally illiberal monarchical regime. That government contributed nothing to a climate of either political or religious liberty for the composition of the *Principia*.

The character of toleration established by the revolutionary settlement at best worked ambiguously for science. The Toleration Act of 1689 did not embrace Roman Catholics or Unitarians. The exclusion of formal toleration for Unitarians even in the absence of formal persecution caused unnecessary difficulty and social stigma for the single most scientifically progressive of all English religious denominations. By the end of the eighteenth century the political and religious hostility toward radical Unitarians played into the hands of the mob who attacked Joseph Priestley's house. But Newton himself had also confronted the problem of possible persecution. He labored under the apprehension that his secret unorthodox Arian views of the divinity of Christ might become public and that he would be attacked for them.[36] Newton had no expectation that his scientific achievement would protect him, just as a century later scientific distinction did not protect Priestley.

The association of Newtonian science with liberty also came about by what was in the eighteenth century understood as a clear connection between Newtonianism and John Locke, who had set forth a theory of liberal politics and religious toleration. While within the context of the day Locke's thought was certainly genuinely liberal and tolerant, it is unclear that his views on toleration had any significant connection to the science of his day. Moreover, for all of its attractive and advanced qualities, there were distinct limits to Locke's version of toleration.[37] It was essentially a plea for toleration among Christians, and as he developed the argument, for toleration among Protestants. Locke's toleration included neither Roman Catholics nor atheists. Both exceptions were fraught with difficulty for the future of science, religion, and liberty. From the late seventeenth century onward, the term "atheist" had a very elastic meaning which would often be used as an ill-defined term of opprobrium against any religious opponent. It is unclear that even Locke would have allowed the public toleration of the theology that Newton worked out in the privacy of his study if such theology publicly discussed would have disturbed the civil peace. In time Roman Catholicism would, as will be seen later, come to constitute one of the most difficult areas for working out a relationship between religious liberty and modern scientific thought.

The climate of early eighteenth-century English religious dispute also revealed the limitations of toleration in theory and practice. Early in the century the London Boyle lecturers, whose lectures had been endowed by the estate of Robert Boyle, attempted to use Newtonian science and the providentialism that had become associated with it to refute and repress deistic freethinkers, such as John Toland. In the minds and rhetoric of the most orthodox Anglicans throughout the eighteenth century, atheists would have included Unitarians. Indeed, early in the century high-church Anglicans attacked the religious orthodoxy of Unitarians just as late in the century they would question their political orthodoxy. Consequently, the tolerant England of Voltaire's reports was certainly more free than France, but its religious liberty was neither unproblematic nor necessarily friendly to those who pursued science.

It is the nineteenth-century British case in which traditionally science has been seen as a force for political and cultural liberation. Indeed such was part of the self-image of Victorian public science. Yet even in Victorian Britain there were distinct limits. Although the British Association for the Advancement of Science provided a venue for religious pluralism, its leaders drew the line at activities of alleged scientific merit that touched upon *new* moral or religious knowledge. The British Association was never willing to open its relatively wide doors to the practitioners of phrenology, mesmerism, or spiritualism.[38] In the first place advocates for each movement made claims that many, though by no means all men of science, regarded as without real empirical foundations despite the claims to the contrary. But there were also other considerations. Although neither phrenology nor mesmerism was an actual religion, the adherents of both did make very considerable moral claims that challenged polite opinion and existing religious authority. The British Association leadership was not about to condone such views. Spiritualism for its part did make claims that related to traditional religious concerns. It was Spiritualism that one scientist after another, with certain notable exceptions, condemned or attempted to prove a fraud. So far as Spiritualism was a new religious movement that claimed to base its authority on scientific evidence, most Victorian men of science, from the United States to Russia, sharply condemned it.[39]

The attacks on Spiritualism were a small part of a wider critique of religion carried out in Great Britain by the spokesmen for Victorian scientific naturalism. This ongoing critique occurred despite their friendships with liberal theologians and their desire to set forth a modern natural theology. John Tyndall and T. H. Huxley, for example, attacked Anglicans, Nonconformists, Roman Catholics, and Scottish Presbyterians.[40] Throughout the advanced scientists' defense of Darwin there ran a strong critique of the intellectual and moral legitimacy of religion and of the cultural influence of the clergy. The cleric-baiting scientists were attempting a social and intellectual redefinition of science that would drive clergymen from the increasingly professionalized ranks of science. Non-clerical scientists were in effect saying that one could not be a good scientist and a good clergyman. The non-clerical scientists quite simply were denying the right of clergy to make serious pronouncements on science. In this regard, the non-clerical scientists were seeking to prevent clergymen from carrying on what for almost two centuries had been a major occupation for a significant group of clergy.

The scientists often covered their activities under the guise of freedom of thought and liberation from tradition and frequently associated socially with liberal theologians. The crusade for Darwinism and scientific naturalism, however, whether in Britain, on the Continent, or in America, did not really represent a commitment to freedom beyond the freedom of professionalizing scientists to establish their own cultural authority. Scientists could and did embrace the general arguments for religious liberty in order to help secular ideas to flourish in a parallel manner. Scientists might encourage liberal theologians to question traditional theology and to embrace scientific methods, but their purpose was to demonstrate the power of science to create a new social and moral world. Scientists gained far more from this cooperation than did the religious liberals, who remained on the defensive within virtually all religious denominations. The theologians ironically needed the scientists and not the reverse. Consequently, that cooperation demonstrated the cultural authority of science over religious thought and at the same time helped to make the religious world less dangerous to science.

The assault on religion by leading scientists and other intellectuals in Britain and elsewhere involved an even more problematic element. Across much of the Western world during the second half of the nineteenth century scientists frequently attacked Roman Catholicism. The relationship of science to Roman Catholicism was and remains a very complex one. Within the history of religious freedom in the past two centuries the subject of anti-Catholicism constitutes a very difficult territory that merits further examination. Anti-Catholicism has been one of the preferred forms of religious and social bigotry often supported by intellectuals in general and scientists in particular of both secular and Protestant outlooks. The Bismarckian Kulturkampf, as seen in chapter 6 of this volume, constituted a clear breach of religious liberty. Attacks by scientists and other intellectuals against Roman Catholicism, however, generally have been regarded more ambiguously.

The sources of the latter anti-Catholic prejudice are not hard to discover. The Roman Catholic Church had long asserted claims to exclusive religious authority not made by other religious groups. Since the religious trauma of the French Revolution, the papacy had been one of the major voices of political conservatism. From the 1850s onward the papacy had assumed both politically and intellectually a sharply illiberal stance. The Syllabus of Errors of 1864 had rejected much modern science. The First Vatican Council had proclaimed papal infallibility. All of these matters placed the Roman Church at odds with modern secular thought, liberal politics, and science. It was not surprising that certain scientists, some of whom had also imbibed anti-Catholicism from other sources such as Protestant national self-identities, replied in a similarly hostile rhetoric.

Scientific thought and scientific naturalism provided an epistemological justification for the social and intellectual attack on Roman Catholicism. The dispute between the Roman Catholic Church and science was repeatedly posed as one of liberty of thought opposing clerical obscurantism and ecclesiastical authority. The issue was one of toleration for science and in turn presumably toleration for liberal and tolerant religions, but such toleration was to emerge through the demise or attenuation of Roman Catholicism itself. In the minds of scientists and of many of their contemporaries, to attack the Roman Church was to strike a blow for both intellectual and religious liberty. One sees this in the rhetoric of Tyndall and Huxley, among continental anticlericals, among the positivists of Latin America, and among American freethinkers such as Ralph Ingersoll. Indeed, vocal anti-Catholicism provided a broad protective cultural cover for scientists whose other ideas and social ambitions might have disturbed the status quo. Anti-Catholicism itself, no matter how sincerely advanced and regarded as progressive, also provided a cultural cover for advocacy of very anti-liberal causes such as British domination of Ireland, American Protestant resistance to Roman Catholic European immigrants, and Bismarck's Kulturkampf, all of which found vocal supporters in the various scientific communities. Much of the rhetoric about the relationship of science to liberal values in post-World War II America also involved no small element of anti-Catholicism. Science served as a cultural vehicle that would lead public life away from too strong an association with both Roman Catholicism and fundamentalism, which had been conservative political forces before World War II.[41]

Although papal power grew within the nineteenth-century Roman Church itself, the institutional authority of that church across Europe had steadily eroded from the era of the French Revolution onward. The Roman Catholic Church, despite the pretensions and rhetoric of the papacy, functioned at the sufferance of national governments of various political shades and was now a religious organization that required guarantees of religious liberty in most of Europe and in the United States. To be sure, there were areas of Europe where the Roman Catholic Church did seek to renew its authority. In other areas such as England and France it was constructing an educational infrastructure that would allow it to compete with other religious groups and with secular alternatives. But everywhere it stood on the defensive against the expansion of secular society. In many respects the anti-Catholic scientists failed to recognize the reality of the situation, but in any case their attacks on the Roman Catholic Church by the late nineteenth century should not be seen as aiding religious liberty. In some cases those attacks actually served to contravene it.

The overt anti-Catholicism of scientists was simply the most extreme element of a general effort on the part of a significant number of scientists in every major Western nation to undermine the influence and practice of traditional religion. When Max Weber wrote in 1919 "That science today is irreligious no one will doubt in his innermost being, even if he will not admit it to himself," he was describing a situation that had prevailed for half a century.[42] This process involved much more than the familiar intellectual controversies carried out in books, journals, and the popular press. There were also very practical ways in which the practice of science and public policies arising from science and medicine challenged the influence of religion and actually inhibited religious liberty. It is difficult to explore this subject because it means the questioning of the power of professionalism from which numerous academic groups not related to the sciences have also socially benefited. It also requires the admission that leading scientists and other respected intellectuals in the late nineteenth and early twentieth centuries actively embraced ideas that are now regarded as simply wrong or morally repulsive.

Once one admits that throughout the nineteenth century and well into the twentieth the idea of race enjoyed a strong and respected scientific pedigree, the entire relationship of science and liberty and more particularly science and religious liberty undergoes a very considerable transformation.[43] Most important, it leads one to consider the impact of scientific thought and activity on religious freedom outside the confines of the debates among Christian denominations.

As is well known, within Europe by the last third of the century racial arguments became directed in particular against Jews. Every aspect of Jewish life, religious practice, and culture was ascribed to race by one writer or another. Whatever legal or customary protections Jews enjoyed in regard to religion or culture could be and were undermined by scientific racism, which gradually pushed the Jew outside the compass and protection of civil society. All of this activity points to the fact that scientific thinking allowed for the persecution of Judaism as a religion as well as of Jews as an ethnic group. Although racial anti-Semitism is today usually described ethnically, it is well to remember that virtually all of the most notable physical attacks on Jews involved not only their homes and businesses but also their places of worship.[44] Racial thinking thus served as a weapon against Jews as a people and against Judaism as a religion that was a central element in that Jewish culture.

The rise of medical science and public health also contributed to a narrowing of the circle of religious freedom. From the opening of the great campaigns for public health there had existed a very real tension between the social goals of medical science and the individualism of nineteenth-century liberal society as medical practice intruded on numerous areas of human freedom. In the course of the nineteenth century public health furnished the grounds for government inspectors to enter the homes and private spaces of Europeans and Americans. Certain public health practices, most importantly vaccination, provided the grounds for the state literally to invade the bodies of citizens. Indeed the term "conscientious objector" originated among the opponents of compulsory vaccination. It was this argument against the intrusion of government into the lives of citizens on scientific medical grounds that would be imitated by religious conscientious objectors in their refusal of service in national armies. This was a case in which the argument for religious liberty that had origins in groups that objected to warfare in the seventeenth and eighteenth centuries, such as English Quakers and continental pietists, was used by secular opponents of medicine and then discovered again by religious groups.

Another direct and often unrecognized impact on religious liberty stemmed from this new authority of medicine and public health. The most familiar case is that of certain forms of medical care, such as blood transfusions, for the children of religious minorities, such as Jehovah's Witnesses. But there has been a much more subtle and ultimately more disruptive conflict. From the third quarter of the nineteenth century onward the sciences associated with public health, eugenics, and medicine began to extend their ideas and the activities of their practitioners into areas of family life relating to fertility, contraception, abortion, and euthanasia. For centuries these were areas of social life that within both Christianity and Judaism had been and would continue to be addressed by traditional religious teachings, authority, and institutions. In the late nineteenth century eugenicists would have introduced far less freedom of choice in all matters of personal life relating to marriage and the family. Some eugenicists saw eugenics as a new form of socially advantageous religion or what has been described as "a form of surrogate religion as a civilizing and disciplining creed."[45] Although eugenics stood largely abandoned by the end of World War I, medical practitioners who were not formally eugenicists nonetheless continued to move forward with other policies, including euthanasia, that touched upon areas of family life often deeply related to religious values.[46]

During the twentieth century the growing authority and persuasiveness of medical science as well as its expanding linkage to the state would lead to further major conflict between medicine and religious teachings in regard to the family. Beginning at least as far back as the 1920s in Europe and more recently in the United States, there arose a new and often not well recognized conflict between a significant segment of health-care professionals, often receiving public funding, and the forces of organized religion. Like the nineteenth-century scientists, the health-care providers of abortion and contraception have often, though by no means always, placed themselves on the side of contemporary political liberalism against what they portray as a conservative or even retrogressive opposition informed by religious ideas. What is occurring in the present-day debate over abortion is in part a repeat of the earlier sorting out process between scientific professionals and religious groups, both of whom claim to stand for liberty. Now as in the past what is largely at stake is a contest for cultural authority between scientific professionals and advocates of religious values. As in the past, the scientific medical community and the various religious communities stand divided. Where

the present conflict differs is in the determination of certain religious
communities and congregations to confront the world of medical science directly through the courts, elections, the forum of public opinion, and violence. In terms of scope, political impact, and social disruption the late nineteenth-century conflict between science and
religion pales before the late twentieth-century conflict between
medical science and religion.

Commentators have traditionally considered religious liberty almost entirely in European and North American contexts. Yet if one
thinks about the impact of the Western powers and economies on the
rest of the world during the nineteenth century, there is an important
connection between science and religious liberty and one that is full
of paradoxes and ironies.

Scientific racism provided arguments in defense of various forms
of servitude and justified much nineteenth-century imperialism and
the governing and in some cases the extermination of races in the
non-European world.[47] Racial thinking undergirded both American
slavery and the policy of the United States government toward Native Americans. Racial thinking, along with sheer greed, allowed
British settlers literally to exterminate the native population of Tas-
mania. Such racism also fostered and condoned the general denigra-
tion of non-European religions and religions not directly related to
the other major religious traditions. The African religion of American slaves was largely eradicated in what Jon Butler has termed "the
African Spiritual Holocaust."[48]

There were, however, other factors at work also related to science
and technology. Virtually all the Europeans, including missionaries,
who interacted with non-European peoples carried with them attitudes of cultural superiority, attitudes which may well have been
more important than concepts of racial superiority.[49] The cultural superiority was rooted in the realm of work discipline, law, technology,
and science. These outlooks along with a traditional sense of religious superiority on the part of Christian missionaries worked to
support the concept of a civilizing mission. The civilizing mission
was deeply related to the technological and scientific superiority of
Western peoples and involved an attitude of disrespect for allegedly
lesser races and religions. These factors led in general to a low es-
teem for non-Christian religions. The civilizing mission in whatever
form it took inevitably worked toward either Christianization or
secularization.

Anthropological outlooks that embodied Enlightenment episte-
mology also delegitimized the religious life of non-Western peoples
who were not part of one of the recognized ancient religious traditions. The scientific analysis of religion created a hierarchy of religions along with a hierarchy of values that culminated in the culture
and religions of Western Europe. There was little or no respect for
indigenous religions on the part of anthropologists who studied primitive non-Christian societies in either the past or the present. Anthropology in general and more particularly the anthropology and sociology of religion also contributed to a clearly articulated hierarchy of
religions. One finds this attitude permeating all of the anthropological literature and brought to the fore in articles such as that on "Religion" in the eleventh edition of the *Encylopaedia Britannica*.[50] At
best the higher religions might be tolerated, but there was a direct
implication that the spread of civilization tied to the concept of
Western science, rationalism, and technology should lead to the
abandonment if not the outright eradication of lower religions.

The great anthropological and natural history museums founded
in the late nineteenth and early twentieth centuries embodied this
triumphalist attitude toward primitive religions.[51] Those museums,
such as the Musée de l'Homme and the Smithsonian Institution as
well as many smaller private and public institutions scattered across
Europe and North America, contain the religious remains of peoples
as separated and diverse as North American Eskimos, Native Americans, African peoples, and South Sea Islanders. These anthropological museums present a curious cultural parallel with the Vatican
Museum. Over the centuries the Vatican Museum has gathered vast
collections of the remains of ancient pagan temples and gods. The
Vatican has literally imprisoned those remains to display to visitors
as a sign of the triumph of Christianity over its Roman predecessors.
In a similar fashion the anthropological museums of the early twentieth century, into which were poured relics of religious practices of
less civilized peoples and even the bodies of ancestors torn from
sanctified graves, portrayed the triumph of modern science over what
nineteenth-century anthropologists regarded as animism or ghost
worship. That such museum collecting did represent an attack on
religious liberty, especially of Native Americans in the United States
and Canada, can be seen by the efforts of later generations of these
people to reclaim the bodies and relics of their ancestors in order to
return them to sanctified ground.

Consideration of the *cultural* impact of science upon religious liberty should not, however, distract from recognition of the impact of *political* life on science as it has related to liberal freedoms. As noted at the opening of this chapter, throughout much of the mid-twentieth century scientists and their public advocates have emphasized the relationship of science to free and open societies. Yet it is not at all certain that empirical consideration of the relationship of science to government in the past two centuries will sustain that viewpoint. The mid-twentieth-century writers linking science to an open society were seeking to reassert a traditional liberal concept of freedom rooted in the free actions and associations of the individual. Theirs was a reassertion of the Enlightenment vision, but between the Enlightenment and their restatement of its goals there had arisen alternative definitions of freedom to which many scientists had tied themselves.

Within the last three centuries the definition of freedom and of religious freedom has undergone various changes in Western society. By the close of the nineteenth century freedom understood as freedom for individual action was giving way to new definitions and a new vocabulary of freedom based on collective ideals. Freedom became for many people the possibility of realizing self in a manner that was congruent to some ideal held by the community. Many scientists and physicians believed they could through their knowledge and skills contribute to those new collective forms of freedom. As Woodruff D. Smith and Paul Weindling have traced in such certain detail in the German case and William H. Schneider in the French, the sciences related to medicine, heredity, and anthropology were in the middle of the nineteenth century associated with liberalism and even political radicalism.[52] By the turn of the century these disciplines had become increasingly professionalized bodies of scholars and researchers who had accepted the outlook of organicist nationalism and state support for science. As these scientists sought to serve the state or the larger nation, they tended to become increasingly less liberal and much less concerned with individual rights.

Furthermore, those collectively defined modes of freedom to which many scientists attached themselves were often tied to bold utopian political experiments, which called for a radical transformation of humanity and which were inherently opposed to religious liberty and traditional liberal values. To the extent that scientists of any

field and specialization associated themselves with those visions—
whether the Jacobinism of the French Revolution, Comtism, nationalism, radical socialism, communism, fascism, or national socialism—those scientists and their ideas worked against religious liberty
in particular and liberal freedom in general. Quite simply, many
scientists over the years became the creatures of the political structures and ideologies to which they had given their loyalties from sincerely held political conviction or selfish personal ambition or in the
hope of improving the situation of the scientific enterprise.

In the case of both Germany and the Soviet Union it would appear
that significant portions of the scientific community at any given
moment were willing to receive financial support from the state and
give political support in return. From early in the nineteenth century scientists throughout Europe presented German science as the
model for emulation in terms of the funding and government support
that it received. Yet at no time during the nineteenth century did
science in Germany flourish under liberal political regimes. The
German science associated with philosophical materialism in the
writings of figures such as Vogt, Moleschott, and Büchner was noted
primarily for its atheism, anticlericalism, and support of the Kulturkampf.[53] The German scientific community found little difficulty
supporting the Kaisarreich during World War I. The favorable relationship of much of the German scientific and medical communities
to the Nazi political regime is well known.[54]

Some writers arguing for the necessity of an open society for scientific progress point to the disasters brought onto Soviet science and
agriculture by the career of Lysenko.[55] But no other political structures of the twentieth century were as deeply rooted in scientific,
materialist views of both physical and human nature as those associated with the Soviet Union and its post–World War II satellites. The
Soviet Union for some time had near technological military parity
with the Western Alliance in numerous areas of research. And while
pursuing intense technological programs related to both military
and economic production, the Soviet government, like the Nazi,
moved strongly against religious liberty and embraced policies of
anti-Semitism.[56]

Throughout the nineteenth century the goal of most of the various Western scientific communities was to achieve significant state
support for science. Over the course of the century and into the next,

they achieved that goal. By the last quarter of the nineteenth century the scientific communities of all the major European nations and the United States generally believed that only governments possessed the financial resources to pay for modern science. Since that time no other group of intellectuals has been so successful around the world in tapping government resources. This important emerging relationship of science to the state and the implications of that relationship for science and liberal politics have not been widely explored as a cultural or political matter.

On a more general level, the impact of state support of science has quietly and not always with intention worked against religious pluralism, especially in education. The necessity of funding scientific education and research put new financial burdens on education from the secondary through the college and university levels. For a time religiously oriented secondary schools, colleges, and universities were able to finance their science programs, but as the cost increased, they like other secular institutions received government support. The receiving of that support in turn drew those institutions in both Europe and North America into the arena of government regulation not only about science policy but about other areas of institutional life. This situation along with other factors of educational life and policy in the twentieth century has led to a profoundly secular character for nearly all institutions of higher education if not all secondary schools.[57]

Certainly during the past three-quarters of a century in the United States science and religion have often not contributed to mutual understanding and respect. From the early years of the century onward various religious groups have attempted to prevent the teaching of evolution in public schools.[58] Similarly, scientists have opposed those efforts. On the other side, professional medicine and public health have steadfastly resisted the pursuit and application of alternative forms of medicine. The issue at hand may actually relate as much to the problem of freedom and professionalism as religion and science, but in either case the activities of significant portions of both the religious and the scientific medical communities have sought to limit the liberty of the other. Yet for the present there is little doubt that the influence of science has on the whole limited the influence of religion more than the reverse, though under modified political conditions in which religious fundamentalism prevailed or significantly influenced science policy that situation might change.

The twentieth-century relationship of science to the state has established a cultural situation for science that is the mirror image of that which once pertained to religion. A science-directed culture has to a considerable extent replaced a church-directed culture. Scientific establishments of differing institutional structures have achieved the privileged cultural positions once held by religious establishments. Whereas in 1750 religion had more cultural authority than science in the Western world, the reverse is now the case. In 1750 various religious bodies retained and would continue to fight to retain political privileges assuring their existence and respected status; such has now become the situation of science and medicine. In 1750 established religious groups generally sought to use the authority of the state to limit or even repress the activities of alternative forms of religious life; government-funded scientists today seek to use the authority of the state in terms of funding and regulation to limit alternative forms of scientific and medical activity. For the purposes of this chapter, what is relevant is that whereas from roughly 1750 to 1875 progressive scientists and liberal religious groups and liberal religious thinkers remained on a cultural trajectory whereby the freedom achieved by one could possibly aid the freedom of the other vis-à-vis the state, that situation changed dramatically with the success of science in linking itself to the financial resources of the state. Having become part of the cultural and political establishment, the scientific community no longer needed to operate from the stance of a beleaguered social group seeking toleration. It had become the new cultural authority.

In closing, it is well to return to Voltaire's comments on the manner in which the multiplicity of religious sects assured the religious freedom of England. The plurality of the number of religious groups in the modern world since the early eighteenth century and the slow but virtually complete demise of effectively established religions has created a vast social realm of religious competition. Indeed now throughout the Western world, in contrast to Voltaire's day, it is more likely that religious groups will seek to influence the state than the reverse. In the world of science, however, there are a vast number of specializations, but not a vast number of sects. Scientists tend to see their truth when achieved or when believed to have been achieved as unitary and as embodied in well-recognized structures of professional organization and publication. And so long as that is the case, and one version of science cannot share social and intellectual space with another version of science, there is little possibility that science in and of itself will create a realm of freedom. Scientific knowledge may remove abuses, but it cannot and has not yet created a brave new world or more to the point a free world. The point of science is, among other things, to reach an agreed-upon truth which may be debated and challenged in pursuit of refinement or even refutation as another mode of agreed-upon truth is achieved. Such is not the character of either political or religious or cultural life in a liberal society. In the later arenas, the point is to let as many diverse opinions as possible be peacefully voiced without the necessity of achieving an agreed-upon truth. Science can make the case for its own freedom, but it is unclear that its arguments can be transferred to the wider social and political sphere. The same may also be said, of course, of various modes of religious fundamentalism.

The relationship of science to freedom is a relationship that exists and develops within the nexus of a multiplicity of cultural and political relationships. Science can contribute to freedom if the larger society within which it is pursued is itself structured for freedom, but science as a body of knowledge or scientists as scientists cannot rise above the values of the society in which they are embedded. Because men and women are scientists or scientifically educated, they will not necessarily associate themselves with a liberal vision of society, just as those persons who are religious or religiously educated will not necessarily advocate religious liberty. Scientists are likely to adhere to liberal toleration either because it is instrumentally necessary for their own professional pursuits or because they value such toleration in other areas of their lives. Such would seem to be the real historical link between science and religious liberty. Nor, on the other hand, can a society rise above its own dominant political and religious values in dealing with science and scientists, which to return to the opening of this chapter may explain the dreary fates of Priestley and Lavoisier two centuries ago.

Which Freedom for Early Victorian Britain?

J. P. ELLENS

I T IS THE THESIS of this chapter that there were two quite distinct views of freedom facing early Victorians. Traditionalists (who before 1832 included Tories, most Whigs, Churchmen, and most Protestant Dissenters) understood freedom as it *had been* understood for centuries in Christendom, and earlier by the Hebrews, as the gift one received when one submitted to God and to his laws. The description of freedom given in the encyclical letter on human liberty in 1888 by Pope Leo XIII fairly captures the traditionalist view of freedom still prevailing in Britain early in the century. According to Pope Leo, one finds freedom in "obedience to some supreme and eternal law, which is no other than the authority of God." This authority of God over human beings, rather than diminishing liberty, "protects and perfects it; for the prosecution and attainment of their respective ends are the real perfection of all creatures; and the supreme end to which human liberty can aspire is God."[1]

This traditional understanding of freedom derives from two sources which had been intermingled in the Middle Ages. The first is rooted in classical thought formulated by Aristotle and reformulated in a Christian framework by Thomas Aquinas. According to this definition each creature could find freedom only by being true to its own nature. Men and women, as rational beings, forfeit their freedom if they act irrationally or autonomously, failing to accept their rightful place in a rational cosmos in subjection to their sovereign creator. The second source of traditional freedom is rooted in the Hebrew and Christian scriptures and the theology of St. Augustine. Most fundamental to this teaching is that man is born a slave; men and women are by their *fallen* nature enslaved to passions and self-will or self-love that lead away from perfection. One finds freedom only when one's self-love is transformed into love of God through atoning and liberating communion with him.

The second distinct view of freedom, proclaimed by liberal spokesmen and women such as Thomas Paine and Mary Wollstone-craft, was that man is *born* free. Rapidly growing transatlantic liberalism, using the language and imagery of the seventeenth-century radicalism of the Levellers, Thomas Hobbes, and John Locke, redefined what it was both to be free and to be human. In the words of the late Canadian political philosopher George Grant, "man's essence is his freedom."[2] Liberal freedom was a subjective individual right possessed originally by the individual. In contrast, according to traditional thought, *God's right* established the "matrix of divine, natural and human laws" as the objective moral and political order in subjection to which man finds freedom.[3]

These two views of freedom between which early Victorians needed to choose were not the "two concepts of liberty" of Isaiah Berlin's classic treatment of liberty. Berlin distinguished between "negative freedom," in which one is free from the coercion of others; and "positive freedom," which allows the human subject "to be his own master."[4] Berlin's two freedoms are two sides of the same modern liberal conception of freedom. Its single focus is the autonomous individual, unrestrained from coercion *and* enabled to exert its rational will.

Traditional freedom reflected a different paradigm. Its focus was not the free individual but the good society. The traditional conception was, as Peter Miller has shown, that individual goods, including individual liberty, were subordinated to the "common good." The traditional formulation of individual aspirations finding their fulfillment, and limitations, in a virtuous community is given by Thomas Aquinas: "All who are contained in any community are related to it as parts to a whole. The part is what it is in virtue of the whole; therefore every good of the part is to be directed towards the good of the whole . . . Since every man is part of a state, it is impossible for any man to be good unless he is well adapted to the common good."[5]

Nineteenth-century debates about political reform can be properly understood only in light of changing views of the meaning of freedom. Traditionalists valued the inherited social order—with its aristocratic leadership, social hierarchy, and confessional boundaries guaranteeing the Anglican character of corporate bodies, including schools and political institutions—as the societal and institutional means by which a nation could be *made* virtuous, and hence free. Radicals and growing numbers of Whigs and Protestant Dissenters, on the other hand, came to emphasize the priority of the free individual, although Dissenters continued to value local expressions of community in family, town, and chapel. Reformers became preoccupied with freeing the individual from the constraints of inherited institutions. They sought free and equal institutions suited to men and women who were, *by nature*, free.

At the beginning of the nineteenth century, traditional conceptions of freedom, and a willingness to submit individual interests to the common good, remained pervasive. Since the radicalism of the 1770s and 1780s a number of events had reinforced traditional commitments to the common good, including the prerogatives of the Church of England. The French Revolution, Romanticism, and the renewed Evangelical Revival each contributed to ensuring that traditional conceptions of freedom continued to engage the thought and imagination of early Victorians. Gladstone's anguished "Pilgrim's Progress" in politics from traditional toryism to liberalism may be seen as a case study in the devolution of traditional freedom.[6] Gladstone's pilgrimage took him from the moral world of Aquinas, Hooker, and Butler, in which freedom was predicated on virtue and religion, toward, although never fully into, the untrammelled freedom of modern liberalism.

Churchmen and Dissenters alike in the early Victorian period turned away from, and indeed often seemed to forget the meaning of, traditional conceptions of freedom. Among no group was the adoption of the individualistic and subjectivistic character of liberal freedom more rapid, more complete, and more paradoxical, than that among Protestant Dissenters. At the very heart of the creed of evangelical Dissent was the traditional Christian understanding that men and women were, by their fallen nature, enslaved to a fatal self-love that presented an impassable barrier to communion with God, and hence to freedom. The gospel message that Christ's atoning power could free the human heart from subjugation to love of self was the key to salvation and to that enormous Dissenting activity in evangelization, chapel and community building, and missionary enterprise throughout the Victorian period.

It was in public affairs that Dissenters came to pursue a concep-

tion of freedom at odds with that of traditional Christianity. Increasingly after 1832 they followed the example of their radical forebears
of the 1780s to become voluntaryists, rejecting all state entanglement with religion,[7] while becoming deeply shaped by the desacralized political assumptions of liberals, including John Locke, John
Stuart Mill, and Herbert Spencer. Dissenting attachment to political liberalism grew, ambiguously, out of the Puritan and Dissenting "gathered church" ecclesiology of the sixteenth and seventeenth
centuries, and from even older late medieval millennarianism.[8] Under Locke's tutelage Dissenters jettisoned the traditional view of the
state as a political community ordained by God to teach public virtue (and hence happiness and freedom), for a liberal view of a con-
tractual institution subject only to the wishes of a sovereign people.

The great goal of Dissenters in politics was to be freed from external constraints: in trade, land, politics, and religion. Voluntaryists
often had an unbounded optimism that a people liberated from state
and Church controls would usher in a period of unprecedented prosperity and harmony—the millennium. Voluntaryist Dissenters could
be devout Augustinians when engaged in mission work, while cheer-
ful Pelagians in politics. In public life human nature was assumed to
be, for practical purposes, without sin, good and free. Evil was located
externally, in government and ecclesiastical coercion. To be sure,
voluntaryist Dissenters were inconsistent. Many continued throughout the Victorian period to seek state sanctions to compel the public
observance of the Christian Sabbath and to promote temperance. In
doing so they reverted to traditional beliefs about human weakness
and sinfulness and to the age-old practice of using law to enforce virtue as a condition for freedom. But the larger political legacy of Dissenting Voluntaryism was the movement away from the traditional
understanding of freedom found in submission to God toward the
unfettered freedom of liberalism's autonomous individual.

The conflict between traditional and liberal freedom was waged
for several decades before the newer definition came to prevail. Later
configurations were given a blueprint by the events of 1828 to 1832.
The "constitutional revolution" brought on by repeal of the Test and
Corporation Acts in 1828 and Catholic Emancipation in the following year, followed by parliamentary reform in 1832, dislodged the
foundation on which rested the old order.[9] The giving of legal enti-

tlement to Protestant Dissenters to hold Crown offices and Roman Catholics to sit in Parliament fractured the symmetry of Richard Hooker's ideal of an Anglican nation in which one belonged at once to the political and ecclesiastical communities.[10] Enlargement of the franchise opened the House of Commons to people neither accustomed to believing, nor disposed to agreeing, that freedom could be found in one's allotted place in the social hierarchy.

The middle decades were raucous ones as reformers took advantage of the unsettling of the traditional assumption that freedom ought to be qualified by social and religious boundaries. Reformers increasingly demanded freedom from restraints still imposed by a traditional society. Protestant Dissenters demanded freedom from all laws which discriminated against them: which compelled them to be married and buried according to Anglican formularies, which compelled them to pay church rates and tithes to support Anglican parish churches, and which tied the taking of degrees at the universities of Oxford and Cambridge to Anglican religious tests. Jews and their supporters demanded the freedom to sit in Parliament. Economic liberals demanded free trade. Political liberals and radicals called for household suffrage, manhood suffrage, or female suffrage, depending on the degree to which they had traveled from the traditional assumption that eligibility to vote was a matter of custom or prudence to one focusing on the natural rights of man.

By focusing in the following section on the Victorian controversy concerning university reform we shall illustrate that central to this issue, as to others in church and state, was the question of which freedom was to prevail. The ancient universities were unusual in that within them traditional assumptions about the nature of freedom continued longer than in most other areas of Victorian life. In our analysis of university tests, therefore, we will give particular attention to traditionalist arguments that assumed the legitimacy of limiting individual freedom by the constraints of religion. We shall study, in addition, debates about the legitimacy of providing tax support for the Established Church, and briefly, the effects on Dissenting theology of support for free trade. Developments in both of these areas will illustrate that liberal versions of freedom increasingly came to shape the outlook of Churchmen as well as Dissenters by mid century.

≺ I ≻

The Ancient Universities

Before 1854, matriculation at Oxford University and eligibility to earn a degree at either Oxford or Cambridge University were restricted to those who subscribed to the Thirty-nine Articles of the Church of England. Beginning in the 1830s, Protestant Dissenters and university reformers of many religious affiliations looked to Parliament to end the exclusively Anglican character of the universities. Especially during the early years of that controversy protagonists differed not only on whether to end the confessional exclusivism of the ancient universities but also on what were the actual conditions of intellectual and religious freedom. Reformers charged that a confessionally defined university by definition lacked the primary condition necessary to give intellectual and religious freedom. Traditionalists insisted that it was only when the university based its learning and teaching on the Christian faith, as defined by the Thirty-nine Articles, that members of the universities could be led into the truth, and hence, become free.

When, in 1834, members of the House of Commons debated W. P. Wood's motion to admit Protestant Dissenters to Oxford, reformers were quick to point to the implications of the repeal of the Test and Corporation Acts and the coming of Catholic Emancipation. Edward Buller, a Whig M.P. for North Staffordshire, argued that what the Dissenters demanded was consistent with the spirit of the times and with the spirit of the constitution. He contended that the constitution formerly had been exclusive but that with the repeal and emancipation all offices of state were opened "to all citizens, without reference to their religious faith or opinions."[11] Thomas Spring Rice, the Whig chancellor of the exchequer, had taken a similar position three months earlier and contended that in light of the ending of religious exclusion as "a general principle in our laws" it was now "preposterous in principle, and indefensible in practice" to maintain "this invidious test."[12]

The strength of Spring Rice's language underlines a significant difference in emphasis between reformers and traditionalists in university reform. Reformers tended to focus on the "rights" of the dissenting individual to intellectual freedom; traditionalists emphasized the freedom of a confessional university to take the steps necessary to retain its religious character. Speaking as a traditionalist in 1850, W. E. Gladstone protested the appointment of a parliamentary commission to investigate the universities of Oxford and Cambridge "as dangerous to all the liberties of the subject."[13] Writing to Gladstone in 1838, Samuel Wilberforce presciently predicted that Gladstone might one day come to "wield the whole government of this land" and urged him to view himself as "the maintainer of [the] Church and of its liberties."[14] The same emphasis is found in the diary notation of the Reverend John Hill in June 1835. The vice-principal of St. Edmund Hall, Oxford, noted that a university convocation had been held to petition the House of Lords "against Lord Radnor's bill to prohibit the Universities from the right of requiring subscription to the 39 Articles before the age of 23."[15] The Convocation had voted by 91 votes to 4 to send the petition.

In an anonymous pamphlet of 1854 a writer who styled himself "A Priest of the Church of England" argued that religious exclusiveness in a university would not offend a religious Dissenter who valued religion as of central importance in education, as in the rest of life. The writer furthermore contended that religious freedom existed where it was possible to have confessional universities. He explained that the basis of academic freedom was found in the freedom of a university to gather to itself those who came voluntarily on the basis of a shared faith. He stated that "Every body or corporation exists, as such, by the virtue of certain principles of which it is the incorporation . . . and that such bodies are increased, *not* by conforming their views and principles to those of individuals who differ from them, but by the voluntary aggregation of individuals who conform and wish to promote the principles held by such [a] body."[16] He continued by stating that so long as there was a continuation of "the relation existing between the Church and the nation, through means of the universities . . . true and practical liberty of conscience may be enjoyed by every man in the dominion of Her Majesty." He warned that if this relation were severed, as it would be with the admission of Dissenters to Oxford, "too late will Dissenters discover that what they sought was not freedom, but licentiousness,—not equality, but domination."[17]

The competing versions of what constituted a free university were mirrored in fundamental disagreement about the nature of freedom of inquiry and learning. Reformers were coming to insist that inquiry and teaching should be unconstrained by confessional boundaries. Traditionalists insisted that learning and teaching could be a liberating force only if they were clearly directed toward the telos of communion with God. In that spirit Oxford University's Hebdomadal Board, its chief executive body, formulated a petition in April 1834 to oppose a proposed parliamentary bill to abolish religious tests. The petition pointed out that religious tests were essential to maintain the university's very purpose as laid down by Royal Charter: "the maintenance of good and godly literature, and the virtuous education of youth."[18]

Henry Goulburn, an Evangelical and Peelite, spoke as M.P. for Cambridge University in March of 1834 to defend religious tests. He remarked that at Cambridge Dissenters were admitted to read, although not to take degrees, as a privilege, on the condition that "they conformed to the existing system of discipline, which was based on the doctrines and principles of the Church of England."[19] Goulburn insisted that Dissenters ought not to be allowed to proceed to degrees because they would then become part of the governing body of the university, thus fundamentally altering its character. The university would then no longer be able to give instruction according to Church principles, "but it would proclaim, that it was an establishment formed for general education . . . without any references to religion . . . At present the university was a seminary of sound learning and of religious distinctions." It is noteworthy, although few Churchmen noticed, that Goulburn identified religion with Church teaching. The historian can only conjecture to what extent Dissenters might have rallied to join Churchmen to maintain an undenominational Christian university defined by a religious test referring to the historic creeds shared by Dissenters and Churchmen.

It would be woeful, declared Goulburn, if the university were to "set the example of separating education from religion . . . if it were to confine instruction exclusively to the propagation of what was vulgarly called knowledge, which was knowledge without religion, and was not the sound instruction which the University now dispensed. If it taught science and excluded that which alone was a saving religion—which fitted a man for the ultimate object of his being."[20] In language and spirit, despite considerable differences of theology and culture, Goulburn's Evangelical conception of freedom resembled that enunciated a half century later by Pope Leo. Like Leo, Goulburn assumed that one's purpose is given in the very structure of one's nature. Freedom is rooted in submission to God's order and is completed by recognizing, as did Pope Leo, that "the supreme end to which human liberty can aspire is God."[21]

Academic reformers, at the same time, were beginning to claim that any confessional test in the university ruined the university as a place for free inquiry. Proponents of intellectual liberty were coming to define it in a sufficiently absolute and abstract manner that the traditionalist claim, that well-ordered freedom was compatible with the structural limitations imposed by human nature and the authority of biblical revelation, was beginning to appear intolerable and even incomprehensible. In this spirit Stephen Lushington, Liberal M.P. for Tower Hamlets and judge of the Consistory Court of London, disparaged, in April 1834, the Oxford University requirement that "youths of sixteen or seventeen" needed to subscribe to the Thirty-nine Articles of the Church of England as a condition of matriculation. He saw that obligation as "a solemn mockery, and injust imposition upon the human conscience."[22] Two months later Edward Buller addressed the question of religious tests for youth; they "appeared to him to be most monstrous. He trusted, that the time had come when they should get rid of all tests in the Universities, and that the only declaration taken would be on entering the University, merely to the effect that the person taking it was anxious and willing to learn."[23] Buller assumed quite simply that a student admitted purely on his declared wish to learn would achieve his desire, and the university would fulfill its purpose.

Traditionalists warned that the act of subscription to articles of faith was a necessary condition of sound learning and teaching. Only by rooting the academic enterprise in acknowledgment of God, the source of all things knowable, could the student's knowledge be grounded in the truth. Only this knowledge, claimed traditionalists, could make one free. Victorian liberals, and Dissenters who increasingly were speaking in the language of liberalism, found such confessional and contextual language too restrictive; they demanded untrammelled liberty. One impatient spokesman for such a liberal view of academic freedom was John Wilks, Radical M.P. for Boston. In a debate in March 1834 on the full admission of Dissenters to Cambridge, Wilks charged that the issue was clear: "the principle was one of intellectual liberty and liberty of conscience." He concluded his peroration with the preface to John Locke's *Essay on Toleration*: "What we want is liberty; absolute liberty; just and true liberty; equal and impartial liberty. More than that the Dissenters need not ask; with less than that they would never be contented." [24]

John Locke's spiritual progeny in the universities were finding that anything less than "absolute liberty" seemed painfully coercive. In one of a series of letters to Edward Hawkins, provost of Oriel College, Oxford, A. H. Clough, a fellow of Oriel who ultimately resigned his fellowship in objection to religious tests, described subscription "as a painful restraint on speculation." [25] Hawkins's reply provides a clear traditionalist contrast to Clough's demand for absolute intellectual freedom. Hawkins acknowledged that adherence to the Thirty-nine Articles restrained intellectual freedom but he saw this as a force for good, not for ill. He suggested "that they impose *some* restraint upon speculation may be an *advantage* . . . I am afraid of unrestrained speculation tending to general scepticism—a very unhappy state and one for wh[ic]h God did not design us. In truth you were not born for *speculation*. I am not saying a word against full and fair inquiry. But we are sent into this world not so much to speculate as to serve God and serve man." [26] For Clough, any religious restraint on speculation infringed absolute intellectual freedom and limited the autonomy of the thinker. According to Hawkins, men and women were so designed by their creator that only by orienting all their faculties, including their intellects, to his service could their nature be fulfilled.

Traditionalists and reformers disagreed about whether truth was found in the community or in the individual. When Lord Radnor brought in his bill in the House of Lords in 1835 to free men below the age of 23 from obligation to subscribe to religious tests he, and other reformers, assumed that any declaration of assent to a statement of beliefs had legitimacy only if the subscriber had come to an independent judgment about his confession. Frederick Oakeley, an Anglo-Catholic who later went over to Rome, denied that it was necessary for a young man to have analyzed and judged for himself every point of doctrine before he could subscribe to the confessions of the Church. Oakeley asserted "he is either a member of the Church of England, or he is not. If he be, it may surely be expected of him, that he should allow the authority of the Church, in which he has been educated . . . to supply his lack of minute personal acquaintance with the subjects involved in the Articles."[27] Oakeley argued that it was in the nature of religious subjects that "we must believe a great deal more than we can perfectly understand."[28] Oakeley placed his trust in the communal authority of the Church over the insight of the individual, asserting that "those views of Scriptural truth, in which the wisest and best men of every age . . . have agreed in maintaining, are of far greater authority than any ordinary person's private interpretation of the work of God." He viewed this position as the middle way of the Church of England between Rome, which attributed infallibility to the decrees of its councils, and ultra Protestantism, "which makes each man's reason . . . the rule of his faith."[29]

How the authority of the Church might function in directing thought was described in an influential pamphlet, *Subscription No Bondage*, published in 1835 by Frederick Denison Maurice. Maurice, a Broad Churchman who had come to the Church from Unitarianism, argued against abolishing university tests, urging that they served as guides to truth. The Articles, Maurice claimed, "contain the terms, according to which the teacher agrees to teach and the learner to learn." The Articles served as "conditions of thought, primarily designed to assist education by warning students against superstitions, which have hindered, and are likely to hinder, the pursuit of knowledge, and the attainment of truth."[30] Maurice's "conditions of thought" appealed to many contemporaries and they continue to have an appeal in our own time for those who are not satisfied by the claims of Positivism. On the other hand, Maurice's "conditions" also referred to standards that limited the freedom of the individual intellect and were, therefore, unacceptable to those who demanded a more unqualified freedom of thought.

Traditionalist defenders of a confessional university cherished these "conditions of thought" because they took seriously Christian teaching about fallen human nature. Charles P. Eden, a fellow of Oriel College, asked whether the Articles did not give "the benefit of Self-Protection; protection of self against self; protection of your proper self against the thousand extravagant fancies which will run away with you if they can?"[31] He went on to say, in a way that must have seemed incomprehensible to liberals who championed human autonomy, that if a student *commenced* his studies by submitting to the authority of the Thirty-nine Articles he would be protected from slavery to error. Eden declared: "to start with a sentence of orthodoxy *within* you, gathered, as you would not yet be qualified to gather it, from remote sources, from all the corners of Scripture, and from the ocean of history, was not to drag a chain, but to carry with you a charter of liberty."[32]

Early in the nineteenth century the contrasting judgments about the nature of intellectual freedom were stark. Reformers were adamant that a religious test as a condition of admittance to any degree or of the right to teach in colleges or the universities was an intolerable infringement of intellectual freedom. To require subscription to the Thirty-nine Articles in the universities was, reformers believed, "to drag a chain" which hindered a student or teacher from realizing the freedom which was his by nature. For traditionalist Churchmen, however, the religious test was an indispensable guide to each student and teacher. Academic work was part of the soul's hazardous ascent to truth. The ascent was hazardous because each person's natural inclination was to look away from heaven and to slip and fall into the abyss of folly, delusion, and superstition. To abolish religious tests appeared to traditionalists analogous to the decision of the novice mountain climber who dismisses his experienced guide and then rejoices in his new-found freedom as he is left clinging to the precipice, forced to scale the sheer face of the mountain alone.

By mid century newer views of freedom, based on the principle of realizing the natural rights of the individual, had become widespread. In the universities, however, traditional views displayed great staying power. In 1854 and 1856 parliamentary acts reforming first Oxford and then Cambridge went far in the direction of opening fellowships and scholarships to competition and merit and urging the universities to pursue academic excellence. The religious exclusivism of the universities was loosened by granting non-Anglicans the right to take bachelor's degrees in both universities without the necessity of subscribing to the Thirty-nine Articles. But in both universities the M.A. degree, and hence the power to teach and to contribute to the governance of the universities, remained dependent on subscription to the Anglican confessions.[33] That bulwark of the Anglican university was not seriously challenged until the 1860s, and not ended until 1871. Until the passage of the University Tests Act of 1871, liberal educational reforms were incorporated in the old religious framework. The reformed statutes and ordinances governing

Oxford colleges after 1854 often defined the colleges as places of "religion, learning, and education."[34] In that spirit the reformed Regulations of Lincoln College retained old directives such as the one stipulating that "the pupils shall obey their tutors, and honour and reverence as fathers those whose efforts, labour, and diligence are expended in training them to piety and knowledge."[35] On such a basis traditionalist churchmen carried their fight against liberalism's definition of intellectual freedom into the second half of the nineteenth century. Here traditionalists continued to defend the view that submission to religious confessions was not an infringement of intellectual freedom but an essential guide to find it.

≺ II ≻

Church Rates

Disagreements about what it meant to be free were never more pointed or more personal than during the Victorian church rate conflict.[36] At issue was the church rate principle, the dictum that all ratepayers (local property taxpayers) in England and Wales, whatever their own denominational allegiance, were obliged to pay church rates to contribute to the physical maintenance of the parish churches of the Church of England. At the heart of the church rate conflict, which began in 1832, was the issue whether the existence of an established church and its compulsory support were compatible with religious freedom.

Traditionalists in 1832 insisted that the maintenance of an established church was harmonious with religious liberty. Most Englishmen, indeed, Whigs as well as Tories, Wesleyan Methodists and many Protestant Dissenters, liberal as well as traditional Churchmen, were convinced at the outset of the conflict that an established church was the essential capstone of a Christian nation. They rested on the settled assumption that both the church and the state were needed to encourage a life of virtue, the prerequisite of freedom.

The Tory view of this position was presented well by Gladstone early in his political career. In 1838, in his *The State in its Relations with the Church*, Gladstone promoted a state church as the instrument by which a national community possessing a personality and a national conscience could sanctify "the acts of that personality by the offices of religion."[37] This commitment to the justice of a tax-supported church establishment was strongly held by conservative Anglican laymen in the 1830s. During the 1834 parliamentary session more than 1500 petitions were signed supporting "A Declaration of the Laity of the Church of England" that pledged to maintain the Church of England "unimpaired" and declared the conviction that "the consecration of the state by the public maintenance of the Christian Religion is the just and paramount duty of a Christian people."[38] Freedom, according to traditionalist Anglicans and most Wesleyans in the 1830s, was the result of submitting to the Christian faith.

Whigs who saw themselves as defenders of liberty were no less committed than Tories to the belief that compulsory payment of church rates and maintenance of the Established Church were compatible with freedom. Although the Whig-Liberal party came to the conclusion by 1856, for political reasons, that non-Anglicans ought to be exempted from compulsory payments to the Church, the Whigs had supported church rates since the church rate conflict had begun a quarter century earlier. As late as 1859 Lord John Russell would still speak in the House of Commons defending the legitimacy of tax support for an established church based on "the general benefit to the community at large."[39]

Before 1832 Protestant Dissenters had also generally assented to the validity of both church rates and the Established Church, although a number of their ministers and other intellectual leaders had begun to agitate against religious establishments in the 1770s and 1780s. The Dissenting *Eclectic Review* observed in 1832 that most Dissenters probably did not oppose the existence of the Church Establishment. Evangelical Congregationalists, Baptists, and Wesleyans cooperated with evangelical Churchmen in the London Missionary Society which was organized in 1795 to spread the Christian gospel and to combat atheism. According to Herbert Skeats, almost all the most prominent Congregational ministers early in the century had close ties with Anglican evangelicals, and there was a "tacit compact that the Church should not be attacked."[40] Dissenters agreed with Churchmen that the national submission to God was a higher good than individual freedom from the restraint of ecclesiastical taxation. The willingness of Dissenters, between the French Revolution and 1832, to accede to the church rate principle

against their own immediate self-interest can be explained as the result of habit, fears of reaction in a revolutionary era, or lack of self-
confidence. It is also an indication of the extent of commitment in
the nation to the traditional understanding of freedom.

That Dissenting understanding of freedom began to shift fundamentally in the 1830s along with the altering social and political
landscape in which Dissenters lived. By 1832 Dissenters, including
especially Unitarians, Baptists, and Congregationalists, joined their
voices to those of Radicals to demand deep-reaching reforms in the
Church of England and redress from disabilities under which Dissenters lived.

Factors leading to change in the orientation of Dissenters were
many and varied. In 1811 Dissenters were alarmed by the aborted bill
introduced by Lord Sidmouth to regulate more closely the registration of Dissenting ministers. The "new Dissent" that was born out
of the renewed evangelical revival at the end of the eighteenth and
the beginning of the nineteenth centuries led to the formation of the
Congregational and Baptist unions as engines for evangelism and missions as well as platforms for posing a more assertive political stance.
In the 1820s Congregationalists and Baptists, led by Unitarians of
the older Dissenting tradition, campaigned successfully to repeal the
Test and Corporation Acts. Quite quickly Dissenters moved from
their traditional pleas for toleration to demands for equality.[41]

The campaign by Dissenters, in particular by Congregationalists
and Baptists, for relief from Dissenting grievances led very soon to
demands for the separation of church and state. Politically active
Dissenters were coming to be motivated by a new ethos of voluntaryism. Voluntaryists repudiated compulsion in religion and consequen-
tially denied the validity of religious establishments. Unlike older
Dissenters, however, whose concern for religious freedom focused
on freedom of conscience and liberty to practice faith that were compatible with religious establishments, voluntaryists aggressively denied the validity of compulsion in religion and turned to politics to
force religiously based institutions, including churches and schools,
to separate from any state connection. During the reform crisis in
church and state in the early 1830s Churchmen proposed reforms of
the Establishment and Whigs were ready to redress Dissenting grievances. The *Patriot*, a newspaper established in 1832 as a national
voice for evangelical Dissent on public issues, declared that even ex-

tensive reforms would not reconcile Dissent to the Church. In June 1832 the *Patriot* indicated how voluntaryism was reshaping the rationale of Dissent: "that which is daily becoming the chief reason for Dissent—namely, a conviction that religious establishments of all kinds are unfavourable to the progress of religion—would operate with undiminished force . . . Our ancestors quarrelled with the church, because it was not reformed up to the point at which they could conscientiously join her; whereas we cannot enter her, let her be ever so reformed in other respects, while she remains the ally—or mistress—or rather the slave of the state."[42]

The growing objections by Dissenters to paying compulsory church rates provided a litmus test to gauge quickly changing views of the legitimacy of the use of compulsion in religion. By the spring of 1834 the church rate had caused sufficient turmoil in the parishes of England and Wales that Earl Grey's Whig government attempted to replace the rate with a fixed parliamentary grant for maintenance of parish churches. On April 21 Lord Althorp, chancellor of the exchequer, announced the government's plan to substitute for the rate a fixed sum of £250,000 from the land tax. Althorp argued that his proposal placed maintenance of parish churches on a more reliable footing, reaffirmed the establishment principle that the legislature was obliged to maintain the nation's churches, and recognized that the rate was unfair to Dissenters.[43] Although the Whigs continued to believe that a religious establishment contributed to a good society, they were beginning to question whether the church rate principle was an undue restriction of the freedom of non-Anglicans. The government quietly dropped Althorp's proposal after Dissenting organizations mobilized to complain that the plan was particularly objectionable because it deprived vestries of the power they now had to refuse to make rates.

In light of Althorp's failed church rate plan, and because of disappointment with what they considered an unsatisfactory marriage bill, Dissenters became disillusioned with the Whigs and increasingly made voluntaryism their rallying point. They differed greatly, however, on the degree to which they wished to act on their voluntaryism. Moderates believed in principle that church establishments were wrong and sought relief from particular grievances, such as church rate obligations, as steps toward separation of church and state; militant voluntaryists demanded that Dissenters should make disestablishment of the Church their immediate political objective.[44]

The differences between moderate and militant voluntaryists spilled into public view on May 8, 1834, when Dissenting delegates from throughout England and Wales met in London to demand abolition of church rates. Militant delegates from Manchester and Nottingham spoke out to say that they had been sent pledged to seek a public declaration demanding disestablishment and that any petition they signed against a particular grievance needed to indicate clearly that redress was looked for merely as a means to secure the full separation of church and state. The meeting finally supported a resolution that called for repeal of church rates with an amended prefix that praised "the great and leading principle of full and complete separation of Church and State, as the true basis on which equal rights and justice can be secured to all classes of his Majesty's subjects."[45] Dissenters, moderates as well as militants, had now stated publicly that in principle true freedom was impossible without separation of church and state.

By the end of 1836 cities and towns were in turmoil as moderate and militant Dissenters acted in public meetings to call for the abolition of church rates. In cities and towns church rate abolition societies were formed and petitions were sent to both houses of Parliament declaring that compulsory support for religion was alien to the Christian faith and demanding the abolition of church rates.[46] Only occasionally now did traditionalist Dissenters still speak out in public to maintain that the operation of the church rate principle and the existence of the Church Establishment served the common good. According to a minority of Dissenters the chief end of the nation was to submit to God; that act of obedience, whether corporate or individual, made one free. Most Dissenters had adopted a newer conclusion. They were coming to see freedom as an end in itself; one could not be free if subject to external constraints.

The church rate question divided Churchmen at the same time that most Dissenters were mobilizing to repeal rates. A considerable number of Churchmen attended the meeting of the Church Rate Abolition Society, a predominantly Dissenting group, on February 1, 1837. At that meeting 400 delegates, representing numerous church rate abolition societies and Congregational and Baptist congregations, called for the full abolition of rates. The Churchmen present, mostly liberal Broad Churchmen, agreed and argued that the rate should be repealed as a way of strengthening the Church. Conservative Churchmen, both Evangelicals and High Churchmen, were astonished that fellow Anglicans might consider giving up rates when, in the words of the Reverend E. Tottenham, one knows "that the general levying of a Church rate is the only existing way whereby the government really recognizes its obligation to provide for the religious instruction of the people."[47] Conservative Churchmen countered the abolitionists with a public meeting of their own, motivated in part by a report in the Whig-liberal *Morning Chronicle* that the government intended to bring in a church rate bill to force the Church on its own resources. On February 18, 1837, a meeting of some 2000 people, chaired by the Evangelical Lord Ashley, pledged their support for the rate. The meeting called on the government to acknowledge that the Church's resources were inadequate to keep up with the expanding population and called on Parliament to grant additional funds to the Church to enable it to meet the spiritual needs of the country. This strong defense of the church rate was based on the fundamental premise of the traditional view of the state, adopted as the first resolution of the conservatives' meeting: "it is the bounden duty of a nation to establish and preserve the public worship of Almighty God."[48] The contrast with the anti-church rate meeting was striking. The focus of the abolitionists' meeting was on individual freedom from church rates; that of the conservatives was on the nation's first duty to establish the worship of God. True freedom, they believed, would follow when primary religious duties were fulfilled.

In the spring of 1837 Spring Rice introduced a bill in the Commons to abolish church rates and to maintain parish churches from a fund of at least £250,000 which was to come from the surplus that the government claimed could be realized from the more efficient management of Church lands. That was to be accomplished by transferring the control of ecclesiastical lands to a new commission. Dissenters were delighted with this proposal. The Radical M.P. Joseph Hume approved because "it placed the burden of maintaining the fabric of the Church on its own property." For just that reason the Evangelical ultra-Tory Sir Robert Inglis opposed the plan. Even if such a fund as the government proposed would suffice to meet the maintenance needs of the parish churches, he argued, "yet the nationality of the Church of England would be destroyed, and it would be considered as a Church not supported by the nation, but by itself."[49] The Whigs' attempt to placate Dissenters foundered on the Church's determination to maintain intact the establishment principle. Aroused Churchmen, including rural clergy, bishops, and Whig gentry, accounted for weakened support for the bill by the time of its second reading and the government's decision quietly to drop it.[50]

By the fall of 1838 it had become quite clear that the Whig government did not intend to alienate the Church to satisfy Dissenters with church rate repeal. In reaction, even moderate Dissenters began to lose confidence in the Whigs and began to become more committed voluntaryists. In April 1839, under the impetus of Josiah Conder, moderate Congregational editor of the *Patriot*, Dissenters formed the Religious Freedom Society (RFS) to advance the cause of voluntaryism.[51]

The growing commitment of Dissenters to voluntaryism could be seen in their increasing insistence on full religious equality. That development was encouraged by the eighteen-month imprisonment of John Thorogood of Chelmsford, Essex. Thorogood was imprisoned in January 1839 for having disregarded a ruling by London's Consistory Court that he must pay a small church rate to which he was liable. A year into Thorogood's imprisonment Thomas Slingsby Duncombe, the Radical M.P. for Finsbury, attempted unsuccessfully to bring in a bill to discharge Thorogood and to amend the church rate law. He proposed to exempt from church rate obligations those Dissenters who declared that they conscientiously dissented from the Church and would agree not to participate in vestry meetings dealing with Church affairs. Lord John Russell objected strongly to Duncombe's description of Thorogood as a prisoner of conscience. Furthermore, Russell repudiated the proposal of exemption for Dissenters. He defended the church rate principle on the same Broad Church grounds that he had always used. Church rates were "for the common good, and that was a principle which entitled them to ask for that burden to be laid upon all."[52]

As Russell was speaking out against exemption for Dissenters, voluntaryist Dissenters themselves were concluding that mere exemption from church rates would not satisfy them. The *Patriot*'s initial response to Duncombe's proposal was that it could be satisfied

with either exemption from, or full abolition of, rates. Duncombe
said in the course of the debate that leading Dissenters whom he
had consulted found his exemption plan equitable. However, three
months later, the moderate Dissenting deputies spoke out publicly
against a similar exemption plan and insisted on the full abolition of
church rates. In January 1841 the *Patriot* announced that it now had
come to the same position, that only the entire abolition of church
rates, and not mere exemption from them, could satisfy the demands
of voluntaryism.[53] By 1841 even moderate Dissenters had become
sufficiently voluntaryist that they felt that their freedom was restricted by the existence of a system of compulsory church rates even
if they were exempted from contributing to it.

While moderate voluntaryists were coming to deny the legitimacy of the church rate system by 1841, militant voluntaryists were
taking steps to attack the Church Establishment itself. Militants,
who did not have confidence that the existing moderate Dissenting
press would seek the disestablishment of the Church in a way acceptable to them, formed a newspaper to preach the separation of
church and state. The *Nonconformist*, first published in April 1841,
was edited by Edward Miall, who gave up his Congregational pastorate in Leicester to devote his life to seeking the disestablishment of
the Church of England.[54]

In the first issue of the *Nonconformist* Miall addressed the question put by moderate and conservative Dissenters, was it possible for
Dissenters to retain their spiritual integrity while they gave themselves to a long political campaign for religious freedom and equality?
Yes, so long, he said, as Dissenters kept their political principles
consistent with New Testament teaching. Miall pointed to what he
believed was one such New Testament principle—liberty—which
Dissenters ought to reclaim: "at present we have government in
excess . . . Restriction meets us everywhere—regulates our mar-
kets, impedes our commerce, cripples our industry, paralyzes our
religion . . . The utmost liberty, compatible with social order, we take
to be the inalienable right of all men."[55] Militant voluntaryists such
as Miall rarely questioned whether the freedom they pursued was
embedded in the vision of the Christian gospel or of eighteenth-
century political liberalism. Militant voluntaryists, as optimistic
historicists, assumed the visions to be identical. In this they were
faithful heirs of the Evangelical Revival which itself, as D. W. Beb-

bington has shown, was profoundly shaped by the spirit of the Enlightenment.[56]

It was especially in their view of the state that militant voluntaryists showed their reliance on the Enlightenment tradition. The Anti-State-Church Association (ASCA), formed in 1844 by militant voluntaryists to seek the disestablishment of the Church of England, regularly promoted a view of the state that was indistinguishable from that of political liberalism. In its influential *Anti-State-Church Catechism* the ASCA inculcated the lesson that a state church was false because its existence reflected a misconception of the proper ends of government. Its catechetical answer as to the proper end of government stated: "civil government is the means by which members of a community combine to seek certain ends. These ends are temporal, and only temporal. They are such as the members of the community naturally appreciate and desire, viz., the preservation of life, liberty, and property. Religion is not one of them."[57]

The ASCA championed both an independent spiritual church true to the Christian tradition and the creation of a this-worldly state demanded by liberalism, quite unconscious of the divergent authorities for each. This view of a state unconcerned with the transcendent was still spurned by many Tories at mid century; and it still was shunned by Dissenters in 1834, when the *Congregational Magazine* explained that in seeking separation of church and state Dissenters wished only to prevent the state from favoring one denomination over another. They did not wish to divorce religion from the concern of the state. If "church" were understood as the universal church, then "the Dissenters were anxious that the union between the Church and the State should be still more intimate; that the obligations of the Christian religion should be recognized by all in authority and enforced by public homage and example; that the civil observance of the Christian Sabbath should be secured by protective enactments."[58] This older evangelical Dissenting ideal of an undenominational Christian state and society was repudiated by the ASCA and militant Dissenters. It was spurned because it clashed with the this-worldly liberal vision of the state that had become an integral component of militant voluntaryism. Militant voluntaryists were coming to view any restriction of their individual freedom by constraints imposed by a vision of the common good, including an undenominational version of a confessional state, as unacceptable.

Militant Dissenters continued their preoccupation with disestablishment through the 1840s, but by February 1852, when Lord Derby's Conservative government replaced Lord John Russell's Whig-Liberal administration, militants joined moderate voluntaryists in campaigning to abolish church rates.[59] More important than the combined weight of moderate and militant voluntaryist Dissenters, however, for prospects for reform of the church rate principle, were changing views of the value of the rate and the establishment principle within the Church itself. In the summer of 1852 Derby received several recommendations to reform the church rate system from Churchmen. Lord Stanley, heir to the earl of Derby, wrote to Disraeli, who was chancellor of the exchequer, that Churchmen might give up universal church rates in exchange for restoration of Convocation, which Anglo-Catholics looked to as a way of giving self-government to the Church. On the same day C. J. Blomfield, the Protestant High Church bishop of London, wrote Derby that Churchmen as well as Dissenters now generally felt that it was urgent to bring in a speedy reform of the church rate system. Blomfield later sent Derby a detailed plan of reform which entailed exempting Dissenters from church rate obligations in return for giving up their parochial rights to receive the sacraments or to participate in the governance of their parish church.[60]

On May 26, 1853, R. J. Phillimore, the Anglo-Catholic Peelite M.P. for Tavistock, actually moved to bring in the Commons a bill similar to the plan proposed earlier by Bishop Blomfield. It would exempt Dissenters from church rate obligations while removing their rights to participate in vestry meetings dealing with church matters. In response, Sir William Clay, an Anglican voluntaryist Liberal M.P. for Tower Hamlets, introduced an amendment, similar to the Spring Rice plan of 1837, that church rates be abolished and replaced by pew rents and the surplus from better managed Church lands. It was a telling sign of how the attachment to full religious liberty was developing among moderate as well as among militant Dissenters; although the Dissenting Deputies and the ASCA actively supported Clay, they insisted that Clay make it clear to the House that the part of his plan that provided a substitute for the rate was his own and not the will of Dissenters. Dissenting M.P.s in the House generally attacked Phillimore's plan and supported Clay's. Oxford's Sir Robert Inglis opposed both Phillimore and Clay, but in keeping with his old Protestant High Church convictions, he took exception in particular to Phillimore's exemption plan, declaring that if the Church relinquished the compulsory support of the nation it would cease being the church of the nation.

Both motions lost but it was significant that also among Churchmen there was now interest in amending the church rate principle.[61] In May 1855 Clay's bill to abolish church rates for the first time passed the second reading in the Commons.[62] As in the year before when it had been introduced unsuccessfully, the abolition bill no longer made any provision for a substitute for a repealed rate. The abolition bill owed its success to effective political pressure, both inside and outside Parliament, applied by the Liberation Society, the new name given to the ASCA in 1853 when it was refashioned into a well-honed pressure group. In addition, most Churchmen now agreed that some reform of the church rate was needed but they were still far from agreeing on how to amend the law.

Clay's bill did not proceed beyond the second reading; Clay withdrew it in light of Lord Palmerston's objections to it. Equally noteworthy as the progress made by Clay's abolition bill was the fact that two days before the second-reading debate, the Evangelical archbishop J. B. Sumner introduced a bill in the Lords to reform the law on church rates. The bill proposed to abolish the rate in parishes where it was no longer levied and to exempt Dissenters in those parishes where rates continued to be made. Although the bill was disallowed by the speaker who ruled that it was a money bill, and therefore could originate only in the Commons, it was remarkable that a bill to exempt Dissenters from church rate obligations should have been proposed. The Liberation Society later expressed amazement that "the Primate of the Church himself had reached the position occupied in 1840 by the Radical member for Finsbury [T. S. Duncombe]."[63]

By the winter of 1856 there was, according to *The Times*, a civil war raging throughout the land in the church rate conflict. Again Sir William Clay introduced in the Commons his bill to abolish church rates. Lord Palmerston's cabinet attempted to find an alternative to abolition.[64] On March 5, when Clay's abolition bill was given its second reading, Sir George Grey spoke for the government to announce that the government proposed to reform the church rate law by introducing amendments to Clay's bill rather than its own legislation.

Grey's proposals included "immediate abolition" in parishes where the rate had not been levied for some time, and "prospective abolition" where parishioners might demand it. The government hoped that in most parishes, especially in rural areas, the rate would be maintained unchanged subject to the right of Dissenters to be exempted from church rate obligations on the simple declaration that they were not members of the established Church.[65]

Palmerston's cabinet had listened to the public pressure and had given up the traditional Whig commitment to universal liability to church rates. Only Lord John Russell stood apart from the new consensus to exempt Dissenters. Russell continued to argue that the Church served the common good and as the national Church was entitled to public maintenance, but Russell was isolated and Palmerston publicly dismissed his views.[66]

Grey's amendments caused great confusion among voluntaryist Dissenters. For a decade they had been demanding that only full abolition could satisfy the demands of voluntaryism. Finally, and with great reluctance, Dissenting leaders agreed to accept the amendments as the best they could achieve without losing the leadership of the moderate Clay and the cohesion of the anti-church rate coalition. Militant voluntaryists were angered that the executive of the Liberation Society should agree to accept Grey's amendments. The Reverend H. Toller of Market Harborough charged that the executive had taken a position "inconsistent with the great principle of the Society, which was, that Government should not interfere in any way with the religious opinions of its subjects; whereas the Amendments it was proposed to accept recognised that right of interference by offering exemption from church-rate on profession of Dissent from the Establishment."[67]

The divisions among Dissenters were healed when the government held back from supporting the Grey amendments to the Clay bill at the committee stage and Clay withdrew his bill on June 27. The Liberation Society declared itself, with considerable relief, no longer bound by its commitment to abide by Grey's exemption amendments. The *Liberator*, the official organ of the Liberation Society, claimed, not unfairly, that voluntaryists had won a victory over the government: "whether so intending or not, they have really given up the principle of church rates, and have furnished us with a reason for rejecting in future a halting measure."[68] Palmerston's Whig-Liberals had indeed relinquished an important part of the church rate principle. They continued to value the Church Establishment as defining the common good confessionally but they had lost confidence in their old belief, still held by Russell, that compelling non-Anglicans to help pay for Establishment churches was not an infringement of their liberty. While voluntaryists were now reunited to seek the complete abolition of the rate, it remained to be seen how Conservatives would respond to the pressures on the church rate.

The Conservative party was compelled to propose its solution to the church rate question when it fell to the earl of Derby to form a Conservative administration in February 1858. Derby needed to act because the church rate abolitionists were gaining increasing support for their solution. A bill to abolish church rates, introduced by J. S. Trelawny—an Anglican and a Liberal—who had assumed the abolitionist cause after Clay stepped down after 1856, passed the second reading and, for the first time, went all the way to the House of Lords, where it was defeated.[69]

On February 21, 1859, shortly after the opening of Parliament, Spencer Walpole, the chancellor of the exchequer, introduced the government's bill to attempt to deal with the church rate question. This first government attempt since 1837 to address the vexed conflict stood as an alternative to Trelawny's bill to abolish the rate. The government's aim was to free Dissenters from church rate obligations and to defend the Church Establishment. Walpole's bill proposed to establish a permanent fund to maintain churches as an alternative to the rate. The bill would encourage landowners to commute the rate into a permanent rent charge on their lands, which tenants could then deduct from their rents, ensuring that landlords, who tended to be Churchmen, and not Dissenting tenants would pay the church rate equivalent. Where church rates would continue to be necessary anyone who declared a conscientious objection to paying the church rate could be exempted from doing so. Unlike Grey's plan of 1856, this bill did not require Dissenters to declare themselves to be Dissenters in order to claim an exemption. Dissenting objections to "ticketing" themselves had been heard. Now exemptions would be based simply on conscience; nothing would prevent a voluntaryist Anglican from claiming the same right.[70]

Walpole's bill was attacked by Lord John Russell who took deep exception to Walpole's repeated assertions that those not benefiting from the Church should not be compelled to maintain it. During the previous session, Russell himself had become a reluctant convert to exempting Dissenters; but he now defended the establishment principle on Broad Church grounds because of the general benefit that the Establishment gave to the entire community.[71] Walpole denied that exempting Dissenters implied a rejection of the establishment principle. That principle was fulfilled, claimed Walpole, when they had "throughout the country, places of worship and ministers of religion to meet the spiritual wants of the people." Walpole went on quite remarkably to claim that exemption did not contradict the establishment principle unless that principle meant "that it was right to enforce on those who did not belong to the Church a compulsory payment of the rate."[72]

This was an astounding explanation by a Conservative chancellor of the exchequer. From the beginning of the church rate conflict defense of the rate had depended on the axiom that universal church rate obligations were merely the financial implication of the establishment principle. Tories had typically asserted that the church rate was a legitimate means of providing for man's highest good—the worship of God; Whigs, more impressed with the temporal significance of the Church, defended the rate as the legitimate share to be paid by all ratepayers for the common good—a moral and orderly society. Both Whigs and Tories had agreed that the compulsory rate was no real infringement of individual freedom. Walpole's assertion that it was symbolized how the church rate question had changed by 1859. Even the Conservative party was well on the way to viewing the church rate issue in voluntaryist terms. Although it was another nine years before the church rate controversy was resolved, with the abolition of the compulsory rate in 1868, the issue was essentially won by the voluntaryists in 1859 when both Conservatives and Whigs had come to assume a new conception of freedom.

≺ III ≻

Free Trade

Protestant Dissenters were children of the Evangelical Revival *and* heirs of the Enlightenment. Their ceaseless work of evangelization at home and on the mission fields throughout the British Empire was

a witness to the historic Christian view of freedom: mankind is naturally born enslaved to sin and requires faith in the atoning blood of
Christ to be set free from sin and eternal punishment. The same understanding of freedom could lead Dissenters and other Christians to
become involved in politics. Opposition to African slavery could, for
example, be pursued from the evangelical premise that it was illegitimate to keep ensnared in legal and economic bonds those whom
Christ had set free from the bondage of sin. But increasingly in the
nineteenth century, Dissenters' views of freedom derived more from
the Enlightenment than from the Christian tradition. Dissenting beliefs about freedom and individual human autonomy were based on
liberal doctrines of human rights that became subtly intertwined
with their older Christian beliefs.

At times the two sets of beliefs appeared to complement each
other powerfully. James Bradley has shown persuasively that in the
late eighteenth century Dissenting church polity, with its emphasis
on consent, became "the basis for the idea of consent in civil matters,
and in this way the ecclesiastical principles of the Dissenters had a
direct bearing on their political principles." He goes on to say that
"ecclesiastical polity was the primary ground for political radicalism
among orthodox and heterodox alike."[73] It needs to be mentioned,
however, that although there was a "direct" link between Dissenters'
emphasis on consent in church matters and consent in civil affairs,
this linkage was often made through the Enlightenment language of
natural rights, in which, as Bradley observes, Dissenters, both orthodox and heterodox, were regularly instructed from their pulpits.[74]
D. W. Bebbington has pointed to the influence of Enlightenment optimism in shaping the evangelical doctrine of assurance of salvation which he identifies as a key to the dynamism of the Evangelical Revival. Bebbington claims that "the legacy of the Puritans, in
both faith and practice, was modified by the temper of the new era
(the Enlightenment) without losing its grasp of central Christian tenets."[75] It may be that Bebbingtion is too sanguine about the comple-
mentarity of the Enlightenment with Christianity. We have already
seen ways in which Dissenting voluntaryism came to redefine the
traditional Christian view of the state. When we focus on a Dissenting paean to free trade, in the following pages, we shall see evidence
that this commitment to economic freedom, rooted in the Enlightenment, led those who followed this route to redefine teachings at

the heart of the Christian faith in light of Enlightenment liberalism.

A publication that illuminates the way in which Enlightenment assumptions reshaped segments of Dissenting theology is *The Charter of the Nations; or, Free Trade and its Results,* by Henry Dunckley, a Baptist minister at Salford.[76] In the first part of his essay Dunckley carefully charted the economic effects of free trade on textile production and shipping. It was when he turned to the social, political, and religious results of free trade that he became truly enthusiastic. It was also here that one can see indications of significant revision of Christian teaching as a result of economic and political liberalism. One such example is Dunckley's treatment of wealth. He contrasted aristocratic and mercantile wealth in a way that was common among political liberals.[77] Dunckley reassured those who feared that wealth of any kind was dangerous to moral health and that it could lead to national ruin. Dunckley called such fears "happily absurd." He claimed that it was only "wealth, wrung by conquest from downtrodden nations" by aristocratic imperialists which would end in "debauching the minds of the victors." Here Dunckley echoed an earlier claim by Richard Cobden that wars "have ever been but another aristocratic mode of plundering and oppressing commerce." Dunckley concluded optimistically: "Thus, the immoral and emasculating influence of prosperity is not its necessary result, but depends altogether upon the source from which that prosperity springs."[78] Dunckley quite brazenly emasculated the strong and troubling warning of the Bible, which he professed to believe, that "the love of money is the root of all evils."[79] The free trade movement, of which Dissenters were an enthusiastic part, domesticated the uncompromising language of the Bible to suit their class interests and their commitment to economic liberty.

Dunckley's passionate advocacy of free trade and his zeal to liberate anything which was "crippled by the iron bondage of monopoly" allowed him to range far and wide. One of his concerns was the restriction of university fellowships to Anglicans in holy orders. Dunckley called for "the removal of the intellectual and religious monopolies which disgrace our age" and continued that "the destruction of these monopolies is logically included in Free Trade."[80] He noted that in a country "abounding with religious sects" the academic advantages of the universities were confined to one, and he asked, "is it just? is it in harmony with the principles of Free

Trade?"[81] In fairness to Dunckley and to Dissenters (and to historians such as D. W. Bebbington and J. E. Bradley who appear to be relatively satisfied that Dissenters were able to synthesize tenets of the Enlightenment with those of evangelical Dissent without harm to the integrity of historic Christian thought),[82] it should be noted that in this case Dunckley's free trade sentiments helped him to call for a more equitable distribution of academic benefits to all Christians and that his commitment to liberty here may have advanced, rather than undermined, Christian teaching.

Dunckley also questioned the rightness of restricting university fellowships largely to the clergy. He asked: "Is there any reason why the communication of secular knowledge should be delegated to clerical hands? The system is a relic of the dark ages, when a baron could not sign a bill or write a letter without the aid of a clerk, and may be regarded as a symbol of those mistaken views, elsewhere prevalent, by which the development of the intellect is regarded as the proper work of the theologian; but where is the wisdom of retaining in the nineteenth century the prejudices of the age of Charlemagne?"[83] On the surface Dunckley merely was voicing the anticlericalism that was an established feature of Dissent. But he went further than that. He also rejected the view that "the development of the intellect" should be led by theology. He, and many other Dissenters who were understandably preoccupied with ending Anglican control of education, gave little thought to how the universities might remain Christian, even in an undenominational way, once the primacy of the Thirty-nine Articles was done away with. In his enthusiasm to gain equality with the Church of England, Dunckley gave little heed to the possibility that his attachment to intellectual liberty might leave him and his fellow Dissenters with universities more fit for this-worldly liberals than for evangelical Dissenters.

The transforming power of Enlightenment themes became less subtle in the last part of Dunckley's essay, in which he examined the "Probable Influence of Free Trade on the moral Renovation of the World."[84] Dunckley declared himself a believer in a coming millennium, reflecting the growing millennialism that was, according to Bebbington, coming to characterize Evangelicalism after the 1830s.[85] What was striking about Dunckley's millennialism was the role that he expected free trade to play in bringing on the period of a thousand years when Christ would rule on earth with his church.

Dunckley expected that free trade would contribute to the coming of the millennium in three ways. First, it would promote economic growth and social well-being which gave the best basis for "every political and moral virtue." Second, it would foster the growth of "purer political sentiments" because "commerce is the emancipator of mankind—it creates wealth, it inspires with energy and self-respect, it fosters habits of justice and moderation." Third, free trade would spread Christianity. Here Dunckley claimed that he would speak only of the temporal impact of Christianity and not what was revealed in Biblical revelation. He referred to a faith that, he believed, was now thriving in Britain and the United States: "a faith which tells us that man's destiny is practically in his own hands; which stimulates inquiry and independent thought, asserts the equality of all men in the sight of God, and bases all virtue on an intelligent appreciation of his will."[86] It is difficult to escape the sense that Dunckley's faith had more to do with human autonomy and human power than with God's grace.

In his conclusion, Dunckley assumed a full consonance between free trade and Christianity. "In proportion as mankind accepts the principles of Free Trade," claimed Dunckley, "they will admit the morals of Christianity, and may be the more easily led to adopt the doctrines from which they spring."[87] In his final sentence it becomes apparent how deeply Dunckley's understanding of the nature of God-given freedom had been recast in the light of liberalism. The essay ends on a note of triumph. With the final victory of free trade would come the long-awaited epoch of earthly perfection—the millennium: "the figments of superstition will then vanish, priestly sanctities and impostures will be scorned away, and man everywhere stand up erect, wearing the image, and blest with the liberty of God."[88]

It would be a mistake to dismiss this statement as a mere rhetorical flourish. According to classical Christian orthodoxy, the image of God in man has been radically warped by original sin. God's image in man can be restored only through the cleansing of Christ's blood. At the core of Evangelicalism is the belief that this atonement, and the restoration of God's image, is a divine gift that is appropriated by faith. According to Dunckley, however, man recovers God's image by standing upright, of his own power, as a free, equal, and autonomous moral agent who has emancipated himself through free commerce.

However much Dunckley, and his fellow Dissenters, might continue to use the traditional language of sin, and freedom through salvation, in their worship and mission work, when they dealt with economic and political matters they were becoming Pelagians with little sense of the power of the original sin that they confessed in their chapels. This meant, in effect, that they now used two quite distinct definitions of freedom. Having adopted the Enlightenment belief in the natural human power to free oneself, at least in the public domain, Dissenters at mid century could aspire comfortably to become a constituent part of the Liberal party that was evolving from the more traditional Whig-Liberal party of Palmerston and Russell.

≺ IV ≻

Summary

In the course of the reform debates in church and state during the first half of the nineteenth century there had been a profound shift in the concept of what it meant to be free. That understanding of the nature of freedom was tied to beliefs about how individual men and women ought to relate to the good—to the common good, and ultimately, to God. At the beginning of the century Tories, Whigs, Wesleyan Methodists, and many Protestant Dissenters continued to hold in many ways to the centuries-old belief in the common good. Traditionalists at the beginning of the nineteenth century assumed, as Peter Miller has pointed out, that it was not a contradiction to seek justice and liberty for individuals in the context of the common good where it was understood that priority would be given to the security of the community.[89]

Giving priority to the community was of special relevance to questions touching the prerogatives of the Church of England. When the privileges of the Church, and its established status, became subjects of political debate by 1832, as they had been during the American Revolution, Tories and Whigs came to her defense in the name of the common good, and the highest good. They denied that the requirement of religious tests as a condition of taking a degree at the ancient universities, and the church rate principle, were infringements of the freedom of those who dissented from the Church. They defended the rights of the Church not only because of their own vested interests in her welfare (which were real enough) but because they continued to believe that "it was impossible for any man to be good unless he is well adapted to the common good."[90] For Tories that meant maintaining the Established Church as a corporate obeisance to God as the way of finding true freedom for the nation, and for the individuals constituting the national community. For Whigs church rates or religious university tests were a legitimate price for individuals to pay to contribute to the common good in terms of promoting a moral society.

It is more surprising that many Dissenters at the beginning of the nineteenth century should have shared much of the traditional sense that individual claims ought to be subordinated to the general good of the community. They, unlike Churchmen, did not have a vested interest in maintaining the Establishment. Indeed, their more militant leaders had taken the lead in the tumultuous 1770s and 1780s in beginning to demand individual liberty over the claims of the Establishment.[91] But the Dissenters of the early nineteenth century had been deeply shaped by the Evangelical Revival. Partly for that reason they too held to the traditional view of freedom that only obedience to God would give salvation and freedom. Many Dissenters were willing, therefore, to subordinate their own political and economic interests to tolerate the priority given to the Church Establishment that most citizens believed to be the best means of shaping a Christian society.

After 1832 older understandings of individual freedom as subordinate to the good of the community, and subject to God, were eroded. Dissenters took the lead in demanding equality with Churchmen. As they adopted voluntaryism in their political contest with the Church they increasingly made use of the language of liberalism that derived from the Enlightenment and which had already in the eighteenth century begun to shape their thinking.[92] By mid century even their theology was showing the imprint of the Enlightenment insistence that freedom was an individual matter based on natural rights.

During the prolonged church rate conflict the Whigs had attempted to placate Dissenters while maintaining their traditional insistence that a compulsory rate was not an infringement of Dissenting rights. By 1859 in Palmerston's government only Russell argued that rates were for the common good and therefore not illegitimate.

He gave up his support for the rate in that same year, having concluded that defending the rate was a danger to the Church.[93] The change in conceptions of freedom was seen most starkly in the Conservative party. Spencer Walpole, in arguing for his bill to exempt Dissenters from church rate obligations, took for granted that it would be wrong to expect a Dissenter to pay a tax for a church that was not his own. So in a few words he dismissed the very heart of the church rate principle that Tories, and Whigs, had insisted on at the beginning of the church rate conflict.

For all segments of the community the definition of "the good" had changed by the middle of the century. The shift that Peter Miller believes to have occurred in the course of the eighteenth century, and that J. C. D. Clark believes to have been completed by 1832, the movement of emphasis from the community to the individual, had made real headway only by the middle of the nineteenth century. In the second half of the century there was established a new definition of the common good in which "the natural right of human beings to think and pursue truth had to be taken as the basis of civil society."[94] Because it was now the individual citizen who determined the definition of "the good," freedom could no longer be seen in submission to the community or to God. The Enlightenment's autonomous individual was now at the center and liberal reformers after mid century worked zealously to expand freedom in terms of the natural rights of the individual. Conservatives, largely having adopted the same definition of freedom, used their efforts after 1850 primarily to slow the process of change.

The Limits of Religious Liberty: Theology and Criticism in Nineteenth-Century England

R. K. WEBB

THE HISTORY OF toleration from its enactment in 1689 to the repeal of the Test and Corporation Acts in 1828 and the passage of Catholic Emancipation in 1829 involved primarily the liberties of groups or interests—the corporate rights of non-Anglican denominations to worship freely and the rights of individuals, as members of those groups, to full participation as citizens. Thus, at the end of the 1760s, Joseph Priestley called for doing away with all ties between Church and state to guarantee the legal parity of all religions, including Roman Catholicism and Judaism. But in arguing for moving beyond toleration to religious liberty, he added a powerful plea for the freedom of individuals to pursue truth wherever it might lead, without interference from secular or religious authority: to shackle debate, he insisted, could only make mankind the poorer.[1]

In the unsettled years after 1790, such free expression of opinion, whether in religion or politics, was subject to constant scrutiny and frequent restraint, a hardening of attitudes resulting not only from fear of revolution but from a clearer drawing of inter- and intra-denominational lines. In much of the eighteenth century, despite differences in social position and religious experience, Dissenting groups had a found an easy accommodation among themselves, while a considerable *rapprochement* took place between Dissent and elements in the Church of England. In an ordination sermon in 1777, the Unitarian William Enfield told the ordinands that, whatever theological course their studies might dictate, they would be welcomed by their Dissenting brethren; he also foresaw (echoing the seventeenth-century ideal of "comprehension") a Church "constructed on such liberal principles, and placed on so extensive a basis, as to invite within its inclosure christian ministers and people of every denomination."[2] Latitudinarianism in the Church of England had adumbrated that possibility, and even when religious differences appeared deep, friendly exchange remained possible. The most celebrated of Evangelical laymen, William Wilberforce, worked with and admired many who differed from him doctrinally, while in one after another provincial town Dissenters and Churchmen joined in the new literary and philosophical societies, in charitable activities, and, where law and custom allowed, in local politics.[3]

In behavior, "as well as in everything else," Enfield told the young ministers, "let me caution you against the extreme." Within a few years, however, extremes were commonplace. Evangelicals, priding themselves on their "seriousness," were not only strong in their faith but determined to bring others to the same safety, through concerted action in the legislature and reforming societies and through untiring efforts at individual persuasion. At the other end of the spectrum, as Latitudinarianism in the Church began to falter, Unitarians began to speak out as plainly as did evangelicals: "I am inclined more and more to think," wrote the Unitarian higher critic Charles Christian Hennell in 1831, "that it is better to run the risk of offending people by candour than to compromise one's veracity by politeness (this however is a great *quaestio vexata*, & what we decide in theory becomes very awkward in practice)."[4] This new stringency is reflected in the establishment of denominational propaganda agencies, in threats to some once-accommodating interdenominational philanthropies, in the rupture between orthodox and liberal Dissent, in the growth of competing and hostile parties in the Church, and, specifically, in the abandonment of William Wilberforce's accommodating spirit in the inward-looking and outwardly belligerent attitudes of his sons, Robert, Samuel, and Henry.

William Wilberforce warned Samuel against his tendency to hasty judgment but to no avail: to all three sons, as to High Churchmen generally, Dissenters were no longer merely separated brethren but schismatics, who, Samuel said, lead the awakening "from sobriety of mind, to feelings and fancies and I fear spiritual pride." Samuel and Henry were amused to think of the "unimpassioned endurance" that Robert would have displayed toward an annoying Unitarian farmer in his parish at a dinner he would gladly have avoided. Invited in

1846 to speak at the Manchester Athenaeum, which had a policy of inviting well-known and ideologically balanced pairs of speakers—Disraeli and Cobden had been guests in 1844—Samuel refused to appear with the radical Birmingham Baptist George Dawson, who he insisted had delivered an un-Christian speech at the Free Trade Hall. When the Athenaeum board protested that on that earlier occasion, Dawson had "that liberty of speech and expression" he would not have under the rules of the Athenaeum, he loftily replied that conscience forbade his sharing a platform with anyone who had maintained principles hostile to Christianity.[5]

This heightened sense of separateness was reinforced by the new importance given to points of theology. Evangelicals, Anglicans and Dissenters alike, put increasing stress on the "peculiar doctrines" of the gospel—"the corruption of human nature, the atonement of the Saviour, and the sanctifying influence of the holy spirit," in the formulation of William Wilberforce so contemptuously dismissed by the converted Calvinist Thomas Belsham in his first, notorious effort as a Unitarian controversialist.[6] High Churchmen developed and defended points of dogma that had hitherto been comfortably assumed and gave the Thirty-nine Articles and the Creeds a new centrality in defining their faith.[7]

Re-emphasis on doctrine was one response to what all sensitive observers, in England and abroad, recognized as a critical rather than an organic age. Amidst a stunning expansion of intellectual resources, deference to the established gave way to a reign of opinion, marked by questioning, rapidly shifting allegiances, and a measure of incomprehension and despair.[8] The rise of such individualist thinking was reinforced by Romanticism, which stressed the insights won in lonely and often agonizing struggle, while a new sense of the vastness and unembraceability of nature and mind altered perceptions of truth, attainable only through partial insight or perhaps never, except as the object of a quest.[9]

As a clash of ideas threatened to break through farther and farther limits, new urgency was given to a question that may itself have been so altered as to be new: how far could liberty extend, within established religious traditions and institutions and in the larger society, when intellectual corrosion had become commonplace? The traditional centering of religious liberty on what groups or their members were permitted to *do*—by no means a dead issue, as demonstrated in chapter 3—was being joined or surpassed in importance by the question of what individuals could be allowed to *say* or even think.

Faced with conflicting authorities, many, indeed most, believers fell back on received and formulaic ways. Others, deeply touched by a compelling idea or a profound experience, responded no less formulaically. For such ordinary Christians, freedom to maintain their ideas and practices, however misguided they seemed to critical minds, was largely conceded. But for the educated and articulate, the newer sense of religious liberty—freedom to think, speak, and write as study and reflection might dictate—made inherited conventions of toleration obsolete.

No single chapter can encompass all the varieties of religious liberty in nineteenth-century England, whether in its older, communal understanding or its newer, individualistic version. Thus, Roman Catholicism will scarcely appear in this chapter, although Victorian Catholics repeatedly confronted questions of individual liberty within their own communion, and despite the fact that, as the hated other, Catholics were the principal contradiction to Britain's reputation as a tolerant country. So, too, I have excluded the liberty claimed for irreligion to oppose religion: the risks run by nineteenth-century free-thinkers and atheists, from Richard Carlile through George Jacob Holyoake to Charles Bradlaugh, were well understood, and the history has been frequently told. The more extreme case of blasphemy is logically and historically quite separate from the question of *religious* liberty.[10] Rather, with procrustean selectivity, I have chosen to illustrate the general question through similar crises of thought and discipline in three denominations—the Church of England, Unitarianism, and Quakerism—within a single decade, the 1860s.

To invoke the metaphor of crisis courts misinterpretation. The 1860s are the *locus classicus* of "the nineteenth-century crisis of faith" usually ascribed to advances in physical and biological science and specifically to Charles Darwin's *On the Origin of Species*, published in 1859. Recent historical scholarship has done much, if not to displace then to complicate that phenomenon. Not all Victorians suffered or were even aware of a crisis; abandonment of religious observance or faith was usually gradual or generational, not catastrophic; and the few who experienced a sudden collapse of their religious world were confined to a small, significant, and mostly (but not entirely) intellectual segment of the population. Within that segment, there were virtually as many crises as there were individuals, arising from different causes and coming at different times. Moreover, for much of the century, scientific developments were more likely to reinforce and be reinforced by religion than to force its rejection. To speak of a single, overarching crisis in this or that decade or generation is, therefore, historical nonsense.[11]

At the same time, Victorian intellectual history cannot be reduced to mental and emotional biography. The striking similarities that emerge in the confrontations within three denominations differing so widely in structure, theology, and religious sensibility surmount the perils of fragmentation to reveal some general contours of the development of religious liberty in the century.

≺ I ≻

The Church of England

The crisis in the Church in the 1860s was preceded by a number of clashes, varying in impact, like premonitory shocks before an earthquake. The granting of Catholic Emancipation in 1829 by a Tory government sparked a rebellion among ultra-Tories and particularly among resurgent High Churchmen that led to the rejection of Sir Robert Peel, the minister who had carried the Emancipation bill, as member of Parliament for the University of Oxford.[12] The reform agitation of 1830–32 appeared to threaten the Church as much as the unreformed constitution, and much of the country drew back in consequence. Then, in 1836, Lord Melbourne's Whig government chose Renn Dickson Hampden—a Latitudinarian associated with the liberally inclined "Noetics" in Oriel College, Oxford—as Regius professor of divinity in the University, unleashing a violent protest fuelled by the general condemnation of liberalism in the nascent Oxford Movement. Hampden's Bampton Lectures in 1832 had offended High Churchmen by questioning the validity of human formulation—by medieval schoolmen—of dogmatic teachings, some of which glowed with new fire in those heady days; Hampden had alarmed his opponents even more by advocating the admission of Dissenters to the University. In 1847, Lord John Russell made things worse by appointing Hampden to the bishopric of Hereford.

But no other pre-sixties incident had the repercussions of the

Gorham judgment of 1850. The powerful, combative High-Church bishop of Exeter, Henry Phillpotts, refused to institute a clergyman, G. C. Gorham, to a living because Gorham held evangelical, and in Phillpotts's eyes heretical, views on the doctrine of baptismal regeneration.[13] Defeated in a suit he brought in the Court of Arches, the court of the archdiocese of Canterbury, Gorham appealed to the Judicial Committee of the Privy Council, reorganized in 1833 to hear appeals from colonial courts and courts with civil-law jurisdiction, church courts among them. The single bishop and one layman on the Judicial Committee as then constituted dissented, but the majority, on narrowly legal grounds, reversed the earlier judgment. Joined to the two Hampden incidents and other instances of what was deemed lay dictation to the Church on matters of belief and discipline, the decision alarmed committed Churchmen.[14] Following John Henry Newman's notorious conversion to Roman Catholicism in 1845, a number of similarly oriented minds were drawing closer to Rome; for some—among them Henry Manning, then archdeacon of Chichester and the leader of late-Victorian Roman Catholicism—the Gorham judgment gave the final push.

The events that concern us here turn on a volume, *Essays and Reviews*, published in March 1860 and embracing seven independently conceived but temperamentally linked chapters by six churchmen and one layman.[15] Frederick Temple, headmaster of Rugby School, led off with "The Education of the Human Race," in which, like Lessing and others, he likened the mental history of mankind to that of an individual whose progression from infancy to maturity entailed changing ideas and interpretations of the world. Rowland Williams, vicar of Broadchalke in Wiltshire and vice-principal of the Anglican theological college at Lampeter in Wales, offered a comment on the biblical criticism of the great German scholar Baron Bunsen. Baden Powell, Savilian professor of geometry at Oxford and, like Hampden, a link to earlier Latitudinarians, dealt with evidences of Christianity, miracles in particular.[16] Henry Bristow Wilson, a former Oxford don and professor (of Anglo-Saxon) who was vicar of Great Staughton in Huntingdonshire, unfavorably contrasted an "individualist" Calvinism to the inclusive, "multitudinist" church he advocated. C. W. Goodwin, the sole layman, wrote on the impact of geology on the Mosaic cosmogony.[17] Mark Pattison, about to become rector of Lincoln College and one of the liberal pillars of Victorian intellectual life, contributed a dismissive survey of eighteenth-century theology, a chapter surely more likely to provoke disagreement today than at the time. The list was concluded by Benjamin Jowett, Regius professor of Greek at Oxford and a future master of Balliol College, whose essay gained notoriety at least in part from his already immense reputation but more from his choosing to elaborate on how the Bible was coming to be read critically, in a famous phrase, like any other book.[18]

Most of the essays had been anticipated in earlier publications by their authors, who were known to be, in a new and fuzzy term, Broad Churchmen and sympathizers with the new theology—"neology" in the jargon of the time—that had emerged in Germany over the past three-quarters of a century. But what might have been expected from the writers as individuals was compounded by the whole, self-consciously addressed to a public beyond the universities and offering startling and disturbing conclusions. Even Temple's irenic vision seemed to offer no firm resting place for belief; while the others demolished one certitude after another: the inspiration of the Bible was questioned by Williams and Jowett, while Williams (through Bunsen) dismissed the prophetic books; Baden Powell rejected miracles as historical events, as scientific possibilities, and as evidences of Christianity; Wilson cast doubt on the doctrine of eternal punishment of the wicked; and Goodwin confirmed the testimony of geology to the age of the earth, a conclusion some were still inclined to resist.

Although the volume attracted little immediate notice, the Positivist Frederic Harrison, in the *Westminster Review* in October 1860, reproved the authors for not rejecting Christianity outright and accused them of clinging to a Church whose teachings (in the Thirty-nine Articles they had subscribed) they had questioned. In the *Quarterly Review* for January 1861, Samuel Wilberforce, now bishop of Oxford, mounted a slashing attack from the High Church perspective, and A. P. Stanley, the most celebrated of Broad Churchmen and a potential author who had escaped the net, offered no more than a lukewarm defense in the *Edinburgh Review*; lesser periodicals followed, in praise or (mostly) blame, while clergymen and laymen rushed pamphlets into print. One instance may suffice. The book, an anonymous author wrote, was "an experiment to decide how much heresy the people of England will stand"; "freedom of thought is all very well in its way," he said, and Mormons, Chartists, and all manner of reformists could claim it, but to accept Church revenues with one hand, while writing like the atheist George Jacob Holyoake with the other was despicable.[19] The challenge was widely dealt with in episcopal charges, and early in 1861, all 25 bishops—including the three reputed liberals on the bench, with Hampden the most vehement—issued a letter of condemnation.

Except for Goodwin and Pattison—and for Baden Powell, who had died shortly after publication—worse was in store. Accused of being unfit to head a school, Temple forbade his boys to read the book. Firm in his immediate response to Stanley's tepid support, he eventually temporized and some years later formally withdrew his contribution, by which time he was on his way to the archbishopric of Canterbury, though his sins were not forgotten when Gladstone first raised him to the bench in 1869. An effort to try Jowett for heresy in the court of the University vice-chancellor failed, but when Jowett's friends tried to increase his scandalously low salary as professor, a vote of Congregation, the University's ultimate legislative body swollen by M.A.s who flocked to Oxford to show their displeasure, defeated the statute.

As clergymen with parochial rather than academic posts, Williams and Wilson were most vulnerable. Williams, whose parish (a college living) lay in the diocese of Salisbury, was accused of heresy by his bishop, Walter Kerr Hamilton, who brought nineteen charges relating to conflicts between what Williams said in his essay and the Thirty-nine Articles, the Creeds, the Prayer Book, and appointed lessons. A similar case, with three charges, was brought against Wilson by a fellow priest in the diocese of Ely. By agreement, the cases were removed from the two diocesan courts to be tried together in the Court of Arches. The judgment was delivered in 1862 by the Dean of Arches, Sir Stephen Lushington, a civil lawyer and judge of great distinction—a liberal in politics (he had been among the defenders of Queen Caroline in 1820) and a supporter of the Hampden appointments—who had been one of the majority in the Gorham judgment.[20]

Lushington rejected most of the charges against the two men, limiting his purview to the single test of conformity to the Thirty-nine Articles. On that score, defining what he saw as the clear sense of the Articles, he proceeded to find against both defendants on the question of biblical inspiration; against Wilson for advocating universal restoration and for denying that the wicked would suffer everlastingly in Hell; and against Williams for rejecting the propitiary nature of the Atonement and for his views on justification by faith.

Lushington's decision moved inevitably to the Judicial Committee, now reorganized to include the two archbishops and the bishop of London, the liberally inclined A. C. Tait. In a judgment handed down in 1864, Canterbury and York voted to uphold the lower court decision, and Tait voted with the majority to dismiss all the charges: once more a predominantly lay court outraged High Churchmen chafing under state domination.[21] The majority argued that the Thirty-nine Articles were so loosely drawn that the defendants' views simply could not conflict with them. Given that reasoning, the Judicial Committee was certain to rule in the same way when, in 1865, they decided the contemporaneous case of J. W. Colenso, bishop of Natal, who had been deprived and excommunicated for a book that questioned the account of creation in the Book of Genesis.

In 1864, in reponse to the first Privy Council judgment, eleven thousand clergymen of the Church of England signed a manifesto proclaiming their belief in the literal truth of the Bible (even in matters of physical science), though it was widely noted that the number did not include the more intellectually reputable of their order: Bishop Thirlwall was reported to have said scathingly that "he considered them in the light of a row of figures preceded by a decimal point." To liberals, in the churches and outside, the *Essays and Reviews* and Colenso decisions were hailed as guarantees of the freedom of all Englishmen, clergymen as well as laymen, to say and write what they pleased without fear of reprisal in the form of accusations of heresy and loss of employment.[22] In fact, in neither case did the Committee's judgment, based on quite narrow legal grounds, raise the question of freedom. But freedom dominated public discussion of the case and appeared prominently in argument of counsel in the Court of Arches.

Although Wilson was the most radical of the essayists, and although his contention about eternal punishment gave rise to the most frequently quoted witticism about the judgment—that the Judicial Committee had "dismissed Hell with costs"—the case against Rowland Williams looms larger, because the charges against him were more numerous and more provocatively worded and came with

the authority of Bishop Hamilton, a much-admired High Churchman. Williams's case is also the better documented, in his own published advice to his counsel, in a remarkable sermon following Lushington's interlocutory judgment, and in the published speech of his
most famous lawyer, James Fitzjames Stephen.

Williams was a spiky and difficult man. He did splendid work at
the theological college at Lampeter, but he was offended by criticism
of a published volume of sermons and was a trial to Bishop Thirlwall
who, as visitor to the college, was attempting to maneuver a soft
landing. But spiky and difficult, even outrageous, personalities are
likely to be the protagonists in confrontations such as these. Personality apart, Williams was a thoroughgoing Latitudinarian out of his
time, who, as is suggested by lists of reading he recommended to
friends, drew his inspiration from a wide range of historical, critical,
literary, and theological sources, being particularly indebted to the
spiritual insight of the early Quakers as "living vehicles of an abiding
power of spiritual truth."[23]

In instructions to his counsel, Williams repeatedly emphasized
the argument from truth: formularies enforced by ecclesiastical dictation could not possibly carry authority, surely here an echo of
Hampden's Bampton lectures. Rather, authority flowed from "whatever persuades the mind," and analytical methods were the means to
overthrow the "floating tradition of error" imposed on the clergy by
violence. Bishop Hamilton, Williams said, seemed to call for fetter-
ing critical research and theological conclusions by falsifying primary facts, which "as they belong to literature, the man of letters has
an *a priori* duty to report": if a clergyman were compelled to say that
all the psalms were written by King David, the statement would lack
any moral value, because extorted against the weightier verdict of
biblical scholars. Williams insisted that he believed the Thirty-nine
Articles, but "it is one thing to sign a proposition as humanly true,
or to accept a large series of not quite consistent propositions, as being the best settlement of complicated problems which their many-
sided aspects admit of," and it is something else to maintain that the
propositions had "fallen down from Jupiter, a revelation stereotyped
forever, and neither containing accretion of human thought, nor ad-
mitting speculative modification."[24]

This concern with the reach of ecclesiastical discipline, above all
with respect to freedom to study and publish the results, is at the

heart of the penultimate sermon Williams preached at Lampeter, on May 25, 1862, following Lushington's judgment.[25] There he staked out more fully the claims of reason, so long as arguments are "disciplined by conscience and sobered by judgment" and rooted in the freedom found in primitive Christianity and exemplified among saints and schoolmen, in the Lutheran reformation and among the Quakers, and in the "ennobling freedom" that Nonconformity asserted against the imperfect freedom of the Church.

If Williams's sermon seems broader in its rhetoric and implications than his instructions, the change may have been influenced by the arguments of R. B. Kennard, rector of Marnhull in Dorset, who had published a protest against Hamilton's action. In an appended letter to Williams, Kennard argued that the case was important to clergymen not only as theologians but as citizens, threatening as it did mutual toleration and "the true Catholic and Christian freedom of inquiry and discussion" accorded to both clergy and laity, which was to be abandoned for "an irrational and self-destructive dogmatism."[26] But it is even more likely that Williams was carried along by the arguments of his most celebrated defender.[27]

The lead counsel for the defense in 1862 was James Parker Deane, an ecclesiastical lawyer of great reputation. In 1845, Deane had pointedly warned clergymen whose scruples might tempt them to alter parts of the liturgy against thus violating the canons of the Church and the Act of Uniformity.[28] But the concern about schism and the finality of episcopal authority that Deane had insisted upon in 1845 was hardly to be found in 1862. He rebutted the charges against Williams point by point, mounting an essentially technical argument with impressive legal and theological learning and magnificent irony. Any state church, he said, must "either shut up confine and cripple the human mind within an arbitrary strict set of precepts and doctrines," thus running the danger of infidelity or Romanism, or it must have a "freer, more rational and reasonable system" that would allow all those believing the great Christian truths to come together. Was Williams, authorized by his ordination to preach and teach, to be "a mere dumb dog," silent on the great matters prohibited by neither Articles nor liturgy and canvassed by every thoughtful Christian? Rather it was the duty of every minister of the Church to use all available means to increase knowledge and wisdom.[29]

The lawyers on the opposing side opposed neither liberty nor the increase of knowledge, differing only on where lines were to be drawn. R. J. Phillimore, lead counsel for Bishop Hamilton, pointed out that the country's greatest intellects had flourished within the expansive confines of the Church and dismissed the essayists as reviving the "discarded trash" of early heretics and later Deists, filtered through the "borrowed infidelity" of a school of German writers: the essays were thus a plagiarism of a plagiarism. But if the threat of these exploded ideas was real, then an unlearned church was better than a dishonest one and the articles and canons might better be swept away than to allow subscription to be dismissed as subterfuge and sophistry and so corrupt faith and morals.

It was left to Deane's junior, James Fitzjames Stephen, to argue the case on a broader plane. Concentrating on the question of biblical inspiration, Stephen demolished arguments for infallibility and cited famous churchmen from Hooker through Baxter, Warburton, Paley, Horsley, and Marsh in earlier times to Whewell and Whately in his own to show how much latitude of interpretation had in fact been assumed, almost from the foundation of the Church of England. He showed how many questions had been left open, how flexible were the Articles, and how irrelevant or incompetent were Hamilton's charges and the arguments of the prosecution, when judged by legal standards.

Stephen was a rising barrister and an already well-known contributor to periodicals; he was also at the apogee of a trajectory from an Evangelical upbringing to utilitarian free thought, before the authoritarian implications of his later work had settled into intellectual habit.[30] It was, then, personally as well as professionally appropriate that his argument was so often couched in terms of liberty—the right of clergymen "to that unfettered liberty of opinion which belongs to them as subjects of the Queen of England"; a liberty of interpretation going beyond the secrecy of the study and the disguises of "devotional phraseology"; security against the "ignorant panic" of public feeling used as a pretext "by a cynical and sceptical minority . . . indignant that a clergyman of the Church of England should dare to use his mind, and should not be punished as a criminal for having done so"; and (in his peroration) "the very right and truth of the cause . . . of learning, of freedom, and of reason—the learning of the most learned, the freedom of the freest, and the reason of the most rational church in the world."[31]

This expansive view of liberty was probably widely assumed

among educated and informed laymen but was far less persuasive
to Churchmen, whether through conviction or experience. The Oxford Movement had originated a generation earlier in hostility to
such views and their consequences. Contemplating the eighteenth-
century theorist of establishment, Bishop Warburton, John Keble rejected his "overweening talk of human dignity and civil liberty . . .
the fashionable quasi-idolatry of that era, perhaps we might say, of
our country, for a century and a half,"[32] an attitude not lost by the
1860s; in some ways, perhaps, it had become even more widely and
rigorously held. In 1847, Samuel Wilberforce insisted that he gave his
clergy "a large circle to work in," and that he did not interfere if they
stayed within it.[33] In 1853 he was evidently distressed by the im-
pending removal of F. D. Maurice from a professorship of divinity at
King's College London following publication of *Theological Essays,*
in which Maurice appeared incidentally to deny eternal punishment.
He worried whether the matter could stop short of removing Maurice
from his chaplaincy at Lincoln's Inn as well as from the professorship
and risking a trial of a famously saintly man. Might a committee of
divines, he wondered, report on the book and hear Maurice in his
own defense? And he did what he could to intercede with R. W. Jelf,
the college principal, to avoid the calamity, in vain. But *Essays and
Reviews* was far worse than the Maurice episode, and Wilberforce
took the lead in issuing the bishops' declaration in 1862 and in organizing the manifesto of the clergy in 1864 against the Judicial Committee's decision.[34]

The Maurice affair suggests a consideration that went beyond the
accusation of reserve with regard to subscription, the hypocrisy of
remaining in a church whose beliefs were rejected, or explaining
away authoritative texts: the obligations and consequences of teaching. Jelf's hand was forced by bishops who refused to accept graduates
of the relatively new King's College as candidates for ordination so
long as Maurice remained in his post. Even as he tried to defuse the
situation, Wilberforce told Jelf that if the *Essays* offered a "fair
sample of [Maurice's] theological teaching, I should think him so
unsafe a teacher of youth that I should acquiesce with great pain in
his removal."

The English university was neither a center for research nor a forum for the free exchange of ideas, but an engine for the inculcation
of received truth. It would, therefore, be anachronistic to invoke the

concept of academic freedom, which was only beginning to emerge in mid-nineteenth-century Germany. From there, it migrated to the United States at the end of the century. It was gradually domiciled in England following changes in the structure and purpose of universities after 1870, but in a sort of absence of mind.[35] To most Victorian understandings, above all among the clergy, teaching had to be protected from untrammelled liberty, as is evident in the demand for Church control and financing of national education and in watchfulness over the universities and the pulpit: departure from orthodoxy posed a threat to religion and civic order.

"We know exactly what Truth is," the traditional High Churchman H. J. Rose had written many years earlier.

We are going on no voyage of discovery. We know exactly the extent of the shore. There is a creek here, and a bay there,—all laid down in the charts; but not often entered or re-surveyed. We know all this beforehand, and therefore can lay down our plans, and not, (as I think), feel any uncertainty where we are going, or feel it necessary or advisable to spread our sails, and take our chance of finding a new Atlantis.[36]

The dangers in a new cultural context had been flagged as early as 1831 by Samuel Hinds, later bishop of Norwich, who warned that chaos of opinion, serious at any time, had risen to a crisis level as an uneducated community had become educated, alerted to free enquiry, and aware of "all that darkens and deforms the subject," while spiritual knowledge had not kept pace with worldly knowledge.

What is sufficient . . . for an uneducated person, becomes inadequate for him when educated; even as he would be crippled and deformed, if the limb which was strong and well-proportioned when he was a child should have undergone no progressive change as his bodily stature increased, and he grew to manhood.[37]

It was in that vein that, when Samuel Wilberforce had refused to join George Dawson at the Manchester Athenaeum in 1846, he had pleaded that he dared not incidentally "expose the young and the half-learned to the seductions of . . . a shallow Pantheistic philosophy; which may rob them unawares of their faith in him who died for their redemption."[38] So, too, a fearful pamphleteer who wrote in the sixties that the essayists had sent out a volume worse than outright disbelief: "They have given so 'free' a 'handling' to the Bible . . . as to sow seeds which must germinate in infidelity and deism; in others, of pantheism or atheism."[39] The distrust that most Churchmen felt for their flocks and their pupils was palpable. But that Victorian, or Anglican, attitude, if it did not disappear, soon became far more complex.

In 1861, Bishop Hamilton had brought charges against Rowland Williams because he and his unrepentant colleagues had gone beyond the bounds of toleration: Hamilton had to keep his clergy within those limits, lest "our children . . . inherit the conclusion that such teaching, though possibly most repugnant to the religious sentiments of their fathers, was . . . admitted to be not unlawful."[40] The essayists, he continued, had in effect told the clergy that their authority was limited, that they should concentrate on outward tasks, sympathize with human infirmities and not judge harshly, be all things to all men—a warning that might prove a blessing if in response the clergy became more active, grew in grace, and attempted to bring all men together "in a temple founded on Jesus Christ the Lord."

Three years later, Hamilton tried to salvage defeat in exactly those terms. Because the power of Convocation had survived the Judicial Committee, he said, it might be possible to rewrite the Thirty-nine Articles, but the risks were too great, among them the likelihood of yet another reverse in the courts, however ill adapted they were, as he had said in 1861, to weigh such questions "in the fine balance of Truth." Religion is not, he insisted, a matter of opinion or sentiment but of faith and demonstrable truth, though asserting its claims is one thing and proving them another. Both clergy and laymen had, therefore, to be made newly aware of the authority of the Church's teaching through preaching, missions, pastoral letters, and the sacraments. Hamilton's 1867 charge dealt almost entirely with the sacerdotal powers of the clergy, suggesting a shift from sweeping efforts at suppressing advanced thought to better securing internal cohesion.[41]

Within a generation remarkable changes had transpired. To be sure, the old style of sectarian exclusiveness was still to be found. H. J. Liddon, a widely admired High Church preacher who had encouraged Bishop Hamilton to his action, refused repeated invitations from his old friend A. P. Stanley, now dean of Westminster, to preach in the Abbey, for Stanley had cast his net too widely for Liddon (who had heard that Maurice and Jowett had been invited) to accept without compromising himself, and eventually Stanley simply stopped asking.[42] Again, in 1870, the distinguished Unitarian scholar G. Vance Smith had been invited to join the committee appointed to revise the translation of the Bible; Dean Stanley, characteristically, made sure that Vance Smith attended when the committee took communion in the Abbey. That a Unitarian was not only present but shared in the Eucharist infuriated High Churchmen.[43] By the eighties, however, Oxford divinity had been won for the liberals to a sufficient extent that Nonconformist colleges could agree (though not without considerable dissension) to move there without grave risk to their mission or their students.[44] Jowett's death in 1893 diluted that confidence, but there was still fairly easy accommodation at the universities of theologians of differing inclinations.

Even more significant was the publication of a new volume of essays, *Lux Mundi*, in 1889. Resolutely High Church, its authors readily accepted the practice and the conclusions of science and the higher criticism; there were protests, notably by Liddon, but they were insignificant compared to what had happened in the 1860s. As if enacting Bishop Hamilton's revised agenda, the new essayists sought deeper insights into the Church, and when that Church looked outward, it was not to secure the dogmatic base of a nation at prayer but to seek a reconciled society.

The overt social concerns of *Lux Mundi* and the contemporaneous founding of the Christian Social Union by Bishop Westcott, among the most adventurous of English biblical critics, point to a new preoccupation that quickly swept across the religious spectrum.[45] This shift in concern from dogma to society—even Liddon was something of a social reformer—offers a curious confirmation of a hunch of Benjamin Jowett's. The Church, he said, no longer numbered really great men in its ranks, for great men could not accept the constraints of creeds: "[A] great man in high Ecclesiastical station" might better "drop all dogmatic theology and . . . fill his mind with great schemes for the regeneration of mankind."[46]

≺ II ≻

The Unitarians

The insignificant place of Unitarianism in the English religious scene in most of this century obscures the key role it played in the nineteenth. Never large in numbers, Unitarians weighed more than they measured, as one Unitarian journalist felicitously put it[47]—in Parliament, in political and cultural circles in large provincial towns, in education and journalism and the formation of opinion. The orthodox readily dismissed Unitarianism as not Christian (a view Unitarians strenuously fought), viewing it as one step short of atheism and a certain path to it. Yet Unitarianism could not be so simply dismissed. Though it was socially more inclusive than most historians have recognized, the presence of wealth, economic and political leadership, and intellectual power within its ranks puzzled contemporaries: how could such respectable people hold such an unrespectable theological position?

Discrimination had made Unitarians fervent defenders of freedom of religion and freedom of thought in the widest sense and reinforced their overwhelming support of the Liberal party, and Unitarian newspapers and periodicals welcomed the decisions of the Judicial Committee in the *Essays and Reviews* and Colenso cases. By a curious irony, however, this most liberal of denominations faced its own doctrinal crisis in the 1860s, on a question of biblical criticism.

As a denomination, Unitarianism resulted from the merging of two main strands in the latter years of the eighteenth century—an increasingly heterodox Presbyterianism and a breakaway group of Latitudinarian Anglicans headed by Theophilus Lindsey and John Disney. In 1774, Lindsey established the first openly Unitarian place of worship in the country—in Essex Street in London—at a time when denial of the Trinity was still proscribed by law.[48] The most significant figure in these years was the scientist and theologian Joseph Priestley, who came to Unitarianism by gradual stages from a Calvinist background, completing his conversion in 1768. Over the next two decades Priestley set out the theological and philosophical groundings of his new faith, and with the losses he suffered in the Birmingham Riots of 1791, Unitarianism gained a new martyr.

Although Priestley was a materialist and denied freedom of the will in a philosophical sense, he never saw these positions as a necessary consequence of Unitarianism. He was more important as a historian of formidable persuasiveness, charting the corruptions of Christianity from its primitive origins: structurally, the involvement of religion with the secular power; theologically, the doctrine of the Trinity. To Unitarians, Jesus was not a god but a perfect man, whose example encouraged his followers to make themselves perfect. It followed that they rejected a substitutionary atonement, which they believed denied human responsibility, and that they came to accept the certainty of universal salvation and perfection, if not in this world, in the next.

Continued belief in the Resurrection and a future life undergirded the Unitarian claim, so fiercely contested, to merit the Christian name. These certainties rested on the Bible, the traditional reliance of Dissenters, and on the miracles that attested to the divinity of Christ's mission and to His (and so our) resurrection. At the same time, as rationalists, Unitarians were committed to science—which in the assumptions of the time could not, rightly understood, conflict with Revelation—and to close study of the Bible, to sort out the genuine from the corrupted and illegitimate.

From the 1830s, however, a number of younger ministers found the Priestleyan paradigm increasingly unsatisfactory: it seemed too scientific, cold, and earthbound in a Romantic age; moreover, with increasing critical sophistication, reliance on biblical testimony and promises was becoming more and more difficult to sustain. The most prominent of these young men was James Martineau, then minister at Hope Street, Liverpool. He signalled the new movement in 1833 with a brilliant, appreciative though devastating article on Priestley; his later thinking can be traced through a succession of brilliant articles and reviews following *The Rationale of Religious Enquiry* of 1836. Martineau's close associates, John James Tayler and John Hamilton Thom, moved even more rapidly than he toward a refounded Unitarianism, which, drawing much of its strength from German theological and critical teachings, stressed the inward sources of belief as against the Priestleyan concern with natural religion and evidences. Martineau's more tortuous course was compulsively masked. He would stake out extreme positions, long before catching up to them in his own thinking, combatively assailing inherited views and so alienating many old friends and teachers, while assuring them in equally unmeasured terms that his respect and affection for them remained entirely unchanged. This rhetorical violence held a powerful appeal to young men, whose support established him as the unquestioned leader of the "New School" as opposed to the "Old School" of the Priestleyans.

Although most Unitarians had been deeply influenced by the

emotional rhetoric of the American Unitarian minister William El-
lery Channing, and although they cooperated warmly in establishing
domestic missions in large towns, the tensions between Old and
New Unitarians grew. The rupture was distressing to many laymen,
among whom there was real interest in theological matters, and the
supersession of older ministers by younger ones frequently left congregations disoriented and unhappy, for a time.[49]

The rift between the two schools was most pointedly evident in
Martineau's lifelong campaign to eradicate the Unitarian name: the
denomination, he insisted, risked isolation if it chose to be identified
with a theological position which development might prove tran-
sient, though his own loyalty to both denomination and theology
was never in doubt. He was openly hostile to the British and Foreign
Unitarian Association, founded in 1825 and the closest thing to a
central organization the denomination was to have before 1928, although Robert Brook Aspland, editor of the theologically conservative *Christian Reformer* and secretary of the BFUA after 1857, reported that Martineau had characteristically assured him that he did
not want to discourage those who would promote Unitarianism, "if
we wd in consideration for his scruples open our door sufficiently
wide for him to come in without sacrificing his regard for Christian
catholicity."[50]

The Priestleyans fought a dogged rear-guard action. Their most
forceful exponent was William Hincks, editor of the *Inquirer* from
1842 to 1847, "clear-headed and sensible," in Crabb Robinson's judgment, "[a] zealous Unitarian professing great liberality."[51] In 1844,
Hincks wrote editorially in praise of the clearness of Priestley's "reasoning power, and his union of philosophic calmness of investiga-
tion, with ardour in the pursuit and diffusion of truth." He deplored
the tendency "to substitute the fanciful speculations and bold assumptions of German metaphysics, for [Priestley's] lucid statements
and solid deductions . . . [The] imputation of coldness . . . seems but
a passing wave of public opinion which will sink as it rose and leave
scarcely a trace behind."[52] But in 1849 Hincks, who earlier in his
career had taught natural philosophy at Manchester College, left
England for a professorship at Cork and four years later for a similar
post in Toronto.

Thereafter, the most prominent representative of the Old School
was Samuel Bache, minister at Priestley's old chapel in Birmingham.

James Martineau's eloquent sermon on the Irish famine could still bring extravagant praise from Bache: "so concise yet so comprehensive, so wise yet so imaginative, history, poetry, political economy, Christian benevolence, wondrously combined."[53] Five years later, however, Martineau preached another sermon, "The God of Revelation his own Interpreter," in which he spoke of the world's having escaped from a religion of law obedient to sovereignty and from a religion of salvation with its gratitude for deliverance to a religion of reverence, "which bows before the authority of goodness." This quasi-Comtean scheme led Martineau to deny that Christ was the Messiah, belief in which John Locke had seen as the sole defining characteristic of Christianity. Bache was astonished:

But oh! what a strange compound of crude & erroneous notions! What a strange view of the epistles in pp. 12–13! What an unwarrantable assumption regarding "the choicest servants of God" in p. 14! What a bold denial of Paul's fundamental doctrine in p. 16! . . . and what a substitution of *abstractions* for real persons & relations, such as, if logically carried out, wd lead to atheism just as it here seems to lead to a renouncement of historical Christianity![54]

A counterattack was mounted. Edward Tagart, minister at Little Portland Street in London and Aspland's predecessor as secretary of the British and Foreign Unitarian Association, said in 1848 that "it appears to me more & more necessary to make a firm & vigorous stand in favour of the philosophy & faith . . . worthy of the homage of the intellect & affections, & against the insidious inroads of what may be called the dry rot in our house"; in 1855 he published a book on Locke to reassert the basic philosophical premises of his school. In 1857 John Relly Beard, a prominent minister and Unitarian publicist, asked the Rev. John Gordon to write a popular life of Priestley— "useful at any time but especially now." And when Bache's Birmingham congregation built a new Gothic church in 1861, Bache proclaimed his theology in its name, the Church of the Messiah.[55]

The leading figures in this passionate embroilment belonged to a small, closely interrelated world, much as contemporary Anglican struggles involved men intimately tied by blood, marriage, and schooling. Martineau and Bache were brothers-in-law, married to sisters of Edward Higginson, a prominent adherent of the conservative school; Tagart had married the widow of Martineau's much-loved eldest brother, a marriage Martineau had strenuously opposed.[56] But even without family ties, these were men who had mostly come of age at Manchester College and who regularly met each other in the course of ministerial and professional life, exchanged pulpits, and reviewed each other in Unitarian papers. There was, then, some pressure to decency: "I will try to keep my temper . . . & to be courteous as well as upright," Bache told Gordon and did his best to keep up the relationship with Martineau, saying good things about him from time to time and inviting him to preach. He felt less compunction with regard to Thom and Tayler: "there is no end to the whims & inconsistencies of the men who look up to brother Jas. M. as their leader," he complained; he thought Thom's fulsome praise of Martineau intolerable.[57]

The caution could not be maintained forever. The *Inquirer* had become the organ of the Martineau faction, and Bache lamented early in 1864 that nothing in the conduct of the paper could any longer surprise him. The "infidel character" of the leading article that provoked this outburst was, he thought, clearly inspired by an article by Tayler in the *National Review* questioning the miracles, and he was disappointed to find a weak approval of that position even in the *Unitarian Herald*, which at its founding in 1861 had generally taken an anti-Martineau and anti-*Inquirer* stance. Moreover, the inroads on the Birmingham District Unitarian Association became so serious that Bache resigned, choosing to communicate his reasons in writing, given the kind of persons he would have to deal with: "I feel that the time is *fully* arrived when the essentially miraculous character of the Mission & Gospel of Christ must be distinctly and unequivocally maintained."[58]

Bache had already declared himself in *Miracles the Credentials of Christ*, five lectures given in the Church of the Messiah in early 1863. Increasingly distressed by the spread of extreme views, on May 23, 1866, he proposed clarifying the rules of the British and Foreign Unitarian Association to require as a condition of membership the recognition of God the Father as the only God and only proper object of worship and of "the special divine mission and authority, as a Religious Teacher, of Jesus Christ"—a stipulation Bache certainly understood as entailing the Messiahship and gospel miracles. In seconding the motion, Thomas Madge, minister at Essex Street, argued that any church that denied the Resurrection, the greatest of the miracles, was built on sand. Bache did not deny the right of Unitarians to hold and express dissident views on these subjects, but, with Madge, he denied their right to associate with those who understood the "promotion of the principles of Unitarian Christianity" as that statement of purpose was understood when the BFUA was founded.

Since June 1865, when Bache gave formal notice of his intention, it had been widely pointed out, by friends as well as opponents, that what he was calling for was tantamount to a creed for a denomination that had prided itself on freedom from creeds. When the vote came, only Bache, Madge, and the Unitarian historian James Yates supported the motion. It was widely believed that a majority of ministers and laymen present were in sympathy with Bache's views, but they could not accept the implied abridgment of freedom, an alignment dramatically paralleling the historic decision of the London ministers meeting at Salters' Hall in 1719 against subscribing a declaration in favor of the Trinity—not because they disbelieved in the Trinity (most did not) but because they opposed any form of words that might limit individual freedom to interpret the Bible.[59]

The near unanimity did not do away with doctrinal divisions, any more than the warm tributes to Bache at the close of the meeting made defeat any easier for him to bear. Still, the tendency among Unitarian ministers was clear enough. When Bache died in 1876, John Gordon, who despite conservative theological views had voted with the majority ten years earlier, spoke in his funeral sermon of his friend's "clear and strong intellect," the very narrowness of which "was a condition of its exceptional power." Those, Gordon went on, who thought of Unitarianism as a necessarily loose collection of thoughts might learn otherwise from Bache's example. But, he asked, was Christianity "ever designed to be thus dogmatic, thus precise?" Might it not be less a matter of defined positions and more "a manifestation of principles and influences and spiritual tendencies and affections?"

As in the parallel Anglican crisis, the Old-School Unitarians had worried that the preaching and teaching of the New School would lead to uncertainties and confusion among laymen and the young. As early as 1848, Thomas Rees, a veteran denominational administrator and enthusiastic Unitarian, deplored the prospect that Francis W. Newman, John Henry Newman's radical brother who at that point was closely involved with New-School Unitarianism, might become warden of University Hall, which housed Unitarian students attending University College London. The swell of opposition in the fifties to the domination of Manchester College by Tayler and Martineau was predicated on the probably malign effects they would have on a future generation of ministers. When Tayler became principal of the College (then still in Manchester) in 1853, an agitation began for a third professorship for Martineau alongside Tayler and the biblical scholar G. Vance Smith—a cabal, Aspland wrote, of a "little knot of youths" who wanted "to supplant theology for the metaphysics of Coleridge and Carlyle." Edward Tagart, who saw the prospect of Martineau's coming to the college as "symptomatic of a fatal division in our body," did not know what to do about exchanging pulpits with him should he settle there: "I am afraid," Tagart told his daughter, "that Mr. Martineau would not give my people a quiet, devotional, comforting sermon."[60]

Again as with the Anglicans, the partial resolution of the crisis in 1866 was followed by a time of ambiguity and then by reorientation. Scriptural Unitarianism was only scotched in 1866. Martineau complained to John Gordon in 1872 that, despite encouraging signs among a younger generation, there was a "growing sectarian consolidation" of Unitarianism by those "busy bodies," the denominational people, with the new secretary of the British and Foreign Unitarian Association, the Rev. Robert Spears, "a truly worthy, well-meaning man," leading the bluster with entirely mischievous results.[61] Spears surely saw matters differently, for in 1876 he resigned the secretaryship over the determination of his committee to republish under BFUA auspices the works of the American radical theologian Theodore Parker. And so the battle see-sawed. Martineau and his disciples dominated Manchester College in London, while the biblical school were pretty firmly entrenched in the new Unitarian college in Manchester; the *Inquirer* was balanced after 1876 by *Christian Life*, launched by Spears on his leaving the BFUA.[62]

On one occasion after another James Martineau saw victory mixed with defeat. His campaign in the 1860s to rechristen his denomination as Free Christians made little headway; although he trumped the BFUA in 1876 by securing the creation of a parallel National Conference, to meet every third year, his proposal in 1887 for drastic denominational reform was overwhelmingly rejected in congregational votes around the country. Especially to the newly liberated, the Unitarian name remained a badge of escape from orthodoxy, a perspective Martineau, coming as he did from an old Dissenting and Unitarian family of unimpeachably high bourgeois credentials, could never understand.

Martineau's reputation rose higher and higher as he got older and older—he died at the age of 95 in 1900—but his views were rapidly outmoded. His great books on religion and philosophy in the 1880s, based largely on lectures he had given twenty years earlier, came too late, it has been argued, for them to have the impact on the evolving field of English philosophy that he might have had, had he published earlier.[63] His admiring biographer and, in time, successor as principal of Manchester College, J. Estlin Carpenter, gained his greatest fame and his stature in Oxford University as a scholar of non-western religions. Carpenter's enthusiasm for comparative religion was entirely lost on Martineau, who had some characteristically dismissive things to say about it, while a variety of competing enthusiasms among Unitarian ministers, from spiritualism to outright humanism, were utterly alien to his universe.[64]

As in the Church of England, the crucial turning came in the 1880s. In the earlier Victorian period, Old and New Schools had agreed on the importance of domestic missions in bringing the most benighted of slum dwellers to education, to a sense of responsibility, and in some instances to a new appreciation of religion. The goal was reformation, not of society but of the individual, by, as J. H. Thom put it, the action of "heart on heart, mind on mind, soul on soul." Thom and Martineau never abandoned that ideal and, like their disciple Charles Beard, remained skeptical about state intervention or any genuine alteration of social arrangements.[65]

Younger ministers saw matters differently. Symptomatically, the *Inquirer* changed its subtitle in 1909 from *A Journal of Religious Thought and Life* to *A Journal of Religious Life and Thought*, explaining the change in priorities at length. Though the new belief in the possibility of fundamental changes in society owed much to a Christian sense of obligation and to the moral force that attached to Gladstonian liberalism, its inspiration often came from outside religion. Indeed, the greatest of early twentieth-century ministers, Philip Henry Wicksteed, the son of one of Martineau's collaborators, insisted that religion was helpless to deal with the social problem from its own resources and had to turn to sociology. In 1920, L. P. Jacks, who had succeeded J. Estlin Carpenter as principal of Manchester College, admiringly effaced the differences between the Old and New Schools of the early Victorian decades, seeing in them both a single religion of vision based on the idea of a perfect God, of whom man is an imperfect image. The truly new (and, he implied, less admirable if inevitable) Unitarianism of his own time looked rather to a perfect world, of which our own is but a mutilated fragment that could be restored to social wholeness.[66]

Tensions could still arise between ministers and congregations, particularly when a minister favored a reform that traditional Liberals in his congregation might regard as socialistic, or, a bit later, when support for the Labour party might be at issue, and, of course, during World War I.[67] But such tensions did not involve *religious* liberty. That concern belonged to a time when individual salvation, the relation of men and women to their God, even the very existence of that God and the authority of His communication with His creatures were central questions for the churches.

<< III >>

The Quakers

The Society of Friends, better known as the Quakers, was descended from a radical sect founded by George Fox in the middle of the seventeenth century. Confident in the "inward light" vouchsafed by God to individual believers, and determined to put an end by witness and example to the world's wickedness, Quakers were severely persecuted during the Restoration period and found in that persecution a source of remarkable cohesion. After Toleration in 1689, and the further installments of privilege they quickly attained, Quakers emerged in the eighteenth century as quietists. Though remarkably successful in the expanding economy, they deliberately set themselves apart from the wider society as a "peculiar people," distinguished by dress and speech, the absence of a paid ministry, the silence of their meetings, rejection of music and art, and resolute opposition to marriage outside the denomination.

These rigid restrictions, compounded by emigration, led to shrinking numbers, calculated on the basis of the religious census of 1851 at about a quarter of membership of the Society at the end of the seventeenth century. Numerical decline was further complicated by an endemic tendency to schism, perhaps to be expected given a defining doctrine so firmly individualistic. Similar disruptions in the larger Quaker movement in the United States echoed across the Atlantic. In 1827, the anti-evangelical protest of the American Elias Hicks, with renewed emphasis on the inner light, produced the largest schism of the century in both countries.[68]

The increasing influence of Quaker evangelicals from the last decade of the eighteenth century of course reflected the broader impact of the evangelical revival. The Quaker turning in that direction was led by Joseph John Gurney, a member of a prominent Norwich banking family who abandoned his career to work for a gospel-based regeneration of Friends on both sides of the Atlantic. Like evangelicals in other denominations, Quaker evangelicals insisted on the literal truth of the Bible and on the centrality of Christ's sacrifice on the Cross by which converted believers were assured everlasting life, while also finding in their faith a renewed stimulus to social action. A new sense of purpose and direction was thus given to what had become a drifting, passive denomination—thought by many to have been spiritually weakened by the introduction of birth-right membership in 1737. Evangelicalism also fostered a sense of closer fellowship with other Dissenters and offered new opportunities for personal development, particularly as practices anathema to traditional Friends, such as hymn-singing, a more conventional ministry, and a missionary movement, began to make headway.

But evangelicals could overreach themselves. In 1835, Isaac Crewdson, a Manchester businessman, published *A Beacon to the Society of Friends*, so extreme in its biblicism as to question the very doctrine of the inward light. The highest governing body in Quakerism, London Yearly Meeting, despite an evangelical majority, had no choice but to disown such shocking skepticism, whereupon Crewdson and his relatives and friends withdrew into a short-lived schismatic body scarcely distinguishable from other evangelical Dissenters.

Both traditional and evangelical Quakers—one essentially mystical, the other emotional and literalist—tended to be anti-intellectual. In a competition anonymously established in 1859 for essays on the Quaker decline—judged by three non-Quakers led by F. D. Maurice—the winning entry was *Quakerism, Past and Present* by John Stephenson Rowntree, a young member of a distinguished Quaker clan.

Providing important statistical corroboration of the losses and advancing the reasons noted above in explanation, he also called attention to the defectiveness of education among Friends for much of their history until the expansion of Quaker schooling following the founding of Ackworth School in 1777. In offering a modestly hopeful answer to the question "Has Quakerism a future?" Rowntree suggested, very much in passing, that all these pitfalls might have been avoided had Quakers recognized

the great importance of a well-proportioned theology, and had they carefully guarded against the danger of obscuring or undervaluing any portions of Divine truth—whether revealed in the inspired volume, or in those "facts of nature" which "are the words of God"—through excess of zeal for exalting a part, rather than the whole, of Christian truth.[69]

In a furious point-by-point rebuttal running over several issues of the traditionalist journal *The British Friend* in 1860–61 and reprinted in its evangelical counterpart *The Friend*, Joshua Richardson accused Rowntree of misrepresenting, out of lack of sympathy, the seventeenth-century Quaker attitude toward reason, while noting that its exercise at any time must wait upon the manifestation of God's will. But the impatience of younger, educated, and more worldly Friends with this sense of priority was demonstrated almost at once, when David Duncan, a manufacturer and a convert to Quakerism, was asked, as a last-minute substitute, to lecture on April 12, 1861, to the Friends Institute, an adult-education and self-improvement association connected with the Mount Street Meeting in central Manchester. Duncan's subject was *Essays and Reviews*.[70]

Although he summarized each of the essays, Duncan disclaimed critical competence; rather, he described his talk as a protest against the intolerant spirit that had greeted the essays, a spirit contrary to the principle of free inquiry that lay at the heart of the Protestant Reformation. "Christianity is a life rather than a formula," he insisted, and "life involves thought and freedom." The traditionalist *British Friend* reviewed the lecture favorably, while the evangelical *Friend*, predictably, took a less benign view, criticizing Duncan's implication that evangelicals placed the Bible above the Spirit and dismissing *Essays and Reviews* (quoting E. B. Pusey) as largely refuted by the body of Christian scholarship.[71] Greatly appealing to the young, generally anti-evangelical Quakers who frequented the Institute, Duncan continued on his radical course. In 1862, the group voted to purchase Colenso's commentaries on the Pentateuch; the next year Duncan returned to the fray with a paper contrasting bibliolatry with the principle of the inward light and calling for a new reformation that would do away with any authority other than God's as revealed to the individual spirit.[72] Over the next few years, the Duncanite position was reiterated by other young Mancunian Friends, and moderate attempts to qualify the radicalism were scornfully rejected.

From the moment of Duncan's first paper there had been deep uneasiness among the evangelicals who dominated the parent Mount Street Meeting, and profound concern had quickly surfaced in the London Yearly Meeting: the worry about unsettling teaching was as evident here as among Anglicans and Unitarians. In 1871 Joseph Bevan Braithwaite, the successor to J. J. Gurney as the evangelical leader of British Quakerism, superintended the preparation of a statement of belief to be applied as a test to the Manchester liberals. The next year steps were taken to disown Duncan, who with his friends then invited Charles Voysey to speak; Voysey was an Anglican clergyman recently deprived for questioning eternal punishment and the infallibility of the Bible. Then, shortly after his disownment, Duncan suddenly died of a virulent attack of smallpox—"a marvellous winding up" of the case, Braithwaite confided to his diary: "How clearly may we trace the Hand that has graciously guided and thus far protected our little Society from the inroads of a dangerous scepticism." Duncan's family and some of his friends joined the Unitarians. In 1873, another Quaker, Edward T. Bennett, was disowned for supporting Voysey. He was the last British Quaker to be disowned for theological reasons.

In 1887, a conference in Richmond, Indiana, produced a manifesto known as the "Richmond Declaration"; it was drafted by J. B. Braithwaite, the chief British delegate who, toward the end of his life, discouraged his children's efforts to interest him in new currents of thought by saying firmly that his views had been settled 60 years earlier.[73] Astonishingly, the London Yearly Meeting refused to accept it. Although evangelicals remained in outward control of the denomination, that refusal signalled a generational shift. In 1884, three Friends—Francis Frith, William Pollard, and W. E. Turner—had published a liberal manifesto called *A Reasonable Faith*; ten years later, Frith's *A Quaker Ideal* appealed against entrenched conservatism by calling for rejection of scholastic theology and substitutionary doctrine, for a new directness linking God and individual, and for escape from superficial Christianity to a thoroughly dedicated Christian life. There were many other signposts in the intervening decade, among them the change in editorial direction of the *British Friend* from traditionalist to liberal: the weekly admonition in the paper's masthead to stand in the old ways gave way to the assertion that the kingdom of God lay not in word but in power.[74] Then, in November 1895, a conference in Manchester, summoned by the London Yearly Meeting, confirmed an overwhelming liberal victory, carefully planned but not the less dramatic for that. The retreat of theological commitment before a wave of social concern was unmistakable. On this new dispensation, reinforced by major re-examination of Quaker history, was built the "Quaker Renaissance," a rebirth not only in cohesiveness and sense of mission but in numbers.

≺ IV ≻

Conclusion

In this chapter, I have considered a moment in nineteenth-century England when a new—one is almost tempted to say last—effort was made to assert the universal applicability of faith as inherited from the earliest Christian centuries and, as much as might be among Protestants, as transmuted into dogma by largely self-appointed guardians of specific forms of Christianity. Control over teaching—from the pulpit, in missions, or through approved scholarship—was, as I have suggested, crucial to this effort, even among the Quakers, though compared to the Church of England entrenched in the ancient universities or to the Unitarians as heirs of the great eighteenth-century Dissenting academies, they were newcomers in the institutionalization, and even in appreciating the importance, of teaching. But teaching, in both its broad and narrow senses, proved difficult and ultimately impossible to control, and the churches were forced to seek new grounds for self-definition.

At least internally, the Church of England retained some of its dogmatic economy, and the question of limits for the clergy has from time to time reasserted itself.[75] But such matters have counted for little in the work of the Church in the world, whether that work was seen as social betterment or, eventually for some, as pursuing ecumenical goals. The failure of Priestleyan Unitarians and evangelical Quakers to impose inherited (though not so ancient) deposits of faith and interpretation upon their fellow-worshippers was less dramatic, but scarcely less fascinating and moving. With time and space, parallel occurrences could be traced in the same generation among English Congregationalists and Baptists and in the Church of Scotland.

If the dogmatic ground for religious fellowship—the particular province of clergy and ministers—had been undermined or supplanted in the latter part of the nineteenth century, what could believers themselves contribute to defining their denominations? The Church of England has always been in large part a civic religion and has remained such for most of its members, particularly for those nominal believers whose sense of belonging entails no regularity of attendance. For Unitarians and Quakers, the bond of union became little more than habit or the personal satisfaction to be drawn from the association, though in both cases (and to a lesser extent among Anglicans) the satisfaction is often cast in terms of what the denomination stands for politically and socially—all this, in Bishop Hamilton's language, a matter of opinion or sentiment, not truth.

The standard of dogmatic truth has been far less diluted in modern Roman Catholicism, while it has been re-erected in the multiplicity of evangelical sects that have transformed the twentieth-century religious landscape. In such circumstances the problem of religious liberty will recur whenever individuals reject or try to qualify some of the tenets of the collectivity in which they wish to remain. But in Protestant England the stakes may never again be so high nor the sweep so impressive as in the challenges to religious liberty in the mid-Victorian decades.

The Jews of Europe and the Limits of Religious Freedom

DAVID C. ITZKOWITZ

THIS CHAPTER discusses some issues that affected and limited the religious freedom of Jews in nineteenth-century Western and Central Europe. Because the actual state of religious freedom for Jews varied from state to state and from the beginning of the century to the end, the discussion does not attempt to be a comprehensive survey of the state of affairs at any given time; it seeks, rather, to identify some general issues and trends and to explore the limits of Jewish religious liberty. The chapter also suggests that the concept of religious freedom, as applied to the Jewish experience, is a complex one that may need some redefinition.

⋘ I ⋙

Freedom of Religion — Some Definitions

In many ways, the nineteenth century was a period in which Jews' enjoyment of religious liberty increased enormously. That it did so was the result of two related developments in nineteenth-century Europe. On the one hand, the period witnessed a general increase in religious freedom, though other chapters in this volume make it clear that this increase was neither uniform nor universal. On the other hand, the history of the Jews in the same period is also one that involves an increase in general freedom. As the ghetto walls fell, both literally and figuratively, as all manner of legal restrictions on Jewish life came to an end, and as Jews became citizens of the nation-states of Europe, options for Jews—economic, social, and political—increased dramatically. For the first time, in most parts of Europe, Jews were free to choose where they would live, what occupation they would follow, and what set of religious precepts they would obey.

Because the Jews are a group of people that has, in the first instance, been defined in religious terms, the increased liberties that Jews enjoyed in the nineteenth century have, at least popularly, been seen as falling under the general rubric of "freedom of religion." This popular view is not entirely inappropriate. There can be little doubt that nineteenth-century Jews enjoyed *religious* liberties that were unprecedented, and nothing that follows should distract the reader from that fact. It may be, however, that the greatest religious liberty gained by Jews was, in fact, what we might call freedom *from* religion, rather than freedom *of* religion. Like their non-Jewish compatriots, Jews increasingly enjoyed the right to ignore religious strictures, and, as has been amply demonstrated, many of them took full advantage of that right. Given the power once held by the organized Jewish community to enforce religious orthodoxy, the importance of this new freedom should not be devalued.

Still, as we have increasingly come to realize, the term *Jew* is not solely a *religious* one, and the ambiguity that surrounds the term is responsible for a lack of precision when speaking of freedom of religion and Jews.

Historians and other scholars have, to be sure, been aware of that ambiguity. In 1974, conferences with the title "The Role of Religion in Modern Jewish History" were held at the universities of Toronto and Pennsylvania.[1] The special examination this topic has warranted is noteworthy. It alerts us to the fact that there is an important distinction between *Jews*, as a people and as a subject of historical inquiry, and *Judaism*, the religion of that people. More importantly it alerts us to the fact that Judaism has not, on the whole, been central to the historical discussion of the experience of the Jews in the nineteenth century. This is, in part, the result of the fact that Judaism was increasingly of less importance to the Jews of the nineteenth century themselves. In this they were not unlike many of the other people of Europe in an increasingly secular age.[2] Taking what they would see as a cue from the subjects of their research, modern historians of the Jews have, I think, not paid very much attention to the practice of religion except as something to be reformed or gotten out of the way, or as the exclusive preserve of an increasingly isolated minority of Jews. No doubt they are right to take this tack. Clearly, religious practice had become of lesser importance to the Jews in the nineteenth century, just as it had for their non-Jewish compatriots. Much of the most exciting work in the history of nineteenth-century Jews has focused on the various ways in which Jews created new visions of what it meant to be a Jew in the absence of religious feeling. In many ways, Jewish communal solidarity persisted in an age in which it was assumed by many that it would not.[3] Still, as Jacob Katz has pointed out, while

admittedly, the role of religion in an epoch that is characterized by its very opposite—secularization—is more problematic than in a generation when religion ruled supreme . . . the waning influence of religion makes the role that it has played and still plays in society an even more important subject for examination, historically or sociologically.[4]

This is particularly germane, of course, to the subject of this volume, and this chapter will focus on the freedom, and impediments to the freedom, of Jewish religion. Religion is here defined as the practice of religious rituals and rites. The discussion is not concerned with religion as the search for meaning in life or as the articulation of the relationship between humankind and God, though Michael Meyer has suggested that it is precisely at the beginning of the period under consideration that individual Jews begin to ask what he called the "novel question," "did the practice of their religion provide spiritual fulfillment?"[5] The religion that is being discussed here is a set of practices that had developed over the centuries, but that traditionalist Jews had accepted as timeless and unchanging. Although within orthodox Judaism, as elsewhere, there might be disagreements about detail, most Jews at the beginning of the nineteenth century had a relatively common set of assumptions and understandings of what the demands of their religion were. Over the course of the nineteenth century, these assumptions would be challenged in a number of ways, and by the end of the century, there was no real agreement among Jews about whether there were any tenets of what we may call normative Judaism.

Let me add here that I am stressing traditional religious practice, what would come to be called Orthodox Judaism, not to privilege it as a kind of normative Judaism. As I have just suggested, the idea of any normative Judaism was becoming increasingly untenable over the course of the nineteenth century. But orthodoxy, because of its relative strictness and inflexibility, can serve as a test case of the limits of religious freedom.

Traditional Jewish religious practice, of course, imposed a great many obligations on the Jew which affected all phases of life. For the observant Jew, the chief among these was the observance of the sabbath and the observance of dietary laws, each of which could provide a considerable obstacle to full integration in European life. Sabbath observance meant that the observant Jew could not work on Saturday or after sundown on Friday and hence was barred from many occupations in which Saturday work was necessary. Observance of the dietary regulations meant that Jews could not easily share meals with non-Jews and thus were debarred from many kinds of social intercourse. From the very beginning of the emancipation period, Jews and non-Jews alike were aware that the practice of Judaism separated Jews from their neighbors. Moses Mendelssohn, the giant figure of the Jewish enlightenment of the eighteenth century, once observed that "the ceremonial laws of the Jews . . . have a . . . purpose to set this nation visibly apart from all the rest and remind it constantly, through the performance of many religious acts, of those holy truths which should be unforgettable for all of us."[6] Mendelssohn, who remained an observant Jew throughout his life, made his observation, in part, out of pride, hence his reference to holy truths. Others were less certain of the benefits of adhering to the law.

This reference to the demands made by Judaism begins to explain why at least one traditional definition of freedom of religion is not entirely useful when discussing the Jews. Freedom of religion, defined as freedom of public worship, is ultimately derived from an understanding of religion that arose out of the experience of European Christians, and especially out of the experience of the post-Reformation period, when the question arose over whether Protestants would be allowed to have the right to worship, as Protestants, in a Catholic country and whether Catholics would have a similar right in a Protestant one. This was not an issue of major importance for the Jews, first, because they always had that right, and second, because, as I hope to suggest, that right was relatively trivial in defining the place of Jews in European society. As the only regularly, if sporadically, tolerated non-Christians in Europe, Jews had the right to worship if they had the right to reside in a particular place. Thus, in his "Constitution for the Jews," issued in 1199, Pope Innocent III forbade Christians from profaning Jewish festivals.[7] In 1247, following a period of increased persecution of Jews, the Jewish community nevertheless managed to obtain from Pope Innocent IV a declaration stating that the Talmud was an absolute necessity for the Jews if Judaism was to continue as a separate religion and burnings of the Talmud were, therefore, to cease.[8] While Jews were frequently persecuted and expelled in medieval and early modern Europe, there was never any question about allowing them to live as Jews wherever they lived.

But because of the way that Jewish religious practices impinge on all aspects of Jewish life, the mere freedom to worship was really quite trivial once Jews were freed from the ghetto and attempted to integrate into the larger European society, though the form that that worship would take was to become an issue.

There is a second definition of religious freedom, which is somewhat broader than the first. This definition of religious freedom does not refer to the right of people to practice religion, but rather to an arrangement in which the practice of religion is not allowed to interfere with civic equality and the integration of Jews into the mainstream of society. It was this understanding of religious liberty that was used by most advocates, whether Jewish or Christian, of what came by the late eighteenth century to be called Jewish Emancipation, the achievement of which is clearly the most significant development in Jewish history in the nineteenth century. It is this second meaning of freedom of religion that is of the utmost importance in understanding the limits to the religious freedom of the Jews. These limits are not defined simply by the restrictions that were placed on Jews, either by the power of the state or by Jewish communal authorities, though, as we shall see, such restrictions persisted. They are also defined by the extent to which privately held religious scruples could interfere with full integration into European life and the extent to which the state was willing to accommodate those scruples.

Under the influence of the Enlightenment, the French Revolution, and the growth of the nation-state, the position of the Jews as an anomalous foreign population in the midst of the national one was increasingly difficult to tolerate. As a result, Jews were freed from various civil disabilities and admitted to full political and economic rights in most of the countries of Western Europe. The progress of emancipation was often slow and proceeded at different paces in different states, but by the end of the nineteenth century legal emancipation had been achieved almost everywhere in Western Europe.[9] Nothing in this chapter should be understood as minimizing the importance of legal emancipation. Clearly the end of legally enforced separation revolutionized the lives of European Jews, and it must be added that emancipation was also a major step in increasing Jewish *religious* freedom, even though emancipation was, in most ways, peripheral to religious issues. By eliminating legal restrictions on Jews, emancipation freed Jews from having to choose between adherence to their religion and acceptance of citizenship. It therefore granted them the freedom to remain Jews, at least in name, without jeopardizing their legal equality. This new freedom may, in a sense, be seen as a complement to the newly gained freedom to ignore religious strictures. Henceforth, at least in theory, Jews were free either to embrace Judaism or reject it without that choice limiting them in other spheres of their lives.

The granting of legal equality to the Jews, however, was seen by many as requiring that the Jews be willing to give up something in return—the particularism that marked them off as a separate people. At the very least, Jews had to come under the operation of a single set of laws that governed all members of society, whether Jewish or non-Jewish, and hence had to give up the separate administration under which many of them lived.

For some emancipationists, Jews had to give up much more. Many assumed that emancipation would ultimately lead to conversion and the ultimate end of the Jews as a separate people. Christian and Jewish emancipationists alike assumed that even if emancipation would not lead to conversion, ultimately the only thing that would come to separate Jews and non-Jews was religious belief and practice. Belief was, of course, seen as a private matter, and practice was generally thought of only in terms of worship, which could also be relegated to the private sphere. In Western and Central Europe, as opposed to Eastern Europe, even relatively nonobservant post-emancipation Jews defined themselves as a religious minority rather than as a separate ethnic or national group.[10] As Dr. Hermann Adler, Chief Rabbi of England, wrote in 1878,

When we dwelt in the Holy Land we had a political organization of our own; we had judges and kings to rule over us. But ever since the conquest of Palestine by the Romans, we have ceased to be a body politic: we are citizens of the country in which we dwell. We are simply Englishmen, or Frenchmen, or Germans, as the case may be, certainly holding particular theological tenets and practicing special religious ordinances; but we stand in the same relation to our countrymen as any other religious sect, having the same stake in the national welfare and the same claim on the privileges and duties of citizens.[11]

Still there was the recognition, usually pointed out by the enemies of emancipation, that various aspects of Jewish life could interfere with that full integration of the Jews into European life that was viewed as the desired end product of Jewish Emancipation. Among these aspects was traditional religious practice.

≺ II ≻

Avoiding the Restrictions of Religion

As is well known, Jews found a number of ways to circumvent the restrictions of religion. The nineteenth century witnessed, after all, the emergence of a series of reform movements within Judaism that attempted to modify religious practice in ways that would, on the one hand, be more appealing to "modern" sensibilities and that would, on the other, let Jews participate more fully in the life around them. In presenting movements for religious reform in this way, I do not mean to suggest that they were simply responses to the dilemmas of acculturation. Clearly these movements originated, in part, from sincere religious feeling. But at least some of the impetus to religious reform came from a sense that the practice of traditional religion interfered with Jews' full acceptance into European society and, hence, had implications for what I have called the second definition of religious liberty.[12]

Other Jews maintained a nominal attachment to orthodoxy but made personal compromises with its demands that enabled them to live more "normal" lives. Increasingly, the place where these compromises with tradition were negotiated was the home.[13] Because orthodox Judaism was an all-encompassing system that regulated domestic conduct as well as public worship and study, the home had always been seen as a place where "Jewish life" was lived. In the nineteenth century the home took on new importance. Although many Jewish men fell away from a strict observance of the commandments and stopped taking part in "public" religious activities like synagogue worship, many of them continued to live in homes where domestic observance of Jewish customs persisted and where women were increasingly seen as the exemplars and carriers of the

Jewish tradition. The reasons for this are complex and reflect the larger issue of the way that developments in the Jewish community were influenced by and intertwined with developments in the larger communities in which Jews lived. The "cult of domesticity" and the feminization of religion that characterized nineteenth-century Christianity was particularly resonant for middle-class Jews for reasons that have been illuminated by recent scholarship. For the purposes of this discussion, however, what is most important is that the domestication of religion provided one more way that Jews were freed from the burden of having to choose between observance and entry into the larger European society. By relegating religious observance to the home, Jews could effectively avoid conflict between religious obligation and the need to fit into the larger society.

Jewish attachment to religion was often seen in terms of community rather than theology. Speaking of his father, who, though a rationalist, continued to be faithful to Jewish traditions, the French Jew Pierre Abraham noted,

He saw religion only in the light of a traditional tie which bound us to the previous generations of Jews. Since in the past the Jews suffered from humiliations, persecutions, massacres, it seemed to him necessary not to cut his bonds of sympathy with a history woven with grief and injustice. The sole means in his power to prove to himself his devotion to his ancestors was to continue the ritual practices which had belonged to them. That is why, his whole life long, he went to synagogue for Rosh Hashanah, he celebrated Passover at home, he fasted strictly on Yom Kipour, and he had a religious education for his children up to their Bar Mitzvah.[14]

Still other Jews drifted away from any religious attachment. In this, they were like many non-Jews in an increasingly secular age, but for the Jew, the drift away from religious practice could be both more "liberating" and more dislocating than it was for the non-Jew, for two reasons. First, the drifting away from religious practice removed far more disabilities than was the case with Christians; and second, as Jacob Katz has suggested, even secularized European society continued to be saturated with the symbols of Christianity.[15]

Conversion, of course, remained the most radical escape from the strictures of Judaism. In the pre-emancipation period, conversion was, in fact, the only way that Jews could remove the legal disabilities under which they lived. Even after the end of legal disabilities, however, there were certainly many Jews who saw conversion as the only path to full integration in European society.[16] To the extent that historians have looked at Jews leaving the religious community, whether by just drifting away or by active conversion, they have, like Pierre Abraham, tended to see the departure in terms of the impact on the Jewish community rather than in the context of any sincerely held religious feelings. Thus, in his discussion of Jewish apostasy, Todd Endelman found it necessary to point out the odd case of a Jewish convert to Christianity who "apparently took his new faith seriously."[17] Clearly, many of those who converted did not take their new faith seriously, but presumably, therefore, they did not take their old faith very seriously either. Conversion for them was simply a convenience to escape the stigma that still attached to being a Jew in many aspects of society.

≺ III ≻

State Power and Religious Reform

For those Jews who stayed within the fold, however, there remained a number of restrictions on freedom of religion. It is important to note that these restrictions could originate either within or outside the Jewish community. In the period before emancipation, one of the most significant forces restricting Jewish freedom of religion was, after all, the Jewish community itself, which had significant power to coerce its members to conform to the demands of religious orthodoxy. In extreme cases the community had the ability to excommunicate offenders, as the Amsterdam Jewish community did to Benedict Spinoza in 1656.[18] The ability to exclude Jews from the community was a particularly powerful sanction at a time when to be excluded from the Jewish community was to leave the Jew who did not wish to convert to Christianity without any community to belong to.

It is important to note, however, that the power of the Jewish community to compel obedience from its members, though it drew its strength and legitimacy from the beliefs and feelings of Jews themselves, was also recognized and sanctioned by the state, which in the pre-emancipation period allowed Jews to run their own internal affairs. Even after emancipation, the relationship between state power and the organized Jewish community remained a complex and problem-filled one, and the story of Jewish religious freedom is, among other things, the story of a complicated dance performed by individual Jews, the Jewish communal elites, and the organs of state power.

Even the most liberal state, after all, never gave up the right to regulate some religious practices, particularly when they related to other matters like public morality, education, or property, areas where the state saw a legitimate role for itself. At times, the "modernization" of Jewish life so as to eliminate Jewish peculiarities, particularly in the economic sphere, was considered such a "legitimate" concern. As Paula Hyman has recently pointed out, "the role of the state throughout Europe in the adaptation of Jews to the conditions of modernity deserves far more attention than it has hitherto been accorded."[19] In these instances, the state did not even pretend to religious neutrality. This must be stressed because, throughout the nineteenth century, it was the coercive power of the state that had the greatest potential to restrict freedom of religion, either directly or indirectly.

State interference in the practice of Jewish religion could take two basic forms, conscious interference and unconscious interference. In some instances, state power consciously intervened in Jewish life, often to either encourage or discourage religious change in the Jewish community. In many of these instances, state power also worked to strengthen the power of the communal authorities, though the particular working could vary tremendously from state to state. In some cases the state worked to strengthen a traditional or orthodox elite against the challenges mounted by reformers inside the community; in other cases, to encourage religious reform as an agent of modernization of the Jewish community.

In her examination of the experience of the Jews of Alsace, for example, Hyman has pointed out that French government authorities intervened in Jewish communal affairs to strengthen the hand of what they considered to be the "progressive" forces within the community. In 1824, to cite one case, the prefect of the Upper Rhine recommended that the seat of the consistory of the department be transferred from the town of Wintzenheim to the city of Colmar, in order to ensure the election of "enlightened" men to the consistory.[20] In 1858, to cite another, the government intervened in a dispute between religious progressives and traditionalists on the side of the progressives and annulled elections for the lay members of the department consistory. In the midst of the dispute, a government ad-ministrator wrote a long note to the minister of public instruction and cults in support of the annulment. The official identified the source of the conflict in the traditionalists' fear that the Central Con-sistory had secret plans to reform Jewish ritual and that the consis-tory's economic plans would be the ruin of Jewish religion. The ad-ministrator argued that it was important to support the progressives because at present

an orthodox Jew cannot be a worker, neither in the fields, nor in the work-shop, nor in the factory. The Central Consistory [was] struck to see that . . . the Jewish population of the Upper Rhine had not furnished one of its own to any profession other than business, dealing in old clothes, and peddling and was living separated [a l'ecarte] from the rest of the French population.[21]

It is interesting to note that traditionalist Jews, who were not al-ways the best friends to freedom of religion within the Jewish com-munity, preferring to enforce orthodoxy whenever possible, never-theless could appeal to the principle of liberty of conscience and freedom of religion in their struggle with the progressives. In 1846, for example, a petition of traditionalists in Alsace expressed the hope that

the Central Consistory will not desire to produce a schism in our religion; and will not seek to deprive us of that precious liberty of conscience that we obtained only after long centuries of persecution. That which our ancestors were able to maintain despite their persecutors throughout centuries of in-tolerance and barbarism, we will not allow to be removed by our coreligion-ists in an era of liberty and emancipation.[22]

This, of course, suggests that for Jews, as for non-Jews, the struggle for religious liberty could involve a struggle within the community, not just the struggle of a national minority against an oppressive alien state. "Progressives" were arguing for liberty from the dead hand of religious tradition; traditionalists were arguing for liberty from the oppressive hand of the "radical" consistory. Still, it must be stressed once more that even with regard to intracommunal struggles, the co-ercive power of the state was of paramount importance, particularly when the state had the power to enforce regulations that governed the financial obligations of members of the Jewish community.

I have mentioned these incidents because it is important to see that even in an age in which most Western European states were giv-ing lip-service to the concept of liberty of conscience, government officials nevertheless were concerned that Jewish religious practice might stand in the way of the modernization of the Jews. This was of concern to them because one of the major impetuses to Jewish emancipation from the perspective of the state was the disappearance of the Jews as a separate corporate entity within society. To the extent that Jewish religious practice might interfere with this process, they saw it as in their interest to do whatever was necessary to encourage changes in it. It must be added, however, that state intervention was not always on the side of religious reform. As has been mentioned, traditionalists in the Jewish community did not hesitate to appeal to state power when they thought it would enforce orthodoxy.[23]

Even in England, where religious liberty was a source of pride, the state nevertheless acted to prop up the religious authority of the Chief Rabbi. Although Jewish marriages were solemnized according to Jewish usages, they were only held to be legally valid if they were performed in synagogues having an officially recognized secretary who was authorized to keep a marriage register. Authorization was granted by the government only to synagogues that were certified by the president of the Board of Deputies of British Jews, the oligarchic body that claimed to represent the Jewish community to the state. The Board therefore had a great deal of power, because without its certification a synagogue could not be empowered to solemnize marriages.[24] The Board, throughout the long period of ascendancy of Sir Moses Montefiore (president of the Board 1838–74), was to exercise this power, in conjunction with the Chief Rabbi, to protect what it saw as the prerogatives of religious orthodoxy in England. When, in 1842, for example, the West London Synagogue of British Jews, the first reformed congregation in England, applied to the Board for certification of their marriage secretary, the Board refused to certify the secretary.[25] The government, in turn, refused to allow the West London Synagogue to solemnize marriages. In this case the government was clearly uncomfortable with its interference in the internal affairs of the Jewish community, and, ultimately, the West London Synagogue was allowed to solemnize marriages. Nevertheless, in its role as guardian both of public morality and the rights of property and inheritance arising out of marriage, the state was willing to interfere in what might be seen as essentially private religious arrangements.

The English situation seems particularly ironic, given that the most liberal of the European states found itself supporting tradition-

alist authority. In fact, the English state had little interest in supporting one faction of the Jewish community against another. But the
elite of Anglo-Jewry, whose "fashionable religiosity" harmonized
with the religious tone of respectable English life, remained at least
nominally orthodox throughout the nineteenth century. In supporting the traditionalists, the English state simply saw itself as backing
the natural leaders of the Anglo-Jewish community.[26]

In Prussia, on the other hand, where, for many years, the government opposed any modernization of Jewish religious services, government opposition to Jewish religious reform was, in part, the result
of Prussian opposition to *any* religious reform, in part the result of a
desire to keep Judaism as unattractive a religion as possible.[27] Thus,
in 1823, the Prussian government closed the Beer Temple, a reformed
congregation in Berlin that was named for the wealthy Jewish sugar
refiner Jacob Herz Beer (1769–1851). King Frederick William III, himself, ruled that the only authorized Jewish services must be held
"without the slightest innovation in language, ceremonies, prayers
or hymns, wholly according to the established custom."[28] In the
years following the closing of the Beer Temple, the Prussian government continued to oppose innovation in Jewish worship because of a
belief that any "sectarianism" was a threat to political stability.[29]

The political motivation for Prussian opposition to Jewish reform
alerts us to the fact that governmental attitudes toward Jewish religion could be motivated by concerns that were only peripherally related to Jews or Judaism, if at all. Following the accession of King
Frederick William IV in 1840, for example, the policies of the Prussian government became somewhat more tolerant toward religious
reform in the Jewish community. The reason for the change, however, is that government thinking was increasingly dominated by the
idea of the "Christian State." According to this doctrine, which had
been developed by the converted Jew Friedrich Julius Stahl, professor
of law at the University of Berlin, Judaism became a matter of no
interest to the authorities. "The Christian State," wrote one official,
"has no interest whatever in whether Judaism sooner or later disin-
tegrates into different sects."[30]

Similarly, over 30 years later the legal status of the Jews of Prussia
was to be changed significantly by legislation inspired by the Kulturkampf, the struggle between the Bismarckian state and the Catholic
Church.[31] The *Law of Separation* of May 1873, which allowed individual Catholics to withdraw from religious organizations without

having to withdraw from the Roman Catholic religion as a whole, was amended in 1876 to allow Jews the same kind of freedom. Under the earlier law of 1847, which had governed the status of Jews in Prussia, every Jew was obligated to be a member of a local congregation. To withdraw from the congregation and to fail to pay taxes or other obligations was regarded as effectively leaving Judaism. Under the amended law of 1876, on the other hand, a Jew could now leave the congregation and remain a Jew. Ironically, though the law did, in fact, increase the religious liberty of Jews in Prussia, many of the leaders of the Jewish community opposed the law because of the fear that this new freedom would lead to the financial ruin of Jewish institutions.[32] As was the case in France, state intervention in the affairs of the Jewish community could increase or decrease freedom, depending on the circumstances. In any event, there was no clear agreement among Jews over the desirability of freedom.

A far more subtle form of state intervention, however, was the situation that obtained when the state acted unconsciously, promoting policies that it considered to be religiously neutral, but that, nevertheless, had an impact on Jewish life. It is precisely because we see this form of intervention operating in the most liberal of the European states that it is of greatest interest to the student of religious freedom, for it suggests limits to the liberal notions of freedom of religion that dominate discussion of this issue. Take, for example, the following story, told by David Landes.

Given the highly selective character of French schooling and the conditions to access of power and to the professions, ambitious Jewish families had no choice but to send their children to the public schools and hence to Saturday classes. Some of them tried to reconcile this necessity with their religious beliefs by asking their children not to write—an impossible and unenforceable constraint. In the end the educational system operated to sever the Jewish child from observance; and while parents (and grandparents) may have deplored this, they viewed it as a necessary (or desirable) avenue of promotion, in other words of happiness.[33]

In Landes's story, we see an example of the limits to emancipation that were, in fact, foreseen during the emancipation struggle. The practice of traditional religion could, in fact, interfere in the attempt by Jews to become full participating members of the modern society. Moreover, as Landes's story shows, state activity was at least implicated in that interference.

As I have mentioned, for an increasing number of Jews in the nineteenth century this was not an issue. By moving away from the practice of traditional religion, either through the Reform movement or by informally falling away from religious activity, they were no longer placed in the seemingly impossible position of having to re-sist integration into the larger society because of their devotion to religion. But what of those Jews for whom the devotion to orthodox religion remained? Was their freedom to practice their religion para-doxically to interfere with their freedom to gain full civic equality? Was there, ultimately, a conflict between the two definitions of reli-gious freedom? This was the knottiest problem that faced emanci-pated Jews and that faces modern historians of religious freedom. I would like to offer here a short description of two approaches taken by the leaders of nineteenth-century Jewry. The examples I will use are those of France and England, in order to show two rather different approaches to the issue. The reasons for the differences are many and complex and it is beyond the scope of this chapter to discuss them in detail. It is important to see, however, that the different reactions of English and French Jewry are intimately bound up with the history and circumstances of the larger society in which the Jews found themselves.

In France, which, under the influence of the French Revolution and Napoleon, was developing a vision of nationhood in which there could be, at least in theory, little toleration of difference, and where for a number of reasons anti-Semitism was far more powerful than it was in England, the leaders of French Jewry, in the words of David Landes, "found it increasingly difficult to reconcile the rules of their faith with the opportunities and requirements of civil education and achievement. And when the two considerations clashed, the Jews—even their rabbis—tended to sacrifice the Law to social, political, and business success."[34] Complicating religious politics in France, of course, was the battle that raged through much of the century be-tween the adherents of the republic and the Church. This battle meant that in France, as in Germany during the Kulturkampf, reli-gious issues could be dangerous even for those, like the Jews, who were not participants in the struggle.[35]

In England, on the other hand, where the development of a uni-tary nationalism was far less advanced, where anti-Semitism was far less a problem for Jews, where the tradition of religious freedom was far more established, and where Jews had been legally British sub-jects, the leaders of Anglo-Jewry, though determined to anglicize the Jewish population, were far more willing in the middle years of the century to assert that true freedom of religion demanded that the larger society be willing to make accommodations for the Jews so as to allow them both to continue to practice a version of traditional religion and to integrate economically and socially into English society.

I have argued elsewhere that the leaders of Anglo-Jewry were among the first to begin to articulate a vision of cultural pluralism.[36] I want to argue here that ultimately a culturally pluralistic vision of society is also the only one that maximized true freedom of religion for the Jews, because it minimized the difficult decision that Jews were faced with. In this atmosphere, freedom of religion did not necessarily mean freedom from religion. This statement, made by a late twentieth-century American Jew, may be seen as anachronistic and ahistorical. Others have been criticized for taking a similar stance.[37] Still, as I hope to show, these issues were, in fact, raised by nineteenth-century Europeans and are, therefore, fair game for historians today.

Organizationally, as we have already seen, there were similarities between the Jews of England and France in the nineteenth century, though the differences between the two communities might have been more significant than the similarities. English and French Jews were both organized nationally. In this, both countries differed from the more traditional pattern of Eastern Europe, where Judaism was a decentralized, congregation-based religion. In France the centralization was achieved through the consistorial system that had been established under Napoleon. Departmental consistories were responsible to the Central Consistory in Paris, which was, in turn, responsible to the government through the ministry of cults. In 1831, Judaism became a state-subsidized religion in France. Synagogue building was financed by the government and rabbis received state salaries. This situation existed until 1905, hence the power of the French state over aspects of Jewish religious life. In England, the national organization of the Jews was far less formal, but, as we have seen, the London-based Board of Deputies of British Jews had at least quasi-official status.

Ultimately, then, the Board of Deputies in England and the Central Consistory in France came to be seen as the representative of the Jews to the state and to the society at large. The powers of the two bodies differed markedly, but both bodies did accept the role as representative of the Jews and attempted to act in that capacity through most of the nineteenth century. In this capacity, the two bodies often had to confront the issue of the extent to which it was possible for Jews to integrate into society and yet continue to practice Judaism. The two bodies took different approaches. To understand this it is necessary to appreciate that though both were dominated by wealthy, acculturated Jews, they nevertheless had very different attitudes toward religion. The Board of Deputies remained nominally orthodox throughout the nineteenth century, reflecting the fact that in England, the leaders of Anglo-Jewry, people like the Rothschilds, Moses Montefiore, and David Salomons, themselves remained at least nominally orthodox. Though, as Todd Endelman has suggested, the orthodoxy of people like the Rothschilds was often rather loose by the standards of Eastern European traditionalists, nevertheless reform made little headway in England.[38]

In France, on the other hand, the Central Consistory was largely dominated by "progressives" who believed that Judaism must be reformed in various ways in order to allow it to become consistent with modern society. The difference between the two bodies was not the accidental result of different personnel. On the contrary, it reflected the different situations that existed in the two countries.

≺ IV ≻

France: Opposition to Pluralism

As Zosa Szajkowski has put it, "French Jews willingly rejected cultural pluralism and accepted assimilation."[39] As a result, when faced with the conflict of religion and society, their leaders tended to choose society even at the expense of those within the community who wished to remain more observant. They did so both because of their own religious "progressivism" and because of their belief that Jewish particularism was not good either for the Jews or for France. On a number of occasions, then, the Central Consistory refused to intervene in disputes between Jews and the state even when that refusal would lead to the harm of Jewish religion. As one leader of Franco-Jewry put it, "a religious minority like our own must above all remain on the defensive, and each one of us, while fully exercising the rights of citizenship, must show great reserve when the political issues in debate touch closely upon matters of conscience."[40]

English Jews were not entirely free of that sort of feeling. In an

1867 Board of Deputies debate over whether to approach the government to seek relief for Jews from a law that mandated Sunday closing of factories, at least one member of the Board argued that

it was undesirable to seek special legislation for the Jews, now that they had been emancipated and were on a par with their fellow citizens; that this would be the means of raising prejudice against them; and precedent showed . . . that it was contrary to the practice of the Board to seek exemption for the Jewish body from the operation of the Acts which religiously affected it.[41]

In fact, however, when it came to the lengths that the leaders of English and French Jewry were willing to go to assert the right of the orthodox among them to participate as fully as possible in national life without allowing their religious observance to get in the way, the response of the two communities was strikingly different. A few examples may serve to illustrate this difference.

Both the Central Consistory and the Board of Deputies were willing to exert themselves to protect what they saw as Jewish rights as citizens. Both bodies carefully monitored pending legislation to see whether it might contain anything that would be to the detriment of Jews. In most cases, both bodies acted on the assumption that absolute equality between Jews and Christians was what was needed. Thus, in 1849, when the French government was preparing a bill on education that would allow for greater freedom of religious groups to establish schools, the Central Consistory pressured the government to assure that rabbis were included on the same basis as priests and ministers as eligible to serve on educational boards.[42]

But as we have seen, absolute equality did not always really result in Jews having equal access to education or other facets of civil life. In France, for example, Jewish students were often under a great disadvantage in attempting to attend the *écoles normales*, which prepared secondary schoolteachers. In many of the *écoles*, boarding was mandatory, and that could pose great problems for Jewish students wishing to observe the dietary laws. Although pressured by local consistories, the Central Consistory refused to try to obtain for Jewish students the right to be boarded with local Jewish families.[43] Interestingly, the consistory was willing to agitate for the provision of food for Jews incarcerated in prisons.[44] Apparently, the fact that prisoners had no choice but to be in prison, whereas orthodox Jews could make the choice not to attend the *écoles*, was the important difference. The consistory was simply unwilling to ask for what might be considered special treatment for Jews. The promise that the French Revolution had given the Jews, that they could be full citizens in return for giving up any special privileges they had enjoyed, was taken seriously by the leadership of Franco-Jewry.[45]

As in the case of education, the area where Jewish special rights might most be sought after was in the area where Jews came into contact with official bodies of one sort or another. In answer to the question of whether official bodies could treat the Jews any differently from anyone else, the Central Consistory's answer always seemed to be "no."

Consider, for example, the case of Jewish burial. Napoleonic law had placed cemeteries in the ownership of municipal authorities. In many localities, there were no exclusive Jewish cemeteries, but Jews were given permission to use portions of the municipal cemetery, over which they had no real control. The consistory, in the words of Phyllis Cohen Albert,

> generally complied with local customs and procedures, rather than insist that Jewish law govern procedures at Jewish cemeteries (or sections of cemeteries). Thus in Paris in 1841 a group of orthodox Jews . . . complained to the Paris consistory about a municipal decision to demolish the temporary graves. The orthodox wanted the consistory to insist that the graves be saved and that the Jewish part of the cemetery be governed by Jewish law, which knows no temporary graves. Religious arguments failed to persuade the consistory to defend Jewish religious interests. Although Adolphe Cremieux, president of the central consistory, supported the religious rights of the orthodox, the Paris consistory disregarded his recommendation and announced that it was important to conform to Parisian ways as much as possible.[46]

It is important to note that this decision was made in the face of a positive injunction of Jewish law about the burial of the dead. There was simply no way that Jews could under these conditions practice what was, after all, a very important part of their religion.

≺ V ≻

England: A Pluralist Model?

In England, on the other hand, the principle on which both the Board of Deputies and the Chief Rabbi operated was to distinguish between what were positive obligations placed on Jews by Jewish law and things that were permitted to Jews. If there was a conflict between the laws of the state and something that was permitted to Jews by Jewish law but forbidden by state law, they unhesitatingly upheld the primacy of the state. One example was the difference between Jewish law and English law over the question of marriage. English law prohibited marriages between people who were related in degrees that would be no bar to marriage according to Jewish law. In those cases, the state made it clear that it could not recognize Jewish marriages that came within the prohibited degrees, and the Jewish authorities, notably the Chief Rabbi and the Board, acquiesced even though they felt it to be a hardship, and periodically raised the possibility of applying to the government to change the law for Jews and Christians alike.[47] Where there was a conflict between secular law and Jewish law that revolved around a positive requirement of Jewish observance, on the other hand, Anglo-Jewish leadership saw no problem in lobbying the government for Jewish exemptions from the law.

In doing this, the Board did not simply seek to make public policy religiously "neutral" as it had done in its campaign to repeal the University Tests, which stood in the way of any other than a member of the Established Church first from taking degrees at Oxford and Cambridge, and then from obtaining a fellowship.[48] Instead, it sought to have the state recognize Jewish distinctiveness so as to allow English Jews to continue to practice traditional religion without having to withdraw from the social and economic life of the nation.

The most striking example of this sort of activity was the campaign, waged in the 1870s, to secure for Jewish factory and workshop owners an exemption from those provisions of the Factory Acts that forbade work on Sunday. This campaign is an interesting one because it represented the limits of Jewish expectations in nineteenth-century Europe. On the one hand, by asking for exemptions from the law, the leaders of Anglo-Jewry were not asking that Jews be allowed to refrain from doing what offended their own religious scruples, as might be the case with requesting that kosher meat be made available to Jewish prisoners. They were, in fact, asking that Jews be allowed to do what offended the religious scruples of Christians. On the other hand, the request for exemption from the Factory Acts was made in a very limited way. The Acts, which prevented the employment of women, children, and young persons on Sunday, had originally been justified on the grounds of protecting the weak from exploitative employers rather than the enforcement of sabbatarianism. As a result, Jews were able to argue that the exemptions they sought could be justified purely on the grounds of fairness, since they limited the number of hours in Jewish workshops to the same number allowed in other workshops. Nevertheless, the request was extreme enough to divide the members of the Board, some of whom were fearful that any such attempt would lead to resentment against the Jewish community.

Despite these objections, the Board of Deputies did, in fact, lend its support to the effort to secure Jewish exemptions from the Factory Acts, and, perhaps more surprisingly, the government agreed to modify the Factory Act of 1878 so as to accede to the Board's request.[49] The act, limited though it was, represents the greatest concessions that nineteenth-century English Jews were able to obtain in order to allow them to minimize the conflicts between the demands of Jewish religious practice and the demands of life in a modern society. Though the leaders of Anglo-Jewry recognized that their victory in 1878 was limited and that hardships continued to exist for many observant Jews, they were reluctant to ask for much more. The Factory Act, for example, applied only to the employment of women and young people. There remained restrictions on other kinds of Sunday labor by adults. When some Jewish workmen appealed to the Board after being arrested for working on Sunday, the Board refused to intervene. "No doubt a hardship is occasioned in most cases in which the Lord's Day Act is enforced against persons professing the Jewish religion who observe the seventh day Sabbath," explained the Board,

but such instances are rare, and the magistrate usually takes a lenient view of the case. He did so in the present instance, for he imposed no fine, but simply ordered the defendant to pay the costs; the Board, however, should watch any legislation relative to Sunday observance, or Sunday trading, and will avail themselves of any opportunity that may be found of endeavouring to secure relief for such cases as the present.[50]

The members of the Board also took pains to publicly distance themselves from those Jewish shopowners who tried to abuse the exceptions that the law allowed.[51] For all their desires to ease the lot of religiously observant Jews, the leaders of Anglo-Jewry recognized that public opinion was uncomfortable with any suggestions that Jews were asking for anything more than to be allowed to compete on terms of equality with their Christian neighbors. It was not until 1911 that the Board of Deputies was to attempt to gain similar exceptions from the Sunday Trading Laws for Jewish merchants, and this time they were unsuccessful.[52]

The limited aims and successes of the English campaigns to accommodate the needs of orthodox Jews are significant for two reasons. When compared to the very different policies of French Jewry, they are illustrative of the profound differences that existed from one Western European country to another in regard to the emancipation experience of the Jews.

More significantly, they demonstrate that nineteenth-century Jews were well aware of the *religious* conflicts created by emancipation. As we have seen, the liberal impulse toward religious freedom could come into conflict with the equally liberal impulse toward the integration of the Jews into European society. For many Jews, a choice had to be made between these two goals. The fact that they were able to choose, is itself a sign of the increase in their freedom. But, as early as the late nineteenth century, there were some Jews for whom true religious freedom implied not having to make a choice. They were in the minority, to be sure, and their success was limited, but they did help lay the foundation for a new conception of religious freedom that moved far beyond mere toleration and pointed the way toward genuine cultural pluralism.

The Kulturkampf: Restrictions and Controls on the Practice of Religion in Bismarck's Germany

RONALD J. ROSS

NOTHING SO WELL illustrates sectarian polarization and the abiding importance of religion in Imperial Germany's cultural life as the segmented character of the German reading public and the appearance and immense popularity of religiously-inspired historical novels. These writings, the product of the years between 1850 and 1920, varied a good deal in literary quality and importance. Some, like German translations of Nicholas Cardinal Wiseman's *Fabiola* (1854), Lewis Wallace's *Ben-Hur* (1880), or Henryk Sienkiewicz's *Quo Vadis?* (1896), quickly achieved bestseller status, and eventually became screen epics in the mid-twentieth century. Others, like Ida Gräfin Hahn-Hahn's *Eudoxia die Kaiserin* (1866), Wilhelm Herchenbach's *Cäcilia* (1883), or Peter Dörfler's *Neue Götter* (1920), to name only a few produced in Germany itself, rarely achieved the same degree of international prominence. Whatever their literary merit, however, all found a wide audience among Imperial Germany's Roman Catholic inhabitants. The popularity of these historical novels among German Catholics—a sizable minority making up about one-third of the population in the Prussian kingdom as in the entire German Reich itself—doubtless owed something to widespread public fascination with the nineteenth century's remarkable archeological discoveries. It owed even more to putative parallels between the sufferings and tribulations of the early Christian church in ancient Rome and discriminatory practices, even persecution, of the so-called Kulturkampf.[1]

≺ I ≻

The Preventive War

Few conflicts in Imperial Germany were more important than the Kulturkampf or "struggle for civilization," a bitter and protracted Church-state dispute that began in 1871, gathered in intensity and bitterness until 1878, and then continued with diminishing severity down to 1887.[2] This dispute reflected Protestant Germany's distrust of Rome, dismay among non-Catholics at Pope Pius IX's Syllabus of Errors from 1864 and the far-reaching claim of papal infallibility promulgated by the Vatican Council in 1870, and liberals' loathing of what they perceived as Catholic backwardness, provincialism, and cultural inferiority.[3] These attitudes hardened as Rome and its German church agents moved swiftly in the months following the Vatican Council to isolate and suppress the so-called Old Catholic movement, a small minority of Catholic dissidents who rejected the new infallibility doctrine because in their opinion it was sanctioned by neither scripture nor tradition.[4] The Kulturkampf also owed much to resentment in governmental circles regarding the reappearance of the Catholic-dominated Center party in the Reichstag and the Prussian *Landtag* (diet or parliament), and to Chancellor Otto von Bismarck's conviction that Catholic clergy used their influence in Prussia's eastern districts to retard the assimilation of the local Polish populace into the German nation.[5] Beyond these concerns and misgivings, as recent research reminds us, the Kulturkampf also represented a strategy of nation-building, "an attempt to consolidate German national culture, to create"—by force if necessary—"a cultural unity, a coherent nation across confessional lines."[6]

What transformed this distrust, fear, animosity, and even hope into political action was Bismarck's decision to launch an "internal preventive war" against the alleged revolutionary potential of Catholics, Poles, and socialists that he believed threatened the consolidation of the newly-unified German Reich.[7] Having just concluded a war with France and faced with the staggering problem of forging a new German nation, Bismarck viewed with alarm and suspicion any group or interest that complicated his task.

Although the pope denounced the Kulturkampf as a "massive persecution" reminiscent of anti-Christian outrages perpetrated in

ancient Rome,[8] the Kulturkampf avoided a frontal assault on religious belief itself in favor of specific limitations and controls on the
practice of religion. In 1871 Bismarck abolished the "Catholic Section" in the Prussian ministry of ecclesiastical affairs—the so-called
Kultusministerium—and amended the Reich's criminal code to prevent the use of the pulpit for political propaganda. In 1872, Bismarck
and his collaborators eliminated ecclesiastical influence in curricu-
lar matters and in the supervision of Prussia's schools, and expelled
the Jesuit Order from Germany. With the *Landtag*'s adoption of the
so-called May Laws in 1873, the training and appointment of clergy
in Prussia came under state jurisdiction. The Prussian government
also introduced compulsory civil marriage in 1874, a step extended
to the entire Reich a year later. Additional Prussian legislation in
1875 abolished religious orders and congregations, choked off state
subsidies to the Church, and deleted religious guarantees from the
Prussian constitution. With Bismarck's sanction, furthermore, Prussian authorities in 1874 and 1875 enacted statutes permitting state
agents to take charge of vacated bishoprics and authorized laymen to
assume administrative responsibilities at the parish level. The Kulturkampf thus asserted secular control over the Church, reduced
clerical authority, and intruded state supervision into the Church's
internal affairs; but it did not prohibit Catholic worship, alter dogma
and belief, or altogether abolish papal supremacy.

This Church-state dispute produced an increasingly pervasive,
almost palpable atmosphere of anti-Catholicism, primarily in Prussia and to a lesser degree in the German Reich as a whole. Sectarian
hostility was so bitter, wrote the prominent Catholic aristocrat and
future German chancellor Count Georg von Hertling decades later,
that it "is difficult to make comprehensible to the present generation what the [anti-Catholic] mood" was like. "The parliaments re-
sounded with the most serious, unjustified reproaches against the
pope, Catholic doctrine, and against the believers who remained
loyal to their church." These charges were also "echoed a thousand-
fold in the liberal press" where Catholics and their church leaders
were routinely vilified with such epithets as *papist* [*Römling*], *Vati-
canaille,* simpletons, "the dregs of mankind," or, worse still, enemies
of the state.[9]

≺ II ≻

Restrictions on Religious Liberty

Within this climate of sectarian hostility, and as a consequence of the Kulturkampf's regulations, the Catholic Church, its leaders, and its adherents suffered grievously. The bishops and lower clergy were the most conspicuous victims of governmental persecution. Before the Kulturkampf came to an end in 1887, no fewer than five of Prussia's twelve bishops were to endure confinement in a prison or fortress. Other members of the episcopate fled the country to avoid arrest and imprisonment.[10] But if the bishops were the Kulturkampf's most obvious victims, it was in fact the common clergy who overwhelmingly dominated the ranks of those arrested and jailed. Priests violating the new church regulations embodied in the May Laws were arrested and led off, either on foot or in a wheeled conveyance reviled as the "culture coach," to jail and eventual trial. Conviction resulted in the levying of a fine up to 100 thalers.[11] But these clerics were unsalaried, and for that reason they could not pay their fines. Nor for that matter did they possess personal property or other assets of any significance (clothing, furniture, and the like) that could be confiscated as an appropriate indemnity.[12] Unable (and unwilling) to pay their fines, therefore, they were expelled from the vicarage, rectory, or parish house and taken into custody. Terms of imprisonment varied a good deal; these could be as brief as one day or as long as several months. And while there were variations around the country, jailed clergy found much the same conditions—overcrowded cells, inadequate food, boredom, squalor, and fetid air.[13]

The Kulturkampf also exacted its toll on Prussia's religious orders, convents, and monasteries. According to a Catholic count, 296 religious establishments, comprising 1,181 male and 1,776 female conventuals, were eventually suppressed as a consequence of the Congregations Law of 1875.[14] Although most of these monks and nuns found alternative ecclesiastical employment in houses of their rule located in other German states or even abroad, having their religious establishments closed or their congregations dissolved was both dreadful and devastating. Nuns turned out without ceremony from suppressed houses—like those in Aachen for example—were brought in closed carriages with drawn curtains to the local railway station, where they were transferred to trains and taken into exile. While the implementation of the Congregations Law in Aachen and elsewhere in Prussia was conspicuously free from acts of brutality and violence against groups or individuals that have characterized almost all suppressions and confiscations of this kind, the "departure of nuns from friends and relatives" in any case "was deeply moving and many an eye was filled with tears."[15]

Following numerous scenes like this, Catholic publicists called attention to the grief, the heartbreak, and the hardships endured by the members, both male and female, of those religious orders who had their lives disrupted and who were forced to leave their homeland.[16] By far the most poignant expression of their outrage was the poem "The Wreck of the Deutschland." Written by Gerard Manley Hopkins, an English Jesuit, it described the sinking of a German ship off the English coast during a storm on December 7, 1875, and lamented the death by drowning of five Franciscan nuns forced to leave Germany by the cloister law.[17]

Laymen, too, were harassed, persecuted, and, on occasion, even imprisoned. Many were punished with fines or jail sentences because they refused to testify in court actions against the clergy or in other ways refused to cooperate with the agents of the courts. For offenses in these categories, according to one statistical sample, 210 Catholic lay people, men and women alike, were convicted during the first four months of 1875.[18] Others were punished for giving assistance to priests who contravened the May Laws[19] or who obstructed the activities of pro-government priests.[20] Following protests and clashes with the police over the arrest of priests accused of conducting unauthorized religious instruction in Upper Silesia in April 1874, for example, eight men and two women were arrested and punished. At Thorn, an old West Prussian fortress town on the banks of the Vistula, a Polish-speaking Catholic was sentenced to nine months in jail because he interfered when the police took a parish priest into custody.[21] In August 1874, on the other hand, several people in Posen Province, a predominantly Polish-speaking territory at the eastern end of the Hohenzollern kingdom, received sentences ranging from one to two years after they interrupted religious services conducted by a renegade clergyman. A year later in neighboring West Prussia, 62 people were charged and 39 were convicted for similar offenses.

Among those convicted, two spent 30 months in jail.[22] In August 1875 five persons received jail sentences of up to one month for obstructing the closing of a Franciscan cloister in Paderborn.[23]

In most cases where laymen became caught up in the Kulturkampf's legal machinery, however, their troubles stemmed from violations of the law on peaceful assembly. Although the total number of such convictions for the whole kingdom has never been worked out, there can be little doubt but that hundreds—more likely thousands—of Catholic lay people were arrested, fined, or jailed for such offenses. To cite a typical example, 49 inhabitants of Stolberg, a community in the northern Rhineland, were fined by a local police court because they formed a public procession of twenty wagons to meet the archbishop of Cologne when he visited the vicinity in 1875. Several persons from the Bursback district near Aachen also received fines because they provided transport for the archbishop. As many as 30 Catholics from Merode, Echtz, Derichsweiler, Merken, Pier, and Gürzenich, small villages in the northern Rhineland, received the maximum fines permitted by law for celebrating a visit from the archbishop.[24] In 1876 a few young men were arrested and taken into custody when they refused a police order to vacate the cathedral square in Münster.[25]

The extremes to which the authorities were prepared to go to cow the Catholic populace into submission were amply demonstrated in 1876 by the Marpingen case.[26] This incident had its origins in widely circulated reports that the Virgin Mary had appeared in a vision to three eight-year-old girls in a small mining community in the Saar district. When long processions of Catholic pilgrims were attracted to the site, local authorities expressed alarm that the whole episode would upset the peace, generate disaffection, and incite fear. District officials, therefore, employed a company of infantry to clear the site of the apparition of all pilgrims and spectators, a task that was completed with unnecessary vigor and brutality. Several people were arrested and taken into custody, the three young children were removed from the control of their parents and placed temporarily in an orphanage, and a contingent of soldiers was quartered in the village. The townspeople were also saddled with an assessment of 4,000 marks, a step, it was said, that increased the community's taxes by 115 percent. So harsh and misguided was the government's behavior that even the subsequent acquittal of all 21 Catholic defendants in the criminal court of Saarbrücken in the spring of 1879 failed to erase the anger, pain, and resentment felt by Prussia's Catholic population.[27]

<< III >>

Limitations on Civil Liberty

Not only did the Kulturkampf restrict religious liberty, it also threatened political freedom in general. No one was more explicit in expressing this foreboding than Wilhelm Emmanuel Freiherr von Ketteler, the bishop of Mainz from 1850 until 1877. The German chancellor, he said, used the Kulturkampf to restore the "old monarchist, absolutist, militarist Prussia . . . in its entirety."[28] For to break resistance to the government's new religious program, Bismarck and the Kulturkampf's proponents were prepared to limit freedom of expression, to narrow the range of civil liberties, to violate traditional standards of fair hearing, and to menace entire categories of individuals.

To a government determined to curb religious liberty and to modify the relationship between church and state, few things could be more troublesome than public opposition from newspapers and other publications, by far the most effective means other than the pulpit itself for influencing the church's rank and file. Although freed from the worst restrictions of earlier press control arrangements by the Reich Press Law of 1874, oppositional newspapers—Catholic and non-Catholic alike—were still burdened by a wide variety of administrative, financial, and legal controls available to the police and other authorities. These ranged from the loss of concession to print official notices for the government to the withdrawal of postal privileges, from censorship to confiscation of offending publications, and from the imposition of fines for press infractions to the imprisonment of stubborn press malefactors.[29]

One of the weapons most frequently employed against the ultramontane press, however, was the charge of libel or slander. Where modern courts in Western Europe and North America protect press freedom against libel claims by requiring a show of deliberate falsehood or reckless disregard of the truth, the Reich Press Law contained no such protections. For that reason Bismarck attempted to stifle criticism of his church policies and to control the denominational press through an endless series of prosecutions designed to exhaust his opponents.[30] The majority of these legal actions involved charges of insulting the kaiser, the Prussian state cabinet, or even Bismarck himself, and most prosecutions resulted in a prison sentence of several months for the accused.[31] No slight was too small to arouse his anger. Few incidents so well illustrate the Iron Chancellor's remarkable sensitivity as his complaint on one occasion that a Catholic newspaper had failed to include the deferential prefix "*Herr*" when it used the name Bismarck![32] So many cases of personal insult were handled—Bismarck himself once admitted to 1,600 of these legal actions[33]—that standardized forms for charge and specification had to be devised to streamline administrative routine.[34]

Comprehensive and accurate statistics about the government's campaign against the Catholic press during the Kulturkampf unfortunately no longer exist.[35] But according to estimates made by the peculiar formula employed in 1928 by the Augustinus-Verein, a Catholic press association, Catholic editors and publishers spent a total of fifteen years and two months in jail and accumulated a total of 40,000 marks in fines.[36] Such statistics, of course, offer general impressions that do not take stock of particular cases like that of Paul Majunke, a Reichstag deputy and combative editor of the *Germania*, who had his parliamentary immunity violated and who was held in Berlin's Plötzensee prison for a year;[37] or of the editor of the Catholic *Mainzer Journal*, Philipp Wasserberg, who in 1874 was sentenced to two months' detention because he allegedly insulted the imperial Crown.[38] In any case, the surveillance of Catholic newspapers was elaborately organized, minute inquiries were launched, and many journalists had to put up with frequent visits from the police who, on the least suspicion, searched offices and homes for incriminating documents. Between January and April 1875, for example, a time when the government was especially zealous in persecuting the denominational press, Catholic editors and journalists were the object of 74 house searches conducted by the Prussian police.[39]

In addition to endless prosecution for libel and insult, the government also attempted to produce financial calamity for the ultramontane press by intimidating and driving away its readers. To this end, the government instructed its employees to boycott all Catholic publications. In November 1872, for example, several teachers employed by the public schools and known to have invested money in the Catholic *Saar-Zeitung* were threatened with disciplinary action if within fourteen days they did not withdraw their investments from this publishing venture.[40] The mayor of a neighboring community also warned his municipal officials and employees that they were expected to spurn the *Saar-Zeitung* in favor of the pro-governmental *Saarlouiser Journal*.[41] Powerful economic leaders also threw their support behind the Kulturkampf's campaign of intimidation and censorship. In another attempt to create financial hardship for the *Saar-Zeitung* and to censor the reading material of his Catholic employees, Carl Ferdinand Baron von Stumm-Halberg, a prominent and wealthy industrialist in the Saar territory, threatened in 1873 to dismiss any of his workers who continued to read the Catholic newspaper.[42]

The obsession with quashing dissent assumed genuinely serious dimensions and generated a momentum that also menaced individual rights. Nowhere was this threat more obvious than in the government's decision to purge the civil service of its Catholic members.[43] Difficulties in enforcing the Kulturkampf had prompted doubts about the loyalty of Catholic civil servants and their commitment to the new ecclesiastical program. "In the Paderborn area," and in Catholic Prussia generally, said a typical report, "the greater part of the administrative personnel—county officials, mayors, policemen, local administrators, village leaders—as well as those magistrates appointed in an earlier period, *even if they fulfill their official responsibilities*" nonetheless "embrace . . . pronounced ultramontane tendencies."[44] The presence of these ultramontanes in the governmental administration unquestionably led to lenient treatment of Catholics charged with contravening the new ecclesiastical regulations.[45] In the western part of the Münsterland, a district in Westphalia, it was claimed that local officials, with but few exceptions, were affiliated with the Catholic Center party and found themselves "in the hands of the clergy" so that they were no longer deemed entirely reliable in implementing the new church policies.[46] Elsewhere in Westphalia, district magistrates and other officials were denounced as "servants of the clergy" who worked against their own government.[47] In the most flagrant cases, it was said, Catholic policemen obstructed inquiries and warned the clergy when arrests were imminent so that apprehension was successfully evaded.[48]

This situation was greeted with concern within the highest echelons of the government, and complaints regarding Catholic sympathizers among the police and within the administration during the Kulturkampf were vocal and widespread. As early as 1875, the liberal deputy Wilhelm Wehrenpfennig chided the Prussian government for its failure to cleanse the civil service of its Catholic officials. "It is indeed clear that when the organs of administration themselves are filled with ultramontane sympathizers," he declared, "the effectiveness of these [Kulturkampf] laws has got to be diminished." It was Wehrenpfennig's conviction, moreover, that the new, more stringent legislation that followed the May Laws would have been unnecessary had the bureaucracy been more reliable and energetic.[49] Rudolf von Bennigsen, another liberal leader, shared this viewpoint. Unreliable officials, he told Bismarck, "continually make illusory all our legal measures" so that "the populace doubts the seriousness of our efforts" against the Catholic Church.[50]

To make the bureaucracy a more reliable instrument for coercing the Church during the Kulturkampf, the government in due course involuntarily transferred or—far more serious—rid the service of many of its Catholic members. Many dismissals were the result of some action or omission on the part of the fired official. In 1874 the Catholic *Oberpräsident* or provincial governor of Silesia was involuntarily retired because he was considered too indulgent in his treatment of the prince-bishop of Breslau.[51] Heinrich Wilhelm von Holzbrinck, a *Regierungspräsident* (district governor) in Westphalia, was forced to resign in the following year because he displayed insufficient energy in combating the ultramontanes.[52] Dismissals were more numerous in the lower reaches of the administration where Catholic officials predominated. In the northern Rhineland police officials at the village level were sacked for failure to press charges against local clergy who violated the new church regulations.[53]

Not all those ousted, however, were judged solely on the basis of some action or outspoken attitude. The government's loyalty program—for that is what it was—also penalized thoughts and mindsets. Even an official's private opinions could bring him down. The long-term mayor of Bonn Leopold Kaufmann came under scrutiny in 1874 when he sought royal sanction for his reelection to another term. After a delay of nearly six months, Kaufmann received not the Crown's confirmation but a summons to appear in the provincial offices in nearby Cologne. There Kaufmann was grilled about his general attitude toward the government's ecclesiastical policy. To these queries Kaufmann replied that he was personally opposed to the May Laws and other legislation designed to coerce the Roman Church but added that these private views did not hamper his ability to implement and enforce governmental policy when he acted in his official capacity as mayor. He had, after all, complied with the Jesuit Law of 1872 and dissolved the Jesuit house in Bonn. In 1873, furthermore, he permitted the acquisition of a Catholic chapel by the Old Catholic sect. But to the outrageous question would he enforce the law with enthusiasm, he naturally said he could not.[54]

Suspicion continued to dog Kaufmann. Dissatisfied with both his answers and his attitude, the Prussian government ultimately refused to confirm his reelection to the mayoralty. Although it is certainly true that other civil servants in Prussia had at one time or another fallen victim to purge, Kaufmann in the opinion of his coreligionists was the first to be ousted for his personal opinions.[55]

Even Protestant officials who expressed misgivings about the Kulturkampf ran the risk of damaging their careers. Ludwig Wiese, Richard de la Croix, and Rudolf Kögel, for example, all orthodox members of the Evangelical Church and senior officials in the Kultusministerium, were convinced that the Kulturkampf's ecclesiastical policies were bringing harm to their coreligionists.[56] To neutralize the consequences of their attitude, the minister of ecclesiastical affairs placed these reluctant and hesitating bureaucrats "on ice," as someone said, "where they were practically not engaged in anything at all" or involved on "unimportant assignments having no practical significance" for their long-term career prospects.[57] Only one Protestant official in Westphalia lost his post as a direct consequence of the Kulturkampf. For confirming the election of a Catholic as a village mayor in his district, Carl von Basse, the *Landrat* (county official) of Kreis Steinfurt, was dismissed in 1876.[58]

Apart from dormant tendencies, latent potentials, private thoughts, and hearsay evidence, the criteria for determining retention or dismissal in the civil service during the Kulturkampf included affiliations and associations. Membership in Catholic organizations was deemed incompatible with governmental employment and often enough it became the yardstick by which loyalty was measured, guilt determined. These voluntary associations, in the opinion of the Prussian *Staatsministerium* or state cabinet, had "acquired a scope and an importance" that demonstrated the inadequacy of existing legal controls. "The number of these associations, according to official inquiries, amounts to about two thousand five hundred, with two hundred thousand members." Whatever their ostensible harmless purposes, the cabinet members agreed, "Most of these associations . . . have assumed a political character and serve the purposes or interests of the pope." As such, these organizations were deemed inimical to Prussian state interests and for that reason the loyalty of their members came into question.[59] No organization, of course, was more suspect than the Catholic Center party. Other suspect associations ranged from Catholic apprentice and journeymen's societies to student groups, and from political clubs like the Pius-Verein or the Constantia to the St. Boniface Society for Catholics of Independent Means.[60]

The largest and by far the most successful Catholic lay organization in Germany and obviously a source of concern to the Kulturkampf's proponents was the so-called Mainz Association, a fraternal society founded in July 1872 and the chief vehicle for mobilizing Catholic popular dissent against Bismarck's ecclesiastical policies.[61] At its peak the association was particularly popular in the western part of the Hohenzollern kingdom, where it had nearly 60,000 members in the northern Rhineland and Westphalia and another 9,000 or so in the southern Rhineland.[62] The indisputable presence of so many of its junior officials in this organization's ranks was naturally viewed in Berlin with growing apprehension and for this reason the government did its utmost to prohibit its Catholic employees and functionaries from holding membership. A pro-Kulturkampf mayor from the St. Wendel district in the Saar territory even suggested that local schoolteachers should be questioned under oath on whether they were or had ever been members of the organization.[63]

A common variant of guilt by association was guilt by kinship. Time and again Catholic officials were confronted with the real or imaginary activities and beliefs of members of their families. A captain in the provincial gendarmerie, to cite one example, was transferred out of the predominantly Catholic Fulda district in Hesse and relocated in a Protestant area because his Catholic wife, in the opinion of local authorities, was identified "with the fanatical wing of this confession."[64] Social rank and station, experience demonstrated, afforded no protection from such measures. Heinrich Johann Freiherr Droste zu Hülshoff, scion of a distinguished family of Westphalian nobility, was dismissed as *Landrat* in March 1874 because his wife signed a letter expressing sympathy for the bishop of Münster when his property was confiscated and auctioned off to pay the fines assessed against him.[65] Even high-born officials on the retired list came under scrutiny. When in 1876 the government learned that the wife of a retired *Landrat* and prominent Catholic aristocrat had visited the apparition site in Marpingen no fewer than three times, the ex-official was severely criticized for allowing his "household and family" to form "a local centre of ultramontane agitation and for the dissemination of belief in the so-called miraculous apparitions" of the Virgin Mary at the site.[66] Local authorities also expressed the hope that "Your Excellency will not close his eyes to the principle that it is the duty of a Royal Official, even one on the retired list, to oppose such conduct on the part of the family." To ensure the former *Landrat*'s cooperation in this matter, the government threatened to deport the family's foreign-born private chaplain.[67]

From the outset, the Kulturkampf's administrative purge was not designed solely to punish obvious dereliction of duty. Through transfers, dismissals, enforced retirements, and the like it also was used to deter potential critics, to intimidate, and to ensure conformity. Many Catholic officials, a number of whom had committed no offense, were therefore made to suffer. Others were cowed into silence. Still others, to the government's dismay, were confirmed in their determination to subvert the Kulturkampf.

≺ IV ≻

The Reaction of the Liberals

Against the Kulturkampf's rising tide of persecution, suspicion, and fear, and its implications for freedom in general, few non-Catholics raised their voices. Nowhere was the absence of protest more obvious than among the lower classes where anti-Catholicism sometimes sank into a mire of obsession and fantasy about Rome and its influence. Conspiracies were seen everywhere; even the death of Hermann von Balan, a Prussian diplomat, and more preposterous still, the death in the spring of 1874 of a popular lion in Berlin's municipal zoo were widely and mistakenly believed to have been caused by Jesuit agents.[68]

If the ignorant all too often displayed a tendency to give credence to every anti-Catholic rumor that came their way, other social classes held to a more informed antipathy established through inquiry into the beliefs and practices of the Roman Church and tested by experience. They were able to represent that church as an institution out of touch with modern society, its traditional beliefs undermined by science and overlaid by an hysterical piety and newly-invented superstitions, of which the apparitions in Marpingen were only the latest example. By portraying Catholics as concentrated in backward and peripheral rural areas, liberals also argued that this very backwardness and marginality contributed to national decadence and decay. No wonder that Rudolf Virchow, an eminent pathologist, prominent parliamentary deputy, and convinced liberal, as early as January 1873 coined the expression "Kulturkampf" and warned his colleagues in the Prussian parliament that what was at stake in this Church-state dispute was nothing less than civilization itself.[69]

However much liberals of all persuasions extended the range of freedoms in the private sphere,[70] reformed the educational curriculum, built new schools, or improved teacher training,[71] their credibility as reformers was seriously compromised by an anti-Catholicism that eroded the foundations of religious liberty and gave momentum to other disturbing political tendencies. They spawned a climate of hysteria and intimidation that undermined civil courage, stifled criticism, and encouraged acceptance of harsher sanctions against their Catholic fellow countrymen. Those countrymen, they implied, were an ignorant, bigoted mob, easily influenced by drink and demagoguery. Catholics demonstrating in 1874, "most with blank, stupid faces," as one liberal newspaper claimed, were made the worse for drink and reeled and staggered through the streets of Cologne in search of trouble. By warning "that the worst could be expected" if this mob ever got power into its hands, the reporter raised the specter of a complete collapse of law and order.[72] All too often, therefore, liberals expressed negative stereotypes, prejudices, and outright hatred.[73]

They also appealed to the use of force and acquiesced in religious persecution. Their newspapers called for the intervention of police and the army, even the stationing of troops on a permanent basis in potential sectarian flashpoints. So appalled was the *Saar- und Mosel-Zeitung* by the alleged events in Marpingen, that it called for military "occupation of the apparition site" even if it "has to go on for years."[74] Others found virtue in their ability to detect Catholic subversives before they could contravene Kulturkampf policy. The driving force behind the purge of the civil service in the Rhineland, for example, was the Deutscher Verein, an organization that probed Catholic influences in the provincial bureaucracy and advocated sterner measures against the Catholic populace.[75] Founded in 1874 by Heinrich von Sybel, a distinguished historian, prominent liberal, and notorious anti-Catholic, the Deutscher Verein boasted nearly 20,000 members, nearly all of whom were recruited from among the Rhineland's liberal intelligentsia.[76]

A few liberals, it is true, expressed unease at the state's coercive methods. Some, like the National Liberal leader Ludwig Bamberger, generally applauded the Kulturkampf in principle but admitted that specific pieces of repressive legislation like the anti-Jesuit bill violated their libertarian sensitivities.[77] Others, the left-liberal Eugen Richter for example, rejected coercion altogether as an instrument of policy. Liberals who advocated force, he warned, threatened to undermine their own position.[78] Foreign opinion shared these misgivings. English liberals, who otherwise expressed hostility toward the Roman Church and support for the Kulturkampf, nonetheless warned their German counterparts against the political peril of cooperation with the Prussian authoritarian state.[79]

A minority of Protestants also spoke out against the Kulturkampf. When the Kulturkampf began, it was easy for Protestants to argue that Catholics, by their religious beliefs and behavior, had alienated themselves from the dominant social milieu and had made themselves intolerable to the majority of their fellow countrymen. Never "in the past ten to fifteen years, but especially since the Vatican Council, has the gulf between the Catholic and Protestant churches been so large and the contrast between both confessions so . . . sharp," a senior Protestant official declared in March 1873. Despite the "outward appearance of peace, a silent and clandestine ongoing struggle" distinguishes the relationship between the two religious creeds. Complaints regarding insufficient "German patriotism" among Catholics have "spread within Protestant circles and animosity against the Catholic Church is very great," he added.[80]

As the Kulturkampf intensified, however, as more clergy and laity fell victim to the new coercive legislation, and as reports of Catholic suffering multiplied, only the most hardened and unremitting advocates of the Kulturkampf could close their eyes to the consequences.[81] Even Willibald Beyschlag, a well-known anti-Catholic theologian at the University of Halle, was shocked by what the Kulturkampf meant in practice. "Despite disapproval of clerical defiance" of the law, he admitted, "it nonetheless made a painful impression when I saw, on a visit to Trier in the spring of 1874, priests under arrest" being "escorted by policemen."[82] But if Beyschlag never wavered in his support of the Kulturkampf, other equally well-known Protestant churchmen were more sensitive to the fate of their Catholic neighbors. They realized, as many a modern government has also discovered, that the abrogation of constitutional rights in the interest of law enforcement carries with it the possibility of transforming lawbreakers from "criminals" into victims and even heroes in the eyes of citizens who sympathize with the motives, if not always the methods, of those arrested and punished.

A number of prominent Protestants, therefore, had no sympathy for the Kulturkampf, and some spoke out against the government's anti-Catholic campaign. "It is a bad thing when the state punishes actions that are considered as purely religious ones and as matters of conscience," wrote Christian Ernst Luthardt, another theologian. And it was especially bad, he added, when "the punishment loses the character of punishment in the eyes of the people and becomes its opposite." For it "hardly promotes the authority of the state and its sanctions when, in the eyes of the better class, even imprisonment begins to be regarded merely as a title to greater respect." For that reason, he concluded, the Bismarckian state "cannot conduct a war against a large part of its own population without causing, on all sides, profound injury of moral consciousness."[83]

Still other Protestant Church leaders expressed opposition to the Kulturkampf because the new ecclesiastical regulations proved as harmful to the Evangelical as to the Roman Church. An increasing number of Protestant clergymen began to feel, as a former minister of ecclesiastical affairs expressed it in the late spring of 1873, that the Kulturkampf and the "sword stroke of the law wounds the Evangelical Church as much as the Roman."[84] The new, more stringent ecclesiastical rules, especially the civil marriage laws and the legislation permitting formal withdrawal from church membership, in fact proved especially damaging to the Evangelical Church because they contributed to a sharp decline in the number of religious weddings and baptisms among Protestants. Ample statistics attested to this trend. By the late 1880s, according to contemporary estimates, 80 percent of Protestant marriages in Berlin were outside the Church and 40 percent of children went unbaptized.[85] No wonder that Rudolf Kögel, a prominent Protestant court chaplain and former Kultusministerium official, complained in 1879 that although "Rome was the target" of Bismarck's Kulturkampf legislation, it was "Wittenberg [that] was hit."[86]

≺ V ≻

Catholic Resistance

In the absence of substantial support from liberals and Protestants, the Church of Rome itself became the Kulturkampf's most uncompromising and effective opponent. Catholics, the Kulturkampf showed, could match governmental persecution with a program, with a church organization, and with a set of beliefs to sustain them during their ordeal and to encourage them in their resistance. That resistance ranged from press criticism of Germany's internal political arrangements or individual statesmen and politicians to systematic and coordinated countermeasures to frustrate the intent of the Kulturkampf's regulations.[87]

Catholic opposition found its most frequent expression, however, in spontaneous attacks on those individuals who directly or indirectly supported the Kulturkampf's new ecclesiastical legislation. In August 1872, during a demonstration protesting the expulsion of the Jesuit Order, an angry crowd in the industrial city of Essen attacked and ruined the home of a despised Freemason.[88] A mob in Münster nearly destroyed the house of a Protestant workman who had collaborated with the court to confiscate the bishop's furniture for subsequent auction and sale.[89] There were disorders in Cologne in March 1874 when bands of Catholics led by *Landtag* deputies from the Center party broke into houses to intimidate those nationalist youths who had the temerity to sing patriotic songs on the king's birthday.[90] But the full force of Catholic wrath was reserved for those who had defected from the Church of Rome's ranks. And no group was more despised than the Old Catholics. In Kühnau, a small town in Lower Silesia, popular dissent became so violent that a renegade priest was nearly assassinated.[91] Early in 1875 the son of a prominent Old Catholic was assaulted and stabbed in Lippstadt, a provincial town in Westphalia.[92] This spirit of lawlessness, turbulence, and even intolerance also manifested itself in March 1876 when Catholics disrupted the funeral procession and interfered with the interment rites for a deceased infant of Old Catholic parents in Gräfrath, a small community in the northern Rhineland.[93] With small variations, these scenes were repeated on scores of occasions as Catholics in both large cities and small towns reacted angrily to the Kulturkampf and to those opposed to their religious beliefs.

Catholic anger and resentment sometimes escalated to the point where it threatened the highest echelons of the government. Prussia's leaders endured constant anxiety about their personal safety, and few more so than Adalbert Falk, the minister of ecclesiastical affairs between 1872 and 1879, who received numerous Catholic threats against his life.[94] Bismarck's wife, Johanna, also admitted that "hate letters and newspaper clippings constantly arrived threatening my beloved's life."[95] The danger was genuine enough, as the most serious incident of this kind demonstrated on July 13, 1874. While heading for the mineral baths in Kissingen, a small town in northern Bavaria and the chancellor's favorite spa, Bismarck was himself the target of an assassination attempt.[96] His assailant was Eduard Kullmann, a 21-year-old Catholic butcher's apprentice. Although Bismarck was only wounded in the hand, the episode not unnaturally stunned the government, shocked public opinion, and gave rise to the fear that Kullmann was part of a broad Catholic conspiracy to murder Prussia's leaders.[97]

≺ VI ≻

A Catholic Contribution to Liberty

With this view of Catholicism and what appeared to be its propensity toward blind, chaotic violence, went the assumption that its absolutist and exclusionary doctrines automatically inclined its adherents to intolerance. In retrospect, of course, it is easy to sentimentalize the Kulturkampf's Catholic victims, to romanticize their opposition, and to criticize their liberal opponents.[98] Because German liberalism failed to sustain the authentically liberal values and standards of tolerance, some historians have been tempted to look elsewhere for a genuinely "liberal" movement that filled the vacuum in Prussian and imperial German politics.[99] These historians find that movement in Germany's Catholic Center party led by Ludwig Windthorst, Bismarck's most able and persistent parliamentary opponent. The Center party "supported every element of the liberal constitution to the fullest," runs this argument, from the democratic franchise to parliament's budgetary rights, from the immunity of deputies from arrest and persecution, to "the protection of the population against arbitrary treatment and exceptional legislation" like that of the Kulturkampf.[100] Windthorst and his coreligionists espoused religious freedom and comprehensive political reform (or said they did) because they themselves were the victims of Bismarck's repressive policies.

To characterize Catholic goals as liberal, however, is to obscure the hybrid and ambiguous character of Windthorst's policies and those of his coreligionists. Their object, the evidence suggests,[101] was to abrogate what they believed were unpopular laws and to prevent the encroachment of the Bismarckian state on the rights of the Catholic population and other minorities. Even where this aim required reforms typical of the traditional liberal program, Catholic goals were not to advance the cause of liberalism, but to obstruct Bismarck and to safeguard the Church's interests. To emphasize the former over the latter is to confuse methods with aims, effect with intent.[102]

Nowhere were Catholic goals more equivocal than in the issue of religious liberty and individual rights. Catholics themselves, events showed, did not always display the religious toleration they claimed was their due. Nor did they regularly respect the civil rights of their adversaries. Despite the experience of the Kulturkampf, Catholics were far from agreed that religious liberty was a good thing and many at one time or another succumbed to anti-Semitic prejudice[103] or acquiesced in the religious or political persecution of their fellow countrymen. That Catholics on the eve of the Kulturkampf in 1867 and again in 1871 advocated the incorporation of religious guarantees from the Prussian state constitution into the national or Reich constitution is sometimes seen as a progressive step. But Catholics, it is good to remember, neither pressed for freedom of religious expression or even association rights nor implied the right of the individual to choose his own religion, guided by his reason. They instead called for freedom of the legally-constituted mainstream churches, not freedom of conscience.

Few episodes did more to reinforce Catholicism's reputation for intolerance in fact than the so-called Braunsberg school conflict.[104] When in 1871 the church excommunicated Paul Wollmann,[105] a young priest and teacher at a secondary school in Braunsberg, East Prussia, because he opposed the new infallibility dogma, ecclesiastical sanctions ostracized him from the society of his former coreligionists. Those sanctions, the government said, not only injured Wollmann's social status, his civil liberties, and his ability to earn a living; they also clashed with the guarantees incorporated in the General Law Code—the *Allgemeines Landrecht* of 1794.[106] That the Roman Church could coerce German citizens on to the path of salvation undoubtedly shocked non-Catholic Germans, provoked a good deal of apprehension, and convinced them that the church was a temporal institution, a machine of government whose claims to authority in the secular sphere should be energetically reined in.

Reinforcing that conviction was the incontrovertible fact that some of the Catholic victims of the civil service purge had themselves been persecutors during the previous decade.[107] The Kulturkampf was not the first time that the Prussian government had initiated a sweeping inquiry into the loyalty of its officials. As a result of Catholic pressure during the constitutional conflict of 1862–64 in Prussia, for example, several Protestant clerks of liberal political sympathies in the Arnsberg local administration were reprimanded and temporarily demoted. August Heinrich Count Korff von Schmissing-Kerssenbrinck, the *Landrat* of Kreis Beckum in Westphalia who was among those purged during the Kulturkampf because of his ties to the Catholic Center party, to cite another case, had in 1863 threatened to oust village foremen and area magistrates for their liberal sympathies.[108] And another victim of the Kulturkampf's purges, *Landrat* Felix Joseph Freiherr von Lilien of Kreis Arnsberg in Westphalia, had himself been in the vanguard of those who in 1863 had ousted the liberal Arnsberg *Regierungspräsident* Friedrich Wilhelm von Spankeren.[109]

Only in retrospect, can one argue, did Catholic opposition to the Kulturkampf blunt Bismarck's authoritarianism and thus by indirection contribute to the idea of religious liberty and the creation of a civil society.

≺ VII ≻

Conclusion

If the message of Wiseman, Wallace, Sienkiewicz, and other novelists
so popular among Germany's Roman Catholics during the imperial
era had a common theme, it was that religious minorities had suffered calamitous persecutions in the past and that they had survived
them all. Although there can be no doubt that the Catholic experience during the Kulturkampf was dreadful and devastating, when
assessed in terms of its larger purpose—as a means to eradicate
Catholicism as a major factor in Germany's political life, to break
Catholic opposition to governmental policy, to forge a common
cultural unity across confessional lines, or to impose a Protestant
version of the German national identity on an unwilling Catholic
minority—the Kulturkampf was a failure and a disappointment to its
proponents. This failure was not the result of anticlerical scruple, reti-
cence, or lack of zeal among Germany's liberals; the Kulturkampf's
proponents were tireless in their politicking against the Church and
unrestrained in their promises of success.[110] It failed instead because
neither the administrative machinery of the Bismarckian state nor
its human cogs functioned reliably and effectively during the Kulturkampf, because the state's institutional and budgetary requirements
made difficult the formation of consistent policy, and because the
state was powerless to counter all forms of Catholic resistance and
to correct jurisdictional anomalies that allowed evasion of ecclesiastical laws to flourish.[111] But the Kulturkampf also failed because the
alliance arrayed against the Roman Church was never as seamless or
as potent as success required and because the Kulturkampf's goals
and aims restricted the kinds of coercion the government might employ against its Catholic opponents.[112]

Like most of his accomplices during the Kulturkampf, Bismarck
disliked the Roman Church, and his own experience with Polish
Catholics, intransigent clergy, and Center party politicians did little
to diminish his prejudice. But for all that, as the bishop of Mainz once
admitted, "Bismarck . . . was not a sectarian fanatic,"[113] and the Kulturkampf was not the result of religious conviction but of political
calculation.[114] "In his own way, Bismarck was a religious man who
sought the guidance of God in his administration of state affairs

(and usually, Ludwig Bamberger jeered, found the Deity agreeing with him)," concludes one assessment; "but he was singularly un-moved by confessional differences, and not at all by the . . . supersti-tious abhorrence of Rome" felt by so many of his pro-Kulturkampf supporters.[115]

Unlike his left liberal supporters, for example, Bismarck did not advocate the strict separation of church and state or claim that reli-gion was a private matter. Nor did he share left liberal hopes dur-ing the Kulturkampf that religion would atrophy and eventually dis-appear altogether. Like his National Liberal allies, on the other hand, Bismarck instead believed the slogan "separation of state and church" found no echo in the German historical experience. For centuries Ger-man religion was organized on the basis of the territorial church. "In the course of this long history," the historian Heinrich von Treitschke claimed in 1873, "Church and state have grown so close together that even today . . . a complete separation is no longer possible." "The *vol-untary system*" of religious affiliation or the notion of religion as a pri-vate matter "corresponds to a concept of state and Church that can never be ours," he continued. "Our Churches were never simple pri-vate associations, nor can they be in the foreseeable future; for us the state is not, as it is for the Americans, a coercive power that must be re-strained so that the will of the individual remains undisturbed." The German state instead is "a cultural power from which we [Germans] demand positive achievements in all areas of national life."[116] In keep-ing with this German tradition of *Staatskirchentum*, Bismarck in-stead preferred a new, heightened state authority over the churches and a more carefully regulated relationship between government and religion.[117] However disturbing the Kulturkampf's measures were to Pope Pius IX, German churchmen, and the faithful at large, it was never Bismarck's intention to destroy the Catholic Church as a reli-gious institution or to expunge all traces of its moral influence. His aims were restorative, not innovative. Throughout the Kulturkampf Bismarck's goal was the restoration of the Church-state relationship that had existed in 1840 before the concessions to the Roman religion made by King Friedrich Wilhelm IV.[118] Bismarck's desire to reduce the role of the Catholic Church in Prussian society to the lowest level compatible with the preservation of its legitimate religious function was in fact a concession that disappointed his liberal allies and imposed constraints on the coercive methods the state might employ during the Kulturkampf.

Without minimizing the indignities and sufferings inflicted on German and Prussian Catholics as a consequence of the Kulturkampf, we can recognize that the Hohenzollern kingdom neither employed wholesale violence and genuinely drastic remedies against its Catholic minority nor persecuted the Roman Church to extinction. Rather, Prussia's Catholics endured a decade and more of constant strain. By the end of the 1870s, when the Kulturkampf began to wane, more than half of Prussia's Catholic episcopate was either in exile or in prison, and nearly a quarter of all parishes were without pastors.[119] At least 1,800 priests were jailed or exiled.[120] The Kulturkampf also cost the Roman Church something like fifteen to sixteen million marks in state contributions.[121] The number of Prussia's monastic houses fell by one-third with the result that 40 to 45 percent of all conventuals, male and female alike, had to seek religious preferment elsewhere.[122] Less severe but painful nonetheless were the hardships that complicated the lives of ordinary Catholics. The dying did not always receive the last rites, burials sometimes became the focus of unseemly quarrels, and regularity of sacramental observance became increasingly difficult to maintain.[123]

As a Church-state conflict, of course, the Kulturkampf does not stand alone. Similar disputes, less well known and on a smaller scale, occurred in the southwest German grand duchy of Baden during the 1860s and in Austria and Spain during the 1870s.[124] Even Prussia itself was the scene of other Church-state conflicts during the nineteenth century. By modern standards, furthermore, Bismarck's methods and the Kulturkampf's sanctions fell short of those of later regimes in Germany and elsewhere. Bismarck's conduct in suppressing Prussia's religious orders and congregations, for example, was not inconsistent with French policy during the Third Republic. Somewhere between 9,000 and 10,000 monks, it has been calculated, were evicted from 261 houses in France during the 1880s.[125] The tally of deaths and injuries was also a good deal shorter in Prussia. When in 1871, to cite another important example of religious strife, New York City authorities confronted Irish Catholic demonstrators protesting an Orange Day parade, untrained militiamen opened fire, leaving more than 60 dead and 100 injured in a single day.[126] The harshness of this American response, with its sweeping appeal to military force, far exceeded the worst violence in the Kulturkampf. Throughout its duration, and in contrast to other social confrontations like strikes and work stoppages in Imperial Germany, not a single person appears to have lost his or her life as a consequence of police action or military repression.[127] Even when Prussian troops were furnished with live ammunition, as they invariably were, the wounds (none fatal) sustained by Catholic crowds came from bayonet thrusts and blows from rifle butts.[128] This is not to say that Prussia somehow embodied an authoritarian ideal which combined collective sternness with individual self-control. But it does imply that Prussian officials believed in the rule of law and rejected suggestions that it might be permissible to step outside its framework. While this preference for the judicial process and its profusion of rules and regulations obviously afforded no guarantees for religious liberty in the contemporary sense, its scrupulous regard for procedure, evidence, and proof nonetheless stood in the way of the Kulturkampf and its successful implementation.[129]

Liberty and the Catholic Church in Nineteenth-Century Europe

RAYMOND GREW

A MONG ALL THE social divisions of the nineteenth century, none was deeper nor more divisive than those defined in terms of religion. To most Roman Catholics, the fundamental aim of the French Revolution—and of most subsequent demands for constitutions or a free press—was to attack religion.[1] To most liberals, the Church's policies revealed it to be the enemy of political liberty and progress. Variously cast as a struggle between Church and state, religion and secularism, tradition and progress, authority and freedom, these battles—despite significant national differences, the changing cast of participants, and the diverse issues involved—were understood on all sides to be part of a larger historical clash at once ideological, political, institutional, and deeply personal. Historians know the picture to be still more complex. The Church was not monolithic, change not unidirectional. Although Catholicism and liberalism seemed two warring camps, there were many Catholic liberals. Despite the liberal commitment to freedom and tolerance, liberal policies often constricted both. The clergy saw themselves combating an age of irreligion or at best indifferentism; yet most nineteenth-century thinkers cared deeply about religion, a concern reflected in their writings and their personal religious crises. Most liberals, aside from some radical secularists, wanted liberty and religion to reinforce each other.

Nevertheless, after all the exceptions have been noted and the variations acknowledged, the fact remains that the contention was real, the distrust and bitterness not entirely misplaced. A Catholic Church struggling to meet what it understood as new challenges to religion and liberals struggling to overcome what seemed almost inexplicable resistance to benevolent progress generally found in each other a persistent and powerful opponent. That conflict constitutes a central theme of nineteenth-century European history. The incompatability between the Church and modern freedom was so widely asserted during conflicts so fiercely fought that a century later it remains difficult to step outside that framework. The effort to do so, however, makes it possible to begin to ponder how the expansion of political freedom affected the consolidation and growth of the modern Catholic Church and how the Church's active presence affected the history of freedom in Europe. Thus a statement that at first sounds like an oxymoron is instead an historical problem: What was Catholicism's role in the development of political liberty in nineteenth-century Europe? This chapter will attempt to outline an answer.

By emphasizing the effects of historical processes, the problem as posed slights much that is fundamental. It largely ignores Catholic theological and philosophical writings on the meaning of freedom, a complex discourse demanding a special erudition.[2] Some excuse for avoiding so difficult a topic may be found in the fact that nineteenth-century Catholic writers could not agree on what practices Christian first principles required, although nearly all conceded (indeed insisted) that liberty in and of itself could never be the primary concern. This chapter similarly turns attention away from liberal writings on religious liberty, important as they were. A partial justification for that lack may lie in the reality that most Catholics doubted the sincerity of the professions of freedom liberals so readily made and that the Church never accepted religious pluralism as desirable, even when welcoming the results. Also slighted is the difference between individual liberty and the freedom of corporate groups because, in their ordinary discussions and their polemics, both sides elided that distinction. To consider instead, as this chapter does, how Catholicism intersected with some of the larger historical changes of the nineteenth century is to emphasize social experience and to treat a question that contemporaries readily answered but rarely asked. They knew the direction of history, either that current trends were fundamentally wrong (and all but certain to end in some apocalypse) or else that history was destined to pass the Church by (and thus no matter how hard believers fought, their position could not hold). The combatants did not see their conflicts as a process of adaptation.

With a little historical distance, it becomes easier to outline what some of the major changes were in politics, society, and the Church itself and then to look at how those intersecting changes affected freedom. By the outbreak of World War I, European political systems were far more similar than they had been a century earlier. Representative assemblies with real power, universal male suffrage, a largely uncensored press, considerable freedom of assembly, and competing political parties were the general European norm. These changes had come about unevenly; and political freedom was nowhere unconstrained, never so full in practice even as formal law implied but rather directly and indirectly restricted in ways that differed in each nation. Nevertheless, the change in a hundred years was extraordinary and its overall direction clear.

Like the larger political trends, the great social changes of the century challenged religion with new threats and opportunities. The growth in wage labor, migration, and urbanization; increased expectations of the family and lengthening childhood; the greater importance of education and the greater need for systematic welfare policies; changes in standards of living, leisure, and associational life all required more people to make more decisions more self-consciously than ever before about such basic matters as whom to marry, where to live, what work to do, how many children to have, what social and political causes to support, and what to say, read, and believe. Given the rising penalties of poverty in a market economy, the widespread sense of economic and social uncertainty, the terrible price and real danger of economic failure, and all the famous inequities and injustices of the era, awareness of choice did not necessarily lead to increased freedom. But it did mean that crises—perhaps the century's favorite word—were simultaneously social, institutional, and moral. They not only affected the Church but raised issues on which Catholicism had more to say and with a clearer voice than it did on politics.

There were great changes in the Church as well, five of which will be mentioned here.[3] The triumph of ultramontanism was perhaps the most important. Increasingly bishops sought direction from Rome and gave the needs and views of the international Church priority over local customs and connections.[4] This change, despite resistance, continued through the century and was part of an institutional reform that increased papal authority and made Catholic practices (including liturgical ones) more uniform, the training of priests more rigorous, and episcopal control more severe. Ultramontanism meant more than organizational efficiency, however, for it was also emotional and intellectual. Obedience became one of the clergy's proudest badges, submission a sign of Grace. In that environment, individual liberty was an abstraction out of place. Perhaps never before had popes been so widely known to the faithful, so consistently seen as the embodiment of a Church under siege, and so loved as spiritual leaders. Intellectually, ultramontanism was part of the extraordinary vitality of Catholic thought and writing, most closely tied to that part of Catholicism that desired a church militant to combat and overcome the errors of the French Revolution and modern society.

The broader intellectual renaissance was a second trend. At various times throughout the century, and in every country, some of the most inventive, admired, and influential writers presented themselves as Catholic thinkers first of all—in an era when they and the Church's critics alike believed that modern thought in science, literature, and the arts ran counter to Catholic teaching. Indeed, the diverse and passionate creativity of Catholic intellectuals became a problem for an ultramontane Church fearful of the dangers of the age. It responded with official support for a campaign to impose neo-Thomist theology, often very formalistically and rigidly interpreted, throughout the Church. Of all the battles in which Catholics engaged, those within the clergy were the most searing, contributing to an atmosphere of tension and intolerance at odds with much of the Church's own traditions and making it more vulnerable than ever to charges of being out of place in the modern world.

Three other trends in Catholic life exposed the fissures within the Church while contributing to the vitality of Catholicism in social life: the extraordinary proliferation of religious orders, the vigorous assertion of Catholic belief by the faithful themselves, and the expansive use of propaganda. The new religious congregations, which were primarily female and dedicated to teaching and social work, engaged social life at an intimate level, amplifying but also sometimes misinterpreting and contradicting the policies of the secular clergy. The expressions of popular belief—in pilgrimages, apparitions, and public devotions—often challenged ecclesiastical control and were themselves a source of tension as well as vitality. Catholic propaganda, disseminated through organized missions and groups dedicated to the printing and distribution of pious literature, expanded in the national and local Catholic newspaper press prominent in every nation. The interpretation of daily events was attached to timeless truth in journalism, in political speeches, and in papal pronouncements that were more frequently made and more widely cited than ever before. Such committed volubility staked out (often conflicting) Catholic positions on every issue.

Together these developments in politics, Catholicism, and society made the interrelationship of religious belief, Catholic political attitudes, and the Church's connection to the state critical to the meaning and practice of liberty in every European country west of Russia (even England). Issues of Catholicism and liberty intersected at every level of society, in nearly every institution and in much public activity. The results for the history of freedom were neither predetermined nor clear cut. Leading Catholics were as diverse and contradictory in their responses to these encounters as were liberals, and there was thus little agreement as to what the Catholic Church demanded of liberty or what liberty required from the Church. There was not even agreement as to where such issues were critically joined, for on all sides claims about what was at stake were shaped more by the course of conflict (or accommodation) than by abstract principle. Almost any discord—over a sermon, the assignment of a priest, a school's curriculum, public dancing, a controversial book, the denial of religious burial—could produce pronouncements that made the issues seem fundamental. Yet millions of similar events took place without such clashes as neighbors, mayors, priests, merchants, politicians, and even intellectuals found modes of reconciliation in daily life. These more benign outcomes might offer useful precedents, but quiet practice proved less memorable than noisy clashes that could later be recalled as having been heroic and used to justify new outbursts of distrust.

As these experiences shaped what freedom would (and would not) mean, the Catholic Church was an engaged participant, institutionally active, socially creative, full of opinions noisily promulgated, and a source of immensely varied responses. The Church in turn was affected by the social developments of the era. Over the century, its parish organizations were strengthened and the laity given more active roles under tight clerical supervision;[5] lay associations and religious congregations created networks of Catholic activity, more interconnected among themselves than most other associations and movements of the time but similar in nature. The administration of the Church itself became more disciplined, centralized, bureaucratic, and hierarchical—rather like the national governments with which it so regularly clashed. Through all these changes, the relationship to liberty of this outspoken, combative, multiply engaged church remained ambiguous.

≺ I ≻

The Church in Opposition

From 1815 on, the Catholic Church was so closely associated with reactionary governments and ideological conservatism that such an alliance in retrospect seems almost inevitable, the natural result of revolution and restoration, a hierarchical institution, Catholic tradition, and resistance to modern change. Such assumptions are more easily questioned, however, when one recalls that the great Catholic intellectual revival in those years produced many who believed not only that the Church would benefit from political liberty but that Catholicism could be its agent. Felicité Lamennais's eloquent fervor had enormous influence in Italy, Germany, and England as well as France; and for a while prominent Catholic figures like Jean-Baptiste Lacordaire, Charles Montalembert, Félix Dupanloup, and the Cochins in France; Antonio Rosmini-Serbati, Vincenzo Gioberti, and Marco Minghetti in Italy; and Josef Eotvos in Hungary confidently imagined a future in which faith and freedom would grow together. Belgium was an important example of that possibility; and to Tocqueville at least so was Catholicism in the United States. "I think," he wrote, "that the Catholic religion has erroneously been regarded as the natural enemy of democracy."[6] Catholic Emancipation in England[7] and the brilliant Catholic writers who soon came to the fore there also often insisted that political liberty and Catholicism were natural allies, a view courageously sustained in noble prose by Lord Acton throughout his long life.

On Daniel O'Connell's death in 1847, his heart was carried to Rome, where a requiem mass for the Irish liberator was conducted by Father Gioacchino Ventura, who eulogized O'Connell for having united what the French Revolution had divided, "true religion and true liberty."[8] In those years, even in Rome, many shared Ventura's optimism; for although Metternich declared that a liberal pope was an impossibility, in 1846 scores of Italian leaders who knew Pius IX and his Church very well were joined by tens of thousands of Catholics, in Italy and beyond, in finding the prospect credible and exciting.[9] In France the short-lived Second Republic enjoyed relations with the Church as nearly trouble free as those of any French government of the nineteenth century. Three bishops, three vicars-general, two canons, and five *curés* were elected, along with Lacordaire, to the constituent assembly, although none of the clerics who ran as republicans was elected. Bishops blessed liberty trees and proclaimed across the nation that liberty, fraternity, and equality were biblical principles (as 50 years earlier in 1796 the future Pius VII had done when, as bishop of Imola, he welcomed the arriving French armies).[10]

This very association of political liberty with religion had its dangers, however; for the advocates of political freedom and social justice often considered some kind of spiritual renewal essential to their programs. That connection was the backbone of what in Italy had come to be called Jansenism, and it ran through a good deal of early nineteenth-century thinking. Acceptable in Manzoni, such concerns troubled the Vatican when they were introduced into the philosophical writings of Romagnosi, Rosmini, and Gioberti. In Abbé Lamennais they proved far too radical, theologically as well as politically, to be passed over in silence or met with merely indirect warnings. The pope hardly needed Metternich's warning that the "so-called religious liberty" Lamennais favored would lead to "civil anarchy" and not the "true liberty" of the Church.[11] Most of the hierarchy similarly found it hard to distinguish political from religious reform, a confusion that increased their opposition to both. Their fears could only be heightened by the attention to religion and its reform among writers outside the Church. Such themes were important in the writings of Giuseppe Mazzini, Auguste Comte, and many utopian socialists. In their programs, the Church could not recognize religion at all.

This conflation of politics and religion widened the gulf between partisans of political liberty, whether Catholic or not, and the Church's formal positions. Issues that advocates of increased political freedom considered to be matters of civil liberty were likely to be treated in Vatican pronouncements (and thousands of sermons) as questions of religious truth, which invited the colorful vocabulary of theological condemnation. Gregory XVI's denunciation of Lamennais's teachings in the encyclical *Mirari Vos* (1832) included opposition "to the unbridled lust for freedom," to a press at liberty to print whatever it liked, and to toleration that granted public acceptance of other religions. By 1850 Pius IX had no doubt that revolution and communism were major threats to religion and that the infiltration of liberal ideas would only lead to discord, the spirit of rebellion, and heresy.[12] Papal pronouncements became increasingly explicit in rejecting the very principles that even the most moderate liberals thought essential. With the Syllabus of Errors, which was attached to the encyclical *Quanta Cura* (1864), the papacy provocatively proclaimed it false to assert that the Church should reconcile itself to modern ideas of liberty and progress. If some of the hierarchy regretted the pugnacity, clearly most bishops, most of the clergy, and most of the Church's politically prominent supporters were more comfortable with such conservatism than with the uncertainty that change would bring.

The language of theological dispute in papal and episcopal pronouncements fell jarringly on the liberal ear. By eschewing the forms of civility so essential to bourgeois politics, the Church reinforced its alienation from modernity. No member of any European parliament would have been permitted the vibrant language of anathema that roared from pulpits, attributing arrogance, insolence, wilful ignorance, and cynical purpose to opponents while charging them with subverting religion. Even within parliament, Catholic deputies could luxuriate in divisiveness, proposing as a resolution to close a day's debate on the separation of church and state in France:

The Free Mason, Protestant, and Jewish majority of the Chamber of Deputies, not planning any further criminal attempt against the conscience of children, against the rights of the family, and contrary to the duties of the state toward registered believers, passes to the order of the day.[13]

Style, more clearly than principle, measured the chasm separating the Church from liberal politics and allowed each side to assert that it was only defending itself from the other's assault.

The often strident pronouncements, disheartening to the Catholic proponents of political liberty who were a principal target,[14] were also difficult to rebut. These statements were presented as not primarily political at all but rather the modest, if firm, declaration of what was required to preserve the faith and the Church itself in the modern era.[15] The Index of Forbidden Books, appalling to nineteenth-century progressive thinking, similarly sought primarily to proscribe doctrines the Church found theologically dangerous.[16] What secularists favored in the name of pluralism and liberals welcomed as toleration, the Church rejected, most absolutely and pervasively perhaps in Spanish Catholicism,[17] where such arguments were treated as akin to heresy, but elsewhere, too, where the gentlest reproach was to see them as at best lamentable instances of religious indifferentism.

All of this was part of a larger, coherent view of history that contrasted the present to an imagined age of universal piety and explained its demise as the result of seductive, bad ideas. These ideas had led to the French Revolution and made it an attack on religion; and it became a central assumption of much Catholic thinking that these dangerous, easily disseminated ideas were the logical consequence of the Reformation, the errors of the Enlightenment, and the teachings of Voltaire and Rousseau. That reading of history, as powerful a myth as that of Comte or Marx,[18] endowed clerical intransigence with an heroic aspect, reflected in Vatican fulminations against the received opinions of the age and in the confident courage of parish priests who marshalled their oratorical and institutional forces to combat irreligious literature and the temptations of the tavern.[19]

These rhetorical traditions and mythic histories fostered in turn a kind of political indifferentism. The Catholic Church declared itself as indifferent to forms of government as secular liberals were to distinctions of dogma. The Church "escapes as a result of its divine origins from social change, history, and the requirements of the age. It is thus politics itself which is radically not considered within the Catholic world, and that is so for explicitly religious reasons."[20] That indifference to politics, a kind of heresy to liberals, did not mean neutrality but freed Catholics to favor whatever regime or party appeared more likely to further the Church's immediate interests. Even while demanding the cooperation of political authorities, every bishop knew that government authorities served different interests and in that sense could not be trusted. The Catholic Church in Ireland may have differed from others in its confidence of popular support, but Irish bishops were hardly more hostile in relations with their Protestant rulers (who respected hierarchy and allowed considerable corporate autonomy) than bishops in Spain, Italy, and France were when faced with liberal governments.

For all his diplomatic tact, Leo XIII would continue to decry freedom of thinking and publishing as the "fountainhead of many evils" and to insist that it was "not lawful for the state . . . to hold in equal favor different kinds of religion" (*Immortale Dei*, 1885). However welcome the Church's favorable situation in the United States might be, the American system was not to be taken as a model; a Catholic state remained preferable.[21] Many French Catholics felt Leo went too far in urging acceptance of the Third Republic, but even as he favored accommodation to varied governments and acknowledged that the people might share in government, he did so by stressing the relative unimportance of political forms. Christian democracy was an acceptable term so long as it was sharply distinguished from Christian socialism, was used in a way "removing from it all political significance," and had nothing to do with parties or changes in administration or regime (*Graves de Communi*, 1901).

Thus the great nineteenth-century campaign for political liberty appeared to have little connection to Catholicism. Even Acton could repair the split only by starting from it:

There is a wide divergence, an irreconcilable disagreement, between the political notions of the modern world and that which is essentially the system of the Catholic Church. It manifests itself particularly in their contradictory views of liberty, and of the functions of the civil power. The Catholic notion, defining liberty not as the power of doing what we like, but the right of being able to do what we ought, denies that general interests can supersede individual rights.[22]

He then broadened the implications of what a Catholic politics might be. "A country entirely Protestant may have more Catholic elements in its government than one where the population is wholly Catholic." Even so, Acton could not find much guidance for his very English liberalism in his religion (and significantly, even that great moralist was slow to see the evils of slavery and did not share Montalembert's concern for the fate of American Indians). Acton found himself confronting papal positions that he could escape only by regretting that the Church so little understood its own history.[23]

Although the declaration of papal infallibility in 1871 had no necessary implication for Catholic political opinions or relations between Church and state, it was received as a sign of medieval intransigence by shocked liberals and concerned chancelleries across Europe. Catholicism and its critics had become highly sensitive to each other's symbols. Although the Vatican could find nothing to admire in freedom for false ideas and insufficient merit in representative government to warrant the sacrifice of other interests, Catholicism and liberalism were nevertheless close, as Acton saw, in their emphasis on individual conscience. They would draw together again and again in their opposition to socialism. The explicitly Catholic liberal economists, prominent and influential in Belgium and France in the first part of the century, never experienced the papal disfavor from which political liberals suffered; and in taking Locke's concept of private property to be a principle of natural law and Thomist doctrine, the Church achieved an accommodation to liberal economic principles it did not attempt with regard to liberal politics. If "by 1891 the official Catholic practice of invoking the authority of the past to legitimate virtually every current belief and practice had been ritualized,"[24] such accommodation to modern civilization stopped short of liberal politics.

Not all proponents of greater liberty shared the Church's distrust of the modern state, but many liberals did. As seen from the Vatican, no threat was more substantial than the enormous expansion in the functions and powers of the nineteenth-century state, a threat exemplified in the policies that followed the unification of Italy and Germany. Even when not antagonistic, Church and state were contesting many spheres of activity. And the Church, while decrying the modern state as a dangerous leviathan, grew more like it, more centralized internationally, more hierarchical and bureaucratic internally—giving bishops increased authority over parish priests, seminaries, and diocesan orders; moving the headquarters of religious orders to Rome; strengthening the authority of the pope and insisting on a uniform liturgy.

The Vatican's preferred mode of protection from the state was to negotiate concordats with it, detailed agreements between sovereign entities that resolved specific conflicts, recognized Catholic sees and congregations, and variously offered some compensation for confiscations of Church property, some guarantees of the Church's autonomous authority in its own affairs, some protection of its role in education, and where possible some assurance that regulations on such matters as marriage would follow Catholic requirements. Agreements made with the governments restored in 1815, after Napoleon's defeat, granted the Church better terms than it had been able to win from him in 1801; concordats were signed with the new republics of Latin America, then with the Netherlands in 1827, Spain in 1851 and 1886, and Austria in 1855. Such agreements were of course attacked by liberals and anticlericals, who considered them instruments of authoritarianism. Concordats, however, were often impossible; and no agreement could regulate all the issues, big and little, in which the interests of Church and state now intersected.

In the course of the century, Church officials, from the Vatican to parish priests, and their lay supporters at every level mastered techniques of attack, resistance, and counterattack. In opposing the tax that supported the Anglican church, Bishop Doyle of Kildare and Leigh urged Irish peasants to "let your hatred of the tithe be as lasting as your love of justice."[25] Indeed, the Church readily spoke the language of liberty when battling proposals that limited the independence of religious orders or episcopal control over congregations and seminaries, a source of conflict even under France's restoration monarchs and the center of bitter conflict in newly united Germany. Catholics also often sounded liberal themes when criticizing an increasingly intrusive state eager to assume functions once largely in Church hands. Sermons and Catholic papers listed examples of the disadvantages that followed from the loss of ecclesiastical control over civil registers and from the substitution of tax-supported welfare services for charity.

But it was public education, the epitome of modern progress, that most often drew the Church, and Catholics more generally, into contemporary politics. The Church viewed teaching as one of its inherent functions and had since the Council of Trent formally advocated the establishment of parish schools. The nineteenth-century demand for universal schooling, however, required more money and teachers and buildings than the Church could provide, even with the great increase in teaching orders. When after the revolution of 1848 Adolphe Thiers proposed that France's elementary schools be run by the Brothers of Christian Doctrine, they demurred, recognizing the task as more than they could handle. If schooling was to be universal and if only the state had the resources to provide it, then Catholics had to accept something less than Church control of all instruction. There were two paths of tacit compromise, and Catholics followed both. One was to work with the state (and maintain steady pressure on its officials) for clerical oversight of public instruction and for the employment, wherever there was a Catholic population, of teaching orders or pious lay teachers. The other was to insist on the right to operate Catholic schools independent of state supervision. The first course engaged Catholics in thousands of minor debates about freedom, for it required perpetual accommodation to local political and social realities, eroding a more consistent and intransigent Catholic position. The second led the Church to defend the existence of a religious sphere over which the state had few rights, but that implied the existence of another, public, sphere and one that was expanding and increasingly secular.

In practice most countries needed the resources of both Church and state to establish the pattern of schooling that eventually evolved into a public system of largely lay schools. Thus the great conflicts over schooling, most extended in France,[26] dramatic in Germany, sporadic and angry in Spain and Austria, were much more than anticlerical attacks on Catholic obscurantism or Catholic denunciations of atheist aggression, although such language was often used. In practice the issues varied—from the use of clerical teachers to clerical presence on school boards, from teaching the catechism in public schools to the right of Catholics to maintain independent schools. Broadly speaking, the sequence in which conflicts arose suggests a decline in the institutional church's influence over the state. Issues of clerical control were followed by questions about a Catholic presence in school, and then the rights of Catholics to have religious instruction. These disputes continued at many levels throughout the century precisely because they involved innumerable compromises in daily affairs and personal lives that were difficult to justify in abstract principles.

The extent and duration of such conflicts between the Church and secular authorities, and their tendency to boil up at any moment (over public ceremonies, prayers for the current regime, the appointments of bishops, or clerical declarations thought to have been political), taught Catholics to perceive, and organize around, communal interests. Catholics learned, in short, to become a political force. When such tensions subsided, the Catholic parties that had been nurtured on conflict with the state were likely to seek from it the sorts of assurances that concordats had provided. They could do so (in Belgium, Germany, and Austria, for example) as parties now essential to a governing majority—a not inconsiderable benefit of parliamentary politics.

Similarly, Church authorities, when denied their claims to a privileged relationship with the state, turned to the language of liberty to argue for autonomy in ecclesiastical affairs. In conflicts over schooling, they cited the rights of fathers to decide how their children should be educated (an argument with remarkable implications of pluralism). Through such habits of contestation (local and regional as well as national and provoked not just by great pieces of legislation but also by issues that could be petty, personal, or largely symbolic) the Catholic Church became one of the century's most effective sources of resistance to the growing power of the state. If the expansion of political liberties resulted from a series of practical compromises, the Church played an important role in that outcome, supplementing what had earlier begun as a classic liberal campaign. By the second half of the century in much of Europe, the outspoken Catholics had replaced liberals as the principal critics of the state, especially where the thrust of liberalism was blunted by rising nationalism or fear of working-class movements emerging on the left. In response to this powerful Catholic criticism, the state increasingly proclaimed its neutrality. Catholics responded by arguing that the state was not truly neutral or not neutral enough and by insisting on their religious liberty to preach and practice their beliefs and organize their activities without interference from government. Not only were these liberal arguments, they furthered the very process of secularization—of the state and of large parts of social activity—that the Church lamented.

≺ II ≻

Catholics and the Expanded Meanings of Freedom

The meaning of freedom expanded in the course of the nineteenth century. Arguments for constitutions and representative government became demands for universal suffrage, a free press, and labor's right to organize. The case for political freedom opened into arguments about social justice. Nor was this expansion merely a matter of ideas. The practice of freedom brought new forms of participation that affected the lives of millions of people, recruiting them to sign petitions, march in demonstrations, and join associations. In all of this, including the new techniques these forms of participation required, Catholics were active leaders.

Throughout the century, there were Catholic intellectuals who argued that Catholicism provided a foundation for political liberty and welcomed it, that liberty was beneficial for religion, and that liberal Catholicism was not just another political party but a broad and positive engagement with modern society. Such views seemed at times, in Belgium and in the *Raillement* in France, for example, close to the official position of the Church; and figures like Lamennais, Montalembert, Newman, Acton, Ketteler, Manzoni, and Fogazzaro, all of whom knew the icy power of Vatican disfavor, had a lasting impact both on Catholic thought and public life. Never really triumphant, liberal Catholicism refused to die but remained an inspiration and comfort to many thoughtful Catholics who found reason for hope in the modern world. Henri Wallon was best known for his pious biography of Joan of Arc, but it was his amendment that established the Third Republic. Efforts to build liberal Catholicism into active political movements, however, ran into trouble in Spain, Germany, Italy, and France.[27] Viewed with suspicion by the hierarchy and many Catholic conservatives, none of these movements had the success or longevity of Germany's Center party, unattached to liberalism and not officially Catholic, which benefited from the weakness of liberal alternatives. Liberal Catholicism nevertheless remained a kind of possibility, tempting to secular and Catholic liberals alike, that helped domesticate representative government within the Catholic world and soften liberal attacks on the Church.

Catholics joined more confidently in the growing recognition that representative government and specific civil rights were not enough to assure freedom for all. At least from the 1830s on, discussions of freedom always encountered what contemporaries called the social question, discussions in which Catholic concerns were pervasive. Utopian socialists denounced the Church's ties to reactionary politics but called upon Christian ideas of justice;[28] Catholic pulpits rang with fulminations against the materialism and avarice of unfettered capitalism and its disruptive effects on the family and on communal ties. A great deal of what the middle classes reluctantly learned about the realities of working-class life came from the inves-

tigations of Catholics like Frédéric Le Play; the campaigns of lay organizations like the St. Vincent de Paul Society, which required its
prosperous members to visit the poor; and the well-publicized work
of new religious orders like the Society of St. Francis de Sales founded
in Piedmont. Catholic writers, with their nostalgia for guilds, fixed
prices, and just wages, joined the clergy in moralistic prescriptions
that were more effective in describing alternatives to a market
economy than creating feasible solutions; but they struck chords
that resonated deeply among the people and had considerable impact
on European political and social theory.[29] The economic doctrines of
Giuseppe Toniolo, Wilhelm Ketteler, and Albert de Mun, incorporated in *Rerum Novarum* (1891), sought a balance between the rights
of private property and social justice for the worker that legitimated
Catholic social activity and trade unions.[30]

This Catholic engagement with social issues is usually treated in
terms of its failures and the more effective movements to which it
later led. Timid and paternalistic, social Catholicism failed to win
significant working-class support, and its more radical and imaginative offshoots were perpetually in trouble with the hierarchy. In
the twentieth century these social concerns would be absorbed into
the great Christian democratic parties, along with their commitment to the protection of property, capital, and the established order.
In the nineteenth century, however, Catholic support for factory legislation, workers' housing, social insurance, and family allowances
made a specific if delimited contribution to modern conceptions of
the requirements of freedom, much as the Church offered a powerful
moral critique of capitalism that easily swept beyond its own teachings. Laws banning work on Sunday may not have offered the social
panacea that preachers claimed; but in making their case, they defined leisure as a right and not only denounced the inhumane treatment of workers but established that the selfishness, love of luxury,
and materialism of employers were both a source of the problem and
a characteristic of modern capitalism. In Catholic societies when
socialists preached that political liberty was inadequate or even illusory without social justice, that agnosticism about political forms
and skepticism about the value of liberal legalism were already
familiar.

If ideology and institutional interests inhibited Catholic engagement with expanding conceptions of freedom in politics and social

issues, the restraints were much weaker when it came to Catholicism's role in the extraordinary, even precocious, recognition of the importance of public opinion in modern society. Programs for disseminating pious literature and reconquering populations considered dechristianized had flourished from the end of the Napoleonic wars. Rooted in religious purpose, they quickly became lessons in political mobilization. The campaigns of preaching, mass confessions, and rededication that swept across the countryside in restoration France included legitimist inscriptions on the crosses planted in town squares and hymns to the Bourbon saviors of the faith. The collection of money for the pope, known in England as Peter's Pence, was an international call to support for a papacy under siege; and it became an annual demonstration in Catholic countries on a scale few other causes could match.[31] The great lesson of the Kulturkampf,[32] was that the loyalty of the faithful properly mobilized could eventually force even the Protestant Iron Chancellor to bend. Such famous protest movements were genuine expressions of communal faith, ones that gained passion and purpose from a sense that the Church was under siege and from attachment to the figure of the pope; but they also reflected a change in the Church itself: "Having once based itself on the state, Rome now sought to further its interests through society."[33]

Catholics also showed a particular talent for the modern journalism they so often decried. In France the legitimist and Catholic provincial press, which gradually became more Catholic and somewhat less legitimist after 1830, maintained a network of ties across the nation that no other political faction could match. Louis Veuillot made his paper *l'Univers* an even more influential international model for a new kind of Catholic journalism. Its witty and vitriolic polemics entertained rural clergy and pious laity alike, enlisting them in a perpetual battle against the evils of the age. Its ultramontanism fiercer and more rigid even than Rome's, it excoriated moderate bishops as compromisers; and its skillful populism won it remarkable influence in Church and politics. In England *The Rambler* and *Tablet*, which did not aspire to so broad an audience, displayed a marked talent for effective disputation. In Bavaria the Catholic press kept up a steady commentary, not just on local issues that affected the Church but on its battles across Europe. When *Civiltà Cattolica* was founded to provide the Vatican with a vehicle for comment on the issues of the day, many expected that it would publish in Latin; instead, Italian was chosen as more suitable to lively comment on current affairs and more likely to gain a large audience. Recognizing the power of public opinion, the Church sought to mobilize it in its own defense, especially against Risorgimento liberalism.

Nearly everywhere this vigorous Catholic press was an outspoken critic of liberal and secular trends. If many of these papers continued in a conservative tradition, like *l'Armonia* in Turin, many of the newer Catholic papers adopted the overheated rhetoric of Veuillot. As northern Italian provinces became part of Italy, new Catholic papers in city after city lampooned ministerial mistakes and used taxes, crime, or unpaved streets to denounce those now in power as the enemies of religion. In Spain an aggressive Catholic press broadcast every governmental affront, while simultaneously helping to nudge the Church from its Carlist associations and to draw Catholics into ordinary national politics.[34] Later in the century, the Assumptionists pioneered a sensationalism that included anti-Semitism and gave *La Croix* an appeal comparable to the yellow press developing in England and the United States. In Germany and Italy beleaguered governments lumped Catholic newspapers along with socialist ones as threats to public order—for the Catholic press shared with radicals the capacity to transform specific incidents in the daily news into dramatic, concrete examples of dangerous historical trends that exposed the erroneous foundations of contemporary society. Effective propaganda, mass demonstrations, and above all the ability to reach ordinary people (even in rural villages) were important in the democratization of European public life; and Catholics were among the pioneers of that development.

Freedom of association was also central to nineteenth-century conceptions of liberty, and associations were heralded as agents of progress and a means for creating that civic culture essential to a responsive and orderly society. A burgeoning associational life was everywhere a source of pride. Yet efforts to restrict religious orders occurred in nearly every continental state, from Spain and Portugal early in the century to Austria at its end. Needing special justification wherever the state laid claim to liberal principles, such restrictions were awkwardly supported with arguments (not unlike those often used against trade unions) that Catholic orders were not really voluntary and hid secret purposes. In the face of such charges, Catholics became adept defenders of the liberty of association, even while bishops and the Vatican extended their claims to control Catholic associations. The hierarchy was hesitant before the risks inherent in lay organizations, insisting through most of the century that they have clerical direction; but the growth of lay associations, like the extraordinary growth of religious orders devoted to social service, was impressive evidence not merely of the continued vitality of the Church but of its social role.

For the history of European liberty, Catholic associations had special importance. Through them, and the need to defend them, Catholics acted as a powerful pressure group for associational freedom. Like the members of O'Connell's Catholic Association in Ireland in the 1820s, they also enthusiastically took part in broadening the exercise of that freedom. At first authorized for specific purposes, primarily devotional or charitable, Catholic associations came to undertake much more. Like those that represented peasant interests in Brittany, Bavaria, and the Veneto, they blurred through their varied activities the distinctions fearful governments sought to establish between political, economic, regional, and religious associations— helping to establish that freedom must apply to all.

The associational life that expanded freedom in secular society also furthered freedom through its impact on Catholics. In country after country their choral societies, sports clubs, cooperatives, and youth groups proclaimed the right of Catholics to enjoy the benefits of increased leisure and common interests, in short to share in civil culture, while preserving their special sense of religious community. Catholic associations, often defensive imitations of socialist and laic organizations, were designed to protect the faithful from bad influences and to reassure them that religious faith did not require sacrificing the respectable recreations and pleasures others enjoyed. In practice, they brought Catholics, as Catholics, into modern social and public life. While outsiders resented their exclusiveness and the prominence of priests within them, always suspecting a political purpose (not entirely unfairly, for Catholic associations did regularly remind their members of Catholic political interests), such associations also taught Catholic citizens some of the practical procedures of public affairs. The Catholic laity, male and female, learned about organized cooperation, the conduct of orderly meetings, and the dignity of holding office; priests learned how to encourage political participation at a time when civic life required just such skills.

In the latter part of the century these organizations expanded still further, especially in the form of movements for social action and associations aimed at the young, like the *Association Catholique de la Jeunesse Française*, the *Volksverein*, the *Opera dei Congressi*, and *Gioventù Cattolica Italiana*. Many of these ventures were reined in (and often declined as a result) under the suspicious attention of a nervous hierarchy uncomfortable with lay initiatives and eager not to risk worse relations with political authorities. For all that, they contributed renewed vigor to Catholic life, constituted important pressure for a greater openness within the Church, and demonstrated both the benefits of liberty to religion and the consonance of Catholicism with civic life.

While contributing to society's expanded experience of freedom, Catholics were themselves drawn into a changing society. As masters of mobilization and propaganda, they brought significant advantages to mass politics. The possibility had been there since the French Revolution, visible and not a little frightening in the anti-Jacobin massacres in Naples and the guerrilla warfare against Napoleon and later the Carlist wars in Spain. No early example was more impressive than O'Connell's achievement in Ireland, where "mass politics was, in fact, created by him in order to realize the power and to mask the poverty and ignorance of his constituency."[35] Later in the century Catholic political participation no longer came primarily in protests or anti-governmental campaigns but through more stable parties, likely to become the backbone of cautious governments and destined to become the principal opponents of the socialists. Catholic political participation, which had seemed all but unique to Belgium, developed in Germany through the Center party, became the goal of French Catholics who hoped for a Catholic republic,[36] led to the idea of a Catholic Association that could be active in Spanish national (liberal) politics, and emerged in Italy with Pius X's cautious support for Catholic action and removal of the ban against voting in Italian national elections. The Church's relationship to political liberty had come to be very differently conceived when the pope could urge Catholics to join in altering society because they, too, should take advantage of "social science, the institutions of the times, and those rights of citizenship which modern constitutions offer to all" (Il Fermo Proposito, June 11, 1905).

≺ III ≻

Catholics and Daily Life

As Catholics shared in the great changes taking place in nineteenth-century society, they responded in ways related to their beliefs and concerns. Expressions of popular piety and the creation of Catholic subcultures reflected (and created) distinctively Catholic experiences, but so did ambivalent Catholic attitudes toward the appeal of nationalism and the rising consciousness of what was called the woman question. In each of these responses, ordinary social life and general attitudes combined with religion in ways that proved powerful at particular moments of contestation and over specific issues. In each, groups of Catholics moved beyond the official positions of the Church; and all of these movements, which raised issues of freedom and divided Catholics, affected both daily life and society at large.

The vitality of nineteenth-century religious life came less from leaders than from the faithful, for whom piety was related to births and marriage and death, infertility and illness, crop failures and good fortune, family and kin and community. It was primarily through these concerns that they related their faith to their understanding of the changes they observed and the news they heard of revolutions and kings and presidents, of urban opportunities and moral dangers. This sense of connectedness was expressed in their prayers and devotions, the ceremonies they attended, the amulets and medals they treasured. The clergy, committed to fostering a faith theologically informed and cleansed of superstition, often found the fervor awkward and embarrassing. They were trying to teach their parishoners not to expect the ringing of church bells to protect the fields from damaging hail storms nor to seek in local grottoes a guarantee of fertility; yet they could not remain unmoved by such demonstrations of faith, deny their own respect for miracles, nor in many cases resist popular, and in essence democratic, pressure. There was, after all, an important kind of personal freedom to be experienced in apparitions, devotions, and pilgrimages—experiences beyond the regulation of state, school, or officialdom and outside the ordinary realm of harsh necessity. Popular piety had special significance for and presented a particular challenge to believers in a hierarchical church.

Recently, historians have come to underscore the importance, for the history of religion as well as social history, of these widespread demonstrations that were expressions of popular religion and deeply held conceptions of the world. They were also protests against unresponsive officialdom, as in the tragedy of the Great Famine in Ireland, and more generally against external pressures from the marketplace and, especially, from a secular state.[37] It was the people who defeated the skeptical medical officers at Lourdes, the stony-faced soldiers at Marpingen, and the makers of inventories following the separation of church and state in France. Martyrologies enjoyed great popularity among nineteenth-century Catholics, combining the appeal of romanticism with lessons of immediate relevance in encouraging Catholic resistance. Radical, socialist, and labor movements have received more scholarly attention; and it is easier to weigh their importance because of their clearer goals, their belief that history was on their side, and their eagerness to bring about the future through agitation. Catholic demonstrations and Catholic resistance, in contrast, were usually responses to immediate affronts and appeared sporadic, however recurrent. Yet the number of citizens who took part in pilgrimages and public protests on issues touching religion was at least as great as the number who went on strike or marched on May Day, and local politicians rarely forgot their potential power.

Faced with the probability that peasants were unlikely to vote for them, liberals, many democrats, and (until the end of the century) socialists feared and often exaggerated clerical influence over peasants and women. This Catholic capacity to mobilize local loyalties was not simply at the beck and call of the clergy, but Catholicism was likely to be involved when mobilization occurred in strongly Catholic areas. There, the existing networks, the subcultural sense of a community at odds with the larger society around it, and traditions of resisting the state tended to come together, providing disaffected groups with the infrastructure necessary for political organization, a dignity of purpose, available leaders, an appeal across class lines, and often a fervor that few other non-elite groups could match. The effects were felt on more than religious issues. These advantages, for example, made the Church a crucial element in the enduring regionalism of Brittany, the Basque provinces of Spain, Bavaria, the Veneto.

Much in nineteenth-century society encouraged sharp distinctions between what is political and what is not, a religious sphere and a secular one, individual rights and social responsibility. Most ordinary citizens probably made no such distinctions in their daily lives, and Catholics especially preferred seeing society whole as a web of relationships with religion at the center. Catholic devotional life had always woven the rituals of daily life and markers of the life cycle into larger connections of family, occupation, politics, and the ultimate meanings of Christian theology. In the nineteenth century, however, the renewed vigor of devotional life in its lay elaborations brought something new: the creation of a subculture in which distinctiveness from the larger society was a source of strength[38] and comfort. Devotional demands were greater and more frequent, and the coherence religion gave to individual lives was extended to the cohesiveness that Church-sponsored organizations and activity could give to a whole community, cutting across differences of gender, age, occupation, and wealth.

In organizing and promulgating more demanding expressions of belief, the Church was in effect raising the standards of conduct expected of believers. Ordinary, relaxed observance, generalized respect, and affection for religion only occasionally accompanied by anguish or passion seemed in contrast to be—and was often denounced as—secularism. An integrated subculture provided the harmonious vision of a social life in which every secular activity would be linked to religion. Within Catholic subcultures, criticisms of the era for its materialism, alienating individualism, and decadent permissiveness had a resonance that fueled arguments about the meaning and value of personal and political freedom.

Others might think that the increased choices people had in life meant greater freedom, but the clergy from top to bottom saw instead temptations to error and sin. Among the rural clergy, resistance to new styles of behavior was often expressed in outraged shock that associated theater and state schools with taverns, blasphemy, criticism of clerical fees, and anticlericalism.[39] Catholic subcultures sought to go beyond verbal criticism to institutionalize opposition to secular society. Important effects followed. Integralist arguments justified (and to the most uncompromising therefore demanded) explicitly religious stands on almost every public issue, thereby dividing Catholics and increasing the range of conflicts with others and with the state. To support Catholic subcultures in public debate was to inflame ideological conflicts by defending a conception of society that to outsiders, including many Catholics, appeared rigid, priest-ridden, intolerant, and obtrusive.

As conflicts unfolded, the Church felt it necessary to defend the search for an organized, wholly Catholic way of life against less integral expressions of Catholic belief as well as against secularists and the state. In doing so, Catholics invoked religious freedom, but there was an unintended dynamic in such claims. The Church could hardly accept that Catholicism itself should have the status of a subculture; yet insistence that it must remain independent of all external demands, including those of the state, meant redrawing the boundaries between the religious and the secular, making Catholicism an agent of that secularization it condemned. Both the arguments and the religious practice of those reluctant to recognize any realm of society indifferent to religion had the effect of forcing governments and politicians to define with excruciating clarity what they required of and permitted to their citizens, what in short they meant by freedom.

Toward nationalism, the position of the Catholic Church might have been expected to be clear and free of contradiction. The Vatican never lost sight of nationalism's inherent dangers, including its tendency to reliance on force, hatred of foreigners, and excessive admiration for the state. Nationalist revolutions were consistently opposed, even in Poland, although Catholic loyalties were at the core of nationalism there. From Rome, especially, nationalism was seen as a dangerous source of international instability and a stimulus to revolution. Experience in Italy literally drove the point home, and most of the citations in Pius IX's syllabus of errors were taken from his earlier denunciations of Piedmontese policies and the Risorgimento's threat to the temporal power.

Nevertheless, the victories of the Risorgimento were celebrated with Te Deums, and Catholicism never lost its place as part of Italian national identity.[40] There were German Catholics, too, who felt little conflict in rejoicing at German unification and taking pride in German might, even at the price of being ruled by Prussian Protestants.

In practice, then, Catholicism thrived quite consonantly with nationalism which, like regionalism, appealed to a Catholic sense of community. Members of Spain's hierarchy readily cited that nation's special dedication to the Catholic Church as they urged the state to keep its ban on the public worship of other faiths and protested every assault on the Church's privileges in the name of patriotism as well as religion.[41] Catholics were leading nationalists in Poland, Slovakia, and Croatia; Catholic nationalism became a call to arms in Belgium, Switzerland, and the Tyrol. In Ireland arguments for and against organized resistance had Catholic support, and the hierarchy did not hide its disagreement with papal policies that too readily acknowledged the British as the established authorities.[42] At Maynooth, the rigorist theology taught to young Irish priests combined quite easily with intense patriotism.[43]

In Catholic lands, this sympathy for and accommodation to nationalism tended to favor certain expressions of it over others. Where military officers were likely to be from the aristocracy and among the Church's most reliable supporters, Catholics gladly noted that priests and soldiers shared an appreciation of order, discipline, and hierarchy. Often under attack and often accused of foreign loyalties, Catholics were quick to insist, in France and Spain and Belgium as well as Germany and Italy, that their youth groups and their schools inculcated the virtues essential to military strength and patriotic loyalty. Catholic apologists in France emphasized that Catholic schools produced the best soldiers and eagerly declared defeat in the Franco-Prussian war to have been a public lesson on the penalties for abandoning religion. In the following years, Catholics contributed significantly to that nationalism of the political right that rose to compete with an older nationalism loyal to the Revolution and the republic. This conservative and Catholic nationalism embraced anti-Semitism in the years of the Dreyfus affair.

Although generally opposed to the expansive claims of the national state, the Church eagerly embraced its role in official ceremonies, interpreting its public presence to be, like the appointment of chaplains in armies, prisons, and hospitals, an acknowledgment of its importance. Catholics were especially drawn to nationalism when it promised to strengthen community, emphasized the value of social order, and extolled personal honor, discipline, and sacrifice. Then Catholics, like nationalists, could accept ambiguity about how far freedom and toleration should extend so long as the position of the

Church was assured. A target of some nationalisms, Catholicism selectively contributed to others—paradoxically, ones that emphasized the military and favored a strong state. Here, too, Catholics took part in shaping society, despite distaste for much of the result.

The growing nineteenth-century tendency to consider women a special category for social and religious concern produced within Catholicism ambivalence, internal divisions, and paradoxical results as great as those that accompanied increased popular piety and nationalism. When the talk was of change, the clergy generally asserted, of course, that no change was needed, that the proper model was well in place. In defining that model—which they did at length from pulpits, in schools, and in print—they shared and reinforced the century's emphasis on family and child rearing and on motherhood as the font of morality in the home. Catholic social theorists like Louis de Bonald and Le Play had reinforced such points in theory and field work; and every Catholic social agency, lay and religious, frequently reported examples of the frugal wife who saved her husband from drink and the pious mother who against all odds raised her children to be honest, hardworking, and respectful of authority.

In this emphasis on the moral authority of the wife and mother, the Church reinforced a theme dear to the nineteenth-century bourgeoisie. It came especially easily to Catholics for whom it was related to established teachings and associated with devotion to Mary; it represented nevertheless the warm embrace of a potentially awkward social change, which was facilitated by calling it traditional. Among Catholics this admiration of the woman's role in the family gained in credibility and political appeal from the strength of female piety. The feminization of religion was one of the phenomena of the century. It was women who filled the pews, were most publicly devout, and thronged to join the new religious congregations. Essential to popular religious practices and the activities of Catholic subcultures, they were crucial to clerical success in coopting both. Women's closeness to their priests, which worried anticlerical writers and perhaps many males more generally, would in Catholic countries become a major reason for denying women's suffrage. Even some Catholics criticized excessive priestly influence as an objectionable intrusion in family life, and many in the laity held contrasting views on celibacy, marital sexuality, contraception, and mixed marriage that made those issues a further source of conflict and may well have driven males from confession and attendance at church.[44] All that may have contributed to the feminization of religion, but there is no simple explanation for this striking phenomenon. It may also have had to do with creating an equilibrium in the family. With families dependent upon cash and men the family's principal source of income, women's greater closeness to religion strengthened their authority in the family. Where women, too, needed to work for pay, religion asserted the continued centrality of their family role. Although civic life was constructed as a largely male sphere, women could find an alternative sphere and some significant autonomy from their husbands through their activities in the Church.

On the whole, the Church regretted women's working outside the home, discouraged talk of women's careers, and argued that limited formal instruction should suffice for most. Nevertheless, Catholic schools, recognizing economic needs, systematically taught girls the crafts (mostly but not entirely traditional ones) by which they might earn a living by sewing, making lace, weaving rope, decorating hats, or painting china. As to careers for women, the Church provided the most visible role models, especially in the newer orders devoted to service; and the training of nuns became in turn more professional. Most girls in Catholic countries received elementary instruction from nuns, and for most of the century nearly all who attended a girls' secondary school or a teachers' college attended a Catholic one. The principal respectable careers that opened to (usually lower middle-class) lay women were those their religious sisters had pioneered: teaching, nursing, and social work (and significantly, celibacy often continued to be thought a requisite for the successful fulfillment of those careers). If the changing role of women was part of the expansion of freedom in the nineteenth century, Catholicism took part in that change, too, and even contributed to it without ever welcoming it.

If the Church did not exactly speak for those without power, it did at least remind the larger society of their presence. It was often a representative of local loyalties and of deeply rooted popular sentiments (even as it sought to reshape them); and it served, however inadvertently, as an agent for introducing some of the concerns of peasants and women into public discourse as its organizations gave them greater prominence and voice. Indirectly, it helped prepare them for a larger role, despite the disquieting implications that carried, much as it taught literacy in the national tongue and fostered better hygiene. The clergy so busy denouncing drink and misspent Sundays were also in fact insisting on the importance of individual free will; and while most of them favored very illiberal measures for circumscribing the moral dangers of modern (urban) life, they were in fact advertising an expanding array of personal choices and placing an emphasis on individual moral responsibility which was appropriate not only to the social changes of the era but to an ethos of individualism and liberty. Much as Catholic teaching facilitated the creation of a modern workforce by urging acceptance of one's lot and the value of hard work and thrift, it contributed as well to an engaged citizenry ready to go to the polls in support of its understanding of liberty.

In responding to popular piety, nationalism, and the changing roles of women, Catholicism went further to accommodate modern society than the Church's formal positions allowed. Catholicism participated in and contributed to social changes its clergy continued to denounce from pulpits. It took part in the era's expanding liberties and in their redefinition. It protected Catholic subcultures that divided Catholics and defended its own autonomy with arguments that made a case for secularization. It supported nationalisms that favored the strong, self-interested national states the Vatican criticized and combatted. It honored women and fostered changes in their roles while seeking to resist changes perceived as disastrous and immoral. All these positions and practices, the practical as well as the theoretical ones, raised questions about the meaning and extent of liberty. As these were debated, the Catholic Church remained indifferent or opposed to some liberties, much as it regretted and resisted many of the changes that others hailed as progress. At the same time the Church defended and helped redefine other liberties, and above all it was not, as its opponents so facilely charged, out of touch with the times.

≺ IV ≻

Institutional Outcomes

As the cacophony of opinions grew louder in the latter part of the nineteenth century, institutions increasingly helped contain centrifugal forces. Industrial firms, labor unions, and political parties

grew in size and in a sense shared power with governmental institutions, which themselves grew larger, more impersonal, and more
clearly structured in functional hierarchies. Similar organizational
forms were adopted by educational and cultural institutions, banks
and insurance companies, and many other public associations. The
Catholic Church, which had activities in common with all these organizations, shared in this trend. An ancient model of bureaucratic
organization, it had been modernizing and centralizing its own institutional structures throughout the century. It found in contemporary
institutional forms new and reassuring ways to mobilize the laity, as
democratization required, yet control their activities; and the Catholic hierarchy was quick to recognize the advantages of having its relations with secular society regulated through orderly negotiations
with other institutions. By the end of the century, Catholic participation in the major currents of social change was likely to occur
within institutions and, like official Catholic responses to those
changes, was very much shaped by institutional concerns.

The institutional focus narrowed Catholic concern with issues
of freedom and sharpened disagreements within Catholicism over alternative responses to modern challenges. It also facilitated accommodation between Church and state, an increase in Catholic political activity, and the enforcement of ideological conformity within
the Church itself. Each of these trends, however, raised additional
issues of Catholicism's relationship to liberty.

The practical and logical outcome of a century of conflict between Church and state was their tendency to operate as if in distinctive realms. Disagreements over the placement of crosses in public
squares, religious processions, and the ringing of Church bells were,
after all, arguments over two definitions of freedom; they could only
end in stalemate or the compromise effected through separate spaces
and specified exceptions. The possibility of legal separation was at
various times a critical issue in Belgium, Italy, France, Germany, and
Spain; and there were some important Catholic advocates of separation in these nations. The fact remained that the principle of a free
church in a free state, much advertised in Belgium and Italy, was
never accepted by the Vatican; and while arguments over separation,
particularly in France and Italy, brought frequent references to the
benefits separation had brought to the Church in the United States,

popes continued to declare that American practice was not ideal (*Longinque Oceani*, 1895).

The separation dramatically enacted in France in 1905, with the angry confrontations that followed, was taken on all sides to indicate the direction of the future. The law of separation was understood by many then and has usually been interpreted since as the culmination of anticlericalism. Bitterly opposed by most spokesmen for the Church, it was the climax of 30 years of conflict over restrictions on religious orders and Catholic schools and a blatant punishment for the political prominence of Catholics in the campaign against Dreyfus and the Republic. Yet many French anticlericals, like anticlericals elsewhere, [45] had not wanted the state to surrender its power over the Church; and some Catholics (Bishop Le Camus was a prominent example) recognized that separation might actually benefit the Church. (Nearly a century later, most historians would agree that it did.) [46] Many on the left had grown increasingly aware that anticlerical campaigns were a threat to stability and an unwelcome distraction from other, especially social, issues. When public opposition forced the state to abandon the inventory of objects in the churches and papal opposition nullified the plan to create a system in which corporate bodies of lay Catholics could serve as legal owners of Church property, such issues were simply allowed to die. A new modus vivendi was established and tensions then declined with surprising speed as republican figures and priests alike felt themselves less threatened than before.

That sort of accommodation—resulting from pragmatic politics, a rejection of old conflicts as counterproductive, and a concern for new challenges, domestic and foreign—was closer to the general European pattern than the ideological debates with which the movement for separation had begun. Much legislation restricting the Church was simply overlooked; civil marriage remained a supplement to but not very often a replacement for the religious sacrament. By the outbreak of World War I, the Church in Europe generally enjoyed more freedom and better relations with political authorities than it had for most of the previous century. This significant gain for the Church was also in a sense a victory for liberalism, but it occurred more from exhaustion and calculation than from agreement on liberal principles. It mattered nevertheless that both sides now argued in terms of liberty. The division within the Catholic community was also significant. There were clergy and laity everywhere who welcomed the Church's improved situation with its opportunities for greater social and political activity, and everywhere there were Catholics who found in this erosion of its official status a further insult to the Church and renewed inspiration for combating the dangerous errors of the age. In the 1920s and 1930s, the desire for a strong state supportive of the Church, one that would end division and oppose socialism, made many Catholic bishops and priests far more generous in granting fascist regimes the benefit of the doubt than they had been willing to be with regard to the less threatening liberal governments of the pre-War period.[47]

There were similarly contrasting responses to what can be called the institutionalization of Catholic politics. In Ireland, Germany, France, and Spain Catholics increased their political weight through electoral politics and the influence of a strong Catholic press in national politics. They had done so, from the 1860s on and especially in the 1880s, while defending the Church but generally not addressing questions of regime, despite their disaffection.[48] Liberals and moderates fearful of socialism, worried by the rising influence of workers' movements, found growing interest in reaching an understanding with Catholics, who had shown such ability in the mobilizations that political democracy requires. Through party-to-party negotiations and the political compromises they practiced without admiration, Catholic parties were drawn into the political mainstream. It was "a remarkable fact" that in Ireland a Catholic party developed as a form of defense against the state became essential to the survival of government,[49] and something similar happened through the Belgian revolution of 1830 and in Wilhelmine Germany.

By the turn of the century, Catholic politics had revealed the tendencies of two distinctive futures. The direction followed would depend very much on the extent to which Catholic parties cared about political freedom. Europe's Catholics can be said to have laid the groundwork before World War I for the parties of Christian democracy that would blossom after World War II and for the Catholic contribution to a European community. Even by the turn of the century, Catholic politicians like Matthias Erzberger in Germany and writers like Charles Péguy, with his lyrical love of France's Third Republic, were emerging as important figures in national political life.[50] Catho-

lic parties could offer a welcome new outlook on Europe's classic
social divisions with their effective critique of social injustice accompanied by a firm attachment to non-threatening solutions and
their sensitivity to the appeal of nationalism while recognizing its
dangers.

That was not the direction that found the greatest institutional
support, however. Catholic social movements were quickly suspect
and often led (as had neo-Guelf enthusiasm on the election of Pius IX
in 1846) to rapid disillusionment. The democratic socialism of Marc
Sangier's *Sillon* was condemned in 1910, and Italy's burgeoning Par-
tito Popolare, with its hints of a social Catholicism, was openly dis-
trusted and even subverted by the hierarchy and the Vatican. Catholic social movements had a better chance of survival when they
seemed to eschew politics; and Catholic parties proved more acceptable when defenders of authority and when, like the Church itself,
they were associated with those in power and with social order. To
many Catholics, appalled by the threat of intellectual and social
upheaval, liberalism was hard to differentiate from anarchy and defenders of an independent secular sphere or of pluralism difficult to
distinguish from enemies of religion.

Thus corporatism gained favor in some Catholic circles as an alternative vision of society, one in which the very conflict of interests
that liberalism fostered would be replaced by harmony. Communities of shared interests would realize the myth of a medieval world
in which faith and freedom were combined through voluntary submission. Such visions of future concord stimulated aggressive rejection of current compromise. In the pages of *La Croix* in France or
Baron Karl von Vogelsang's *Vaterland* in Austria, the traditions of a
virulent press readily amplified hostility to the secular state in terms
all could understand. Sensitive to the precarious position of many
parish priests, their campaigns reverberated more broadly to all the
stresses of social change. In that context representative politics and
freedom of opinion had little to offer, compromise looked like corruption, and absolutist views were reassuring. Catholic institutions
of parish, press, and party were reluctant to antagonize such vocal
Catholic circles even as they sustained a systematic and explicit
anti-liberalism that embraced anti-Semitism.[51]

It was within the Church itself, however, that the institutional
dynamic had its greatest effect; and only internal preoccupations can

explain the direction it took. It is true, of course, that the Church had seen itself engaged in formal conflict with modern society throughout the century; but it is also true that by the end of the nineteenth century, the freedom of the Roman Catholic Church had greatly increased. Less closely attached to or dependent upon particular governments or any single social class than in the past, it benefited from a liberty it had not sought. Its organs published more or less freely in every European language; its laity exercised the freedoms of association and speech to great effect; its clergy were trained as their bishops wished them to be; and the Vatican exercised an authority over hierarchy and clergy, both regular and secular, as unimpeded as ever in Church history. Yet this was the moment in which the Church indulged in an almost unprecedented campaign of repression against its own clergy.

The justification was the need to combat what was called modernism, a loose term that easily acquired far broader implications. Although its initial focus was on biblical interpretation[52] and theological issues, the drive to extirpate modernism quickly became a campaign of fear that reflected other fears not unrelated to the Church's own increased freedom, and it was never far from politics. As a young Catholic politician in the Austrian Trentino enthusiastically explained to his readers, papal guidance would now check those who wished to transform Christian democracy into a movement for the reform of philosophy and the sacred sciences, those who, under the pretext of reform, favored reformism; "under the pretext of modernity, modernism; under the pretext of liberty, liberalism" as part of a process that ultimately was "nothing but the infiltration into Catholic ranks of the most ardent, liberal protestantism."[53]

The war against modernism as "the synthesis of all heresies" (*Pascendi Gregis*, 1907) may well have been more an institutional battle than a theological one, but its extension into politics was psychologically and ideologically natural. Once again Catholic political liberals and social activists risked being labelled dangerous to the faith itself;[54] and the movements led by Romolo Murri in Italy, Sagnier in France, and George Tyrrell in Britain found themselves under a shadow or formally condemned. Anti-liberalism became a part of the anti-modernist self-definition, while integralist positions flourished in the populist anti-modernism of *L'Univers*, *La Croix*, and *Vaterland*. Revival of the intransigence associated with the Syl-

labus of Errors reinforced Vatican strategies of control.[55] A flourishing Church was divided and constrained by internally generated rumors, hints of heresy, and secret conspiracies made more effective by
the improved communication and centralization that were among
the Church's modern gains.[56] The Christian tendency to see the present as a period of moral decline from earlier eras had been vastly
strengthened in the nineteenth century by the general preoccupation with historical change and among Catholics by the belief that
these changes threatened the Church, the faith, and morality. Para-
doxically, a better educated clergy, more effective organization, and a
more international reach increased a troubling awareness within the
Church of the great diversity of outlook it contained. As the repression of modernism shook the Church, freedom was clearly not what
mattered most.

≺ V ≻

The Implications for European Liberty

If delimiting the state was important to the development of political
freedom in the nineteenth century, then Catholicism made significant contributions to that development. Anti-popery, anticlericalism, and opposition to religion reached levels that endangered civil
liberties, and in that climate Catholics became formal and effective
defenders of legal freedom and often of representative government as
well. More generally, in protecting the Church's autonomy, Catholic
schooling, and lay Catholic organizations, Catholics alerted society
to the state's expansive tendencies and by doing so joined in the dissemination of liberal ideas about restraining it. As for the Church, on
the whole it succeeded remarkably in preserving and even expanding
its own liberty, despite the growth of the state and the success of
policies the Church opposed.

If democratization was part of the growth of political freedom,
Catholics contributed to that growth as well without necessarily
embracing democracy. As outspoken critics of the state, Catholics
exposed the contradictions of liberalism and (less consistently) of
nationalism. They in effect often forced societies to debate, more
fully and more publicly than they might otherwise have done, the
proper role of the state and the meanings of freedom. At the same

time, Catholic success in political mobilization and mass politics pushed liberal political systems to seek support beyond their traditional, narrow base, although the real and imagined influence of the clergy remained in the eyes of many an additional reason to restrict political participation. The Church helped, in short, to bring the masses into political life and proved more effective at doing so than traditional liberals.

If increased concern for social justice and programs to support it were part of liberty's expansion, then the Church contributed to that expansion, too. Its charities were the model for many social programs; its welfare activites made powerful appeals for government subsidies before state agencies dominated the scene. Equally important, the Church informed society of the social conditions that resulted from industrialization, urbanization, and poverty, urging the necessity for immediate remedies. Catholic writers and clergy joined in a powerful moral critique of capitalism that undoubtedly strengthened demands for reform and then for more radical solutions, most of which the Church opposed. The Church's failure to become a vital force among most of the working class left socialism as the major expression of moral concerns Catholic teaching had helped to formulate and make familiar.

Catholics were also as effective as Marxists in unmasking the liberal state's claims to neutrality, claims essential to its legitimacy. In that respect the Church contributed to the weakness of liberal regimes in Catholic countries, as it often did by direct opposition. Even so, the Church indirectly facilitated the development of a supposedly neutral public sphere, as a space left open and secular by the creation of strong Catholic subcultures. These, Catholics of course argued, should remain outside the reach of government; and governments vulnerable to charges of anti-Catholicism found their most convincing defense in the assertion that they treated all religions equally. In that somewhat perverse sense, nineteenth-century conflicts between the Catholic Church and a secular state contributed to religious liberty in many countries, as governments interfered less and less with the Church and as it acquiesced to the public presence of other religions. If religious liberty was achieved on much of the Continent, it resulted more from tired necessity than intellectual principle. That was all the more remarkable because political pragmatism and compromise remained especially vulnerable to criticism in Catholic societies, where the Church insisted on (and taught society at large to value) arguments that began from first principles, developed logically, and were not subject to negotiation. That emphasis on broad (and in important respects apolitical) principle coupled with disdain for politics allowed Catholic parties great tactical flexibility. For all their own political success, however, Catholics rarely found much to admire in political parties, viewing them as mere agents of selfish interest unless they maintained a consistent ideology. In Catholic eyes Marxists did but liberals with their emphasis on law, procedure, and tolerance did not meet that requirement.

Catholicism played a major role in sharpening the divisions between left and right in continental societies, for it was at the heart of deep and bitter conflicts for much of the century in France, Germany, Italy, Spain, and the Habsburg Empire, and more briefly in Great Britain. The association of Catholicism with conservative regimes, bourgeois elites, and the peasantry made the conflict between the Church and anticlericals divisive in practical politics as well as intellectual argument. Equally divisive was the Catholic tendency to present the Church as the sole barrier to socialism, communism, republicanism, liberalism, atheism, and immorality—all treated as parts of a single trend.[57] Political liberty was in many respects broadened as a result of these conflicts between left and right, but the practice of liberty also benefits from civility. Catholicism contributed little to that. The target of conspiracy theories about reactionaries, Jesuits, and clerical intrigue, it was an important source of conspiracy theories about revolutionaries, Freemasons, and atheists.

Catholic ideological propaganda, enriched by a century of polemic, combined the vocabulary of theological anathema with modern journalism to create a superheated rhetoric that increased tension and promulgated apocalyptic visions against which mere liberty seemed a pale and minor issue. The scars of a century of conflict, and the sense (largely erroneous) that the Catholic Church was a consistent loser in the social and political changes taking place, affected Catholic attitudes toward politics. Integral Catholicism, reinforced by the campaign against modernism, suggested theories of corporatism and a mythic Christian harmony from ages past as an alternative to fractiousness and relativistic uncertainty. Where alternatives narrowed, the Church became the rallying ground for political opposition to democracy as well as socialism and communism.[58]

A Church eloquent in behalf of private property yet insistent that social justice was a moral imperative, that stressed the importance of the family but also the social responsibility of the state, had said much of importance throughout the nineteenth century. In varying degrees Catholic policies addressed the needs, or at least some of the needs, of every social class. But without a more positive view of political freedom, Catholic political interventions were likely to find themselves crippled or lurching to the right. Catholic social practices were similarly limited by more than continuing ties to conservative groups and a traditional favoritism toward rural life. While formally respectful of individual conscience,[59] Catholicism was reluctant to extend that principle to society at large or to recognize abstract merit in pluralism. In retrospect, the ambiguous relationship between political liberty and Catholicism during the nineteenth century can be seen as part of the necessary tension between individual conscience and religious truth. At the time, few Catholics felt they could risk such equanimity.[60]

Changing Religious Establishments and Religious Liberty in France
Part 1: 1787-1879

C. T. McINTIRE

THE HISTORY OF religious liberty in nineteenth-century France is usually told according to a plot which originated amid the trauma of the French revolution of 1789 and culminated in the events surrounding 1905 which the story calls the separation of Church and state. The story details a titanic struggle not only for religious liberty but indeed for the very character of the nation. The two great combatants are the French Catholic Church and the French state. The tale varies according to which side of the struggle the teller takes, but, either way, the line is much the same. On one side, the Church, led by bishops, clergy, religious orders, and the pope, fights for religion and the union of France with the Church. On the other side, the state, by means of successive republics and republican governments, contends for the separation of France from the Church. Each views the other as the enemy of liberty. Both construct the story around a series of paired and opposing symbols: Church and state, Church and revolution, clericals and anticlericals, reaction and progress, religion and secularization. The sides represent *les deux France*, two different nations of France joined in protracted combat.

The principals agree on the bold master thesis which drives the plot: from 1789 to 1905, *les deux France* wage their warfare, concentrated in violent episodes—the revolutions, the Dreyfus affair, the school conflicts. By this means France transforms from a society dominated by the alliance of religion and the state into a secular society with the church and the state separated. One France experiences the process as the loss of the ancient Gallican liberties of the Church and the demise of the glory of Catholic France. The second

France experiences it as the inexorable rise of modern liberty and the birth of a new society in which the state is neutral toward religion and those individuals who wish religion may have it as a matter of personal concern and private voluntary association.[1]

There is a credible basis to this hegemonic image of the history of religious liberty in France in those years. Conflict between the French Catholic Church and the French state occurs again and again. Bishops, priests, nuns, and monks as well as the pope exercise enormous power within French life, and they undoubtedly count the republicans as their arch enemies. The French state is inescapably at the center of the question of religious liberty, and when the republicans gain state power they reveal unmistakable anti-Catholic animus. There occurs during those years a fundamental transformation from a state bound to the Catholic Church to a state in many ways disconnected from the Catholic Church. It is easy to interpret these changes as secularization, and in some sense an achievement of religious liberty. There are moments of truth in the dominant historical interpretation of the history of religious liberty in France during those years.

But this view of the history of French religious liberty is also distorted. First, there are not merely two Frances in bipolar conflict. Instead, we encounter complex religious and political diversity, and the diversity increases over time. Second, the events from 1789 to 1905 do not make up a single productive process with an achievement at the end. It is not simply a case of the Catholic Church declining, a secular state appearing, and religious liberty abounding at the end. It is not self-evident that religious freedom is lacking during the period, or that religious freedom indeed issues from the events, or even that the separation of church and state occurs in France around 1905. We discover instead complex processes and surprising paradoxes about religion and religious liberty, both along the way and at the end of the road.

These initial observations lead us to reconsider religion, the state, education, and society in France from 1789 to 1905, with the aim of proposing a reinterpretation of the history of religious liberty in France during the period. We find we must stretch our period beyond the standard limits, starting just before the French Revolution and ending soon after the events of 1905, that is, from 1787 to 1908. We must also extend the religious geography to include Algeria in the years after 1830 when the French conquered the region and enveloped it into France. Our strategy is twofold: first, we scan French religion and politics in order to identify what religious communities and political expressions were involved with the question of religious liberty; and second, we peruse the process of events from start to finish to discover how religious liberty fared, looking especially for crucial moments when the structures and issues pertinent to religious liberty changed. The analysis is divided into two parts. This chapter pursues the subject through the early 1870s, while the following chapter completes the picture to 1908 and its aftermath.

≺ I ≻

Political and Religious Diversity in France

To begin, we consider the presumption that the story is a matter of two sides, *les deux France*. If we ask who are the people actually involved in the question of religious liberty, whether in politics or religion, we find that our vision quickly enlarges beyond two sides. We discover remarkable political and religious diversity in France between 1787 and 1908, and we realize that the dynamics created by religious and political differences affected religious liberty.

If we readily grant that religious liberty turned on what the state did, or rather what certain people invested with state authority used state power to do, we must immediately add that the French state was not one thing. It is repeatedly significant that laws and public policy played out differently on the three governmental jurisdictions we encounter—the 38,000 local communes, the 83, later 87, *départements*, and the national government, whether in Paris, the provinces, or Algeria. Local mayors and communal councils; prefects heading *départements*; members of the national legislature, the national Council of State, and the state ministries; and the heads of state themselves exercised different functions that affected religious liberty. Moreover, the French government did not act as one thing over time, but operated according to various politics over the long period. Successive government authorities differed in their politics and religion, and they sought to achieve different things, even opposite things, from their predecessors. Over the long run from 1787 to 1908, the political positions people took in France were myriad, and they often changed as the circumstances and issues changed. We are familiar with this political variety because every version of the political historiography of France includes it to some degree. We need only recall it.

The variety was marked at the national level. Republicans exercised great political power in France, but at all times republicans formed only one of many political movements, preferences, and parties. Moreover, the republicans were not one movement, but many.[2] In the first revolutionary period there were Feuillants, Hébertists, Girondists, Montagnards, Jacobins, Thermidoreans, and many others in addition to Bourbonists and constitutional monarchists. During the Restoration, the July Monarchy, the Second Republic, the Second Empire, and the revolutionary moments in between, there were legitimists, Orleanists, Bonapartists, liberals, republicans, democrats, and socialists, and each of these came in various kinds and mixes. During the Third Republic the parties proliferated across a very broad political spectrum, including conservative, moderate, and radical republicans; monarchists of several shades; and degrees of clericals and anticlericals. When we look below the surface of national politics, the political tendencies multiply still further, varying by commune, department, gender, social stratum, religion, and regional identity, whether Breton, Basque, Provençal, or something else. France was a changing world of political difference.

We may also acknowledge at the outset that the Catholic Church of France—the Église de France—dominated the religious world of France.[3] In 1787, the Église de France comprehended nearly 98 percent of the population of France, estimated at around 25 million, with all of France organized into parishes and dioceses under the care of about 37,000 clergy and 141 bishops and archbishops. Supplementing these were the eleven great religious orders, among them the Dominicans, the Augustinians, the Carmelites, and the Cappucins, as well as many religious congregations, including the Frères des Écoles chrétiennes, the extensive lay teaching order.[4] Most of the people of France alive at that moment had received baptism according to the rite of the French Catholic Church. Church affairs were defined by a concordat between the pope and the French Crown which had lasted since 1516. The monarchy of France was Catholic, the French Catholic Church was the state church, the bishops and clergy formed a privileged estate, the schools of France were dominated by the religious orders and their teachers were mostly nuns and monks, the national economy and many regional and local economies were heavily affected by the Catholic Church, which, with the religious orders, was, in the aggregate, the largest landowner in France.

By 1900, after all the contortions of the intervening years, and with the territory of France differently arrayed, the Catholic Church had only 84 bishops and archbishops, in addition to three in Algeria, but it still comprehended nearly 98 percent of the population of France, which by then had grown to nearly 40 million. The number of priests had increased to 55,000 and there were thousands of religious orders and congregations, with perhaps 150,000 members, integrated into every diocese. The political, economic, social, and even religious powers of the Church were articulated differently from 1787 but continued to be monumental nonetheless.[5]

This dominance by the Église de France did not mean that there were no other religions in France or that the other religions were inconsequential. Neither did it mean that the Église de France could be treated as simply one thing. There were always other religions in France during our period, and the dominant church as well as the other religions always carried internal subgroups and subtendencies which modified and increased in number over time. The French state called the other groups collectively *"les cultes non-Catholiques."* There was religious pluralism in France in the nineteenth century long before we knew to call it that. Once we acknowledge it, we start to see religious liberty as a matter of many churches and religions, each with a different identity and make-up, and each with significant internal variation. The members of these churches and religions founded further organizations and societies, which they considered expressions of their religious faith. They believed them to be useful, or necessary, to the free exercise of their religion. We shall look at these religions one by one.

For a time, and a very important time, after January 1791, the Église de France split into two churches. One was the official church containing the bishops and clergy who accepted the Republic's Civil Constitution of the Clergy of 1790. The other was the non-juring church, an illegal church, embracing the bishops and clergy who did not swear the oath of loyalty required by the Civil Constitution. The split nationally was about 50–50, but regionally each church retained 80 percent or more in certain areas. The clergy and bishops of the government church enjoyed liberty and remained on state salary. The state continued to own and maintain all church properties which were not sold to non-ecclesiastical purchasers. The clergy of the non-juring church, something like 18,000 priests, lost their liberty along with their parishes, their regular sacramental and pastoral ministry, and their income. Thousands of these priests went into exile; but in the chaos of the times, many thousands remained in their towns and villages, and many continued to exercise their ministry apart from the official church. In May 1791, as a gesture of toleration, the government permitted non-juring priests to use church buildings, including even the parish church, for worship.[6]

Beginning in 1801, a third Catholic church appeared, known simply as the Petite Église. This involved the bishops and supporting clergy who refused to accept the implications of the new concordat made in 1801 between Napoleon, now first consul of the French Republic, and Pope Pius VII. The arrangement sought to end the split in the French church by creating a reunified Église de France. As part of the agreement, the pope requested the resignation of all the non-juring bishops still claiming their pre-revolutionary sees. Forty-eight resigned, but 37 bishops, scattered around France, refused to do so. In November 1801 they were removed by the pope. These now twice-refusing bishops and their priests were denied their liberty, but nonetheless continued to minister. The last of the original bishops died under the Restoration, leaving no canonically ordained bishops or priests, but the Petite Église persisted outside the national church throughout the century. Another Catholic split in the 1880s produced the tiny Église Catholique française.[7]

Within the new Église de France, especially after the defeat of Napoleon in 1815, important subgroups and tendencies arose which varied over time. Fundamentally the Church divided into Gallican Catholic and Roman Catholic tendencies. The Gallicans, including some of the bishops and especially government officials, wished to maintain the Gallican Articles of 1682 and the traditional powers of the state over the Church as well as the traditional limits on the power of the pope within France. The Gallicans gave a strict reading to the Napoleonic concordat with emphasis on government priorities concerning the Church and on the acceptance of the centralized administrative and constitutional structures instituted by Napoleon.

The Roman Catholic tendency was propelled by a religious revival on an enormous scale from 1815 onward. The revival heavily influenced the course of religious liberty. It gave rise to new spiritual communities whose members professed beliefs and practiced religious expressions not known before or during the Revolution. Roman Catholics reoriented the church toward the spirituality and ecclesiastical forms associated with the universal church under the headship of the pope of Rome. They claimed the freedom for the French church to operate without state domination and urged the state to serve the maintenance of the Catholic Church within France. From the 1830s onward, those who insisted on a particularly intransigent form of the pro-papal movement became known as Ultramontanes. We can reserve that title for the intransigents, and use the name Roman Catholic to identify the vast mainstream movement oriented towards Rome.

The Roman Catholic revival took many forms.[8] Above all, the church sought to do in a renewed spirit what the church most normally does—provide pastoral care, worship, baptism, marriage, burials, education, health care, and welfare for the people of France—and in so doing needed to repair and extend the ancient parishes and cathedrals, and to create large numbers of new ones to serve the increasing population. Particularly important was the recommencement, or commencement, of the great religious orders in France—the Jesuits, Dominicans, Benedictines, Assumptionists, Carthusians, and the like—and the creation of hundreds of new religious congregations for women and men, many dedicated to contemplation and prayer, others to education, health, and welfare. These congregations opened and operated thousands of schools on the pre-school, primary, secondary, and normal school levels as well as educational boarding homes called *pensionnats*. They created institutions of health and welfare by the thousands.

The impact of the religious orders and congregations on the church and society far surpassed that of any other segment of the Catholic Church. In a sense, each of them, especially the larger ones, represented a different denomination of religious observance, power, and belief.[9] Millions of ordinary Catholics—the faithful—became more intentional about their Catholicism as a liturgical revival transformed their worship, a devotional revival took hold of their spiritual imagination and practice, and new forms of popular religion attracted them. Catholic education became infinitely more important to them, as did obedience to the Holy Father, especially after his Temporal Power came under attack from the 1840s to 1870.[10] New tendencies emerged as Catholics sought to relate to the revolutionary and republican movements and the new industrialization. Liberal Catholics, Catholic democrats, social Catholics, Catholic socialists all appeared from the 1830s onward.[11] Simultaneously, intensely conservative Catholics sought to push the church in a more authoritarian direction. The authoritarians represented a hardening of the Ultramontane direction in the 1860s, after the loss of the pope's temporal power in Italy. Under the Third Republic, they appeared first as aggressive Catholic monarchists, and later as integralists and anti-modernists. They were especially visible in defense of Catholic schools and religious orders when the republicans pursued their attacks from 1880 onward.[12]

There were other Christian churches in France, most of them varieties of Protestants, whom Roman Catholics regarded as heretics, plus a very few Eastern Orthodox, called schismatics by Roman Catholics. The largest of these were two Protestant churches whose history linked them with the Reformation of the sixteenth century. The Église reformée de France, known historically as the Huguenots or Calvinists, had existed within the territory of France continuously since the Reformation, in spite of long periods of persecution. The Église de la Confession d'Augsbourg, the Lutherans, had been attached to France since the mid-seventeenth century. In 1806, after the worst of the French Revolution was over, these churches together numbered about 700,000, or just over 2 percent of the national population, with about 480,000 Reformed and 220,000 Lutherans. By 1868 the number had risen to about 560,000 Calvinists and nearly 300,000 Lutherans, still representing something over 2 percent of the now larger French population. Because of the French defeat in the Franco-Prussian war of 1870–1871, France lost possession of Alsace and most of Lorraine, and with it most of the French Lutheran population. In 1892, the Lutherans counted about 80,000, the Reformed about 600,000. When Alsace and Lorraine rejoined France in 1919, as a result of the Treaty of Versailles after World War I, the Lutherans regained their strength. In Algeria, the Reformed and Lutherans, compelled by the French state, joined together in a single church, known as the Consistoire Central Protestant à Alger.[13]

The Reformed, by virtue of their larger size and greater role in

French history, tended to lead the Protestants; in the eyes of the Catholics and the French state they were often regarded as the only Protestants. They were strongest in the Midi, where in some departments of Languedoc and Provence Reformed populations amounted to more than 5 percent of the whole. By 1793 the Église reformée had virtually collapsed in France as an organized church, a victim of a century of intermittent persecution. It gained new life in 1802 under Napoleon and began to experience a revival that went on for generations. In due course, it divided into evangelical, center, and liberal tendencies, with some congregations splitting away altogether. The evangelicals eventually created the Union réformée évangélique in 1879 after a clash with liberals at the national synod of 1872. The liberals then organized the Union libérale in 1882 as their response to the evangelicals.

The Calvinists were prolific in founding institutions attached to their local churches as well as groupings they called religious societies. These organizations in a Protestant way carried out the same kinds of ministry that Roman Catholics did through the religious orders and congregations detested by the republicans. There were hundreds of schools at all levels—primary, secondary, normal schools, and *pensionnats*, as well as a theological faculty at Montauban.[14]

The Lutherans were located almost entirely in Alsace, Lorraine, and the former principality of Montbéliard, with a small, but important, presence in Paris. In Alsace they numbered about one third of the population. Nearly all of these Lutherans became part of France in 1648 as a result of the Peace of Westphalia, and they remained under a separate legal regime defined by that treaty. This status saved them from the horrific calamities that the state heaped on the Huguenots. The Lutherans of Montbéliard joined France in 1793. Lutherans, too, carried out the same sorts of works as the Catholics, operating a vast number of religious societies as well as organizations connected with local churches. These included schools at all levels, a theological seminary at Strasbourg until 1871, thereafter Paris, and other groups for missions, health, welfare, and education.[15]

In addition to these two large Protestant bodies, there were other Protestant churches in France whose presence, though small, was vital for religious liberty.[16] The French Protestants themselves called these groups collectively "les églises indépendentes." The title marked their independence from the state, rather than their independence from any organized denomination of churches. Most were small denominations in their own right. They are often hard to identify, or count, because of the fluidity of their connections among themselves as well as the desire of many of them to keep their whereabouts blurred to the eyes of the state. In the 1860s, by one count, the independent Protestants included 195 worship locations and about 100 pastors, with perhaps 10,000 people. By including churches, chapels, "stations," "lieux de culte," and religious workers of various kinds, the number rises to nearer 400 churches and church-like sites and perhaps 25,000 people. Their church sites, many of them private dwellings, were found throughout France, with more in the cities than in the countryside. They, too, opened churches and missions in Algeria. Many of them published periodicals and operated schools as well as religious societies for missions, evangelism, welfare, and education.

The longest standing of the "églises indépendentes" in France were the Mennonites, derived from the sixteenth century Anabaptist movement. Perhaps 2,000 lived in Alsace and Montbéliard and came with those regions when they were incorporated into France. The Unité des frères moraves, related to a pre-Reformation reform movement in Moravia, entered France in the mid-eighteenth century. By the 1860s, there were at least three congregations in Alsace and Montbéliard and two others in the south of France. Separations from the Église réformée, noticeable from the 1820s onward, led to free-standing congregations that were Reformed and evangelical in character and vigorously opposed to any connection with the state. These were joined by other congregations produced by Reformed evangelization. They later banded together in various groupings. The largest of these was the Union des Églises évangéliques de France, founded in 1849 under the leadership of Frédéric Monod, with at least 60 churches and chapels in the 1860s. They were known as the *libristes* because of their insistence on independence from the state. A reorganization in 1883 created the Union des églises évangéliques libres de France.

There were other groups: the Église évangélique de Lyon began in 1832, the Églises indépendentes des Alpes-Maritimes became part of France in 1860, the Églises réformées indépendentes included nine churches and chapels in the 1890s, the Églises indépendentes du Littoral grouped six churches together in the 1890s, the Églises libres isolées had one church in Angers and another in Nice in the 1860s. Added to these were several very small churches resulting from missions from outside France, especially from Great Britain, Protestant Switzerland, and the United States. The biggest of these was the Église Methodiste de France, organized in 1852, but whose presence in France dated from the late eighteenth century. In the 1860s they listed about 180 "lieux de culte." It is likely that Quakers had also been in France from the same period. The first group of what became the Églises Baptistes met in the 1830s. Other bodies included the Église évangélique hinschiste based in Nîmes from the 1830s, the Irvingites from the 1840s, Darbyite Brethren from the 1840s, and, from the 1880s onward, the Salvation Army, Adventists, Mormons, Nazarenes, and Jehovah's Witnesses.

Scandinavian and German Lutherans, the Church of England, the Church of Scotland, English Congregationalists, English Methodists, German Methodists, and various American groups all maintained churches in France, chiefly for the benefit of their compatriots, but some French people attended. Two other bodies which strictly speaking were not churches maintained "stations" which sometimes functioned as churches—the Société évangélique de France, founded in 1833, and the Société évangélique de Genève. The Eastern Orthodox presence was focused on the Russian embassy in Paris and, by mid century, the Russian Orthodox Church in Nice which served compatriots. By the end of the century a very small number of Eastern Orthodox immigrants entered France from Russia, eastern Europe, and the Middle East and set up public worship. The Orthodox were loosely classed with the "églises indépendentes."

Outside all these Christian groups were the Jews, with a history in France extending well back into the medieval period. In the 1860s, the Jews had ten high rabbis and 130 rabbis and precentors, serving a Jewish population of 90,000, including 50,000 concentrated in the southwest around Bordeaux, Provence, and Paris, 40,000 in Alsace and Lorraine, plus 30,000 in Algeria. The loss of Alsace and Lorraine to the Germans hurt the Jews in much the same way as the Lutherans. Jews in the south were Sephardics who represented migration from the western Mediterranean since the 1550s. They were known in French law in 1790 as "Portuguese, Spanish, and Avignon Jews." Jews in Alsace and Lorraine, and most in Paris, were Ashkenazis who migrated from Germany and eastern Europe. They had been in

France since the 1550s at Metz, and since 1648 in the rest of Lorraine and Alsace.

Amid this old variation, new differences arose during the nineteenth century over liturgy, ideology, and politics. There were assimilationists and non-assimilationists; Consistorial Jews and those who resisted the state-imposed Consistories; and Orthodox, Conservatives, and Liberals late in the century. In addition to the synagogues and rabbinic institutions, Jewish social institutions were numerous, including primary and religious schools, a school for rabbinic education at Metz and later at Paris, and societies for health and welfare.[17]

The Muslims formed a special case. Throughout most of the nineteenth century very few Muslims could be found in France, that is, France in Europe. But after France began to move into Algeria in 1830, the mental and legal understanding of what was included in France altered radically. Almost from the first the French state treated Algeria differently from the rest of the French empire. By 1848 the government took the line that Algeria, located just across the Mediterranean, was not a colony, but "the continuation of metropolitan France." From that date, the state officially began to incorporate Algeria into France in various ways. By these acts the state catapulted 2.5 million Muslims, their religious leaders and their mosques, in addition to the Catholics, Protestants, and Jews of Algeria, into the middle of the question of religious liberty in nineteenth-century France. Moreover, after at least 1870 Algerian Muslims were migrating into metropolitan France, especially Paris and the Mediterranean region. According to one estimate, Muslims in France may have numbered 50,000 by 1900.[18]

We dare not leave this inventory of the religious identities in France during our period without reference to the wide assortment of people who abandoned the explicit teachings and practices of Christianity but retained religious commitments. Most remained committed to a spirituality focused on God, the immortality of the soul, and a universally valid morality. These embraced *la morale républicaine* and, later, *la morale laïque* and *la foi laïque*, what we might call universal moral religion. Many of these called themselves Free Thinkers as a way to emphasize their separation from organized religion and creedal dogma. Others left out the references to God, but devoted themselves to religion-like alternatives. Included in a wide assortment at various times were Deists; devotees of the Cult of Reason, of the Cult of Liberty, and of the Cult of the Supreme Being; the Theophilanthropists; philosophical spiritualists; the supporters of the Positivist church; the Free Masonic Order; the Ethical Society; and the Universal Religious Alliance. The Société pour l'instruction élémentaire in the 1830s and, from 1866, the Ligue de l'enseignement championed schools shaped by universal moral religion. In 1900, by one estimate, perhaps 120,000 could be counted as Free Thinkers, secularists, or atheists.[19]

Our review of the most salient political and religious allegiances in France during our period shows us, not *les deux France,* but mounting diversity in religion and politics. We find not just "church," but churches, synagogues, mosques, dioceses, parishes, consistories, religious orders and congregations, religious societies, and much more; and not just "state," but communes, departments, and the national government as well as many political tendencies, and much more. The reality of this religious and political variety and the interaction among these communities and institutions are essential to our understanding of religious liberty in France in our period. We focus on six moments when significant changes occurred in the structure of religious liberty.

≺ II ≻

*From the Old to the New Gallican
Religious Establishment*

To begin we look to the years surrounding 1789. In this period the ancient way of handling the religions and liberty was destroyed, and a new structure, similar to the old yet opposed to it, took its place.

The year 1787 places us in the ancien regime under the Bourbon monarchy. In November 1787, Louis XVI granted the Edict of Toleration which improved the civil position of the Reformed Protestants within the French state.[20] In that event we encounter two opposing meanings of religious liberty—the Gallican liberties of the Église de France and the religious liberty of the Huguenots of France.

The edict first of all reaffirmed the historic Gallican liberties of the Catholic Church and evoked the interpretation of French history which fastened on the Gallican Articles of 1682 as their most potent symbol.[21] The fundamental Gallican liberty claimed the freedom for the Catholic Church in France to flourish as the religion of the state and, by consequence, for the Catholic faith to be the common profession of the subjects of the kingdom. The Gallican Articles also affirmed other liberties. They acknowledged the preeminence of the king in matters civil and religious within the French realm. They declared restrictions on the pope's authority—it was limited to spiritual matters, subject to church councils, and, within France, subject to the ancient regulations, customs, and constitutions of the Gallican church. The Catholic religion alone would enjoy the rights and honors of public worship.

With the Gallican liberties secure, the edict then went on to acknowledge that there were those who did not profess the Catholic religion. They would not be granted the liberties of public worship, and they would not be permitted to have pastors. Indeed, the king would continue to use all means, except violence, to induce these people to convert to the Catholic religion and insure thereby the unity of the kingdom. But the Calvinists would be granted civil liberties, deemed to derive from nature. Henceforward, they would not be barred, by virtue of their religion, from holding property, receiving inheritance, exercising their occupations, and marrying and registering the birth of their children. By extension, the Calvinists were permitted to participate in the affairs of the state, including acting as electors and holding public office. It is noteworthy that the Reformed received their civil liberties from Louis XVI, the Bourbon monarch, under the Old Regime.

This was not religious liberty as understood within the Calvinist definitions. In their interpretation of history, religious liberty was fixed by the Edict of Nantes of 1598, by which Henry IV ended three generations of civil and religious war in France between the Catholics and the Reformed. The Calvinists received full civil recognition within the kingdom and full freedom to exercise the Reformed religion within designated towns and regions. Their ministers received a state subsidy. For nearly a century they flourished in France. Then, in 1685, three years after the Gallican Articles, Louis XIV revoked the Edict of Nantes. France returned to what the other states of Europe regarded as normal. The maintenance of civil peace and good order demanded that within any one realm there must be only one religion. The Crown determined that France must be unified in the

Catholic religion. The revocation prohibited the Calvinists from having public worship, closed their churches, required their pastors to convert or leave France, withdrew their civil rights, and mandated that their children must receive Catholic baptism and education. In the name of the Gallican liberties, the state persecuted the Calvinists for most of the eighteenth century.

Such mistreatment resurrected deep memories of the Massacre of St. Bartholomew in 1572 when thousands of Calvinists were murdered in Paris. After 1685, tens of thousands of Calvinists emigrated from France to England, the Low Countries, Germany, Canada, and the United States.[22] The Reformed unequivocally associated the Catholic Church with tyranny and perpetuated Protestant anti-Catholicism into the nineteenth century. The Reformed repeatedly referred to the Edict of Nantes as the measure of religious liberty and to the massacre and the revocation as religious oppression.[23]

The text of the Edict of Toleration in 1787 referred to the king's "non-Catholic subjects," not simply to the Reformed, but the authorities applied it principally to the Reformed. The Reformed celebrated the edict of 1787, though second best to the Edict of Nantes, as an emblem of their liberty.[24] The Lutherans in Alsace, covered by the traditions of the Treaty of Westphalia of 1648, benefited by the clarifications the edict provided. The authorities simply overlooked the other Protestants. They ignored the Jews, rendered invisible by the mentality and the view of history which put the Reformed in the villain's role as the threat to Gallican liberties.

In 1789, by virtue of a broad interpretation of the edict of 1787, some Reformed were elected to the Estates General; they later became members of the National Assembly, which superseded it. The National Assembly continued the process of securing the civil liberties of the non-Catholics, in December 1789, by explicitly opening all civil and military offices to them. The Jews, however, were not included in the law.[25] The Jews only came into view a little later. The National Assembly, following on the precedent with the Reformed, approved a decree in January 1790 which applied to "all Jews known in France under the name of Portuguese, Spanish, and Avignon Jews." The decree reaffirmed all rights granted them by previous letters patent, and further granted them "the rights of active citizens." The National Assembly later extended the rights of active citizens to all Jews, including the Ashkenazis, and specifically terminated "all privileges and exceptions previously introduced in their favour." Both decrees were promulgated by the Bourbon monarch. Jews in France achieved their civil liberty by these decrees, and Jewish historiography thereafter named this the moment of Jewish emancipation. Because of this series of decrees, the Reformed, Lutherans, and Jews tended to give their support to the National Assembly, and many were enthusiastic about the Revolution.[26]

The National Assembly changed the terms of discourse about liberty with the adoption of the Declaration of the Rights of Man and Citizen in August 1789.[27] The declaration seemed to convey two messages at once. Both were contained in the opening article: "Men are born and remain free and equal in rights. Social distinctions can only be founded on common utility." In one voice it announced the universality of liberty, while in another it admitted restrictions on that liberty for reasons of common utility. Subsequent articles sounded the universal voice again: "liberty, property, security, and resistance to oppression" are "natural and imprescriptible rights of man" (article 2); liberty consists "in being able to do whatever does not cause harm to another" (article 4); and "the free communication of thoughts and opinions" is "one of the most precious rights of men" (article 11). But they reiterated the restrictive sounds as well: the law can place limits on liberty, and the law, which is the premier act of the state, determines itself (article 4). The universal voice of the declaration proclaimed a new identity for all people of the realm: the "citizen" of the nation of France. But the restrictive voice denied thereby the primacy of any other identity the people might enjoy—regional identities like Breton, Basque, and Provençal, and religious identities like Catholic, Protestant, and Jew. Because of this duality, those who appealed to the declaration hereafter could use it to promote liberty or justify constraints on liberty, since the state, as the maker of the law and the voice of the citizen, was all-powerful in the realm of law.

For civil liberty, the declaration was apparently liberating, and, judging by the decrees that followed for Reformed, Lutherans, and Jews, the National Assembly acted accordingly. For religious liberty, however, the declaration was constrictive. The National Assembly deliberately chose to exclude religious liberty from the text. The first and second versions of the text which the Assembly debated included overt references to the need for religion and public worship to be free. The final version, however, removed the reference to public worship: "No one may be disturbed for his opinions, even religious, provided that their manifestation does not trouble the public order established by law" (article 10).[28]

The same National Assembly, without a pause, and without the consent of the pope or the Catholic Church, approved a series of decrees which asserted the state's authority over the Catholic religion and radically altered the structure of the Église de France.[29] The decrees can be understood as a reinforcement of the monopoly position of the Catholic Church, and even as a continuation of the traditional overlording role of the state in the exercise of the Gallican liberties. But they also meant state intervention in the affairs of the Catholic Church in a way that destroyed the Gallican liberties, and were distinctly anticlerical. The Assembly moved against the economic base of the Catholic Church, first, in August 1789, by abolishing the church tithe, the primary feudal source of revenues supporting the clergy. In November it authorized the confiscation of all ecclesiastical properties and goods and placed them under state ownership and maintenance. As a kind of compensation, the government assumed the funding of Catholic worship and the relief of the poor, and placed all Catholic archbishops, bishops, and priests on state salary. In February 1790 the Assembly attacked the religious orders by withdrawing recognition of monastic vows for both women and men, and abolishing all religious orders not engaged in education, health, and welfare.

The acts of the Assembly destroyed the old order for religion. Something was needed in its place. In July and August 1790, the Assembly approved the Civil Constitution of the Clergy, which perpetuated the status of the Église de France as the state religion.[30] This was designed to consolidate the unity of the realm under one religion in the tradition of the Old Regime. But the church constitution also produced something quite new. Acting without papal knowledge or consent, the Assembly abolished the diocesan and parochial structure of the Old Regime, including the 135 bishoprics and archbishoprics, and replaced them with 83 new dioceses and a new circumscription of parishes. The dioceses matched the new centralized administrative units called *départements* which the Assembly erected to replace the ancient provinces, like Bretagne and Provence, which it also abolished. The church constitution put the selection of bishops

and priests into the hands of citizens holding the civil vote, and retained the clergy on state salary. In November 1790, to insure that
the church worked properly with the state, the Assembly agreed to
require all clergy to swear an oath of loyalty to the nation and to the
church constitution.[31]

The many laws and decrees about religion since 1787, taken together, first altered the old religious order in France. They gave the
Reformed, Lutherans, and Jews their civil liberties, but not religious
liberty, and destroyed the ancient Gallican liberties of the Catholic
Church. They went on to abolish the old order. In place of the state
establishment of the ancient Gallican Church, the Assembly erected
a new Gallican religious establishment, one subservient to the interests of the all-powerful national state and inimical to the interests
and liberty of the Catholic Church, the religious orders, and the pope.

< III >

Religious Collapse and the Establishment
of Moral Religion

Between 1791 and 1795 the question of religious liberty went into
utter turmoil. Instead of securing the unity of the realm, three religions were reproduced out of one. The enforcement of the oath of
loyalty was the instrument that split the Église de France into two
Catholic churches—the established government church and the unofficial non-juring church. The oath-taking occurred during the spring
and summer of 1791, with many clergy retracting their oaths during
1792, resulting in the approximately 50–50 division among the
clergy. The religious question divided France as nothing else had
done since 1789.[32]

The text of the new French state constitution of September 1791
explicitly proclaimed "the liberty of every man . . . to exercise the
religious worship to which he is attached" (article 1).[33] But the actions of the new Legislative Assembly and the government spoke differently. Repression of the non-juring church continued, and even
the government church began to suffer. In August 1792, the government abolished all remaining religious orders. For the time being, the
teachers and hospital workers were kept on as lay individuals. In September 1792, the National Convention, the next legislative struc-

ture, abolished the Catholic monarchy of France and founded the Republic in its place with the government church attached. In January 1793 it executed the king. Louis XVI made his last confession to a priest of the unofficial non-juring Catholic Church. Also in September 1792, while eliminating the monarchy, the Convention reaffirmed the act of September 1791 which abolished church marriages, a sacrament for Catholics, and instituted civil marriages to be performed and registered before municipal authorities. Divorce was legalized, against Catholic teaching. In June 1793 another French state constitution explicitly guaranteed "the free exercise of worship" (articles 7 and 122), but the government never formally implemented it. Simultaneously the government moved toward what we know as the Reign of Terror, and an active campaign of dechristianization.[34]

In the middle of this crisis, a third set of religious actors emerged from the Église de France—the devotees of moral religion, historically related to Deists of the eighteenth century. The government soon elevated various forms of the new religious expression into a state religion, supplanting both Catholic churches. The several versions of the new moral religion shared three central beliefs: God, the immortality of the soul, and the moral goodness of humanity. This was the same triad of doctrines espoused by the Free Masonic Order.

The new religious expression took several forms and unfolded in stages. In October 1793 the National Convention abolished the Christian calendar and adopted a new calendar which reckoned time from the establishment of the French Republic. In November local authorities were given the power to renounce Catholicism. During 1793 and 1794 many *représentants en mission*, the national agents in the provinces, undertook to enforce dechristianization throughout their spheres of influence. The movement affected Protestants and Jews as well as Catholics. The commune of Paris instituted the Feast of Liberty and Reason in the Cathedral of Notre Dame and closed all churches except those devoted to the Cult of Reason. Elsewhere festivals devoted to the Cult of Liberty, the Cult of the Supreme Being, or the Cult of Reason sprang up. In April and May 1794 the government mandated the observance of the festival of the Supreme Being, and the National Convention issued a decree declaring that "the French people recognize the existence of the Supreme Being and the immortality of the soul." During 1793 and 1794 large numbers of priests in the official government church moved in unison with the government by resigning their priesthood and marrying. The tally across France came to about 20,000 resignations by August 1794. In September 1794, all clergy were cut off from their state salaries.[35]

Simultaneously the National Convention directed attention to the schools, with implications for religious liberty. The Convention issued a series of laws and decrees which reconstructed the schools of France in keeping with the revolutionary republican agenda. In December 1793, the National Convention dechristianized the schools, removing Catholicism and instituting in its place what they called "*la morale républicaine.*" The Convention proclaimed in its decree, "Education is free" (article 1). Any citizens, male or female, could exercise the "liberty of education" and, by following the set procedures, open and operate schools. All schools were counted as public, and all were bound to seek the same overriding aim: the transformation of the children of "the fathers, mothers, guardians, and caretakers" of the Republic into citizens of the Republic. The government created a list of books and other materials containing knowledge deemed "absolutely necessary" for this purpose. The citizen teachers, female and male, were required to teach in conformity with the approved list, and they were enjoined not to teach "any precepts or maxims contrary to the laws and *la morale républicaine.*" The National Convention reinforced the point in November 1794 and required all schools to give "elementary instructions on *la morale républicaine.*" Liberty of education did not include the freedom for Catholics, Protestants, and Jews to open schools which taught their religion and morality.[36]

Intellectual support for liberty of education during the National Convention came particularly from the thinking of the marquis de Condorcet, the rationalist and liberal devotee of moral religion, whose political links were to the Girondins. Condorcet's plan for a national school system, as examined by the National Convention's Committee of Public Instruction, laid out how he understood the liberty of education. The historical enemy against whom liberty needed to be asserted was not the state, but the Catholic Church. Any citizen would have the freedom to open a school, the teaching would include the free expression of opinions, and the father of the family of the child would have a say in the selection of the teacher. Combined with this, however, there would be an absolute ban on the teaching of the Christian religion in the schools. In its place, the school would teach what he called *"une morale laïque"* which embraced the triad of cardinal beliefs of moral religion—God, the immortality of the soul, and humanity. Although religious in character, it would be neutral toward the traditional religions.[37]

During 1793 and 1794 the public exercise of all the religions virtually collapsed. During 1795, however, the National Convention decreed, in February, that "the exercise of no worship can be disturbed"; in May, that the government desired "more and more to assure the free exercise of religions"; and, in August, in a new constitution, that "no one can be hindered from exercizing, in conformity with the law, the religion he has chosen" (article 354). But the very same acts, as well as another decree in September, created a network of restrictions and prohibitions that worked against the free exercise of religion: worship was permitted only in a limited number of designated places; no government-owned property could be used; no signs were allowed; no invitations to worship could be offered; no religious vows were recognized as valid; no one could serve as a priest, pastor, or rabbi unless he swore an oath subscribing to popular sovereignity and promising submission and obedience to the laws of the Republic, including all the restrictive laws; no clerical dress could be worn in public; and so on. Besides all this, the state retained the property confiscated from the churches and religious orders, while simultaneously cutting off the salaries of the clergy.[38] With respect to the schools, in October the National Convention reinforced the mandate to teach "the elements of *la morale républicaine*" as one of four pillars of the curriculum, along with reading, writing, and arithmetic.[39]

In the vacuum created by the meager public presence of the traditional religions, the new government defined by the constitution of 1795, the Directory, decided to give special favor to the Theophilanthropists, a small religious group founded during the Revolution by Chemin-Dupontes. Theophilanthropists were a milder version of the moral religion of 1793–94. Their religion emphasized the familiar triad of beliefs common to the various forms of moral religion: God, the immortality of the soul, and the moral goodness of humanity. They eliminated explicitly Christian content, although they mirrored Christian style in their public worship, with an altar, sermons, and their own saints. They preached a religion of common morality based on universal maxims drawn from the example of the lives of great men and from nature. Supported in particular by La Révelliere-Lépeaux, a member of the governing group, the Directory granted Theophilanthrophy the use of ten churches in Paris and for a moment considered making it the state religion.[40]

The split in 1791 in the new Gallican Church establishment, only recently constructed by the Civil Constitution of the Clergy, was the start of religious collapse. The events of 1793 and 1794 virtually completed the process. Amid the chaos arose various forms of moral religion, both in public worship and in the schools, installed as a new state establishment to replace the new Gallican establishment. Like the Bourbon monarchy and the state under the initial phase of the National Assembly, the republican governments of these years intended for the new religious expression to maintain the unity of the realm. None of the other religions had any reason hereafter to prefer the republic over the monarchy. The initial support that Protestants and Jews tended to give to the Revolution nearly dissolved. The Directory of 1795, while gentler, nonetheless repressed the traditional religions and continued the establishment of moral religion, focusing particularly on the schools.

≺ IV ≻

Quadrilateral Establishment of Religion

Between 1801 and 1808 the French state headed by Napoleon, now first consul and dictator of the French Republic, stumbled on a new way to handle religious difference and religious liberty. The purpose was the same as that of previous governments—to secure the unity of the realm through an enforced unity of religion. This time there was a new departure.

The center of the government's religious policy was the Concordat of 1801 between Napoleon and Pope Pius VII, defining the arrangements for the Catholic Church of France. It became French law in April 1802. Included in the law were the Organic Articles of 1802, a document containing regulations for Catholic ecclesiastical affairs, drawn up without the pope's knowledge and issued without his consent.[41] The new and united Église de France resulting from this Catholic settlement resembled both the pre-revolutionary Gallican church and the new Gallican church created by the Civil Constitution of the Clergy.

The Gallican marks were clear. In keeping with the Gallican liberties, the concordat proclaimed: "the Religion Catholic, Apostolic, and Roman will be freely exercised in France; its worship will be public, conforming with the police regulations which the government will determine are necessary for public tranquility" (article 1). The agreement maintained previous limits on papal power, particularly the government's primacy in the nomination of bishops, and the stipulation that papal documents required government authorization before publication in France. The Organic Articles explicitly protected "the liberties, franchises, and customs of the Gallican Church," and required all professors in the seminaries of France to subscribe to the Gallican Articles of 1682.

The continuities with the revolutionary period, and particularly with the Civil Constitution of the Clergy, were also clear. Their effect ran contrary to the Gallican liberties in placing a tight net around the Catholic Church. Like the Declaration of 1789, the liberty granted in one breath was taken away in another, in this case, by the "police regulations," decrees, and laws which the state may dictate in the interests of "public tranquility." Diocesan and parochial structures were made to conform to state needs. The clergy again became civil officials on state salary. Church buildings remained state property with workshops to maintain them. Even an oath was included. The archbishops, bishops, and priests had to swear obedience to Napoleon's government, and were required to inform the government of anything contrary to state interests. A prayer for the Republic and Napoleon was mandatory at the end of the Divine Office, and the wording was prescribed. There must be one liturgical rite, and the government would have to approve it. There must be one catechism containing the Church's teaching, and the government would have to approve that. Clergy must wear French-style ecclesiastical dress.

The settlement contained the acknowledgment that the Catholic religion was "the religion of the great majority of French citizens" as well as "the personal faith" of the Consuls of the Republic, and no longer the religion of the state. In spite of the shift in rhetoric, however, the particulars of the settlement positioned the Catholic

Church as a religion established by the state's law and treasury. Since
the settlement gave priority to the state's interests, it did not satisfy
the pope and the French bishops, and the Organic Articles in particular deeply aggravated them. Under the circumstances, however, and
given the religious disasters of the last decade, the pope and the
Catholic Church accepted the settlement as advancing the interests
and liberties of the Catholic religion in France. It was a paradox: the
economic, political, ecclesiastical, liturgical, and theological controls by the state over the Catholic Church were greater and more
extensive than at any other time in French history, yet these very
measures ensured a high degree of religious liberty for the Catholic
Church. The work of rebuilding the Catholic Church carried on in
earnest. The state continued to suppress the religious orders, but
made some allowances for new female congregations in education
and health care. The Frères des Écoles chrétiennes resumed their
work in education, and Catholic schools began to reopen.

With the Catholic Church moving rapidly back into education,
the Napoleonic government acted to bring education under state authority. In May 1806 the government founded an unusual institution
called the *Université de France*, the aim of which was to create a
state monopoly of education at all levels.[42] The *Université* was a public monopoly, with no private schools permitted, and it was Catholic.
The bases of instruction were "the precepts of the Catholic religion,"
fidelity to the government, and obedience to the statutes of the
teaching corps (article 38). The object was to achieve uniformity of
instruction and, "for the sake of the state, to form citizens attached
to their religion, their ruler, their fatherland, and their family." All
seminary professors continued to be bound to the Gallican Articles
of 1682. The *Université* solidified the leading accomplishment of the
revolutionary governments in education—the monumental shift in
authority from the Catholic Church to the French national state. Napoleon and his government understood what previous republican
governments also realized, that the schools and the school teachers
gave the government a permanent presence in the 38,000 communes
of France which might offset the independent influence of the Catholic Church.

While constructing the Catholic settlement, a way to handle the
Protestants occurred to Napoleon and his government. It sprang from
Napoleon's monopolistic mentality and had no precedent anywhere

in Europe and the Americas. Historically French governments had followed a series of strategies toward the Protestants—civil war, liberty within regional and local boundaries, persecution, exile, annihilation, heavy regulation. Napoleon now authorized a religious settlement with the Protestants which mirrored the arrangements with the new Catholic Church. Acting on Napoleon's initiative in 1800, a group of Protestants based in Paris cooperated in talks with Jean Portalis, who as a member of the State Council was assigned to deal with the religions. The result was the Protestant Organic Articles for the Église réformée and the Église de la Confession d'Augsbourg, attached to the Catholic settlement in April 1802.[43]

The Reformed and Lutheran churches were now officially established by the state alongside the Catholic Church, giving France three state religions. Like Catholic bishops and priests, their clergy became civil officials paid by the state, and they were compelled to swear the same loyalty oath to the government as the Catholic clergy. Their doctrines, catechism, and creedal statements required state approval, and their clergy were required to offer a prayer during public worship for the prosperity of the government of the Republic. They were absorbed into the state's apparatus, with an organizational structure matching the centralized format created for the Catholic Church, the *Université*, and the *départements*. The legislation arranged the churches into local consistories and area synods for Reformed and inspections for Lutherans, and, against Reformed tradition, prohibited the formation of national synods. Most of their church buildings were the property of the state which the state gave them permission to use. The number and the location of the churches were regulated, as were the number and the selection of their ministers. The number, location, and regulations of their seminaries, their professors, and their teaching required government approval.

The Protestant settlement, like the Catholic, was a paradox. Protestant churches, seminaries, creeds, polity, finances, and ministers came under the state, but the Protestants achieved thereby the freedom to exercise their religion as never before. Both Reformed and Lutherans welcomed the settlement in spite of the controls.

When Jews learned of the Protestant settlement and saw the extraordinary stimulus and operational freedom it gave the Reformed and the Lutherans, they petitioned the government for similar treatment. The government had so removed the Jews from view that the idea of a Jewish settlement had not occurred to anyone. However, within the new monopolistic mentality of expanding the religious establishment, the government was quick to see the merits of a Jewish settlement, although slow to make it fully parallel with the others. Napoleon authorized Portalis to assemble a commission of Parisian Jews in 1805 to produce a plan. The government convoked an Assembly of Jews in Paris in 1806 to pursue the matter. The outcome was the *Réglement* of 1806, which, after some delay, the government promulgated and implemented in March 1808. Simultaneously, however, the government issued what the Jews knew as the *décret infâme* which laid down new civil restrictions.[44] The *Réglement* created an elaborate system of organization for synagogues and rabbis that matched the Protestant and Catholic systems. It regulated the number, location, and structure of synagogues, created consistories to govern them, prevented the creation of any other religious organization among Jews; prohibited the founding of any other synagogues without government approval; regulated the number and placement of rabbis and defined their functions; created a central consistory in Paris under the eye of the government; required rabbis to pray for and to preach obedience to the government; and placed all Jewish affairs under government surveillance. The *décret infâme* impeded Jews in commerce and finance, and their movement into and around France, until the government repealed it in 1818. The Jewish Assembly had requested that rabbis be put on state salary, but the government resisted. Eventually in February 1831 rabbis did go on state salary, completing their transformation into civil officials.[45] Although the Jewish settlement took time before matching the others, the Jews welcomed it as an enhancement of their religious liberty. Judaism, too, became a religion established by the state, unprecedented anywhere in the world. Jews experienced the same paradox as the others: the state control over their public religious life was extreme, but they received thereby more religious liberty than ever before in French history.

The government either deliberately excluded or neglected the remaining religious communities of France. The Petite Église was forced outside the system. By agreement with the pope, the government banned Theophilanthropy from using church buildings held by the state. The result was the virtual elimination of the religion.[46] The few independent churches were overlooked, although the new Penal

Code of 1810 affected them incidentally. Articles 291–94 restricted religious groups and other associations which met regularly in private dwellings.[47] If there were more than twenty people involved, both the group and the person whose home they used had to secure prior government approval each time they met. Participants were banned from doing or saying anything that could be construed as inimical to the government.

The outcome of the Napoleonic religious settlements was a surprise. France now had four state religions, a quadrilateral establishment of religion. In the legal terminology of the time, the four were called the "recognized" religions. The state perpetuated the ancient strategy of securing the unity of the realm by means of the unity of religion, but with a twist. It was a composite religious unity, one which absorbed, and co-opted, the new Catholic Church, the two large Protestant churches, and the Jews. All four religions accepted the paradox of membership in the religious establishment as the way to increase their religious liberty. The neglect or exclusion of other religions served to define the system. The arrangements created a uniquely French response to the reality of religious difference, even as they sought to contain the variety of religion in France. It was a unity of four in one, but no more than four.

The state's powers to regiment the religions were legally extensive, and affected not only their external relations and temporalities but significant matters of their internal affairs and religious life as well. For the system to work, successive governments were obliged to exercise their powers permissively, and not as tyrants, and the religions were obliged not to press for an extension of their liberties. The religions understood the conditions of their new-found liberty: the state held a reserved power at all times, there to be used, strictly or loosely, or left unused, as the state saw fit. They enjoyed religious liberty at the discretion of the state. In practice the application of the restrictions depended on the policy and behavior of successive regimes, particular ministers, directors, departmental prefects, and even local communal officials. Napoleon created a permanent *Ministère des cultes*, a ministry of religious affairs, in 1804. Under various names, the ministry lasted over the years, linked at different times with the ministries of interior, justice, fine arts, or education. The funding of the religions was channeled through the *Budget des cultes*, which included the salaries and pensions for the religious personnel sanctioned by the government, expenses for the preparation of religious personnel, and costs for the repair and construction of religious buildings designated by the government. Most of the time, the system ran smoothly, and the symbiosis among the religions and the state held up, to the advantage of the parties involved.[48]

≺ V ≻

Adjusting the Quadrilateral and the Extension into the Schools

The religious peace created by the Napoleonic settlements made possible the revivals of the Catholic, Reformed, Lutheran, and Jewish religions as well as the increase in religious diversity which occurred throughout the century. Between the 1830s and the 1850s, these religions were free to shift their primary attention from the liberty of their churches and synagogues to the schools, and to what participants called the *liberté de l'enseignement*, broadly, the liberty of education. *Liberté de l'enseignement* was, above all, a question of religious liberty. For those groups not in the system, however, public religious practice remained a problem. It became a particularly serious matter for the independent Protestant churches, and the Muslims in Algeria.

Independent Protestants experienced frequent harassment during the 1830s and 1840s, stemming from a broader application of the restrictions in article 291 of the Penal Code.[49] They recounted their troubles in their oral histories and written remembrances. The Églises baptistes, for instance, told of departmental prefects and mayors of communes repeatedly refusing authorization of their meetings or bringing charges against them in the law courts for holding unauthorized meetings. The authorities also impeded their evangelistic activities and distribution of religious literature.[50]

The Constitution of the Second Republic, the product of moderate republicans, was the first public text to acknowledge the religions beyond the quadrilateral in a positive way. It contained a sweeping provision linking the freedom to profess one's religion with the practical means to be able to do so within the religious system. The exercise of everyone's religion, it said, receives equal protection from the state, and the ministers of every religion, whether the religions currently "recognized" or "those which would be recognized in the future," possess "the right to receive a salary from the State" (article 7). The attitude associated with this provision gave the independent Protestants a rush of freedom to operate.

The government of the Second Empire under Napoleon III reintroduced a period of repression but nonetheless was the first to acknowledge the independent Protestants in the national law. The effective decree, in March 1859, was designed in the first instance to toughen the constraints on the official Protestants.[51] The official Protestants were no longer to apply to the mayor of local communes or departmental prefects for authorizations to open new churches and chapels. They now had to secure authorizations from the emperor himself, acting in the Council of State, and upon the recommendation of the government minister of religions. The decree went beyond the state Protestants, however, and explicitly included the "unrecognized" religions, in this case, the independent Protestants. It required members of "non-recognized" religions to apply to the emperor, with the Council of State, for authorizations to exercise public worship. The applications had to pass through both the minister of religions and the minister of the interior, who was responsible for the police and government surveillance. These "non-recognized" religions were placed under particular provisions of the Catholic and Protestant settlements.[52] Specifically, they were forbidden to hold deliberative councils without expressed government approval, to have relations with a foreign authority, to employ ministers who were not French citizens, and to bring charges against persons or the other religions recognized in France. The decree represented a kind of settlement with the independent Protestants, adjusting the quadrilateral establishment to enable the state both to notice and to deal with them. Whereas the effect of the decree on the state Protestants was greater restriction, the decree actually gave the independents a way to relate to the state. It was the same paradox experienced by the four state religions: the state's imposition, and their acceptance, of controls resulted in the expansion of their religious liberty.

The encounter with the Muslims of Algeria went much further, and led to greater adjustment of the state religious establishment. After the French capture of Alger in July 1830, the French immediately undertook two initiatives toward the Islamic religion. First, they issued the Convention of 1830 which declared, "The exercise of

the Mahomedan religion will remain free . . . the religion will be under no attack." Second, they ordered the confiscation of the lands and
buildings which produced income for the public exercise of Islam,
and simultaneously set the French army to work destroying mosques
and expelling Muslim religious leaders. To the French these were not
contradictory things. Both applied the French religious system to the
Muslims, and recapitulated the treatment of the Catholics, Protestants, and Jews in France from 1789 to 1795 when the religious system was first being defined. By 1848, when the French occupation of
the fertile, inhabited regions of the north was complete, the French
had extended, and adapted, the French religious settlements to the
Catholics, Protestants, and Jews of Algeria. While the declaration
of religious liberty for Muslims remained in effect, the French destroyed well over half the mosques of Algeria, confiscated all Muslim
income-producing properties, closed most of the Islamic schools attached to mosques, and restricted the annual pilgrimages to Mecca.[53]

In exchange for depriving the Muslims of their income, the regime began, albeit haphazardly, to supply funds to Muslims for their
religious operations. In April and May 1851, the government of the
French Second Republic formalized the funding of the Muslims and
extended French-style religious controls to the organization and operation of the Islamic religion in Algeria. Islamic schools began to
appear in the public system. The French designated 78 mosques for
preservation under French organization and funding. They provided
salaries, and sometimes lodgings, for the muftis and imams assigned
to staff the mosques. These religious personnel were named and
monitored by the French, and arranged in a hierarchy which the
French created. In 1868, the government organized a Muslim consistory for Algeria, akin to the organizations for the Protestants and
Jews. The government funded these expenses for the Islamic religion
from the income of the confiscated Muslim properties, and through
the 1850s processed the costs through provincial and regional bud-
gets in Algeria, leaving the national budget of France untouched.[54]

French government policy toward Islam in Algeria gave the religion status as an established religion which reflected, but did not du-
plicate, the position of the quadrilaterals in Algeria. In this the government acted consistently with the Constitution of 1848 which
provided for an extension of the state religious system and the payment of clerical salaries to additional religions. There were two big

differences, however. First, the French government treated Islam as the fifth state religion only for French Algeria whereas the French-connected religions operated as state religions in France as well as French Algeria. Second, the Algerian Muslims were a conquered people, and the French establishment of the Islamic religion, with its official clergy and official mosques, represented to them not religious liberty, but tyranny. Moreover, the French-established version of Islam touched only a fraction of the 2.5 million Algerian Muslims. The vast remainder exercised their Islamic life quite apart from the government's intrusions. It was a paradox of a different sort. The French government thought they were achieving with the Muslims the same resolution of the religious question as with the other state religious settlements, but they were not. The more they did for the Islamic religion, the more unsatisfied the Muslims became. It was the paradox of benevolent tyranny.

The *liberté de l'enseignement* raised new questions about religious liberty for the established religions. The Constitutional Charter of 1830 brought the issue to the top of French politics with its promise of a law providing for "public instruction and the liberty of education" (article 69).[55] The initiative for placing education in the Charter came not from Catholics, but from members of the Legislative Assembly who followed the tradition of Free Thought and moral religion. By appealing to the liberty of education they deliberately recalled the educational laws of the National Convention in 1793–95 when the term was first used, and, in particular, the thinking of Condorcet. Liberty of education meant opposing the influence of the Catholic Church and the religious orders in the schools, and resisting the state monopoly of education insofar as it sanctioned the Catholic presence. They would replace it with a state monopoly in the schools for what they called *"la morale laïque"* and *"la morale républicaine."*[56]

As the campaign for the liberty of education developed, the advocates of traditional religion in the schools took the initiative away from the followers of Condorcet. The meaning of *liberté de l'enseignement* switched from opposition to the church within the state system to resistance to the state monopoly. Pushing the new campaign were Catholics, Protestants, and Jews who maintained, or desired, schools with a character and personnel different from the authorized schools within the *Université*. Each of these groups acted on the con-

viction that their religion was not limited to certain authorized practices. For each of them, religion was central to life as a whole and
specifically included the education of their children and the perpetu-
ation of their religion into the next generation. True education was
permeated with religion.[57]

The *Université* was still officially Catholic, in the sense that the
system operated in tandem with the Catholic Church and with the
hundreds of new or revived female and male religious orders, and
the teaching rested on "the precepts of the Catholic religion." The
Catholic presence more than kept up with the immense expansion
of primary schools after 1815, when the number of primary schools
rose from about 23,300 to about 36,200 by 1829.[58] In spite of the
Catholic character of the state monopoly, however, Catholic bishops
were not satisfied. They objected to the state's monopoly of the authority to make the decisions about the schools. After the state
placed severe restrictions on the Jesuits in 1828 and the anticlerical
voices increased their power in the legislature in 1830, Roman Catholics began to call for the liberty of education. They opened a large
number of schools without state authorization. The liberty of education meant to them the power to create schools under religious
authority, with Catholic teachings as the basis, with a Catholic environment, and with clerical teachers.[59] In October 1830 the new
group of liberal Catholics, in the first issue of *L'Avenir*, issued a call
for liberty of education. They intended the marriage of "God and Liberty." To show what they meant, they ostentatiously opened a liberal
Catholic school in Paris in May 1831 in defiance of the governmental
monopoly. The government laid charges against them in the law
courts and closed the school.[60]

Protestants were not satisfied with the monopoly either, even
though there were Protestant schools in the *Université*. The problem
was that the Protestant schools existed by state forebearance, without a secure footing in law. Since 1809, in response to high-placed
Protestant inquiries, the government had allowed the phrase "the
precepts of the Catholic religion" to be loosely interpreted to mean
"the precepts of the Christian religion." An ordinance in February
1816 had loosened the interpretation even more. It permitted the organization of Protestant schools within the monopoly that were fully
Protestant in teachings, spirit, and staff. It provided for Protestant
local school committees with the power to appoint teachers for

the local school, and authorized the Protestant pastor to act as an inspector of the local school in place of the local priest in areas where the Protestant population warranted it. Perhaps four or five Protestant schools began under Napoleon, some more in 1815, and many more after the 1816 ordinance. One report in 1828 counted 392 Reformed schools, mostly in the Midi, not including unauthorized schools. There were another 280 Lutheran schools, mostly in Alsace and Montbéliard. Yet for these Protestants, the liberty of education meant two oppositions at once, often in tension. Like Roman Catholics, they resisted the state's power over schools; they also feared Catholic domination within the government schools.[61]

The Jews also had schools within the *Université*. Their position was even less secure than the Protestants'. Jewish schools were permitted by virtue of a government decision in May 1816 to stretch the references to Protestants in the 1816 ordinance to include Jews. Jews tended to educate their children at home. For them, it was a matter of preserving Jewish identity, practices, and teachings within an overwhelmingly Catholic society. The Protestant school movement gave Jews the impulse to act. With planning underway in 1817, the Jewish consistory of Paris founded a Jewish primary school in 1819. The Metz consistory organized one in 1818; twelve more such schools opened around France by 1821, and more opened through the 1820s. These were all authorized, although, unlike the Protestant schools, they received no funding. The number of unauthorized Jewish schools also increased. The school ordinance of October 1830 specifically included Jewish schools, with the intention of containing the schools within the system. The strains within the system were palpable and worked to rouse Jewish interest in the liberty of education.[62]

A remarkable coalition endorsed legislation on the liberty of education in the early 1830s—devotees of moral religion and *la morale républicaine*; Catholics, both Roman and liberal; Reformed; Lutherans; and Jews. Each group in the mix meant something different by the *liberté de l'enseignement*, and each had good reason to suspect the intentions of one or more of the others, but they had a common foe in the too-powerful state enforcing things about religion they did not like.

The first part of the promised legislation, on the primary education of boys, was completed in June 1833. The second part three years later, in June 1836, extended most of the provisions of the 1833 law to the education of girls.[63] The boys' law bore the name of the chief sponsor, François Guizot, the new minister of public instruction, an Orleanist, a historian, and, most important for the character of the law, a Reformed Protestant. Guizot wrote the law with liberty of education for non-Catholics in mind, and, until Georges Cuvier died in 1832, he had that Lutheran's help. The laws were an attempt by the government to take direction of a situation that was close to chaotic. New schools were opening within the system by the thousands, with many living only nominally within the rules, and untold others operating outside the rules altogether.[64]

In one sense the laws sought to preserve the monopoly that belonged to the *Université* by consolidating the mandatory national structure and adding to its density. In another sense, however, the laws broke up the monopoly, and this was the heart of the matter for the liberty of education and religious liberty. They provided for two tracks of schools, one called "public" and within the *Université*, and the other called "private" and formally outside the *Université*. The schools designated "public" were those placed under the authority of the state, funded in whole or part by some level of government, and mandated for every commune of France. "Private" schools were those operating under a non-state authority, unfunded by the state, and dependent for their existence on sufficient enrollments and funding from other sources. Any suitable person, Catholic, Protestant, or Jew, a minister of religion or a member of a religious order, was free to open and operate a private school. The operating authority was free to set the religious character of the teaching and the school environment. Certain restrictions applied, like the requirement of the *brevet de capacité* for teachers, which kept the private schools within boundaries defined by the government, but the schools had wide freedoms as long as the local officials agreed and higher government authorities did not intervene. The girls' law of 1836 dispensed with the requirement of the *brevet* for members of religious orders teaching in girls' schools. The law added that every department must have a normal school for the training of male teachers for boys' schools, but made no mention of training for women teachers.

The required curriculum gave public schools a specifically religious character. "Moral and religious instruction" was mandatory as were reading, writing, the elements of the French language, and arithmetic (article 1), but nothing said the moral and religious instruction had to be Catholic, as in the 1808 requirements. Protestant and Jewish schools could operate in the public sector in those communities where the Protestant and Jewish populations were sufficiently large. Schools had to follow the wishes of the father, whatever his religion, concerning the participation of the child in religious instruction (article 2). The local priest served on the supervisory committee for the public school, but, the law said, "In the communities where the population is divided among different religions recognized by the state, the priest or the most senior priest, and one of the ministers of each of the other religions designated by its consistory, will be part of the community committee for supervision" (article 17). The other established religions had a member on the regional committee as well (article 19). The effect of these provisions was that almost all schools within the public system were Catholic but that some were Reformed, Lutheran, or Jewish. In addition there were Catholic, Reformed, Lutheran, and Jewish private schools.

Regulations issued in April 1834 described the religious and moral content mandated for all public schools and the duties of the teachers.[65] The expectations were the same for all teachers, both those who were members of religious congregations and those who were not. Teachers were required to devote their every word and action to the end of "putting into the soul of the pupils the feelings and the principles which are the safeguard of good morals and appropriate to inspire the fear and love of God." The school day included acts of religious worship: prayer, the reading of the Christian scriptures, recitation of the gospel appointed for Sunday, and exhortations by the teacher. Students were expected to attend the Divine Office in the parish church. The moral and religious instruction included the Catholic catechism, scripture, sacred history, and Christian doctrine. In Protestant and Jewish schools the appropriate substitutions were permitted, and Protestants and Jews attending religiously mixed schools were excused from Catholic worship and teaching to attend their own religious exercises and instruction.

The state religions approved the new educational system and used their new liberty of education to stabilize or augment their roles in education. By 1843, there were about 17,100 private schools, representing about 29 percent of all schools in France. The vast majority of the private schools were Catholic, including about 3,000 run by religious orders. Reformed and Lutherans maintained at least 702 schools, public and private, with about 81,000 pupils. Jewish schools increased as well.[66] To prepare the teachers, both Catholics and Protestants began setting up training courses for men and for women, while the *départements* continued the movement for normal schools for men.

The new educational laws broke up the monolithic and officially Catholic system of primary education within the *Université* and replaced it with the schools of the quadrilaterals, both public and private. In so doing, they replicated for primary education the paradox the religious settlements created for public religious exercise. More religious control produced more religious freedom. The state wrapped both public and private schools, authorized and unauthorized, in a system of uniformity surpassing anything previously attempted; the effect was to ratify, instead of oppose, a process of diversification already underway in the schools of France. Excluded from the public system were schools set up by the independent Protestants, since they were not a recognized religion, and schools teaching *la moral laïque*, since the religious instruction demanded by the law meant traditional religion.

After the Guizot laws the question of religious liberty refocused on the liberty of education at the level of the secondary schools. Most of the secondary schools within the *Université*, notably the *collèges*, were Catholic institutions. The school day for all years at the secondary level began with religious instruction, followed by sacred history later in the morning.[67] However, Catholic bishops were just as unsatisfied with the *collèges* as they were with the old state primary schools, and for the same reason: the authority over them belonged to the state and not to the Catholic Church. Bishops were free to found ecclesiastical secondary schools outside the monopoly for boys intended for church vocation, and, against the restrictions, especially restrictions laid down in 1828, these *petits séminaires* were opened to other boys. It continued to be illegal to operate other secondary schools outside the monopoly, although during the 1830s and 1840s government enforcement was lax and unauthorized private secondary schools were numerous. Catholic pressures for liberty of secondary education were intense, and Protestants desired secondary schools free from Catholic influence for their youth.[68]

The government's response was a new education law in March 1850, the Falloux law, promulgated during the Bonapartist period of the Second Republic. It was comprehensive, embracing both primary and secondary education, and it fulfilled the commitment of the Constitution of 1848 to the liberty of education.[69] It extended and adapted to the secondary level the provisions of the Guizot laws for the *liberté de l'enseignement* at the primary level. It legalized what had by then become the practice. Non-state schools at both the secondary and primary levels were specifically permitted, and hereafter were called "free" schools, signifying their independence from the state (article 17). Any suitable person having either a bachelor's degree or the *brevet de capacité* could open a free secondary school or primary school merely by informing the regional authorities of the plan for the location of the school and the object of the teaching. Associations as well as individual persons were now permitted to found schools, and no restrictions were placed against members of religious orders. Non-Catholics were explicitly rendered eligible to open schools. When a non-Catholic sought the *brevet*, the examining jury had to include a minister of the same religion as the candidate. Special free secondary schools to prepare youth for ecclesiastical and rabbinical seminaries were authorized.

Beyond these provisions for free schools, Protestant and Jewish public schools were more clearly provided for than previously, as was the religious instruction of non-Catholics in religiously mixed public schools. Catholic, Protestant, and Jewish religious officials were placed on all levels of governance and supervision of the system. Remarkably, when referring to non-Catholic free schools, the law did not limit its provisions to the "recognized" religions. This left the door open for the independent churches to found their own free schools.

The new law maintained the requirement of "moral and religious instruction" in the primary curriculum for all schools, and, as before, it did not specify that the teaching had to be Catholic (article 23). Every day began with moral and religious instruction in first period.[70] In August 1851, the new national Higher Council of Public Instruction enumerated the requirements for religious teaching and religious practice in the public schools.[71] The requirements applied to both lay teachers and members of religious orders. "The principal duty of the teacher," the regulation declared, "is to give to the children a religious education and to engrave profoundly in their souls the feeling of their duties toward God, toward their parents, toward

other men, and toward themselves." The curriculum, except for Protestant and Jewish schools, included the study of the Catholic catechism, scripture, the history of the church, and moral lessons. The
practices of religious worship continued as prescribed in 1833: prayer,
scripture reading, recitation of the gospel for Sunday, attendance at
the Divine Office in the parish church, and inspirational words by
the teacher, who above all was expected to set a moral and religious
example for the students.

During the debates on the Falloux law in the legislature, Edgar
Quinet, republican and professor in the Collège de France, proposed
an amendment to add after "moral and religious instruction" the
words "without acceptance of the particular doctrines of the diverse
communions." His amendment received no support and did not come
to a vote. Thwarted in the legislature, Quinet soon published his plan
in a book, L'enseignement du peuple.[72] His notion of liberty of education ran counter to the dominant discourse in the debate, and focused instead on liberty from the influence of any particular religion
in the schools of France, especially emancipation from the rule of
priests. He was adamant that his alternative was not atheistic. It was
a moral religion which he believed the public schools were best
suited to instill in future citizens. Quinet may have gained no support in the legislature for his project, but he earned a place for himself
next to Condorcet among the heroes of la morale laïque in France.

The Catholic response to the freedom offered by the law in both
public and free secondary education was immediate. About 250 new
Catholic secondary schools opened between 1850 and 1852, and the
figures continued to rise thereafter. Government figures recorded
that free secondary schools were operated by Jesuits, Marists, Lazar-
ists, Basilians, Picpucians, Doctrinaires, secular priests, and the dioceses. The free Catholic secondary schools surpassed the enrollments in any other category of secondary schools. Protestants acted
as well. Government figures showed thirteen free Protestant secondary schools in the 1860s. Jews chose to send their youth to religiously
mixed secondary schools and took advantage of the improved provisions of the law for separate Jewish religious instruction.[73]

The law facilitated the religions at the primary level as well. In
keeping with the priorities of the bishops, Catholics made particularly strong advances in the numbers of schools run by members of
religious congregations, schools known in the language of the day as

congréganiste. The number of *congréganiste* schools was already rising before the law, from 7,600 in 1843 to 10,300 in 1850, but after the law the figure rose even higher, to 18,300 by 1867.[74] Protestant schools benefited too, rising to nearly 2,000 in number by 1863. In Paris, there were 7 Reformed and Lutheran schools in 1852, 49 in 1862, and 98 in 1875. Jewish schools also increased;[75] and independent Protestants opened their first legally authorized schools, most connected with a local church group, but many sponsored by the Société évangélique. By one count, in 1865 there were 56 free schools throughout France run by independent Protestants; but the figure is probably low. Another report put the figure for the independent Protestant free schools in Paris alone at 14 in 1862 and 23 in 1875.[76]

Like the Guizot laws of 1833 and 1836, the Falloux law ratified, rather than trying to suppress, diversifying trends already well underway. The state religions welcomed the Falloux law, like the Guizot laws, as an advancement of their religious liberty. At the same time, because of the looseness of the references to non-Catholics, the independent Protestants also felt an improvement in their religious liberty. The combination of the Falloux law of 1850 for the schools and the decree in March 1859 relative to the public exercise of religion gave independent Protestants the experience of a substantial increase in their religious liberty in both church and school. The application of the education laws to Algeria led to the creation of the Islamic public schools in the French system and gave Muslims some compensation for the destruction of the Islamic religious schools attached to their mosques.

One set of people felt particularly excluded from the schools, however. These were the advocates of moral religion in the tradition of Condorcet and Quinet. During the 1860s and the early 1870s, they gave the liberty of education a test. Appealing to the Falloux law, they created free schools around France, offering instruction in *la morale laïque* and animated by what they called the *ésprit laïque*. At the national level they were given voice by the Ligue de l'Enseignement. Local societies sprang up as well. In the department of the Rhône, for example, the Société d'instruction libre et laïque began in 1869 and by 1873 directed seven schools. The Prefect of the *département* of the Rhône charged the instructors with violation of the Falloux law, claiming that their schools provided "free and *laïque* education outside all religious doctrine." In their defense the teachers appealed to the liberty of education and the Falloux law. The rulings of both the departmental and national councils went against them on the grounds that the law required religious and moral instruction in the traditional sense, and that the requirement applied to both public and free schools. In 1874 the schools of the *ésprit laïque* in Lyon were shut, as were those in Paris, Bordeaux, and elsewhere.[77]

The repression of the schools of the *ésprit laïque* preserved the government's national system of education and demonstrated the limits of religious liberty in education. The freedom of education within the system did not extend to the devotees of moral religion.

The remaining large sector without *liberté de l'enseignement* was higher education. In July 1875, a new law permitted the formation of free faculties and free universities.[78] The Catholic bishops welcomed the law as a further extension of the liberty of the church, and within a few months created the Free Catholic Universities of Paris, Angers, Lille, and Lyon, and the Free Faculty of Law of Toulouse. The Catholic Church retained the Faculties of Theology within the state system at Paris, Aix, Bordeaux, Lyon, and Rouen. Protestants were content with their two theological faculties at Montauban and Paris, and the Jews with their seminary at Paris, all funded by the state.

Changing Religious Establishments and Religious Liberty in France

Part 2: 1879-1908

C. T. McINTIRE

THE PREVIOUS CHAPTER has described the political and religious diversity of France between the Revolution and the beginning of the twentieth century and has looked closely at the major religious players—the Catholics, Reformed, Lutherans, and Jews—up to the 1870s. By then, as we have seen, the advocates of moral religion also had a role, albeit an ambiguous one. After the 1870s, it became clearer and more prominent. At the same time, the government made a major decision about the role of Islam in relation to the French state. In addition, the political and religious control of education and the religious and moral character of the schools became increasingly contentious, and complex, during the next 30 years, with new implications for religious freedom.

≺ I ≻

Another Religion and the Establishment of
Moral Religion in the Schools

The elections of 1879 gave the republicans a majority of the Senate in addition to the majority they had enjoyed in the Chamber of Deputies since 1876. The Third Republic was for the first time in the hands of republicans rather than monarchists, and most of the republicans were anticlerical. The elections of August 1881 returned an even larger majority of republicans in both houses.

The new government determined not to touch the foundational structures of the relations of the religions and the state. In 1879, enunciating government policy, Jules Ferry, minister of public instruction, defended the concordat with the pope as "the surest and best rampart against the undertakings of a certain section of the religious society against the independence of the civil society." Republicans feared a religious war against the state if the Catholic Church were let loose from the constraining power which the concordat gave them.[1] Out of self-defense, the republicans routinely fulfilled the state's obligations to the religious establishment. They named the bishops and principal Protestant officials and rabbis, and with the annual *budget des cultes* they paid the salaries of the 55,000 bishops and priests, 640 Reformed pastors, 70 Lutheran ministers, and 60 rabbis. They constructed new cathedrals, parish churches, and Protestant houses of worship; funded repairs of Catholic, Protestant, and Jewish religious buildings; and underwrote the transportation costs of clergy and rabbis going to Algeria.[2] The government did, nonetheless, introduce measures to constrict some of the public and social expressions of religious life. Between July 1880 and August 1884, the republicans abolished the public observance of Sunday as a day of rest, abolished military escorts for religious processions and withdrew military guards for episcopal palaces, expelled the Jesuits, barred clergy and rabbis from election to local office, gave local officials powers to place restrictions on public worship, reintroduced divorce, and cancelled the obligation of the quadrilaterals to pray for the work of the new legislature.[3]

While remembering the concordat, the republicans did not overlook the advantages of state controls over the Islamic religion in Algeria. Their acts toward Islam stemmed from a policy analogous with their Catholic policy, coupled with their policy to assimilate Algeria into France. Their predecessors in the Third Republic had already reorganized the administration of the region and made it directly responsible to the ministry of the interior in Paris. All the native Jews of Algeria were declared French citizens, and the Muslims were called French subjects. By 1876, what remained of the confiscated Muslim properties yielded so little revenue that the government was faced with either cutting off the Islamic religion or charging the whole of the costs of maintaining it to the national budget in Paris. The government chose to move the Islamic religious expenses into the budget of Algeria within the ministry of the interior. These costs included the salaries of official religious personnel and the maintenance of mosques as well as grants for the construction of new mosques, the administration of Islamic law for Muslims, and provision for Islamic public schools which the application of the Falloux law to Algeria had extended. Only 1 percent of Muslim children of primary school age in the early 1880s went to school, but of those who did, 90 percent attended an Islamic public school in the French system.[4]

The republic of the republicans took the matter further. In August 1881, while debating and then reaffirming the state religious establishments, the republicans placed all the costs related to the Islamic religion, along with the other civil services of Algeria, under the direct authority of the appropriate ministries in Paris, and they authorized the application of all French laws and ministerial instructions directly to Algeria.[5] Islamic public schools went to the ministry of public instruction and fine arts, Islamic law to the ministry of justice, the construction of new mosques to the ministry of public works, while costs of the salaries of the official muftis and imams, and the maintenance of their mosques, were given to the ministry of religions. With this act, they completed the integration of Algeria into France. Algeria remained the exception within the burgeoning overseas empire of France—not a colony, not a protectorate, but France.[6]

With the decree of 1881, the Islamic religion took its position among the state-established religions of France. The *budget des cultes* now displayed five religions in a single list, ordered in this hierarchy: the Catholic religion, the Protestant religions, the Jewish religion, and the Islamic religion.[7] Two profound exceptions continued to apply to the status of Islam. Its establishment pertained only to that part of France which was Algeria; and the Algerian Muslims resented, and did not finally accept, what the French did to their religion. Algerian Muslims protested that the state establishment of Islam in France-Algeria impeded, and did not advance, their religious liberty.

At the very moment when the anticlerical republican government itself was adding Islam to the list of state establishments, the government took the first steps in what became an unmitigated offensive against the French state religions in the sphere of the schools. State power swung from the established religions to the very people whose schools of the *ésprit laïque* were closed by the government throughout France a mere five years earlier. Radical republicans had already made one attempt in 1877 and 1878 to supplant the Falloux law of 1850. They projected an omnibus law on education that would make the primary schools compulsory and free of cost for students, place all teachers on state salary, and eliminate traditional religion and the religious orders from the schools. But as over the motions to abolish the concordat, the government demurred, concluding that this one would risk a protracted war over the schools. The government resolved to handle the matter piece by piece, while keeping the comprehensive outcome in full view.[8]

Ferry, the political leader, was fortified by his own religious convictions and view of history. He had strong Protestant connections. He had married into a Protestant family. He came to power when William Waddington, a Protestant, became premier, and served under the two terms of another Protestant premier, Charles de Freycinet. But he also styled himself a positivist and joined the Masonic Order in 1875. As follower of Auguste Comte, he believed that the course of the ages was an evolution of humanity away from the tutelage of religion and metaphysics and toward a civilization under human self-direction, driven by the love of humanity. Ferry did not need to push and rush. The schools would become free in due course. It was enough for the government to blend its efforts into the natural evolution of humanity.[9]

Behind Ferry was Ferdinand Buisson, director of primary education, and a Protestant from the liberal wing of the Église reformée. Buisson provided the thinking and articulated the arguments driving the campaign. He was a foe of orthodoxy, dogmatism, and sectarianism, and the perpetual enemy of religious officials who usurped the freedom of the ordinary lay member of any religion. He championed the freedom of the individual conscience. In a lecture to public school teachers in August 1878, he summarized "the capital truths" which surpassed the variable creeds of the churches, and which teachers should instill in their school children: "What does not change is the intuition of the infinite and the divine, of moral perfection, justice, devotion, the intuition of this other grand thing which one has never been able to define and which one loves no less because of it: *la Patrie*." The duty of teachers is "to present to your children a sufficient enough image of the moral ideal and to keep up the worship of it in their soul." Buisson went through a religious evolution of his own and found himself passing gradually beyond the

Reformed tradition, but his core beliefs endured. He later named what he espoused *"la religion laïque de l'idéal moral"* and *"la foi laïque,"* and he devised "Seven Articles of Faith" to go with it.[10]

For Ferry, Buisson, and the republicans, as for the Catholic Church, the foremost issue was one of authority, the authority of the state to control education in France at all levels. The Guizot and Falloux laws elaborated a complex system of shared authority, distributed among the communes, the *départements*, and the national government, and among the established religions. This shared regime replaced both the older system of church supremacy and the Napoleonic system of state supremacy. Ferry, backed by Buisson, spoke repeatedly in the legislature about the preeminence of the state in education. His formulation varied with the issue, but the point was the same every time. In 1879, in answer to those who demanded that the government not intrude on girls' education, he responded, "I say (to you), that the education of girls, like all education, is the possession (*le bien*) of the state, the sphere (*le domaine*) of the state."[11] In 1880, speaking in defense of the abolition of fees for elementary schools, he declared, "The duty of the state in the matter of primary education is absolute—the state owes it to all."[12]

In Ferry's view, the Third Republic was the fulfillment of French history, and the Third Republic was obliged to act according to the "principles of 1789," the highest of which was *la Patrie*. The French state has the sacred mission to make all children into citizens of an undivided France. The schools are the medium by which the state performs its work. The schools belong to the state and serve as the agents of the state. The state cannot share its work with religion, since all religions divide. Of this the Catholic Church is particularly guilty, especially the religious orders and above all the Jesuits. Their cause is the counterrevolution, the destruction of the Third Republic. In the face of this, the state must control education so that the youth of France "revere 1789 as a deliverance and modern society as an ideal," and act accordingly as citizens when their education is complete.[13]

The corollary of this absolutist and unitarian doctrine of state power over education was the redefinition of religion as a matter belonging to a purely personal and private sphere. Both the Gallican system before 1789 and the religious settlements still in force depended on the conviction that religion belonged to the public life of

France. The Napoleonic *Université* as well as the Guizot and Falloux modifications constructed the educational system with religion as part of the public order. Ferry and Buisson intended to break with that tradition, and to compel the religions to withdraw from the public order in education. Speaking in 1880 in support of the proposal to remove all religious ministers from the governance and supervision of public education, Ferry enunciated the doctrine of the limits of religion:

> Today, if the State does not permit the (Catholic) Church to invade its rights, it does not allow itself any longer to usurp the liberties of the Church. She is mistress of her sacraments and her ceremonies up to the door of the sanctuary and with the single reservation of the rights that the Organic Articles allocate to the public administration, in the interest of families, the State, and the Church herself. Beyond this, the civil law alone acts and commands.[14]

With this doctrine, Ferry negated fundamental teachings of Catholics, Reformed, Lutherans, Jews, and Muslims alike, all of whom, in different ways, affirmed that religion and life were indivisible. For them, their religions properly informed their existence outside the walls of their religious buildings, most certainly including the education of their children. Ferry was not prepared to challenge the public carriage of the established religions within the religious settlements, but he did reject the role of the churches and synagogues in public education.[15]

Ferry and Buisson's doctrine also entailed a direct conflict with an understanding of religious liberty shared by the state religions within the context of French law. The Catholics, Protestants, and Jews who accepted the Napoleonic religious settlements as well as the education laws did so because they enjoyed relative liberty as religious communities in the practice of their religions and the education of their children. Within the bounds of the constraints laid upon them, they felt protected from attack by the state and each other. Ferry and Buisson reversed the meaning of liberty in two ways. They sought to protect individuals, rather than religious communities; and they gave protections, not against the state, but against institutional religion and religious ministers. Religious liberty did not mean the freedom of religious formation in the schools, but the freedom of individual conscience from religious imposition in the schools.

Ferry began the legislative campaign in March 1879 with two projects of law, both focusing on the issue of governance. The first, approved in February 1880, removed the established religions from the governance of the public system at the national and departmental levels. They were replaced entirely by educators, barring any educator who was a cleric. A later law, in March 1882, removed clerics from local school governance.[16]

Ferry's second project asserted state authority over universities and undercut the free Catholic universities, recently founded after the extension of the liberty of education to higher education in 1875. The original version included article 7, a tangential ban against teachers at any level who were members of unauthorized religious orders. After vehement debate which engulfed the country, the article was dropped. The final version, in March 1880, permitted "free institutions of higher education" to continue to exist, but deprived them of some of the most important marks of a university—the rights to hold their own examinations, to grant degrees, and to use the name university. These rights were given to the state institutions as a state monopoly, and any students in the Catholic institutions who desired university examinations and degrees had to go to the state faculties.[17] In 1885, the government went further and suppressed all five Catholic theological faculties within the state university system; but it retained the Protestant theological faculties at Montauban and Paris within the state system. The Jewish seminary at Paris continued to receive funding.

The offending article 7 took on another form as the government refocused on the issue of the teachers. The aim was to cleanse the schools of clerical teachers and create a professional teaching corps loyal to the state. The republicans feared the religious orders as the greatest threat to republican liberties. Their fears were deeply religious, political, and sexual.[18] As early as 1877 many newly republican municipal councils petitioned the prefects of their *départements* to remove teachers who were members of religious orders from the public schools and replace them with non-clerical personnel. This was called the *laïcisation* of personnel. In many localities this was done, often with intense local battles and court cases, and the movement spread. By 1880 about 70 *congréganiste* public schools were laicized or converted into free schools.[19] Backing away for the moment, the republican majority agreed to pass no new laws, but to ask the government simply to enforce existing law. In March 1880, the government required unauthorized orders to apply for legal recognition within three months, declining to say what would happen if they did not.[20] A second decree attacked the Jesuits, who were given three months to dissolve themselves and vacate their premises, and five months to vacate their schools.[21] The Jesuits did not disband, and during the summer the government sent the police to force the Jesuits from their 37 houses and their many collèges throughout France. The evictions continued in the fall against the unauthorized orders who failed to register. Ferry reported to the legislature that the police expelled 5,643 men religious from 261 religious houses. The women religious were left untouched.[22]

Great as the conflict was, the government came nowhere near the goal of removing the religious orders from the schools. Indeed, if the campaign had succeeded, it would have damaged not only the religious orders, but the schools, especially schools for girls, and the government. In 1876, members of religious orders staffed almost 20,000 schools out of the 71,500 in France, including a big share of the large urban schools. Counting teachers in public and free schools, and including head teachers (titulaires) and assistants (adjoints), there were 110,700 teachers in France. Of these, 46,700 were members of religious orders. There were no replacements on that scale prepared to take over.[23]

The government took the slow route to the goal. The state needed a teaching corps that was trained to teach in the manner and spirit that befit the state's purposes in the schools. With little opposition, in August 1879 the legislature required every département of France to maintain a normal school for the training of women teachers, in addition to the stipulation of the Guizot law of 1833 requiring a normal school for men. By 1876, 78 out of 87 départements, plus Algeria, had normal schools for men, but only 17 and Algeria had a school for women. The new schools were to take over the role of the religious orders in providing teachers for girls' schools, and to replace the many teacher training courses for women run by Catholics. The plan worked immediately, and by 1881 there were already 41 women's normal schools.[24]

To prepare the professors to teach in the new women's normal schools, the government founded the École normale supérieure at Fontenay-aux-Roses in July 1880, and then two more at St. Cloud and Sèvres. The school at Fontenay was the centerpiece. To direct it, Ferry and Buisson selected Félix Pécaut, also a liberal Protestant who was dedicated to moral religion freed from dogma, sectarianism, and clerical influence.[25] The next step was the teacher's certificate, the *brevet de capacité*. In June 1881, the government abolished the provisions of the Falloux law which permitted members of religious orders, priests, Protestant clergy, and Jewish rabbis to teach in the schools without the teacher's certificate.[26] The *brevet* was now mandatory, without exception, for both public and free schools. Teachers without the *brevet* had two years to pass the examination given by the state, or else lose their positions, and all new appointments were required to have the certificate in hand. The requirement fell most heavily on the members of religious orders, particularly women. In 1876, of the 46,700 teachers who were members of religious orders, 37,100, 31,500 of them women, did not have the *brevet*. The timetable for passing the examination was onerous, but nearly nine out of ten succeeded in passing. The others left the schools. After the law on the *brevet*, *départements* opened women's normal schools at a faster rate. By 1886 the number had risen to 81.[27]

In March 1882, almost as an aside, the government blocked one of the avenues for recruiting public school teachers from the state religions. The Falloux law had authorized heads of religious orders and the consistories of the Protestant denominations and Jewish religion to nominate their members as teachers for the public schools. The new law abolished the provision and confined the selection of teachers entirely to the municipal council of each commune (article 3).[28]

The effect of the government's actions between 1880 and 1885 was a loss of 3,500 *congréganiste* public schools. But this was not enough to satisfy the republican majority. It took Ferry's successor, René Goblet, to complete Ferry's legislative program for religious teachers in the public schools. The Goblet education law in October 1886 was straightforward: "In the public schools of every level, teaching is exclusively entrusted to lay personnel" (article 17).[29] While the Catholic religious orders and congregations were the explicit target, Protestant and Jewish religious personnel also were affected. The law authorized further *laïcisation*, what it euphemistically called "the substitution of lay personnel for *congréganiste* personnel" (article 18). Whether or not they had the state teaching certificate, all men religious were banned from teaching in the public schools. They had five years to leave or be removed, to be replaced by non-clerical teachers. Women religious were also banned, but they had no deadline for their removal. During the first twelve months following the law, prefects laicized 553 schools, affecting 24,500 pupils, and transferred 276 *congréganiste* public schools, with 18,000 pupils, to free school status, cutting off their funding. Notices of laicizations appeared in the *Journal Officiel*, day by day, week by week, for years. Between 1885 and 1890 the number of *congréganiste* public schools fell another 2,200, and still another 3,450 by 1900.[30]

The male religious in the public schools were decimated. The previous actions of the government had already reduced their numbers from the high of about 6,900 teachers in 1876, to 4,100 in 1882, and 2,500 in 1886. By 1891, five years after the Goblet law, there were virtually none. The government met the target and achieved a male teaching corps with entirely non-clerical members. The effect on women religious was enormous, but not yet total. Their numbers in the public schools fell from the high of about 20,000 in 1876, to 16,200 in 1882, 13,100 in 1886, and 11,200 in 1891. As with the men, the overall number of women teachers increased much faster than the rate of removal of women religious. In 1876 women religious made up about 60 percent of the girls' public school corps. By 1891, they made up just under 25 percent. The government plan was succeeding here as well, although for pragmatic reasons women religious were still needed as teachers for girls' public schools. The republicans were content for the moment to leave the free schools alone.[31]

The process of securing state jurisdiction over the teachers included two crucial financial steps. In June 1881, the state assumed full financial authority over the public primary system and abolished all tuition fees.[32] In July 1889, the state put all public school teachers on state salary. These acts shifted the balance of power away from the local level to the national, and away from the religious orders to the state. The national budget rose catastrophically with the abolition of fees and the absorption, and increase, of the salaries of teachers not in religious orders; but for the republican government the effect was worth it. The teachers became a national state teaching corps, entirely under the authority of the state, paid by the state, removed from any connection with religious authorities, and no longer subject to religious pressures through the local councils.[33]

On the two issues raised so far, governance and the teachers, the state put severe limits on the free exercise of religion in education. The third issue, the religious content of the curriculum and the religious environment of the schools, imposed still further limits. When Ferry introduced the project of compulsory primary school attendance in January 1880, he intended to treat the question of religion and the curriculum in a separate and later law. The republican majority, however, insisted on linking the religious question with compulsory schooling. The move was extraordinarily controversial, and it took until March 1882 to pass the law. The agitation was not due to the requirement of school attendance, since, on this point, the law simply brought a national full enrollment trend to completion.[34] The controversy attached to the first two articles of the law, which transformed the religious content of the school curriculum and the religious environment of the public schools. The language of the law was abrupt, and, considering the magnitude of its consequences, meager. It began, "Primary education consists of: Moral and civic instruction; Reading and writing; The language and elements of French literature"; and so on, through a list of courses, ending with a line abrogating the curriculum defined by the Falloux law in 1850 (article 1). Public schools were closed one day a week other than Sunday to permit parents to give their children religious education outside school buildings, and private schools could add religious education to their curriculum if they wished (article 2).

The contrast with previous law could not be sharper. For 50 years all primary schools under French law had begun the day as the law prescribed, with "moral and religious instruction." The Ferry law of 1882 altered one word, and with that word changed the religious make-up of the curriculum. A legislative commission chaired by Paul Bert conceived the idea, and, in a stroke, "moral and religious instruction" became "moral and civic instruction."[35]

Ferry, Bert, and Buisson, defending the new wording, evoked four primary arguments against traditional religious teaching in the state public school system. They all assumed the aim of the school to be the formation of future citizens of the one *Patrie*. First, the schools must respect the "liberty of conscience" of both the teachers and the pupils, and cannot impose upon any citizens religious teaching which they do not believe. Second, the schools must be entirely neutral among the religions, and cannot favor any one religious teaching over another. Third, the schools must educate future citizens in the morals and civics common to all civilized people, and cannot instill doctrines particular to any religion. Fourth, the schools must leave religious teaching to the religions and families, and cannot usurp their role in religious teaching.

The government issued the new program and timetable for moral instruction in July 1882, followed by a revision in January 1887 after the Goblet law. Buisson and Paul Janet, philosopher and advocate of moral religion, wrote the text.[36] Moral instruction was one of three parts of the curriculum, along with physical and intellectual education. Moral education, the 1887 text explained, "differs fundamentally in aim and character" from the other two parts:

Moral instruction is intended to complete and bind together, to elevate and to ennoble all the other instruction in the school. While each of the other branches tends to develop a special order of aptitudes and of useful knowledge, this study tends to develop the man himself—that is to say, his heart, his intelligence, his conscience. Hence moral instruction moves in an altogether different sphere from the other subjects.

This is the same sort of function traditionally ascribed to religious instruction. In method too, moral education has the character of religious instruction. It depends less on reason and precision than on "the intensity of feeling, the vividness of impression, and the contagious ardor of conviction" engendered by the teacher. Moral education is "the art of inclining the free will toward the good." The teacher may assume, said the text, that the pupils have received at home and in their religious communities basic familiarity with the idea of God, practices of worship, and eternal and universal morality. The teacher should not oppose these, but should complement them, and, teaching by example and from the heart, lead all the children to live their lives according to "those essential notions of a morality common to all civilized men." The aim is to prepare them so that later in life they will join "in feeling united in that fealty to the good, the beautiful, and the true, which is also a form, and not the least pure, of the religious sentiment."

The 1882 program laid out the moral curriculum in detail. At each level it included religious feeling and religious teachings. In children up through age nine, the teacher seeks, among other aims, to develop "the feeling of admiration for the order of the universe and of religious feeling." For those between ages nine and 13, the teacher must cover the whole range of duties which the child owes toward the family, the school, *la Patrie*, oneself, and others, culminating in the duties the child owes to God. The teachings about God focus on certain divine attributes—God as First Cause, as Perfect Being, as one to be venerated, as one to whom the child owes homage, as the author of the divine laws to which the child owes obedience, as one toward whom the child feels he can do wrong, and as one who warrants respect even when appearing in the various religions in different forms. The teacher helps the child to discern the revelation of the laws of God which comes "by his conscience and his reason." The teachings include belief in the soul.

During the first year of moral and civic instruction Catholic opposition was immense, reaching even to Rome. Catholic rejection of the new curriculum crystallized around four textbooks explaining the new teachings which the Vatican denounced as unsuitable for use by Catholic teachers or children. Bishops circulated the Vatican decree against the textbooks, and, in so doing, violated the concordat requiring government authorization of papal documents before their publication in France. Thousands of priests spoke against the textbooks and the new curriculum in their parishes. Local conflicts erupted in at least twelve *départements*, leading sometimes to violence in the streets and priests refusing the sacraments to teachers. The government reacted by stopping the salaries of some 2,000 priests, including five bishops; interrogating five priests before the Council of State; and threatening to break the concordat. Pope Leo XIII and the French president Jules Grévy combined to pacify the conflict before it went any further. The government's show of force succeeded in restraining the Catholic response to the new direction in the schools.[37]

In November 1883, Ferry addressed a conciliatory letter to the then 88,000 public school teachers of France, but without retreating from the new program.[38] He reminded the teachers that, in morals education, the law commissioned the teacher to act as the representative of *la Patrie*. In the eyes of the legislature, each one of them was, he said, "a natural auxiliary of moral and social progress." He explained how they should fulfill this high role and sought to inspire them in their mission. Moral and civic education was a new form of education for France, he said, and they were the first to teach it to the children of the nation. Their task was "to prepare a generation of good citizens for our country."

The revision of 1887 prescribed the daily exercises that had grown up around moral instruction since 1882. Moral instruction came first in the day and occupied the position traditionally filled by religious instruction. A liturgy evolved. The teacher should present "a lesson in the form of a familiar talk, or an appropriate reading devoted to moral instruction." The lesson might include a moral maxim drawn from general wisdom or a great leader. The teacher would write the maxim where all the pupils could see it, and they would recite it. There might be a song. The teacher should speak in a manner and tone of voice which induces the changes of heart called for by the program.

The model for these morning exercises came from Félix Pécaut, the head of the École normale supérieure at Fontenay-aux-Roses. Participants in his program described them as religious exercises, comparing them to morning prayer, and testified of the religious impression the experience made upon them.[39] Pécaut's commitment was to "train the young teachers of the people to consider themselves devoted to a divine task, in which they are working in the direction of God himself." Buisson professed, "we believe that we are performing not only a moral and philosophical work, but one profoundly religious as well . . . We pity those who, being able to see God only through denominational forms and traditional ceremonies, do not see him in our doctrines, and do not perceive that He is nowhere more present and more profoundly active than in that humble sanctuary of education which they call the school without God."[40]

The features of the program of moral instruction—its content and teachings, its spirituality, its role in the curriculum, the teacher's mission, the methods, the daily exercises, the effect on the lives of the pupils—all indicate that what the government instituted in the schools was not merely a school lesson, but religious in its own right. It was not Catholic, Reformed, Lutheran, Jewish, or Islamic. But neither was it atheist, in the sense of belief that there is no God, or secularist, in the sense of belief that humanity or this world is ultimate, and it was not nothing. Its proponents described it as religious. They named it *la morale laïque* and *la foi laïque*, and the movement promoting it was *laïcisme*. When they used the term *la morale*, they specifically embraced religious content and religious commitment about God, the soul, spirituality, and human nature. They firmly believed that what it represented was neutral with respect to the traditional religions and universal with respect to humanity, even though Catholics found it offensive and unsuitable for their children.[41]

It is worth returning to the arguments Ferry, Bert, and Buisson used to expel the traditional religions from the schools, and seeing how well they matched the effects of the government's legislation. First, the government did not respect the liberty of conscience of all, but instead explicitly imposed universal moral religion on the teachers and the pupils. Second, the government did not render the schools religiously neutral, but favored universal moral religion over the traditional religions. Third, the government did not rid the schools of all religious doctrines that were particular in character, but, with the teachings of the moral and civic curriculum, installed the doctrines of universal moral religion in place of those of the traditional religions. Fourth, the government left to the churches, synagogues, mosques, and families the teaching of the Catholic, Protestant, Jewish, and Islamic religions, but entrusted to the schools the teaching of universal moral religion.

The legislative and educational program of Ferry, Buisson, and the republicans reconstructed the religious identity of the national public school system. By means of the changes in governance, the teaching corps, and the curriculum and daily practice, the government disestablished the state religions in the schools and established in their place the teachings and practice of universal moral religion in the tradition of Condorcet and Quinet. The state religions experienced the moves against them in the public schools as a loss of a significant part of their religious liberty. By contrast, the advocates of *la morale laïque* found the reversal of roles in the schools utterly liberating. They were free to create what they called the *école laïque*, schools animated by the *esprit laïque* in which *la morale laïque* reigned.

In terms of enrollment, most Catholic pupils attended the government's *école laïque*, the only school available in the majority of communes. Most parishes accommodated themselves to the law by providing religious instruction in the church on Thursdays when the public schools closed for that purpose. But next to this trend arose a dramatic Catholic rejection of the government's public schools. Catholics created free schools in large numbers, particularly schools operated by the religious orders, many financed with great hardship without state money. Overall, the total number of schools run by religious orders by 1901 was about 18,300, roughly the same as 1876 and, indeed, the 1860s, but now 80 percent were free schools, more than the reverse of 1876. By 1901, about one-fourth of all pupils in France attended a *congréganiste* free school.[42]

Protestants, excepting the liberals, among whom Buisson was one, were generally suspicious of the *école laïque*, but they felt unable to finance and maintain a Protestant free school system. In any case, lingering Protestant anti-Catholicism made them continue to fear Catholics more than the promoters of universal moral religion. The Protestant response was to establish "Thursday schools" by the hundreds, institutions connected with a Protestant church which gave religious instruction mid week as allowed by the law. Jews likewise responded by adding to the number of religious schools connected with the synagogues.[43]

The case of Islamic public schools in Algeria presented a special problem. The government's immediate impulse was to apply the new school laws to the public system of Algeria without modification. This they did, at least for the Catholic, Protestant, and Jewish schools, by means of article 68 of the Goblet law and decrees in February 1883 and November 1887. But they hesitated to follow through with the Muslims. Muslims raised an outcry against the elimination of Islamic public schools and the stipulation that all Muslim children, including girls, must attend the Republic's *école laïque*. In any case, the logistics of enforcing the new laws in a land where only 1 percent of primary school-age children went to school were overwhelming. The government inserted the caveat in the second decree that the law would only be implemented for Muslims by special order of the governor general in each case (article 14). The Islamic public schools survived, and the republicans even found themselves opening more of them and increasing their budget. The paradox of benevolent tyranny remained, as the Islamic public schools of France-Algeria became the exception in the government's establishment of *la morale laïque* in the public schools.[44]

≺ II ≻

Disestablishment in France and the Ongoing
Establishment of Moral Religion in the Schools

Newly enflamed by the Dreyfus affair, the protracted war among varieties of monarchists and republicans, clericals and anticlericals, burned wildly during the 1890s, destroying the Catholic *ralliement* to the Republic promoted by Pope Leo XIII in 1892. Under President Émile Loubet, a moderate republican, René Waldeck-Rousseau formed a moderate republican ministry in June 1899 designed to pacify national politics. In the elections of 1901, however, radical republicans and socialists gained such strength that the premier resigned. The new government under Émile Combes, from June 1902, was vigorously and stridently anticlerical. Waldeck-Rousseau's government had opened a campaign against the religious orders with the aim to regulate, not destroy. Combes's government transformed the campaign into a battle against the religious orders and their share in French education. The battle unexpectedly escalated into a full-scale war against the state religions, especially the Catholic Church and the concordat with the pope. The outcome, completed under the government of Maurice Rouvier after Combes's resignation in January 1905, initially seemed straightforward but then appeared more and more ambiguous. The relations of the religions, the state, and the schools altered radically, with the schools fulfilling an extraordinarily powerful role.

In July 1901, by the law of association the state ended the toleration of religious orders operating without state approval.[45] The intellectual basis of the law was the notion of an "association," construed as a permanent relationship of two or more individual persons for a common end. The republicans applied the law to religious congregations. Hereafter, religious congregations needed a special law in each case authorizing them to exist, and a special decree in each case permitting them to operate a school or other institution. They could be closed by simple decree. Unauthorized religious orders had three months to secure approval or to be shut, their property confiscated and later sold. New congregations had to apply for approval through a cumbersome process which inhibited their formation. The Catholic Church considered the law so serious a threat that Leo XIII himself intervened twice to oppose it. He objected to the treatment of religious orders as associations of individuals rather than as hierarchically ordered communities of religious men and women bound by vows to God. More pointedly, he protested that the law "restricts the liberty of the Church" guaranteed by the concordat and "hinders the Church from fulfilling her divine mission."[46]

The government began to enforce the law at once. Under Combes, enforcement became severe, driven by republican political and sex-

ual fears of nuns and monks, the people deemed most threatening to
the Republic, the Republic's schools, and the Republic's children.
The effects on the religious orders were devastating. Of the 1,663 religious congregations in France in 1901, 753 were unauthorized; of
this number 305 dissolved themselves rather than submit to the government, and 448 applied for authorization. The government, applying the law harshly, denied approval to most of them, including
almost all teaching congregations. The government closed 2,500
schools connected with congregations in July and August 1902, and
then another 9,500 during 1903.[47]

From the radical republican point of view, these measures were
only partially effective. For the Combes government, the goal became more clearly the removal of all *congréganiste* teaching from
the schools of France and the building up of the universal *école
laïque*. Two further laws, in July 1904 and January 1905, hit directly
at the congregations engaged in teaching.[48] The 1904 law was blunt:
"Teaching on every level and of every kind is forbidden in France
to religious congregations" (article 1). The ban applied to all congregations, whether authorized or not, to teaching orders as well as
those for whom teaching was only one of their objects, and to public
schools as well as free schools. A ten-year period was set for the closure and liquidation of existing congregations and their schools. At
the insistence of the ministers of foreign affairs and the colonies, the
ban was limited to France and Algeria and not applied to the rest of
the world where expanding French imperial interests needed the congregations to supply schools and teachers. To insure the congregations would not use this provision against state interests, the state
would strictly control the number of novitiates.

The new pope, Pius X, protested vigorously. The government
violated the role of France as "the classic nation of liberty and gen-
erosity," he said, and denied thousands of nuns and monks their liberties as citizens. The argument referred to the ancient Gallican
liberties and appealed to the new republican liberties. Buisson himself, now a professor in the Sorbonne, a radical republican in the legislature, and more of a Free Thinker than a liberal Protestant, had felt
compelled to answer the argument when it arose during the debates
on the congregations. Only individuals have natural rights, he said,
not communities. The religious congregations are associations of individuals and, as associations, possess only those rights and liberties

conferred by the state, in this case by the law of associations. Just as the state confers these rights and liberties, so the state may withdraw them, and close the congregations and their schools. Their members cease to be nuns and monks in France, but they remain citizens. If they hold the proper certification, they may continue to teach, no longer as monks and nuns, but as qualified citizens. To the pope and the Catholic Church, this was an apology for state tyranny against the liberties of the Catholic religion.[49]

Acting on the law, the government followed the policy of closing *congréganiste* schools in every commune where the pupils had an *école laïque* to go to. During 1904 and 1905 this meant closing another 3,000 *congréganiste* schools. Altogether in the four years following the 1901 law, the regime shut 15,000 *congréganiste* schools, 3,000 public and 12,000 free, and forceably turned hundreds of religious out of their schools and confiscated many religious houses. For the moment, the government let the remaining 3,000 *congréganiste* schools stay open as an expedient. In 1881, when the republicans began their legislative program for the *école laïque*, about one-third of all French pupils were enrolled in a *congréganiste* school. By 1901 the figure was still 27 percent. Then as a result of the war against the congregations the figure fell to 4 percent in 1906 and 0.6 percent in 1912. By that date, only 27 *congréganiste* schools remained in the public system, and a few hundred remained as free schools, mostly for girls, staffed by nuns. The government reached virtual zero by the target date of 1915. The government's action against the religious orders eliminated their schools, both public and free, and ended the liberty of education as understood in France since 1833. The republicans completed their system of public education with *la morale laïque* installed as the only religious expression permitted in the public schools.[50]

The Catholic Church and the religious orders responded in various ways to this ruin of their religious ministry in education and the imposition of the *école laïque*. From 1905 onward thousands of Catholic men joined associations in communes across France to insure that the *écoles laïques* did not teach anticlerical doctrines or force unsuitable books on their children. In October 1902, during the initial stages of the attack on the congregations, 74 bishops signed a collective letter of protest to the legislature. The government replied by stopping the salaries of the leading bishops. The bishops protested against the 1904 law, and the government responded with more repressive measures. Many schools reopened illegally after their closure, but were quickly shut. Several hundred cases went to court, all of which the religious lost or dropped. Hundreds of religious kept their vows and left France to teach in the colonies and protectorates or, as during the French Revolution, to regroup in Italy, Belgium, and Austria. Most of the bishops released the religious from their vows if they asked, permitting them to live outside the congregations and teach as lay people. In this capacity the newly laicized religious led a powerful Catholic movement to reject the *école laïque*. In perhaps 60 percent of the cases across France, the former religious operated a lay free school in place of the closed *congréganiste* public school, rather than accept the government's *école laïque*. The figure rose to 80 percent and 90 percent in some regions. Enrollments in lay free schools escalated from 119,000 in 1901 to 1,032,000 in 1912, representing an increase in their share of the total pupil enrollment which equaled about half of the pupils lost by the congregations in the same period. The government tolerated the ruse as a temporary expedient, while the religious suffered the awful destruction of their religious vocation and the Catholic Church lost still more of her liberty.[51]

The Combes government initially had no desire to tamper with the religious establishments, since, like every ministry since Napoleon, even this most anticlerical regime found the bonds attaching the religions to the state useful for safeguarding state interests. Well into 1904 both Combes and Loubet were still publicly affirming the concordat with the pope, but a combination of events made them slip into an attack on the religious settlements. Relations between the Catholic Church and the government had been worsening since 1901. Besides the conflict over the religious orders and schools, the two parties disputed the interpretation of the concordat and disagreed over the mechanism for the nomination of bishops. The pope refused names put forward by the government to fill episcopal vacancies, the government nullified the pope's orders to bishops which were not communicated via the minister of religions, the pope protested the insult to papal dignity which he felt from Loubet's official visit to the king of Italy in Rome itself, and each one accused the other of usurping its freedoms and prerogatives under the concordat.

Then, in July 1904, the French government acted preemptively and broke diplomatic relations with the Vatican, which, said the

French, "by the will of the Holy See, were now found to be without purpose." In November 1904, Combes introduced a bill to terminate the maintenance of the religions by the state and define the legal position of the religions thereafter. The government no longer feared religious war. The republican majority had put up with the religious establishments for a generation since coming to power, and now, for the first time, they believed that the Third Republic and the electoral power of the anticlericals were sufficiently secure to survive counterattacks by the Catholic Church and the pope. After vehement debate and criss-crossing accusations, a substantial republican majority in the legislature under Rouvier's government approved a much modified law in December 1905, the one we know as the law of the separation of church and state. A series of government decrees, circulars, and further laws, running into April 1908, interpreted, implemented, and modified the law.[52]

The law of 1905 contained an opening declaration about religious liberty, together with a statement about the limits of this liberty: "The Republic assures the liberty of conscience. She guarantees the free exercise of religions under those restrictions decreed hereafter in the interest of public order" (article 1).[53] The rest of the law was a contradictory network of freedoms given and freedoms taken away which changed the structures but left the religions and the state entwined. The legislators dismantled the system of religious establishments by abolishing the concordat with the pope and the Organic Articles for the Catholic Church, as well as the religious settlements with the Reformed, the Lutherans, and the Jews, and finally the semi-settlement in 1859 for the independent churches and new religions (article 44). However, they expressly declined to abolish the settlement for the Muslims of Algeria, providing simply that future administrative regulations would "determine the conditions in which the present law will be applicable to Algeria and the colonies" (article 43). They prohibited the use of government funds for religious exercises and terminated the salaries of the clergy and rabbis paid by the state, allowing four to eight years for the transition; but they approved government money for religious chaplaincies in public institutions such as *lycées*, *collèges*, schools, hospitals, asylums, and prisons (article 2), and retained Easter Monday and Pentecost Monday as state holidays. They left the payment of the salaries to the religions, but they did not return the properties confiscated from the religions which the religions had used to pay and house their clergy.

Neither did they provide an endowment for the religions to use in compensation for a century of government prohibitions and restrictions against the receipt of non-state funds and legacies by the religions. The state retained ownership of most of the religious buildings of France (article 12). The law acknowledged that some properties and goods did belong to the religions and would remain with them, but the power to decide which was which was given to government agents. The agents were to draw up inventories of the properties and goods of the religions, with a description and estimate of the value of each item. The commission noted that, in many cases, the determination of ownership would fall to the courts.

The legislators also abolished the primary religious institutions— the Catholic dioceses and parishes, the Protestant churches and consistories, and the Jewish synagogues and consistories (article 2). In place of these, they compelled all the religions to adopt a new social structure, called *associations cultuelles*. The religions had one year to transfer the control of their public religious activities and their worldly goods to these *associations cultuelles*. The state would then grant the associations the free use in perpetuity of the state-owned churches and synagogues. As a transitional measure the state would also give them free use of the state-owned clerical houses and goods for two to five years, after which the state was permitted to sell or otherwise dispose of them. Any conflict arising within a religion over the formation of the associations would be adjudicated and decided by the state (article 8).

The sole purpose of an *association cultuelle* was "the public exercise of a religion," involving the finances, organization, and functions of public worship and other religious activities. As with religious orders in 1901, the state now treated churches and synagogues as associations, a social form which befitted a sports club or charitable society but which did not match the theologies or traditional structures of the religions. *Associations cultuelles* were local organizations composed of a minimum of 7, 15, or 25 dues-paying individuals, depending on the size of the commune, and they could form unions with other associations. They were lay controlled, with authority vested in a general assembly of all members, meeting at least once a year.

Associations could own and administer properties and collect funds, but the amount they could hold and the sources from which they could receive them were strictly limited. There were other restrictions: associations were required to make public advance declarations to government authorities for both regular and special worship services or other religious meetings, with the presumption that the government would monitor public gatherings and prevent undesirable ones; they could not erect religious signs or symbols except on buildings designated for worship and in their cemeteries; they could not hold public processions nor ring church bells except under strict regulation; they were forbidden to engage in political acts or speak against public officials; they were banned from doing anything to resist the laws and decrees of public authorities; their clergy were barred from membership on town councils for eight years.

To round out the law, the legislators affixed a series of penalties, ranging from light fines to imprisonment, against any violators of the law, including clergy and rabbis. Moreover, in localities where the religions failed to organize an *association cultuelle* the state would sequester all religious properties and goods not already state owned and give them to the communes for use in public welfare (articles 8 and 9). As a final measure, and just in case there was any doubt, the legislators expressly reaffirmed the restrictions placed on religious orders by the 1901 law of associations and the prohibition imposed by the law of 1904 against teaching in France by members of religious orders (article 38).

To the government's great relief, Protestants and Jews believed they had little option but to go along with the new law, in spite of the grave financial hardship it caused for their pastors and rabbis, their communities, and their activities. The form of the *association cultuelle* required by the state was sufficiently similar to the consistories imposed on them for a hundred years that they regarded the switch to the new structure as simply a prolongation of government regulation of their religious life. The Protestants began to adapt their theology to the new social form, since their classic theology of church government gave extensive authority to lay elders and lay members generally. They gained new freedom to hold regional and national synods usually denied to them under the religious settlements. The evangelicals among them and the Independent Protestants welcomed the new regime for French religions.[54]

The Catholics, however, vigorously opposed it. Pope Pius X, while eschewing religious warfare, rejected the new arrangements as a destruction of the liberty of the church. With encyclicals in February and August 1906 he denounced the law of 1905 as an offense to God, a negation of the divine unity of the spiritual and temporal societies, a violation of international law, and an act of tyranny against the Catholics of France; and he forbade the church to form *associations cultuelles*. In September 1906, the archbishops and bishops of France then announced their refusal to comply with the government order.[55] They protested that the law prescribing *associations cultuelles* ignored the divine authority of the pope, the bishops, and the other clergy; gave final authority to settle church disputes to the state; and imposed a lay constitution which was contrary to Catholic teaching, and this they could not accept.

In the face of this outright rejection, the republicans maneuvered for position, for they also wished to avoid religious warfare. At the last minute, the government found a way for the clergy and faithful to use the state-owned churches and to meet for public worship even after the deadline passed to found *associations cultuelles*. Nonetheless, in January 1907 the legislators authorized the confiscation of the properties and goods owned by the religions in all cases where no *association cultuelle* was organized and approved the termination of all clergy salaries within one month. In April 1908 they set in motion the final arrangements for the confiscation and distribution of all unclaimed church properties and goods.[56] The government shut the *administration des cultes* and distributed the management of religious properties and affairs to the ministries of the interior, beaux-arts, and foreign affairs.[57] Pius X denounced the state confiscation of the goods of the Church and the alliance of France with atheism and proclaimed that he was prepared if need be "to suffer all oppressions and all sorrows" for the sake of the holy and full exercise of his apostolic charge.[58] The Catholic Church of France entered a period of renewed repression, accompanied by an all-out ideological battle of books, pamphlets, newspapers, and public debate which raged until the beginning of World War I.

The government acted with restraint toward the Muslims of Algeria. By an administrative regulation in September 1907, the French authorities in Algeria applied the 1905 law to Algeria, but they did not enforce it, fearing rebellion if they did. The Muslim members of the Algerian administration demanded that the French return to the Muslim religious authorities all the lands and buildings confiscated from them in the 1830s. The French backed away and agreed to a moratorium on the application of the law for ten years, later extended five more years. The French continued to budget state funds for the salaries of the muftis and imams, the mosques, Islamic public schools, Islamic justice, and Islamic welfare. The total amount spent on these items actually increased every year until 1922, seventeen years after the law of 1905.[59]

The actions of the republican state during 1901–8 amounted to the disestablishment of four state religions in France, ending the quadrilateral establishment which had given France religious peace for a century. They did not, however, separate church and state. The partisans for and against the law referred to it that way,[60] but it is significant that the legislators themselves did not use the language of "separation of church and state" in the law. The state retained too many connections with the religions to call it a "separation." The most noteworthy of these included the ownership and control of the use of most of the religious buildings of France and Algeria, the *budget des cultes* for the Islamic religion, the state chaplaincies, the imposition of the *associations cultuelles*, the prohibition of the religious orders in education, the detailed restrictions on ordinary religious activity, and the general repression of Catholics. Moreover, when Alsace and Lorraine were restored to France in 1919 after the defeat of Germany, and large blocs of Lutherans and Jews again became French, the Republic agreed to place the Lutherans and Jews of the region under the religious settlements in effect in 1871 when they were lost to France. In the areas of Alsace and Lorraine, the Lutheran Church of the Confession of Augsburg and the Jewish consistory once again became state religions.

Free Thinkers, secularists, atheists, and anyone who supported *la morale laïque*, revelled in the achievements of 1905–8. For them this was religious liberty in France, and the dreams of 1789 come true. At last the Catholic Church, the priests, the nuns and monks were put out of the public realm into a private space where presumably they were powerless to harm the public order and the public schools.[61] The independent churches experienced little change in their religious liberty in relation to the state as a result of the events. They became subject to the same general restrictions as the other groups, but these were much the same as those laid down in 1859. The religions that arrived from abroad after 1860 met with relatively little harassment from government authorities and generally flourished. The Catholic Petite Église was not affected by the events. Reformed and Lutheran churches and the Jews continued to have more or less the same freedom for the public exercise of their religions as before, although the financial loss they sustained crippled their churches and synagogues and hampered the recruitment of pastors and rabbis for many years to come. Protestants and Jews tried to make the most of a bad thing, and Protestants began to speak again of the laity in their theology. Only slowly did the Protestants come to regard the proponents of moral religion and the secularists of the Third Republic as more of a threat to religious liberty than the Roman Catholics. The Catholics, still making up nearly 98 percent of the population, suffered an enormous net loss of religious liberty, severely harming their dioceses, parishes, bishops, priests, religious orders, and schools. The effects lasted at least a generation. France and the pope did not restore diplomatic relations until 1921. The conflict over the structure of religious authority subsided only in 1924 when the government and the Catholic Church agreed on the formation of *associations diocesans* which respected the episcopacy and Catholic teaching. Not until the 1940s were religious orders permitted to teach again in France and *congréganiste* schools allowed to reopen.

The renewed vigor of the republicans in defending, promoting, and supporting the *écoles laïques*, while simultaneously crushing the Catholic *congréganiste* schools, made it apparent that they intended to maintain the establishment of universal moral religion in the public schools. The law of 1905 pointedly reiterated the 1881 prohibition of all traditional religious expressions in the public schools (article 30). The curriculum for "moral and civic instruction" created in 1881 to replace Catholic, Protestant, and Jewish "moral and religious instruction" remained at the center of the life of these schools. The start of every day continued to feature the daily practice of moral exercises and mandatory teaching about God, the soul, and universal morality. The teachers still functioned under the mandate contained in the program of 1887 to foster the *esprit laïque* through their every word and deed. In spite of the official rhetoric that the *écoles laïques* were religiously "neutral," they were not. And in spite of the insistent allegation by Catholics, and even by the pope, that they were schools "without God," they were not. Writings on various sides of the furious ideological debate during these years focused precisely on their religious character, and the very debate itself served to emphasize that the *écoles laïques* had a religious identity.[62]

By means of the combination of compulsory school attendance, the ban on the traditional religions in the public schools, and the impediments put in the way of Protestant and Jewish schools as well as Catholic free schools, the republicans insured that most of the children of France would be brought up in the *école laïque*. In 1923, when the French government revised the national curriculum for the first time since 1887, and the official school program dropped explicit references to God and the soul, the government wanted no one to think that this meant the elimination of the religious content and spirit from the public schools. As proof the education ministry republished the 1887 directives for "moral and civic instruction" which explained the teachings about God and the soul, and asked the teachers to follow them with sensitivity, and to make them even more effective by integrating them fully into the daily life of the primary schools.[63] In the eyes of the republicans, the public schools continued to be the one institution able to embody universal moral religion as promoted by the Third Republic. They desired for the *école laïque* in every commune of France to surpass, and even co-opt, the influence of the churches and the synagogues in the moral and spiritual formation of the citizens of France.

≺ III ≻

Concluding Observations

We are now in a position to offer a number of concluding observations about religious liberty in France from 1787 to 1908. It is evident that everything pertaining to religious liberty was much more complex and paradoxical than we usually imagine. When we seek to explain why the question of religious liberty kept arising, we are struck chiefly by the persistence of diverse religious communities who were not satisfied with the treatment accorded them by the law and successive governments. The interaction of these religions among themselves and with the various governments affected the process of events so completely that it is not possible to examine the role of any one group apart from the others without distorting our understanding. Amid the variety of religions, no single, or stable, understanding of religious liberty won wide acceptance, and no single group, not even those who took the name "liberal," were the privileged agents of religious liberty.

Instead, alternative, often conflicting voices in changing circumstances appealed for religious liberty, with perhaps as many meanings of liberty as voices. The religious communities, social structures, and issues involved with the question of religious liberty varied markedly over the period. For Catholics, Reformed, Lutherans, and Jews, public religious expression in churches and synagogues was the central issue until the religious settlements; from the 1820s religious expression in the schools and from the 1870s religious orders took precedence for the rest of the century. Independent Protestants and the Muslims in Algeria from the 1830s were concerned about everything at once—their churches and mosques, their schools, and their other public religious activities, especially evangelism for the independents and pilgrimages for Muslims. The advocates of universal moral religion consistently cared most about the schools throughout the whole period. All the traditional religions after 1905 felt challenges to the whole gamut of their religious expression—their institutions of public worship, the schools, the religious orders, their other public religious practice. Instead of the emergence and expansion of religious liberty which we are led to expect from the standard story, we find a series of modifications of religious liberty, with liberty and repression affecting each religion in different ways at different times.

The principal device which mediated religious liberty across the period was the state establishment of religion. The same paradox appeared again and again—the liberty of a religion usually increased with its absorption into state establishment. The paradox served the Catholics, the Reformed, the Lutherans, the Jews, and, in a sense, the independent Protestants, as well as the various expressions of universal moral religion. It failed the Muslims in Algeria. The device represented an extension and adaptation of the pre-revolutionary Gallican religious system. In order to secure the peace of the realm, the state insisted on the unity of religion. The first surprise came when the state absorbed the Reformed, Lutherans, and Jews into the religious establishment with the Catholics. The surprise increased when the state later tried to do the same with the Muslims. The second surprise came in the 1880s when the state established *la morale laïque* as a monopoly in the public schools, but without dethroning the state religions. The third surprise followed upon the disestablishment of the religions by the law of 1905, when, in spite of the rhetoric, the separation of church and state did not occur, and the Gallican-style imposition of religious unity did not end. The state perpetuated the Gallican system by enforcing the establishment of universal moral religion in the state's *écoles laïques*, while simultaneously placing restrictions on the traditional religions and maintaining the Muslims in position in Algeria and the Jews and Lutherans in Alsace and Lorraine. The state mandated the schools to receive the children of all religions into the same classroom where they might be molded as citizens of the same *Patrie*, united in their duty to the common divinity, their assurance of the immortality of the soul, and their devotion to the universal moral ideal.

The outcome by 1908 was not the achievement of secularism, and the religions did not decline. Over the long haul and by a difficult itinerary, the religious transformation of France from 1787 went like this: France moved from a Catholic state church with liberty for Catholics and oppression for others, into state oppression of all traditional religions, followed by a system of state religious establishments with relatively high levels of liberty for most, and emerged not as a secular society with secular schools, but as an increasingly more complex society marked by the diversity of religions, the state establishment of universal moral religion in the public schools, the repression of Catholics, and the experience of moderate liberty and moderate restriction for others in tension with the state. Religious liberty in France after 1787 did not move along a straightforward path that can be called progress, but, rather, circulated in a manner that transcended any single metaphor. By 1908 the experience of general religious liberty within a pluralist society remained to be achieved.

Religious Freedom, Clericalism, and Anticlericalism in Chile, 1820-1920

SIMON COLLIER

IN MANY PARTS of Latin America in the nineteenth century, the issue of religious freedom was closely entwined with a developing struggle between the long-established Catholic Church and the newly emerging republican states.[1] In certain countries, notably Mexico, the struggle assumed very violent forms and was at times (as in 1857–60) one of the key questions at stake in the deadly contest of Liberals and Conservatives. While the same contest between Church and state, between Liberals and Conservatives, was also present in Chile, its characteristic forms were somewhat different. The country followed a uniquely distinctive course in nineteenth-century Spanish America, with its early attainment of political stability and the settled conditions prevailing for most of the time thereafter. Issues such as religious liberty and the role of the Church were fought out as *debates*, above all in Congress—usually fairly civilized debates, which sometimes reached a high level of acrimony. Many of the republic's best minds were engaged in these arguments, which makes it seem possible to examine the whole question as an episode in the history of ideas, as a purely ideological contest.

It probably would be misleading to recount the story in quite this way. Perhaps no ideological contest can ever really be divorced from a wider social or political context. It is true that no great material interests were at stake between Church and state in Chile, but there is nonetheless an interesting sense in which attacks on and defenses of the Catholic Church, and the whole issue of freedom of worship, became caught up in the weave of day-to-day political competition. For the first century after independence, Chilean politicians were drawn predominantly from the upper class and moved in circles where they mostly knew each other, when they were not actually related to each other. They became adept at partisan competition fairly early in their republic's history, arguably to an extent unrivalled elsewhere in Latin America. Religious liberty, when it came, was in many ways the byproduct of a struggle for greater *political* freedom, in the context of the interplay of emergent political parties.

The formal establishment of freedom of worship in Chile in 1865, however, was by no means the end of public debate over the role of the Catholic Church in the national culture. Indeed, in some ways it marked its real beginning. For it was then that a really vocal tradition of anticlericalism developed, and Chilean anticlericals, whose influence on national (notably but not exclusively upper- and middle-class) life was to be so impressive by the early years of the twentieth century, saw the religious freedom they ardently promoted as only part of an altogether larger continuing battle in favor of freedom, democracy, and progress. In their view, the Catholic Church was a distinct obstacle. The cause of freedom *of* religion thus merged with the cause of freedom *from* religion. This theme, too, is an important part of the story to be examined in this chapter.

≺ I ≻

Church and State in the Early Republic

Prior to independence, Chile had been a remote and rather neglected Spanish colony. Its population was barely one million in the 1820s. The new country shared with the rest of the former Spanish American empire the overwhelming legacy of Catholicism. But although the Jesuit order (expelled from the Spanish empire in 1767) had owned and worked haciendas, the Church had never been an important landowner: here the contrast with Mexico is again very notable. Moreover, its position had been somewhat weakened by the wars of independence, during which the hierarchy and clergy (with the exception of a rather small handful of radical clerics) had for the most part taken the Spanish side. Nevertheless, the new republic, as it took shape, was indisputably and consciously Catholic. All its early constitutions (1818, 1822, 1823, 1828, and 1833) made Catholicism the official religion of the state and disallowed other forms of public worship. The Catholic Church thus remained firmly in place as the established church.

The new Chilean state aspired, as did other Spanish American republics, to inherit the so-called *patronato*, the extensive supervisory powers over the Church which had been granted by the papacy to the Spanish Crown in colonial times.[2] The papacy was by no means ready to concede these. A papal mission sent to Chile in 1824 (its secretary was the future Pope Pius IX) failed to reach agreement with the government on the issue. Later attempts by successive governments to secure a concordat also failed.[3] Despite this, an effective modus vivendi between the Chilean state and Rome (including the creation of the new archbishopric of Santiago) was struck by the end of the 1830s, and the government continued thereafter to exercise limited supervisory powers and to nominate ecclesiastical dignitaries until the formal separation of Church and state in 1925.

Intellectual opinion at the time of independence, such as it was, did not on the whole favor religious liberty, although the issue was certainly discussed in the 1820s, when the all-important nineteenth-century ideological divide between Liberals and Conservatives first began to define itself.[4] Certain Liberal writers tended to exalt the virtue of tolerance, and there was a minor note of anticlericalism in the political debates of the period—very minor in comparison with what came later. Yet the early legislators conspicuously failed to include freedom of worship in the lists of individual rights and guarantees incorporated (with enthusiasm) into the early national constitutions. Under the law regulating abuses of the press, enacted in December 1828, writers could be prosecuted for blasphemy as well as immorality or sedition. The 1828 constitution, very much the Liberals' constitution, included a stipulation (article 4) that nobody would be "persecuted or molested" on account of private opinions. This provision, drawn from the Spanish constitution of 1812 and omitted from the long-enduring Conservative constitution of 1833, was something less than a full-blooded statement in favor of religious freedom, though it is interesting that the 1828 constitution was the only one of the period (or any other period) to omit the customary opening invocation of "Almighty God."

Conservative opinion (and perhaps much Liberal opinion also) was inclined to see a connection between religious uniformity and political stability—less a simple assertion of *cuius regio eius religio* than the belief that religion was an indispensable element in social stability. Juan Egaña, the most interesting intellectual of the independence period, and a Conservative of unusually moralistic bent, even wrote a short treatise on this theme, in which he stated the case succinctly: "1. The multitude of religions in a single state leads to irreligion; and this is the tendency of our century. 2. Two religions in a state lead to a struggle which must terminate either in the destruction of the state or of one of the two religious parties. 3. Religious uniformity is the most effective means of consolidating the tranquillity of the great mass of the nation."[5] In the short-lived constitution Egaña managed to foist on Chile in 1823, at the highest point of his political influence, the press was explicitly forbidden to concern itself with the "mysteries, dogmas, religious discipline, and the morality generally approved by the Catholic Church" (article 263). Irreligion, for Egaña, was not much worse than religious diversity. It was conceivable in a nation of traders, as he once put it, but not in a national community of true citizens. The nation of traders he had in mind was England.

In the absence of domestic religious challenges to the Catholic monopoly (there were no Protestant services *in Spanish* held in Chile before the late 1860s), and given the hegemonic position of Catholicism in the national culture, many educated Chileans were content to allow for time to pass before the issue of religious freedom was confronted head-on, whatever their inner wishes might have been. A newspaper of 1820 noted that there might later come a day, "in the darkness of the centuries," when such matters could "safely be discussed in Chile."[6] This was far too cautious a view. It was never at any stage seriously unsafe to discuss such matters (whatever might be the case with other matters) in Chile, and the country did not have to wait centuries before the issue was formally resolved. In legal terms, religious liberty was achieved in Chile in the mid-1860s, though not, as we shall see, in the form of a constitutional amendment as such. Only in 1925, in fact, was the principle firmly entrenched in the highest law of the land, in a formula shifted word for word into the constitution General Augusto Pinochet imposed on the republic in 1980—which can be taken as the ultimate sign of its completely non-controversial nature in the twentieth century.

It cannot be said that the Conservative politicians who forcibly displaced the Liberals in the brief civil war of 1829–30, and who retained power until the late 1850s, were unduly preoccupied by questions of religious orthodoxy or dissidence. There was, it is true, a certain deliberate policy of "reclericalization" in evidence after 1830, with the Church being seen (and used) quite consciously as one of the buttresses of the new Conservative regime. The first of the Conservative presidents, General Joaquín Prieto (1831–41), was a pious man who took religious ceremonies seriously. The dominant figure of the new regime, the "omnipotent minister" Diego Portales, almost certainly did not: "You believe in God," he is said to have told Juan Egaña (or in some versions, Egaña's son Mariano), "while I believe in priests"—a remark (if he really made it) worthy of Napoleon. Portales himself certainly paid close attention to the role of the Church in fostering morality and social stability.[7] But there was never a truly clerical strand in Conservative political thinking, as there sometimes was elsewhere in Latin America. This does not mean that the state forgot the Church or that it failed to take its supervisory role seriously.[8] Nor does it mean that there was not, within the ruling Conservative party, a section of opinion strongly and emotionally attached to the Church. The frustrated presidential candidacy of Joaquín Tocornal in 1841 was in part a bid for the support of this section. What it does mean is that religious or theological reasons were not usually adduced in propagandistic justifications of the Conservative regime, which rested its claims to legitimate authority on much more down-to-earth considerations: order, political stability, the stimulation of material progress, and so on.[9]

< II >

The Affair of the Sacristan

There is, in fact, a real sense in which the Conservative politicians of the 1830s and 1840s can be said to have taken the Church for granted. Doing so proved to be a miscalculation. As the greatest of English historians once observed, "Ambition is a weed of quick and early vegetation in the vineyard of Christ."[10] In this case, ambition played a part, but was scarcely the sole factor involved. The Church itself was stiffened by the uncompromising attitudes radiating from Pius IX's pontificate, and was revitalized in the 1840s and early 1850s by an energetic and combative archbishop of Santiago, Rafael Valentín Valdivieso. Under his forceful leadership (widely though never universally accepted), the Church moved from its previous regalism (acceptance of state supervision) toward ultramontanism, with its aspiration to greater independence vis-à-vis the state. Valdivieso reacted vehemently when the state's essentially regalist attitude suddenly came to the fore in very dramatic fashion in the mid-1850s, in the noisy jurisdictional conflict known as the Affair of the Sacristan (1856).

It was a trivial issue that exploded into a great political event. Over a matter of internal ecclesiastical discipline arising from the dismissal of a junior sacristan in Santiago cathedral, President Manuel Montt (1851–61) supported a supreme court decision that threatened Archbishop Valdivieso with banishment. The commotion was intense: society ladies threatened to tie themselves to the wheels of the carriage bearing the defiant prelate into exile. Although the Affair itself was eventually resolved by behind-the-scenes compromise, the bulk of the Conservative party found the president's attitude to the archbishop excessively rigorous, and defected into opposition, rapidly forming an alliance with the Liberals, who immediately sensed that this was a chance for them to leave the political wilderness where they had languished for more than a quarter century. A serious armed rebellion against Montt swiftly followed (1859); it was defeated, but in due course (July 1862), during the benign and tolerant presidency of Montt's successor, José Joaquín Pérez (1861–71), the Liberal-Conservative Fusion, as the alliance called itself, took over the cabinet from Montt's remaining Conservative supporters.

While the Affair of the Sacristan generated a great deal of pious passion, and a certain amount of impious passion too, there is good reason to doubt whether the Church-state relationship was the underlying issue at stake between Montt and his adversaries. The Affair was in some ways a convenient pretext for conflict. It is tempting to think that in its absence some other pretext would have been found. Montt was an inflexible president who upheld, with unnecessary vigor, the authoritarianism (including frequent recourse to repression) with which the Conservative political settlement had been operated since the 1830s. The country's growing prosperity and the greater exposure of the upper class to foreign, especially European, ideas had inclined many leading Conservatives to the view that government could be exercised in a more tolerant spirit. The opposition Liberals, needless to say, had believed this all along. They had never ceased to clamor for a revision of the 1833 constitution, the Conservatives' much-revered talisman. Thus the central issue in the 1850s was really one of political liberalization, of freedom versus authority.

At the same time, the fact that the political realignment of 1857–58 stemmed *from* the Affair of the Sacristan meant that the position of the Church was brought firmly into the developing political debate. The Church's own militancy was definitely enhanced, with the formation of a "Society of St. Thomas of Canterbury"—priests who pledged themselves to refrain from appealing to the civil courts, as had happened in the Affair.[11] The *cantorberianos*, as they became known, were Archbishop Valdivieso's shock-troops, forming a very solid phalanx among the clergy: in 1868, of 61 parishes in the Santiago archdiocese, 42 had *cantorberiano* priests.[12] The Church was by no means averse from now onwards to exercising political influence. Moreover, the Conservatives, as they defected from the Montt government, began to conceive of themselves as an incipiently clerical party, with a special interest in defending the interests of the Catholic Church. This tendency was one that developed slowly but surely during the Liberal-Conservative Fusion's years in power (1862–73). Federico Errázuriz, the Liberal nephew of Archbishop Valdivieso (and brother of a future archbishop) who aspired to the presidential succession in 1871, was able to win it only by careful cultivation of the "clericalists." Three years before the election, indeed, a pamphleteer described him as "the presumed candidate of his uncle the Archbishop and of the *cantorberianos* of the capital."[13]

≺ III ≻

Foreign Protestants and Chilean Anticlericals

It is against the political developments of the 1860s that the formal enactment of religious freedom has to be set. Implicit in the deal that created the Liberal-Conservative Fusion was the idea of a gradual liberalization of the political system. The climate of discussion was now altogether more open than had been common in the past. Inevitably, in this new atmosphere, the demand for constitutional reform was raised more vigorously, not least by the radical wing of the Liberal party, which had played the most dramatic role in the rebellion of 1859 and which now organized itself as a separate Radical party (1863). The timetable of reform was slow: not until August 1871 was the first constitutional amendment enacted. This was due in part to the cumbersome and longwinded amendment procedure under the 1833 constitution, while President Pérez himself—for all his patrician tolerance, a stout defender of that constitution[14]—was in no great hurry to see it reformed. Nevertheless, with the elections of 1864, a strong Liberal delegation took its place in Congress, part of the large Fusion majority, while five Radicals were elected. The issue could no longer be kept off the congressional agenda. In the following year's sessions the Chamber of Deputies debated the possible amendment of several constitutional articles. Far and away the most memorable debates of this session concerned article 5, the article stipulating the Catholic religious monopoly in Chile. It was the first battleground of the long contest between reformers and their adversaries.

Why was this particular battleground chosen? It was partly accidental: article 5 was near the beginning of the constitution; "reformable" articles were being taken in numerical order; and articles 1–4, defining the national territory and form of government, offered no scope at all for controversy. Over and above this, however, there were perhaps two main reasons why the amendment of article 5 became the first major constitutional episode in the struggle to liberalize the political system. The first was the pressing need to regularize the status of Protestant foreigners now resident in Chile. The second, and perhaps more important, was that political reformers saw the issue as a convenient one from the viewpoint of their long-range program, an issue, not directly political, which could be used to test the practicability of constitutional reform. In addition, of course, anticlericals relished the prospect of a first major skirmish with their Conservative and Catholic adversaries.

From the time of independence onwards, foreign traders had flocked to Chilean ports, especially Valparaiso, which became a distinctly cosmopolitan city. British traders and sailors held Anglican services in private from an early date, and their American counterparts, understandably objecting to the customary Anglican prayer for the British monarch, soon established a congregation of their own. An Anglican chapel was set up in Valparaiso in the mid-1830s,[15] and its opening was attended by two cabinet ministers, both of them staunchly Catholic.

The ministers' attendance was not as paradoxical as it might seem. It was standard policy of Chilean governments to maximize overseas trade, and foreigners occupied the dominant position in the import-export houses that sprang up in Valparaiso and elsewhere; it therefore was necessary to handle foreigners' religious sentiments with some care. Guarantees of freedom of worship for foreign nationals were written into commercial treaties concluded with the United States (1833), France (1852), and Britain (1855). General Bernardo O'Higgins, Chile's strongly pro-British head of state from 1817 to 1823, would have liked to accord them freedom of worship there and then, but prevailing opinion was far too strong. He did, however, grant foreigners the right to open a cemetery of their own in Valparaiso, a measure that did nothing to help him when his enemies combined later on to bring about his downfall. Later governments, notwithstanding this, did not in any way harass the foreign Protestant congregations that grew up in the port.

An important moment in the history of these congregations was the arrival in 1845 of an American Congregationalist, the redoubtable David Trumbull. He was from a distinguished New England family, an alumnus of Yale and Princeton Theological Seminary, and in 1855 he built the first permanent Protestant church in Valparaiso.[16] When Archbishop Valdivieso pointedly, and, one might think, rather unnecessarily, drew the government's attention to the existence of the new-built chapel, the government responded with what can be interpreted as masterly inactivity, though Trumbull *was* required to erect a wooden fence to hide his new Union Church from public view—a restriction also applied to (or perhaps self-applied by) the Anglican church built in Valparaiso a couple of years later.[17] This apart, Trumbull was in no way impeded in his ministry. Many years later (he died in 1889) he was to pay tribute to the "enlightened public sentiment" that had kept de facto toleration alive even before its formal enactment in 1865.[18] Trumbull was an able publicist, and his advocacy of religious liberty and occasional sturdy doctrinal polemics against Catholics[19] made him something of a hero to Chilean anticlericals, although their own agenda was somewhat different.

While foreign Protestants did not suffer very much, except sometimes on the level of verbal abuse, from Catholic Chileans, there were occasional incidents that caused friction. A particularly thorny episode occurred in 1848 when a newly arrived American diplomatic envoy, Seth Barton, married a Chilean Catholic bride in a Protestant service. Archbishop Valdivieso's hostility to this mixed marriage came close to causing an international incident and led to Barton's withdrawal from the country in a blaze of recrimination.[20] It was perhaps natural that opinion in Valparaiso, the main foreign redoubt and often independent in its political preferences, should in general favor freedom of worship. Certainly the thriving British trading community actively supported the idea.[21] Advocacy of religious freedom was a line taken at regular intervals by Valparaiso's most celebrated newspaper, *El Mercurio* (today the oldest Spanish-language newspaper in the world), which regarded itself, as it still does, as peculiarly well qualified to interpret the national interest. In the late 1840s and early 1850s the paper entered into a running battle with the Church's main organ, the *Revista Católica*, founded in 1843 and read widely by the clergy (though not by many others). "Will the *Mercurio* want the Chilean press to discuss the mystery of the Incarnation, Original Sin or the Trinity?" asked the *Revista* in 1849,[22] and later, with obvious relish, it denounced the suspect newspaper in capital letters as "IMPIOUS and HERETICAL."[23]

It is clear that the Church's attitude at mid century to any relaxation of its religious monopoly was marked by complete intransigence. Eloquent statements of its position can be found in the *Revista Católica* in the winter of 1850. In one such article the magazine asserted roundly "(1) that all Chileans have the *obligation* to *believe* and *profess* the Catholic religion, the only one there really is, both *internally and externally* . . . (2) that in consequence they have no *right* to embrace any other religion . . . (3) that they lack the right to ask for toleration of other forms of worship."[24] Three weeks later, the *Revista* reasserted its case, appealing now to considerations of Chilean history and nationality:

Where consciences obey the Catholic faith, Catholicism and Catholicism alone should be admitted; because we Catholics believe that all other religions are false . . . This is the case in Chile. Catholicism, which has ruled for more than three centuries in these fortunate regions, Catholicism which is embodied in the very spirit of the Spanish American race, is the only religion in which we Chileans believe. To invite in others would deeply wound our national sentiment . . . We know well that many Europeans residing in Chile are advocating freedom of worship, but why should we sacrifice the wishes of a whole nation to theirs?[25]

Attitudes such as these were increasingly an embarrassment to the government, and naturally infuriated the growing number who now opposed the Church on doctrinal or philosophical grounds.

It is not easy to pinpoint the origins of Chilean anticlericalism. Clearly some of the leaders of the independence movement, and some of the Liberal politicians who predominated in the pre-1830 governments, were steeped in the thought, including the deistic and atheistic thought, of the European Enlightenment. When Juan Egaña expressed his fears about the growth of "irreligion" in his treatise on religious toleration, he certainly had a number of his contemporaries in mind. The minor note of anticlericalism in the politics of the 1820s has already been mentioned. In policy terms, it might be noted here, the most serious anticlerical measure of the early Liberal period (the reduction of annual religious holidays from seventeen to twelve hardly counts as such) was the expropriation in 1824 of the far from extensive properties of the religious orders. These were restored directly or in the form of compensation after the Conservative seizure of power in 1830.

Certainly by the early 1850s the beginnings of an anticlerical constituency can be noted, greatly stimulated by the revival of Liberalism as a political force in the later 1840s. A number of incidents showed this very clearly. In 1851–52 students at the Instituto Nacional, the key institution where so many leading Chileans received secondary and, indeed, professional education in the nineteenth century, openly revolted when a new and very devout education minister tried to impose an exclusively clerical regime on the college. When Archbishop Valdivieso issued an edict in November 1853 calling for the denunciation of "heretics, the excommunicated, and those who in any way pervert customs," a crowd in the northern city of Copiapó gathered at the railway station and publicly burned the document.[26] The Church itself, to judge from its publications, was by now seriously concerned by the spread of irreligion, and was inclined to view the immediate future with alarm: "Storms and tempests are what we discern in a not too distant era . . . We do not doubt that evil will triumph over good . . . but . . . whatever the philosophers say, the will of God will be accomplished in time, and beyond time."[27]

It would be impossible to count the number of politicians and intellectuals who by this stage were opposed on philosophical grounds to Catholicism, but it seems certain that it was more than, though perhaps not *much* more than, a modest sprinkling. Here it is difficult to relate levels of belief or unbelief to political party. There were many Liberals who were devout, whatever their feelings about the legal position of the Church. Chilean anticlericalism can be seen as having a "statist" wing and a "doctrinaire" wing, the two wings often overlapping, the statists chiefly concerned with laicizing national institutions, the doctrinaires espousing a secularist and rationalist program. By the same token, it certainly must not be supposed that all Conservatives were devout. There were some whose religious position was distinctly suspect to the orthodox. One such was Antonio Varas, President Montt's interior minister and closest collaborator. After the political realignment of 1857–58, it is a fair guess that the number of religious skeptics was higher in the National party of Montt and Varas—the *monttvarista* party, as it was nicknamed—than it was among the defecting Conservatives. The anticlerical thrust from this quarter should not be forgotten. It was certainly not forgotten by the Church, whose principal organ devoted two fierce articles in 1868 to the "blind hatred of the clergy" supposedly evinced by the *monttvaristas*.[28] Clerical influence was also suspected by many in the noisy attempted impeachment of the supreme court (1867–68), whose chief justice was the hated Montt.[29]

Liberals, Conservatives, and Nationals may have been divided in their religious preferences, but with the new Radical party of the 1860s, doctrinaire anticlericalism became closely associated with a political movement. From the outset, however, the Radical party was consistent in its belief in freedom of ideas and universal toleration. It was also consistent in its demand for the separation of Church and state. All of these principles formed part of its program for the democratic advance of Chile—to which, indeed, its honorable historical contribution is quite indisputable.

Here we should also note a strong though not exclusive connection between Radicalism and Freemasonry,[30] which had first taken organized form during the 1850s. In April-May 1862 Chilean Freemasons formed their own Grand Lodge, declaring independence from the Grand Orient of France, then experiencing meddling by Napoleon III. The movement attracted a number of leading intellectuals and politicians. This was the start of one of the more enduring subterranean forces in Chilean political life, influential until at least the early 1970s. (A shift from masonic to Catholic leadership in the Chilean army was certainly one factor, though far from the only one, in the overthrow of President Salvador Allende in 1973). The number of Chilean lodges grew from ten in 1872 to more than 100 by the 1950s.

The ramifications of freemasonic influence have never been properly studied; perhaps they cannot be. The basic Chilean freemasonic principles were defined in 1862, very much in line with international masonic standards, as "the existence of God, the immortality of the soul, and love of humanity."[31] Like their counterparts elsewhere, the Chilean masons often referred to God as the Grand Architect of the Universe, or, in writing, as GADU, the Spanish acronym of this expression. This definition did not prevent the Freemasons from being described as "atheists" by the Church, which, indeed, subjected them to regular and virulent denunciations, although the more fair-minded Conservatives, and even the odd priest, sometimes admitted that the moral precepts espoused by Freemasons appeared to be rather admirable.

≺ IV ≻

Article 5 and the "Interpretative Law"

The arguments over article 5 in 1865 were impassioned in the extreme, with the Church (or at any rate individual priests, notably the combative Juan Ugarte) mobilizing demonstrations, some inside the Congress itself, against the proposed amendment. The congressional record repeatedly notes *desordenes en la barra*—disturbances in the public gallery. The debates themselves were later remembered as classic—"long and luminous," as a minister of the interior was to say eight years later.[32] The politicians divided along fairly predictable lines, Conservatives and Radicals embodying the opposed positions, with Liberals and Nationals falling in between. Federico Errázuriz, whose eye was already on the presidency, opposed the amendment. In the end, the government, "fearful of wounding the religious sentiment of the country and arousing popular passions," as one of its ministers revealed,[33] dissuaded Congress from amending the constitution, proposing instead a two-clause "interpretative law" on article 5. This gave non-Catholics the right to worship in "buildings of private property," and to establish their own schools. In principle, a law of this kind was inferior to a constitutional amendment; it could have been rescinded by a later Congress. That this never happened is a sign that the principal battle had been won. And it had been, although the Church disliked the law and continued to denounce the appearance of new Protestant churches.[34]

It is useful at this point to take a look at the terms in which the debate of 1865 was cast—for many of the arguments used were to be repeated in one form or other in the much more acrimonious congressional struggles of the next twenty years. In general, the reader is struck by the high level of debate, and also by the frequency with which practical rather than theoretical arguments were adduced. Nonetheless, certain common themes were very much in evidence, the reformers appealing to progress and democratic rights, the Catholics and Conservatives basing their case on history and national identity.

Manuel Antonio Matta, the Radical leader, always known as "the Patriarch," opened the attack on article 5 by asserting that it was absurd for a *state* to have a religion at all. "Conceive, for example, of the Republic marching to confession . . . We are not dealing with a theological question, but with an indisputable and eternal right."[35] Underlining his "respect for all beliefs, and respect for the rights of all men," he suggested that religious liberty was an essential aspect of progress, "in accord with the diversity that appears to be a law of the development of human intelligence." Matta argued, too, that persecution was counterproductive: it merely served as a stimulus to new religions. He cited the Mormons in the United States, whose leaders, he noted, "were worth little or nothing as writers and as sectarian chiefs"; they had nonetheless flourished because of persecution.[36] He concluded the second of his three major speeches with a lyrical call for religious liberty in the name of "immigration, which is strength and wealth; democracy, which is liberty and order; civilization, which is light and wellbeing; the Republic, which is law and duty; Religion, which is love of God and love of man."[37] Other deputies, noting that the unity of belief had now been broken in Chile, argued that the only new basis for harmony was, as Juan Nepomuceno Espejo put it, "the unity we arrive at through free and intellectual discussion . . . Tolerance . . . has to make a single family of the human races, a universal family."[38] The Radical Manuel Recabarren suggested that "only in democracy is every man equal before the law; only in democracy can we reconstruct the great synthesis we call humanity."[39]

The Catholic-Conservative defense of article 5 was a formidable one. It included the odd flash of dogmatism: "We believe," said Fr. Joaquín Larraín Gandarillas, the front-running Catholic speaker in the debates, "that our Catholic religion is the true one, and that the truth must be protected for the wellbeing of the country."[40] He came close at one point to demanding that the Protestant churches of Valparaiso be closed down as "unconstitutional."[41] In general, however, Larraín Gandarillas, while citing Plato and Rousseau as authorities in favor of uniformity, rested his case on the "Catholic unity" that was for him an essential attribute of Chile's historical identity. "Chile already has a religion which is the true one," he asserted, "and should preserve its exclusive dominion."[42] The foreign Protestants, he told the Chamber, "come only in quest of temporary advantage."[43] "What would the Republic of Chile be," he asked, "without religion or God? Gentlemen, it would be a society without a head . . . God is the true author of human society. To take away its God is to decapitate it, and to remove its very foundations."[44] "Let us not destroy," he urged, "the basis of the majestic edifice of our civilization."[45]

Another Catholic deputy, Enrique Tocornal, speculated that with religious freedom Chile might "lose its autonomy along with its faith."[46] Federico Errázuriz, as befitted a cabinet minister and would-be president, shifted the argument to "serious considerations of social order": "I want uniformity . . . in religion, just as I do in customs and in all the constituent principles of the social order . . . We find the origins of religious struggles, and all the disasters that are their consequence, in diversity of belief."[47]

Such arguments entirely failed to persuade the reformers: as Manuel Recabarren put it, alluding to a fairly recent event in the United States, "Catholic unity" was being regarded by its proponents as "another Fort Sumpter [sic]" which they believed to be "inexpugnable."[48] Examples and precedents drawn from foreign countries, especially England, France, and the United States, were a prominent element in the article 5 debates, as was to be true of all later arguments on these matters. Catholic speakers and writers, it might be noted here, were particularly well acquainted with developments in France. The French influence on Chilean Catholicism in this period was fairly noticeable, with effects on both church architecture and devotional practice. The reformers were more inclined to look to northern Europe and North America for inspiration. Matta, for instance, length-

ily analyzed the religious clauses in various state constitutions in the
United States, and warned that Mr. Gladstone, favorably cited as a
liberal hero several times in the debates, should not be regarded as a
reliable ally: he was "perhaps the most notable and famous man in
Europe for his financial measures," but was also known for "a decided and mischievous adherence to Anglican exclusivism."[49]

Larraín Gandarillas, for his part, insisted that Chile should *not*
imitate England or the United States, where new religions were being
invented all the time, sometimes by mere "shoemakers and tailors"
("and others by carpenters," interjected Matta at this point, causing
instant uproar in the Chamber).[50] Larraín Gandarillas also dwelt ex-
tensively on the persecution of Catholics in the United States, and
by dint of misreading some statistics in an American almanac, asserted that religious freedom had plunged the United States into
"fearful unbelief."[51] His lack of statistical expertise was soon pointed
out to him by the rising Liberal, Benjamín Vicuña Mackenna, who
noted that religious freedom in England had enabled Catholicism to
make great advances—even in Oxford, "the Rome of Protestantism."
"Is there more patriotism, public spirit and moral and civic virtue in
decadent Spain," he asked, "than in glorious England?"[52] Insisting on
his own Catholic credentials, evoking the "tolerance and enlightenment of the century," and claiming that freedom of worship was "essentially a practical question," Vicuña Mackenna presented the "international" argument most eloquently:

I too have been intolerant, as are all who are born on our soil. I was one of
those children who went in processions to spit on Jews, and at the first sight
of a Protestant in the street I would run with my brothers to hide in the
innermost patio of our house, for such are the ideas which float above the
cradles of all the children who are born under the roofs of the Catholic capital of Chile. But when I grew up and thought about it, and above all when I
left my country and saw, in California, the pagoda of the Chinaman alongside the Catholic chapel . . . when I saw in Paris and London and Vienna,
indeed everywhere, the toleration of worship established as a peaceful fact,
and respected by all . . . I exclaimed: "How is it possible that in Santiago
anyone who merely enunciates the proposition of toleration . . . is declared
impious?"[53]

The government's "interpretative law," when it reached the
Chamber, met with a certain amount of opposition from the most
resolute reformers, including Matta, who admitted nonetheless to a
"secret desire" that it would pass. "Later on," he said, "minds more

daring than ours will know how to establish true democracy in Chile."[54] Antonio Varas, for his part, claimed that he would have preferred "a wise amendment" rather than the new law, which he saw as an unworthy concession to the "religious fervor" and "outbursts of exaggerated religiosity" recently in evidence.[55] But the government wanted the law, and it got it, by large majorities: 43–7 for the first clause, 32–8 for the second. A few stubborn deputies tried to reopen the question in subsequent sessions, but the debate rapidly petered out.

≺ V ≻

Politics and the "Theological Questions"

The debate over article 5 is probably best seen as a dress rehearsal for the wider discussions of constitutional reform that soon followed.[56] These focused on more exclusively political aspects. Cross-party "reform clubs" were organized in several cities in 1868–69, proving especially attractive to younger politicians. Church and state issues did not loom large in their deliberations, though the Santiago club advocated the "elevation of religious tolerance to a constitutional precept."[57] Constitutional reform was, not very surprisingly, the principal business of the congresses of 1867–70 and 1870–73, though rather little was then accomplished in this regard. If what we may call (for convenience) the "religious issue" remained latent during these years, it was always from now on potentially disruptive, and it was destined to play its part in the next major shift in Chilean politics. President Federico Errázuriz (1871–76) had successfully wooed the increasingly clericalist Conservatives in his bid for power, but once in office he found it impossible to hold the Liberal-Conservative Fusion together. One of the consequences of the gradual liberalization of the 1860s was that party competition was now developing its own dynamic, and the religious issue, as it turned out, was far too tempting to be left aside as a means of rallying support: both Catholics and anticlericals found that they could appeal to substantial constituencies within the still very limited, but also now gradually widening, political class.

It needs to be stressed here that Conservatives and Catholics, despite their clerical allegiance, shared fully in the common attitudes

of the political class to such things as patriotism and material progress. Abdón Cifuentes could thus proudly boast that "the least of the
Spanish colonies . . . has managed to place itself among the first of its
sisters."[58] Indeed, the Church itself sometimes implied that its patriotism was more profound than that of its adversaries—"for all our
history and all the cherished traditions of our country are condensed
in Catholicism."[59] Fr. Mariano Casanova, in a sermon for the national holidays in 1863, exhorted his flock: "let us remember our republican credo, and . . . let us swear to its most faithful observance."[60]
The same Fr. Casanova, speaking at a Catholic meeting in 1867, was
positively ecstatic on the subject of material progress: "We all long
for progress; we all want civilization to take root and expand. Forward! May a thousand and one sails plow through our tranquil seas;
may the racket of cities replace the silence of our forests, the noise of
industry supplant the trilling of birds; may the steamship and elec-
tricity open up a way everywhere, shortening distances, levelling the
hills, and joining the remotest peoples."[61] The politician Zorobabel
Rodríguez, fervent Catholic Conservative that he was, was as fervent as any Liberal or Radical in his belief in laissez-faire economic
ideas: he saw competition as "the hand of God in the sea of human
transactions."[62]

The Conservative party's growing clericalism, however, when
combined with the dynamic of party competition, was almost certain to lead to an intensification of the religious issue. The Church's
own behavior, it has to be said here, helped to maintain the pattern.
Two contentious public rows at the start of the 1870s brought what
were labelled at the time *las cuestiones teológicas*, the "theological
questions," to the center of the stage once again. The Church's refusal to marry a minor politician and to bury a popular veteran of the
wars of independence pointed, as far as Liberals were concerned, to
the need for a civil marriage law and for separate non-Catholic plots
in public cemeteries, a change decreed in December 1871. And indeed, there *were* fundamental Church-state questions still to be resolved at the start of the 1870s. While formal freedom of worship had
been conceded in the 1865 law, and was never in serious danger
thereafter, the Church nonetheless retained certain functions which,
in the Liberal view, properly belonged to the state, functions such as
civil registration and marriage.

A further key question, which at this point suddenly assumed great importance, was that of education. A public education system of sorts had been gradually assembled by the early republican governments and placed under the supervision of the new University of Chile founded in 1843. Education was not yet large scale (only about one fifth of the population was literate in the census year 1875), nor was primary schooling made obligatory before 1920. But both the *content* and the *control* of education, over which there had previously been a remarkable degree of consensus,[63] now became a matter of deep interest to Liberal and Radical reformers and to Catholics. The latter were determined to retain as much influence as possible, the former aspired to extend and to secularize state education (very largely accomplished by the end of the century) and, an important point, to supervise the numerous private schools, many of these Catholic, which had grown up alongside the public system. Supervision was principally exercised through state-controlled examinations held under the auspices of the Instituto Nacional.

Two figures in particular played the leading role in the divorce between Conservatives and Liberals in the early 1870s. One was the formidable young Conservative politician Abdón Cifuentes, a devout Catholic who was given the education portfolio in Errázuriz's cabinet in order, so the president hoped, to solidify Conservative support for his coalition. The other was Diego Barros Arana, Chile's most eminent historian, who in 1863 had been appointed head of the Instituto Nacional by President Pérez. As a Liberal, Barros Arana was moderate; as a doctrinaire anticlerical, he was not. As he wrote around this time to his equally anticlerical friend and fellow historian Miguel Luis Amunátegui: "It is indispensable that everyone . . . should contribute to the fight against superstition and error."[64] He was regarded by the Church with particular loathing, though, as with all good anticlericals, his friends included men of the cloth. Barros Arana's reforms at the Instituto included the removal of the daily mass and nightly saying of the rosary which had previously been part of the students' routine. Cifuentes, for his part, decreed "freedom of examinations" in January 1872, thus liberating Catholic private schools from state tutelage.

As with the Affair of the Sacristan, the conflict between Cifuentes and Barros Arana generated high passions and street scenes—at one point Cifuentes's house was assaulted—and we can legitimately see this as much more genuinely a struggle between clericalism and anticlericalism than the earlier Affair, a definite indication of the way in which they had become clearly defined attitudes since the 1850s—attitudes which fed on each other. Contemporaries certainly sensed something new in the air in the early 1870s: "what is being fomented in the country today," asserted Pedro Félix Vicuña, now a senator, "is a true schism, and who knows where we will end up."[65] Vicuña, it is fair to say, was better skilled than most at recognizing purely political schisms; clearly he intimated a deeper conflict in the making.

Only the bare bones of the Cifuentes-Barros Arana story can be presented here.[66] Barros Arana was dismissed from the Instituto Nacional, but the resulting political storm meant that Cifuentes, too, was obliged to resign, and his examinations decree was in due course rescinded. With Cifuentes's resignation in July 1873 the Conservatives left the government and moved (tentatively and then definitely) into opposition, where they remained, with one unimportant exception, until after the civil war of 1891. President Errázuriz, meanwhile, constructed a new governing coalition focused on the Liberal party and enjoying support from the Radicals and at times, thereafter, the Nationals. He was reproved for this by his brother Crescente, the future archbishop, who had earlier told him he would soon be surrounded by "men hostile to religion" and would become "an enemy of the Catholic cause and its persecutor."[67] But the president had no alternative. The new Liberal alliance, however, was far more prone to factionalism than its predecessors.

It was likely, given the nature of the realignment of 1873–75, that the religious issue should intrude fairly frequently into the notable congressional sessions of the period, which saw a sequence of constructive legislation, bringing constitutional amendments, electoral changes, and important legal and judicial reforms. There was more personal attitudinizing in these debates than there had been in 1865. Manuel Antonio Matta scathingly denounced the use of the terms "Catholic" or "anti-Catholic" as "unparliamentary,"[68] but there was nothing he could do to hold back the tide. "I give thanks to God," declared a now prominent Conservative, José Clemente Fabres, "for making me fanatical and exaggerated and for bringing me to this Chamber to publicly manifest my beliefs."[69] The deputy Jorge Huneeus, for his part, proudly identified himself as "militant in the Liberal ranks, or, to speak the truth, in the ranks of the anti-clericals."[70]

Gratuitous sniping was also much in evidence, as, for instance, when
Juan Gandarillas demanded the suppression of the university's theology faculty—since God's attributes were incomprehensible, there
was no point in maintaining "a science which naturally has to be
incomprehensible."[71] Matta, in similar vein, once tried to prevent
payment of the archbishop's salary, on the grounds that the country's
main seminary was "a school of anti-republicanism."[72]

Parliamentary interruptions and more serious "incidents" were
also now more common than previously. A typical interruption occurred in November 1872 in the Chamber of Deputies, when the
Conservative Carlos Walker Martínez, expounding the importance of
confession and last rites for those on their deathbeds, was challenged
by one of the Radical leaders:

GALLO: That is what your excellency believes.
WALKER MARTINEZ: Everyone believes it, Mr. Deputy.
GALLO: No, sir.
WALKER MARTINEZ: Yes sir . . . Even if these sentiments are not to be found
in the upper classes of society . . . they exist, and very sincerely, among the
people.[73]

"Incidents" were not always limited in scale. On one occasion, on
October 20, 1874, order in the Chamber broke down completely (fist
fights; an invasion of the floor by the public; cries of "Down with the
priests in frock-coats!" and "Up with the cabinet!") during one of
the many debates on the proposed new Penal Code. Several articles
of the draft code had incurred the displeasure of the Church, which
had promised "anathemas" to those who voted for them in Congress.
"We are now deliberating under the threat of the Church's thunder-
bolts," indignantly declared the Liberal senator Alejandro Reyes.[74]
But who, asked his distinguished Conservative adversary Manuel José
Irarrázaval, was really persecuting whom? "Is it the Church, with
nothing more than the power of its canons, with no sanction for its
laws beyond the conscience of believers? Or is it the State, the pos-
sessor of force and power, of the judges, of the public jobs, of prisons
and banishments?"[75]

In October 1874 the bishops actually excommunicated all who
had voted for the offending articles, a measure President Errázuriz
charitably attributed to Archbishop Valdivieso's growing senility.
Senator Reyes predictably denounced this new attempt "to exercise

pressure on the consciences . . . of the representatives of the nation fulfilling the most august of their duties."[76] The excommunication was later lifted: the Senate, which had already removed the offending articles, could not be overridden by the Chamber, whose majority wished to retain them. The Church's public posture throughout the reform debates naturally infuriated Liberals, Radicals, and Nationals. As Matta put it, "the undeniable fact, for all to see, which everybody recognizes, is this struggle by the Church to obtain its complete independence while preserving its privileges and prerogatives."[77] This is more or less what the Church *was* doing.

Congressmen in the mid-1870s were perhaps more conscious than in 1865 that their local "theological questions" were part of an international struggle. The Catholics had by now fully assimilated Pius IX's strictures on liberalism, progress, and modernity. The Liberals, perhaps flushed by their new role in government, were more confident than before in their own prescriptions. The rising politician José Manuel Balmaceda saw the conflict as worldwide, as between "the spirits who adore tradition and the past" and "the men of the present, or better put, the men of the future."[78] The Liberal deputy Isidoro Errázuriz, speaking in a debate four years later, saw the triumph of liberalism as inevitable: "our ship is drawn to a safe haven by a powerful and irresistible current . . . the current of history, logic and truth." The remark drew prolonged applause from the public gallery. He then indulged in a typical paean of praise to liberalism and secularization as liberating forces: "For a long time water and fire were used as methods of torment, to drag confession of the error of their ways from the enemies of orthodoxy. Today, water and fire combine to give motion to the locomotive and the steamship, for even the elements have been secularized and placed at the service of science, industry and human progress."[79]

Where they could, the Conservatives responded in kind. "Christian civilization," proclaimed Angel Custodio Vicuña, "will in the end triumph over modern civilization." He predicted that Darwinism, one of modern civilization's "most powerful agents"—with its belief that "it is more glorious to be a perfected orang-utang than a degenerated Adam"—would one day be viewed as the "most lugubrious of romances."[80] A new tone can also be heard creeping into the Conservative pronouncements of these years. It was, after all, easy enough to turn liberal rhetoric against itself—to claim, for instance, that modern civilization was essentially the product of Christianity. "What are our democratic dogmas?" Abdón Cifuentes had asked in 1869. "Liberty, equality, human dignity, respect for law and duty. Well, all these dogmas come from Calvary; they are all title-deeds of humanity as regenerated by the Gospel."[81] "The Catholic religion," claimed José Clemente Fabres, "is the foundation of modern civilization."[82] Manuel José Irarrázaval, likewise, suggested that "the spirit that gives life to civilization, which the present-day world is so proud of, is the spirit of the Gospel."[83] Another line of attack was to insist that the laicizing Liberals were themselves creating a new form of despotism. "The Liberals of 1873," insisted Abdón Cifuentes, "are less liberal than the frankly authoritarian legislators of 1833."[84] Another deputy, José Lira, criticized "the limitless omnipotence and omniscience of the State" he now saw as "a fundamental dogma in politics."[85] More was to be heard of this argument in the next decade.

The mounting economic crisis of the 1870s, and the outbreak of the War of the Pacific (1879–83)—in which Chile inflicted shattering defeat on Peru and Bolivia—diverted politicians' minds from the religious issue, but only temporarily and never completely. As the new president, Domingo Santa María, speculated in September 1882, "the religious questions could well rise up again after the war."[86] They most assuredly did. With the Liberals now at center stage in government, anticlericals saw a golden opportunity to further their program. The Conservatives, for their part, were now forced by the fact of being in opposition to marshal their forces in hopes of an eventual return to power. Here the developing dynamic of party competition needs, once again, to be placed in context. The strongly presidentialist political system created in the 1830s was now coming under increasing criticism from politicians who aspired to a greater degree of congressional control. A particular bone of contention was the shameless way in which the executive manipulated elections. Put crudely, all elections in Chile between the 1830s and 1890s were "fixed." Earlier on, given the government's frequent resort to repression, this had been easy enough to manage. With the liberalization of political life from the 1860s, however, electoral "intervention" (as it was always known) became altogether more difficult for the president and his ministers—one reason why the level of violence at election time rose fairly noticeably in the 1870s and 1880s.

Since opposition parties were seriously disadvantaged by the practice of intervention, the Conservatives after 1873–74 were bound to take up the cause of electoral freedom. They espoused it vigorously. They also now had an obvious stake in further constitutional reform, if only to reduce the overwhelming power of the executive, expressed most flagrantly at election time. The Liberals, for their part, found the position complicated by their newly salient role in government. Both those in office and their followers in Congress, the so-called "government Liberals," found electoral intervention to be far too useful for it to be readily abandoned. But growing numbers of dissident Liberals now opposed the practice as a matter of democratic principle, as did the Radicals. From all sides, therefore, there was pressure by the 1880s to modify presidentialism and to rid the country of electoral manipulation. On this issue, the Conservatives were by no means isolated, and their propaganda in favor of political reform was, if anything, more heartfelt than that of anyone else. Their clerical attachment, however, *did* separate them from other parties, and became increasingly a badge of distinctive identity—as well as a useful banner under which to mobilize electoral support. The Conservatives' organizational efforts in the 1870s, in fact, were rather impressive; they were the first political party ever to stage a national conference (December 1878), at which Abdón Cifuentes crisply summarized their policy: "Catholicism and liberty . . . unbreakable adherence to the faith of our fathers and to public liberties."[87]

≺ VI ≻

The "Religious War" of the 1880s

President Domingo Santa María (1881–86) was faced by the fundamental problem of growing indiscipline in the Liberal ranks. Strong willed and anticlerical, he had been one of the architects of the mid-century Liberal renewal, but in office he was determined to maintain the traditional pattern of presidential power. "I have been called an interventionist," he wrote in 1885. "I am . . . I want an efficient, disciplined parliament that will collaborate with the government's hopes for the public good."[88] Santa María's vigorous methods of intervention, combined with the mounting anti-presidentialist feeling of the time, might well have produced a major political crisis had he not chosen to press forward with the anticlerical program. The president himself was hostile to what he termed "medieval prejudices," and was eager to diminish the still very powerful and pervasive role of the Church.

The pattern for his presidency was set by a conflict between the Chilean state and the papacy itself. Following the death of the once-formidable Archbishop Valdivieso in June 1878, the government had proposed (naively, it seems, rather than maliciously) a priest with Liberal connections, Francisco de Paula Taforó, as his successor. Taforó was of illegitimate birth; Valdivieso had barred his promotion to bishop. Mgr. Celestino del Frate, an apostolic delegate sent to Chile to examine the matter, advised Pope Leo XIII to reject the nomination. Santa María expelled the delegate and broke off relations with the Holy See (January-February 1883).[89] Chilean Catholics responded fiercely, not least the Conservatives, whose anger was heightened by the fact that Santa María was systematically excluding them from Congress by the traditional methods. Mgr. del Frate's train to the Argentine frontier was accompanied by ardent demonstrations from the faithful.

Santa María, quite apart from wishing to put pressure on the pope over the archiepiscopal vacancy, undoubtedly sensed that concentration on the religious issue was the best way of holding his fractious Liberal following together—as a distraction from the disagreeably controversial questions of presidentialism and electoral intervention. As his adversary Carlos Walker Martínez was to put it, "Santa María knew his people and knew how to exploit them."[90] Anticlericals of all colors could joyously unite under the banner of reducing the powers of the Church. The congressional majority now enacted the major secularizing legislation in Chilean history, depriving the Church of its monopoly over marriages and civil registration in January and July 1884. Even more controversial was the law secularizing all public cemeteries in August 1883—the debates cover more than 200 pages in the congressional record. The Church had previously given its blessing to such cemeteries, but now declared them unholy. Some macabre and grotesque scenes resulted. Catholics sometimes spirited corpses away for burial in churches (illegal since O'Higgins's time), while coffins loaded with stones or tin cans were deposited in the execrated cemeteries.[91]

Clerical and anticlerical passions now reached a new pitch of intensity. In fact, something like a religious war raged in Chile during these months, with symptoms of incipient rebellion in evidence. At a great protest meeting held in July 1883, one of many organized in Santiago and the provinces, it was rumored that Santa María had surrounded his house with hussars and placed the Eighth Line Regiment on alert. Santa María himself apparently feared no upheaval: "I have absolute confidence in the people and in the army," he wrote.[92] But the atmosphere was undoubtedly fraught with tension. In January 1885 there was a vain attempt, by means of a parcel-bomb, on Santa María's life. On a lighter note, Chileans long recalled the story of the society lady who told the president that she no longer said the rosary because it included his name—that of the Virgin Mary. While this incident does not seem to be documentable, it sounds entirely credible.

The debates of the mid-1880s, both inside and outside Congress, naturally reflected the intensity of "the political-religious atmosphere, agitated today by a real whirlwind," as one deputy put it.[93] "We are passing through an hour of crisis in which differences of opinion arise in all households," observed Augusto Orrego Luco. "Unity of religious sentiment has been broken, and conflict between the opposing sides is quite inevitable."[94] Not surprisingly, there were numerous angry exchanges on the floor of Congress. The debates, however, give an impression of one-sidedness, largely because the opposition (thanks to Santa María's ruthless "interventions") was only minimally represented in the Chamber of Deputies. This was a matter of regret to at least one deputy, Diego Elizondo. Drawing attention to the "empty benches," he suggested that the government could have shown "more nobility and more gentlemanliness" toward the Conservatives.[95]

The great Radical Enrique Mac-Iver ably summarized the aims of the new legislation during the cemeteries debate: "to base the public organization of the country on scientific and experimental foundations, removing from it any institution that deals with the relations between man and the Divinity; the secularization of the State . . . so as to establish equality in law and justice and liberty for all."[96] Yet liberals were still uneasily aware that the weight of history was an obstacle to their campaign to laicize institutions. "In the countries inhabited by the proud Spanish race," noted Augusto Matte, "it is almost impossible to form a perfectly clear notion of the attributes of the State, because of its long sustained consortium with the Church."[97] Mac-Iver himself acknowledged the existence of "far from contemptible social forces," as well as "the spirit of stagnation that weighs heavily in our country."[98]

Despite such reservations, liberal triumphalism was much in evidence as the new laws went through. Manuel Novoa, evoking "the mandate of liberty and progress" received from the voters, roundly declared: "we Liberals are the law, we are justice, we are the future of the country, we are power, ours will be success, ours will be the victory."[99] Mac-Iver insisted that the majority of Chileans now agreed with "the credo and doctrine of modern liberalism," only regretting that the Conservatives had become "a Catholic political party that will profoundly perturb the normal progress of institutions."[100] Liberals presented the laicizing laws as an epic battle for liberation, part of "the history of all the civilized peoples of this century," as Gonzalo Bulnes put it, and as a battle that would be ended "only when in the last country on earth the last of men possesses for his conscience and his faith the rights which are inherent in his nature."[101]

The formidably confident rhetoric of liberalism can be appreciated in speeches of the time. In January 1884 the Radical Francisco Puelma Tupper recounted a long litany of Catholic misdemeanors: the Massacre of St. Bartholomew, the suppression of the Albigensians and Hussites, responsibility for the reactionary thoughts of De Maistre, Chateaubriand, and so on.

Liberalism, bad as this must be for ultramontanism, will triumph in the whole world, while this retrograde party will have to humbly bend its neck and accept the conditions we wish to impose on it . . . Let it be clearly understood that the tendencies of the clerical party are those of the reestablishment of the Inquisition. The triumph of the great Liberal cause could not be opposed by all the Popes, if they came back to life, or by the Inquisition, with its thousands of victims, if they could restore it . . . What have the Republics had to struggle against? With the Catholic religion and its fanaticism, with the infallible Church with its insatiable desire for power and wealth, with political despotism based on religion as dogma . . . What has been the progress of the Republics? To wrest from the Church, little by little, the fragments of territory it possessed. Freedom of worship, mixed marriages, the abolition of censorship, freedom of the press, abolition of perpetual vows, philosophical institutions of education, freedom of instruction . . . What has been the fate of the Republics that have adhered to Catholicism? Death: Venice, Florence, etc., Paraguay, etc . . . That which is freest, most splendid, most advanced on earth is found in nations which have separated from Catholicism: Germany, Holland, Scandinavia, Switzerland, England, the United States.[102]

As in earlier debates, congressmen in 1883–84 were anxious to take account of what Manuel Novoa called "the lessons and examples offered to us by the most advanced peoples of the world."[103] In general, Protestant countries were taken to be natural allies in the struggle between progress and reaction. Thus Francisco Puelma Tupper applauded the United States, for halting Napoleon III's "Catholic" intervention in Mexico, and the Protestant Hohenzollern dynasty, for having stopped Catholic expansionism in the Franco-Prussian war—"Pius IX himself said that the worst news he had received in his life was the defeat of the French at Sedan."[104] By no means all of the arguments from foreign examples strike the historian as equally persuasive: during the cemeteries debate, Augusto Matte came close to attributing the recent expansion of the British Empire into Egypt to the English cemetery legislation of 1881.[105]

The principal Catholic-Conservative response to Liberal triumphalism was to accuse the government of sheer despotism. Ricardo Letelier, for instance, deplored "the development which the authoritarian tendency is taking amongst us," and denounced the (admittedly grotesque) use of the police during the battle of the cemeteries as "only one of many manifestations of government authoritarianism."[106] In like manner, José Nicolás Hurtado castigated "the Liberal school which exaggerates the attributions of the State, which denatures its faculties, removes it from its proper orbit and makes it invade the sphere of the rights and even the liberties of the individual."[107] In a later session he suggested that Chile was falling into the clutches of "the goddess Reason, [and] the deliriums of the French Revolution."[108] According to a speaker at the huge Catholic protest meeting of July 1883, "Liberal despotism does not wish to recognize that there is anywhere that the action of the gendarme cannot reach."[109] "The cult of the State," likewise asserted Juan Agustín Barriga, "threatens to become a real fetishism, and it carries grave dangers for the future of our free institutions."[110] Carlos Walker Martínez, for his part, contrasting the "entirely Jacobin and theological" Liberals of the 1880s with their more decent predecessors of twenty years earlier, saw the government as reintroducing the despotism of the ancient world: "The God-State is Assyrian civilization transplanted into the nineteenth century."[111]

The opposition to the laicizing laws was probably on firmer ground when it cast doubts on their practicability. Chile was still "essentially Catholic," insisted Adolfo Murillo, and the new laws were out of harmony with social reality. The educated classes might accept them, but Congress had to "legislate . . . for the majority of the country, which is ignorant, and which knows no other function-ary than the parish priest."[112] The answer to this dilemma, suggested the arch-Liberal Miguel Luis Amunátegui, not altogether helpfully, was to "diffuse education and habituate the lower classes . . . to work and thriftiness."[113] Perhaps predictably, the strongest suggestions of impracticability came in connection with the civil marriage and civil register bills. As Tomás Echavarría pointed out, "concubinage" was "an endemic evil in our lower society," and was likely to be worsened by a complicated system of civil marriage.[114] Guillermo Puelma Tup-per argued that "within ten years we shall find ourselves with a great number of illegitimate children."[115] Other arguments bordered on the fanciful. Juan Mackenna, for instance, suggested that state mar-riage could lead to polygamy, for which there were numerous prece-dents—"the happy old times" when men were "surrounded by num-bers of beautiful women," or the recent case of the Mormons, who "live and prosper in the most enviable cordiality."[116] Most Liberals were not prepared to go beyond civil marriage as such. Manuel Novoa tried (and tried very hard) to incorporate a divorce law into the bill, but this was rejected, Enrique Mac-Iver arguing that it would unnec-essarily complicate the issue in "a country where religious ideas . . . still have considerable force."[117]

The logical sequel to the laicizing legislation of 1883–84 would obviously have been the formal separation of Church and state. Most Liberals and Radicals would by now have agreed with Miguel Luis Amunátegui, who in an earlier debate had stated the essential liberal principle: "As long as the secular authority remains linked in any way with any ecclesiastical authority, civil tolerance will not be reached to its full extent."[118] There was no lack of support for the idea in the congressional majority. Congress in 1884 approved a government-sponsored initiative to amend the constitution, elimi-nating article 5 altogether, while retaining other articles which al-lowed the state certain residual controls over the Church. The pro-posed amendment was sent, as it had to be under the rules, to the 1885–88 Congress, but was never ratified. This was partly because Santa María was now hoping for a solution to the archiepiscopal question, but the president also felt that the recently enacted laws needed time to take root, and that an immediate move to separation would "produce a perilous upheaval." He also took account of the desire expressed by many of his friends for "peace in the family and tranquillity in the home"[119] after the storm and stress of the "religious war."

It must not be suggested, of course, that the passionate feelings of Catholics and anticlericals were not perfectly genuine during the Santa María years, and clearly when such passions are involved the issues concerned tend to take on a life of their own. Nor can it be denied that it was necessary by the 1880s to delimit the proper spheres of influence of Church and state. At the same time, it is also legitimate to interpret this episode as closely related to the political dynamic of the period. As Isidoro Errázuriz put it at the time, in the Chamber of Deputies, "the secret of the comedy is inside and outside this hall," by which he meant the interplay of the parties.[120] The Catholic-Conservative opposition was perfectly aware of the political dimension to Santa María's anticlericalism: "the government," one of its publications underlined, "needs to feed the common hatred in order to keep its ranks solid."[121] For his part, Santa María saw the Catholic agitation as little more than a Conservative attempt to regain power. Concentration on the religious issue, it must be said here, should not allow us to forget that some of the more conventionally political disputes of the Santa María years were almost equally intense. Cases in point include the violent and dramatic scenes in August 1885, both inside and outside Congress, after the interior minister, José Manuel Balmaceda, had been accused of flagrant electoral intervention, or the extremely contentious termination of the debates on the tax law in January 1886. The religious issue was by no means the sole factor responsible for the now bitter relationship between government and opposition.

The fact is that the political system created in the 1830s, which on balance had served the republic well, no longer reflected the aspirations of the increasingly well-educated political class, many of whose members, including the Conservatives, now wished to replace presidential supremacy with what they termed a "parliamentary" regime. (When actually instituted after 1891, it bore no real resemblance to European parliamentary systems.) The aspiration had grown notably during the 1870s. Santa María was able to hold the traditional system together only by invoking the religious issue—whether cynically or not must remain a matter of opinion.

Reflecting on the "religious war" soon afterwards, Carlos Walker Martínez suggested that "if armed revolution did not break out then, we can be sure it never will."[122] How wrong he was! It was Santa María's successor, President José Manuel Balmaceda (1886–91), who had to try to resolve the mounting tension within the system. Balmaceda hoped to usher in a new era of concord among Chileans in general and the "Liberal family" (that is, Liberals, Radicals, and Nationals) in particular. He very quickly mended fences with the Vatican, something Santa María had tried unavailingly to do toward the end of his presidency. The archiepiscopal vacancy was filled, by Fr. Mariano Casanova, who had remained aloof from the recent struggles; he wrangled lengthily, though politely, with the president over the precise form of the constitutional oath he had to swear.[123] The "religious war" swiftly abated. But Balmaceda could find no alternative issue with which to unite and rally the disparate factions of Liberalism and to uphold the presidentialist tradition, which he espoused as strongly as his predecessor, despite having been one of its most eloquent critics in his earlier years. When Balmaceda finally lost control of Congress, as he did in 1889, the game was up. All parties combined to resist and attack the president, and the matter had to be decided by force of arms. In this conflict, as in the rebellion of 1859, whatever the individual role of members of the clergy may have been,[124] the religious issue was conspicuous by its absence. It was politics pure and simple—and war.

≺ VII ≻

The Religious Issue in the Parliamentary Republic

The civil war of 1891 was a straightforward contest between president and Congress, and the latter's victory in that tragic conflict in which at least 6,000 lives were lost signified the elimination of strong presidential government. The congressional supremacy achieved in 1891, however, heightened rather than diminished the dynamic of party competition, not least because elections were at last freed from executive control, and party competition at this level was now far less restrained than previously. Here, needless to say, the Conservative party benefited from its clerical connection, and over the next few decades its political strength was much greater than it had been at any time since the 1860s. The religious issue, caught up as it had been for three decades in the weave of partisan struggle, continued to play a significant part in the politics of the so-called Parliamentary Republic, which lasted until the convulsive presidential election of 1920—the end of Chile's "long" nineteenth century.

There were several reasons why it did. Among the most important, perhaps, was the high level of agreement on major questions of national policy as between all major political parties at this period: the Conservatives; the faction-ridden Liberals; the Liberal-Democrats (the opportunistic following of the defeated Balmaceda); the Radicals, whose star was rising; and the Nationals, whose star was dimming. Disagreement on specific issues (the efforts to return Chile to the gold standard in the 1890s, for instance) may sometimes have been fierce, but tended to cut across party lines rather than to reinforce them. The one issue that could stimulate the conditioned reflexes of politicians was, precisely, the religious issue, the Radicals occupying one extreme of the spectrum, the Conservatives the other, and the other parties holding positions somewhere in between. (The main internal division within the Liberal party, significantly, was between "moderates" and "doctrinaires," the latter being more anticlerical than the former.) The Radicals continued to press their demand for a final separation of Church and state, and to advocate the extension of an essentially secular state education. The Conservatives, for their part, resisted all such proposals and defended Catholic interests, also seeking to expand the influence of the Church in the national culture. There were endless little conflicts, many of them trivial, between Catholics and anticlericals in the provincial cities and small towns. The battle flared up at regular intervals in the sessions of Congress. In 1898, for instance, an anticlerical deputy, objecting to public money being spent on repairs to Santiago cathedral, asked the Chamber to note the "wealth and luxury of the archbishop, representative on earth of the poor fisherman of Galilee, of the putative son of Joseph."

The religious issue, in fact, played a regular part in the complicated ballet of congressional maneuvers and cabinet changes that marked the Parliamentary period. The congressional record supplies numerous instances. One example will have to suffice. In 1897 Francisco de Paula Pleiteado, the Radical deputy who made the remark just quoted, objected strongly to a circular issued by Fr. Guillermo Cárter, a celebrated and highly combative priest in the north of Chile, which referred to the civil marriage law of 1884 in scathing terms. "Is it proper," he asked, "for a public functionary to evaluate a law of the Republic in this way? . . . How is it that this Government, which calls itself Liberal, can tolerate these assaults on liberal laws?" Pleiteado won immediate support from other anticlericals, one of whom described the offending circular as "an audacious and violent attack against one of the most beautiful conquests of Chilean liberalism." Pleiteado and his colleagues were seriously annoyed when the responsible cabinet minister refused to reproach Fr. Cárter, and proposed a motion to reprimand the priest. Toned down somewhat, it passed by 43 votes to 28. This led immediately to a vote of confidence in the cabinet, which survived by 39 votes to 36.[125] Not all cabinets were as fortunate: on several notable occasions in the Parliamentary period, use of the religious issue brought governments down. This did not mean very much. Cabinets at the time rarely lasted more than a few months.

There was a distinctly negative side to this persistence in muted form of the "religious war" of the Santa María years. It could well have distracted Chile's upper-class politicians from addressing the serious social problems that came fully into view in Parliamentary times. In this sphere, the record of the Parliamentary Republic has long been seen, and on the whole rightly, as highly defective. What is interesting for our purposes, however, is that both sides in the modified religious war could draw on the support of significant constituencies. This is a point that bears a brief examination.

At the turn of the century, Catholicism was still the religious preference of nearly all those Chileans who had a religious preference at all. In 1920 there were barely 25,000 native-born Protestants in a population that had by then reached 3.8 million; the Jewish community was not much more than 2,000. The Conservatives could depend on strong electoral support from the faithful, as well as discreet, and sometimes not so discreet, help from the pulpit. The Conservative party's "true electoral power," asserted a deputy in 1897, was "the priests and other members of the clergy."[126] The anticlericals' comparable institutional network, probably a stronger one, was the state education system. "Nobody can ignore," reported the *Revista Católica* in 1913, "that public instruction in Chile is almost entirely in the hands of Radicals and Masons . . . [who] in their sectarian obfuscation have come to preach purely socialist doctrines . . . and even proclaim the *emancipation* of women, the greatest horror of all."[127] In the Normal School at Valdivia, the same report noted, all the instructors save one were "masons, anti-religious propagandists, enraged sectarians."[128]

By this stage, secularist and rationalist attitudes had certainly taken hold of a substantial part of the upper and middle classes, especially among men. Alejandro Venegas, author of a justly celebrated essay of 1910, referring to "educated people," observed that *"the great majority is not Catholic."*[129] The first two decades of the twentieth century saw strong growth in both the Radical party and in Freemasonry. Anticlericalism also found a congenial home in the developing student movement of these years. Students were at the forefront in two spectacular episodes of agitation, 1910 and 1913, against an unpopular papal Internuncio, Mgr. Enrico Sibilia, whom they denounced as a "clerical vampire." On one famous occasion they stole his monsignorial hat and paraded it on a donkey down the main avenue of Santiago.[130] Nor did the anticlerical cause lack publicists, the most celebrated of whom was Juan Serapio Lois, from the traditionally Radical northern province of Atacama—which Matta, also from there, once described as "the true school of the most advanced ideas of the modern spirit."[131] The historian Gonzalo Vial, in a recent monumental account of the Parliamentary period, describes Lois as "beyond all caricature."[132] This is not by any means fair. He had a poorly coordinated physical gait, which exposed him to derision, but he was intelligent, able, and extremely influential. "You don't *have* to believe" was one of his recurrent catch phrases.[133] He bore the brunt of numerous attacks by the Church and the Conservatives. Lois, it might be noted in passing, was one of a number of Chilean intellectuals who since the 1870s had assimilated Auguste Comte's Positivism.[134] Its most distinguished local disciple at this period was the great educationalist Valentín Letelier. Letelier's appointment (1906) as rector of the University of Chile, fiercely combated by the Church and the Conservatives, was one of the occasions when the religious issue brought down the cabinet.

Among upper- and middle-class women, anticlericalism seems to have been altogether less marked. Back in 1877, Isidoro Errázuriz had noted that women were "the army of religion, the reserve of the Conservative party,"[135] and President Santa María himself had seen women as the "dynamite used by the clerics."[136] "If there are men freethinkers in Chile," José Nicolás Hurtado asserted in 1883, "there are no women freethinkers."[137] So it was that the strongly Catholic wives of equally strong freethinkers continued to give religious names to their children, as with the boy christened Salvador Isabelino del Sagrado Corazón de Jesús Allende in 1908, although husbands did sometimes prevail on this score: Voltaire and Renan were the first names of two other well-known politicians slightly younger than the future president.[138]

The only mass medium of the period also played its part. With the growth of literacy, the provincial press, much more flourishing at the start of the century than it is now, included a large number of newspapers whose editorial line was anticlerical—a typical example, no doubt, being *El Correo*, a Valdivia newspaper "of liberal affiliation, propagandistic, with characteristics of the most advanced radicalism," valiantly combated by the Conservative *La Aurora* (with its circulation of 3,500).[139] This pattern seems to have been a common one in many provincial cities.

Anti-Catholicism was by no means confined to the educated classes. That it had a more popular following is evidenced in the public excitement aroused by Juan José Julio Elizalde, a renegade priest known as "Pope Julio"—another product of Atacama Province. A man of large build and commanding appearance, he had taken up Positivism, and his riveting anticlerical oratory involved him in several national sensations in the first years of the twentieth century: these sometimes won the attention of the cabinet itself.[140] Likewise, the emergent Chilean labor movement of this period,[141] despite Conservative attempts to channel it toward Catholicism, swiftly developed socialist or anarchosyndicalist, and in due course Marxist, orientations with a definitely anticlerical coloring. In short, the national culture in the 1900s and the 1910s was no longer in any sense homogeneously Catholic in the way it had arguably been in the early republic. It now consisted, we could suggest, of two comprehensive and competitive sub-cultures, one Catholic, one secularist and rationalist. If anything the second was stronger than the first. Certainly the Church thought that it was. When Valparaiso was devastated in the earthquake of August 1906, Archbishop Casanova was not slow to connect the catastrophe to recent national trends: "Chile . . . was moving further from God every day . . . violating the sanctity of the Sabbath . . . despising the sacrament of marriage . . . profaning His temples, blaspheming publicly and solemnly with His holy name . . . the heart of youth has been perverted by an irreligious education; the press has become a source of scandal and a school of dissolution."[142]

It is entirely reasonable to suggest, as does the historian Ricardo Krebs, that the interplay of ultramontane Catholicism and laicizing Liberalism made a major contribution to the Chilean tradition of political tolerance and ideological pluralism.[143] There is also, however, a sense in which the religious issue reached a point of stalemate in the Parliamentary Republic. Neither side could win—or for that matter lose. The competition between the Catholic and anticlerical cultures continued at various levels thereafter. In the state education system, for instance, secularist emphases continued to prevail. No educated Chilean needs to be reminded of the close connection between the Radical party and the teaching profession until the party's sad decline in fairly recent times. In higher education the Catholics had succeeded, despite the reluctance of Archbishop Casanova, in establishing their own private university, the Catholic University of Chile, in 1888. The secularists, led by a distinguished philosopher, Enrique Molina, created a redoubt for themselves in the new University of Concepción (1919), whose proud motto, "For the free development of the spirit," sums up the institution's foundational ethos. And so the competition went on.

The final separation of Church and state in 1925, accomplished without great drama by President Arturo Alessandri, made little or no difference, though it did have the important effect of finally disconnecting the religious issue from mainstream political life. The Church continued to influence politicians, needless to say, but its institutional position was no longer a matter for public debate. Nobody has ever seriously sought to restore the link between Church and state.

It might be remarked in conclusion that the boundaries of the two sub-cultures did not remain fixed or permanent. Anticlerical, secularist, and rationalist attitudes were far more prevalent in the Chilean upper and middle classes in the early twentieth century than was to be the case at the end of the century. In hindsight, the reasons seem fairly obvious. In the first place, the terms of the debate shifted, as the newly salient Chilean Left pressed the claims of social reform and indeed socialism; the Left inherited anticlerical attitudes, but these were never its main *raison d'être*. The most successful political movement of the second half of the century, it must also be noted, the Christian Democrat party, came from a strongly Catholic background, deriving its inspiration from the "social encyclicals" of Pope Leo XIII and Pope Pius XI and from modern Catholic thinkers such as Jacques Maritain. Partly in consequence, the old connection between the Church and the Conservatives was eventually broken, and the Conservatives themselves finally merged with their historic foes the Liberals (1966), in a genuinely new party rather than a temporary "fusion," and one in which the religious issue ceased to be any kind of reference point. And, finally, the long dictatorship of General Augusto Pinochet (1973–90) had the unintended consequence of enabling a certain "reclericalization" to take hold in the national culture as the new democracy of the 1990s came into being.[144] None of these developments, whatever their other effects, has adversely affected religious freedom.

Religion and Imperial Power in Nineteenth-Century Britain

JEFFREY COX

In 1796 THE General Assembly of the Church of Scotland debated—and defeated—the following proposition: "Men must be polished and refined before they can be enlightened in religious truth."[1] The debate was one about liberty by people with contrasting visions of the nature of religion in the modern world. The rules governing religion were changing in the eighteenth and early nineteenth centuries. Under the "confessional" religious settlements of early modern Europe, religion in its public aspect was primarily a matter for political and social elites to settle for the benefit of those under their jurisdiction.[2] Under the "voluntarist" religious settlement in modern Europe and North America, public forms of religion are treated as consequences of the conscientious choices of individual believers.[3] A central issue in the transition to a new religious settlement was the significance of the freedom to make conscientious choices.

The primacy of conscientious choice in matters of religion opened up the possibility of making public space for men and women who choose to be indifferent to religion. In 1690 an alarmed bishop of Chichester was already asking ministers and churchwardens whether there were "any in your parish who, under the pretence of liberty of conscience, wholly neglect all public worship of God."[4] In the late eighteenth-century age of imperial expansion and evangelical revival, voluntarist religion opened up the prospect of men and women not only choosing to neglect religion, but actually changing their religion.

Every religious denomination has confronted these issues at some time or another in modern history. Are men and women free to choose their religion? Or has God organized the world so that some people are freer than others? If so, what was the appropriate religious response to those impediments to conscientious choice? Some individuals were unable to choose because of state power, although that was known to be a removable obstruction. Others, it was asserted in the General Assembly, were unable to choose because of what we now call culture, and methods of eliminating cultural barriers were difficult to envision.

In a sense the debate about religion as conscientious choice was a working out of the implications of the seventeenth-century Baptist confession of faith, which asserted that "The magistrate is not by virtue of his office to meddle with religion."[5] However much it may be asserted that seventeenth-century Dissenters were indistinguishable from their neighbors, their religious principles were revolutionary. Voluntarist Protestants provided a rationale for a new religious settlement that was argued from within the world of religion itself rather than imposed by cultured despisers on the outside.

By the time the Church of Scotland confronted the issue of conscientious choice in religion, the issue of liberty had broadened considerably beyond the boundaries of sectarian Protestantism. The Assembly was debating in the context of imperial expansion, which had caught the imagination of religious men and women, particularly upon reading accounts of Captain Cook's voyages. But it was also responding to the new religious settlement that I have labeled "voluntarist religion" to distinguish it from the "confessional religion" of the early modern period. Beginning with sectarian Protestants in the seventeenth century, broadening as a consequence of pietism and evangelicalism in the Protestant world, strengthened by some aspects of "rational religion" of the eighteenth century,[6] voluntarism has become the dominant metaphor for the discussion of religion in the modern Western world. Even religious groups that reject or resist the principle (notably the Roman Catholic Church for much of modern history) find themselves forced to operate under voluntarist assumptions. Churches where confessional attitudes persist often find themselves at a severe competitive disadvantage in the modern world.[7]

Two metaphors commonly used to understand the history of religion in the modern world distract attention from the voluntarist religious settlement. One is the "free market in religion."[8] Voluntarist religion is not a market in the economic sense, where free and happy consumers in a theoretically unlimited marketplace set prices through consumer preference. Although religious choice is analogous to economic choice in some respects, its significance is fundamentally different in others. The choice made in voluntarist religion is not characteristically a decision to choose a religion when confronted with an unlimited supply of religious choices.[9] It is an internal struggle over whether to take religion seriously, or treat it as a matter for public conformity or even neglect. An element of Christianity for centuries, this internal spiritual struggle took on a new public significance in eighteenth- and nineteenth-century Europe and the Americas. In the modern world such a spiritual struggle determines the character of religious institutions, which are expected to accommodate conscientious choice rather than dictate it through the influence of state power.

A second confusing metaphor is "the downward slope on the graph" that is at the heart of the master narrative of secularization.[10] Whether implicit or explicit, the downward slope describes the fate of religion in the modern world in every secularization story. I have discussed secularization elsewhere, and will only say here that I believe it difficult to overstate the barrier that the secularization story places in the way of understanding the nature of religion in the modern world.[11] In the master narrative of secularization, religion is locked into a competitive struggle with modernity and the latter holds a decisive advantage. Because the master narrative of secularization is teleological, it renders the idea of religion as choice problematic by marginalizing conscientious choice. Furthermore, the secularization story obscures the extent to which modern religion is something new and cannot for all purposes be treated as part of a continuum with older forms of religion.

Voluntarist Protestants of the eighteenth and nineteenth centuries elaborated an alternative to the master narrative of secularization. In their view of the world, it was not science or instrumental rationality or the bureaucratic organization of society or a desacralized vision of the universe that was at issue, but the likely consequences of conscientious choice in matters of religion. This voluntarist vision was shared by theological liberals, evangelicals, and those who attempted to construct some kind of "civil religion" in the nineteenth century.[12] Of the voluntarists, evangelicals were the most aggressive.[13] Bolstered with the self-confidence to proceed without the interference or patronage of the meddling magistrate, voluntarist evangelicals both inside and outside the state churches saw in the decay of confessional religion and the spread of religious liberty, not a peril, but a golden opportunity for their variant of voluntarist religion. It was also an imperial opportunity, as even state-church Presbyterians began to realize. The imperial dimension posed new and difficult issues that defined the limits of voluntarist religion.

≺ I ≻

Voluntarist Religion in an Imperial World

In 1792, the Northamptonshire Baptist minister William Carey published his *Enquiry into the Obligations of Christians, to Use Means for the Conversion of the Heathens*, in which he felt confident enough to argue that "the spread of civil and religious liberty" meant that for the gospel "a glorious door is opened, and is likely to be opened wider and wider."[14] Carey dissented from those eighteenth-century pessimists who saw only perils to religion in the modern world. Was "civil and religious liberty" part of the downward slope on the graph of modern history? Or was it a glorious open door?

The founders of the modern Protestant missionary movement in the 1790s on the whole advocated the latter view. They argued and acted implicitly within an alternative master narrative of religion. Their governing metaphor was not a downward slope on the graph, but *contested terrain*, and they had great confidence in their ability to contest that terrain. They did not intend to wait for men and women to become polished and refined (or integrated into the world marketplace in agricultural commodities, as some mid-Victorian missionary theorists suggested).[15]

If they were right, then men and women in the modern world are not subject to the uncontested hidden hand of secularization. They are free to be religious, or irreligious, if they choose, and their choices determine the course of modern religious history. From Carey's missionary point of view, the historical fate of religion in the modern world was an experimental question that could be resolved only by preaching the gospel, planting Christian institutions, and seeing what happened as God's providential history unfolded.

The missionary impulse was not new to British Protestantism in the late eighteenth century, but (Moravians aside) missionary aspirations had been thwarted by the cumbersome, bureaucratic, confessional mechanisms of the Society for the Propagation of the Gospel (SPG) and the Society for the Promotion of Christian Knowledge (SPCK), and by hostility, indifference, and uncertainty on the part of the British state. Only in the 1790s, with the founding of the Baptist Missionary Society, the London Missionary Society, and the Church Missionary Society (for Africa and the East), did enthusiasts for the glorious open door create efficient bureaucratic mechanisms for religious expansion overseas. They managed to throw off the shackles of state patronage and control, and proceed without the sanction or the funds of the meddling magistrate.

The voluntary missionary society in some ways pre-figured the bureaucratic structure of the characteristic form of voluntarist religious expression in the modern world, the denomination. The missionary movement, consigned to the margins of history in many scholarly traditions, has played a central role in the construction of the new religious settlement of the modern world. Missionaries also played central roles in the multiple cultural encounters associated with the western imperial enterprise. Far more people in the colonized and imperialized world had contact with western religion through missionaries, mission schools, and mission hospitals, than encountered western religion from any other source, bureaucratic, technocratic, or commercial.

The partisans of religious liberty confronted almost at once the facts of the global imperial expansion. After publishing his tract and founding a missionary society, Carey could act on his own advice, set an example for others, and sail to Bengal. John Wesley had declared the world his parish, but voluntarist Protestants could only expand beyond the western world by entering an imperial world, in which fundamentally new forms of inequality and of state power confronted them.

In the world-view of optimistic voluntarists like Carey there was an infuriating indifference to state power. Looking over his *Enquiry*, it is clear that state power was of no concern to him except as a possible impediment, or as an external force that provided providential opportunities. The political dimension, bringing with it issues of power and liberty, simply does not appear as a problem from the evangelical point of view in this period, or at least not from the sectarian or voluntarist evangelical point of view. It was the extreme naivete of the early voluntarist evangelical missionaries that Sydney Smith had in mind when in his widely read *Edinburgh Review* essay of 1807 he referred to the Baptist missionaries in Bengal, including Carey, as "little detachments of maniacs."[16] The *Edinburgh Review* mislabeled them as Methodists, actually, with the characteristic Anglican inability to distinguish one kind of Dissenter from another. Whatever their denomination, they were, in Smith's view, endangering the state in India with their ill-considered fanaticism.

But other imperialists, sensitive to the realities of imperial rule, looked upon Carey not as a menace but as a potential resource. There was a convergence of interests between the early Indian missionaries and the East India Company Servants in Calcutta, who hired Carey as professor of oriental languages in their college at Fort William. Throughout his life Carey viewed his post as a providential opportunity, a glorious open door. That he was being used to promote British rule, from another point of view, seemed to cause no qualms of conscience, despite the fact that he had been selectively persecuted by British rulers during his first years in Bengal and continued to face restrictions on his missionary institutions. Carey seemed to have a blank spot in his brain where the significance of politics and other forms of state power belongs, a characteristic he shared with other missionaries from sectarian or voluntarist denominations.[17]

Missionaries who believed in the centrality of conscientious choice, especially evangelical Protestant missionaries, worked in a context of imperial power, a context which restricts or even denies freedom of choice. Imperial power placed very severe limits on the freedom of conscience in matters of religion pre-supposed by nineteenth-century voluntarist Protestants from England, Scotland, Wales, Ireland, Canada, Australia, New Zealand, and the United States, limits often unrecognized by the missionaries themselves. These men and women provide an instructive test case for a new master narrative of religion in the modern world, one which emphasizes freedom, opportunity, and change rather than static institutions in terminal decline. They also provide an opportunity for us to explore, as they explored, the limits of the transformation of religion in the modern world, limits set by imperial power.

Edward Said has argued that one cannot be neutral about imperialism: one is either for it or against it.[18] As a reminder that twentieth-century scholars have no right to evade moral and political commitments, that is a useful formula. As a way of understanding the relationship between religion and imperial power in the nineteenth century, it ends a conversation that should continue. It is not clear, for instance, that Said's formulation can be deployed directly in a judgment on Carey, since anti-imperialism in the modern sense did not exist. Moreover, Carey was simply more interested in other issues. "One cannot be neutral about the Apostolic Succession: one is either for it, or against it," is a formulation that would have made a great deal more sense to Carey.[19]

On the other hand there is no reason to put Carey beyond the reach of moral or political judgment. Neither he nor other voluntarist Protestants would have claimed such a privilege. Dissent from the exercise of state power was widely known in the wake of the French Revolution. Furthermore Carey came from a religious tradition that specialized in dissenting from the exercise of state power and the entanglement of religion with the state. There is nothing unfair about judging Carey according to standards that were present in his day and that he would recognize and find intelligible. His indifference to his own entanglement with state power was not merely colorful naivete or religious fanaticism, but a stance that opened the door for a fatal compromise between his own voluntarist principles and imperial power.

Unlike Carey, other voluntarist Protestants in an imperial setting worried about politics and imperialism. In 1829 Anthony Norris Groves, one of the co-founders of the Plymouth Brethren, left England for Baghdad, where he intended to live as a simple teacher of Christianity unconnected with any missionary society. His was one of the first "faith" missions, for Groves proceeded without regular bureaucratic support from home, depending upon irregular voluntary contributions from friends.

Groves is useful for providing a kind of "ideal type" of the extreme voluntarist in matters of religion. When in Baghdad he provided a telling commentary on what he regarded as the Pasha's rule, combining a sharp critique of illegitimate state power with a clear assertion of his own lack of responsibility as a Christian for such matters:

This conduct on the part of the Pasha begets an universal system of smuggling and fraud among all classes, so that the state of these people is indeed very, very bad. I never felt more powerfully than now, the joy of having nothing to do with these things; so that let men govern as they will, I feel my path is to live in subjection to the powers that be, and to exhort others to the same, even though it be such oppressive despotism as this. We have to show them by this, that our kingdom is not of this world, and that these are not things about which we contend. But our life being hid where no storms can assail "with Christ in God"—and our wealth being where not moth or rust doth corrupt, we leave those who are of this world to manage its concerns as they list, and we submit to them in everything as far as a good conscience will admit.[20]

So much for non-Christian rule, for principalities and powers with which we have nothing to do. But what about British rule? It was easy enough for a British missionary to condemn non-British rule. Unlike Carey, Groves was too fanatical to co-opt. He would have caused hilarious difficulties teaching at the College of Fort William. But he was a thoughtful itinerant observer who, after leaving Baghdad, traveled widely in India, and he could hardly fail to encounter the dilemmas of British rule for an evangelical Englishman. Groves speculated on the contrast between Englishness and Christianity on his first arrival in Calcutta, April 13, 1834:

We this day made a rapid and delightful voyage up the Hoogly to the city of palaces. The beautiful mansions that adorn the banks, the verdure that relieves the eye, with the variety of foliage which the trees exhibit, created a feeling that I had not been sensible of since I left my native shores. The multitude of shipping that lies on the borders of the water, purely and simply English, gives at once a *home* impression, that the thousand minute differences which strike you, if you enter into detail, do not destroy. The trees, in their variety of forms and richness of blossoms, are not English; the little boats that glide on the river are not English, nor those who so dexterously manage them; still this does not destroy the continual effect of the houses, the gardens, and the shipping. After passing up Garden Reach, where Calcutta first breaks upon the view, it is very, very grand; but when the christian mind begins to analyze the nature of its glory, and the principles to which it owed its birth, the gilded splendour soon vanishes, and the only feeling is, that you are entering a mighty city where God is not known, either in her palaces, or by the myriads over which she bears sway.[21]

The residents of those palaces included the Anglican bishop of Calcutta. Successive bishops had accommodated themselves to the missionary movement, but with great reluctance and skepticism. The first bishop (1814), Thomas Middleton, had in his early years no interest in missionary work in the broader sense, and limited his ministry to the nominally Christian European population among whom, he asserted: "We have work enough for years to come, without interfering with any species of superstition."[22] Middleton presumably adhered to the view of those confessional members of the General Assembly of the Church of Scotland who believed that men, and presumably women, must be polished and refined before turning loose in their midst little detachments of voluntarist maniacs like Groves.

It certainly was not clear to Middleton that Bengali men and women were free to choose in matters of religion, and there is a great deal to be said for his point of view. He shared the defensive, pessimistic suspicion of liberty as a standing threat to religion that is characteristic of confessional religion. Imperial power was a problem for a state-church bishop like Middleton, since he was uncertain of what ecclesiastical authority he could exercise in an imperial setting. Unsure if Indians were even subjects of the British Crown, he refused to ordain them at first. He did not share the views of voluntarists who believed that religion and empire were fundamentally different enterprises.

Carey and Groves were not unaware of the basic facts of imperial expansion. Carey was first inspired with missionary fervor upon reading of Captain Cook's voyages. Groves recognized that his responses to the palaces of Calcutta varied according to whether he was viewing them as an Englishman or as a Christian. But for voluntarist Protestants the British Empire, like the Roman Empire, was providential. The histories of both empires constituted, not merely a record of the crimes, follies, and misfortunes of mankind, but the working out of God's plan for the world. What was new in the voluntarist Protestant point of view was the obligation to take immediate advantage of whatever opportunities God provided. Their attitude to empire has been described as "God-intoxicated opportunism."[23] Empire opened a glorious door of opportunity. New methods of transportation and communication had opened the world to Christian ideas. The spread of religious and civil liberty meant that men and women were free, not only to propagate their religious views, but to accept or reject them.

In this world where power and religion were separate, the master narrative of voluntary religion led back to the Baptist objection to the meddling of magistrates in matters of religious choice. This voluntarist logic posed severe problems for state-church Anglicans who were also evangelicals, for it presumed some degree of formal neu-

trality on the part of the state. Voluntarist Protestants recognized
that the spread of civil and religious liberty was not instantaneous
and was likely to be compromised in practice. They disagreed vigorously among themselves about what did, and did not, constitute
religious liberty, particularly when it came to religious establishments and religious teaching in schools. The proponents of state
churches and religious dissenters drew different lines separating religion and power. Evangelical Anglicans elaborated a considerable
body of theory justifying religious establishments as consistent with
religious liberty, with freedom of choice in matters of religion. Their
acceptance of voluntarist principles was a long time coming.

But voluntarist Protestants, including evangelical Anglicans,
agreed with each other that civil and religious liberty was becoming
more acceptable in the world, even to those committed in principle
to a state church, and there was a good deal of evidence that they
were right. They recognized clearly the new form of religious settlement in the modern world, in which the churches could not count
on state support to maintain their power and influence. The voluntarist point of view was officially enshrined in the imperial context
with Queen Victoria's proclamation of 1858, following the Indian
Mutiny: "Firmly relying ourselves on the truth of Christianity and
acknowledging the solace of religion, we disclaim alike the right and
the desire to impose our convictions on any of our subjects."[24]

As Ainslee Embree has shown, this statement represented a
complicated compromise.[25] A state which supported an established
Christian church in India could hardly claim strict neutrality in matters of religion, a contradiction Queen Victoria recognized herself
when she personally struck out the word "neutrality" from a draft
of the proclamation.[26] But as many fierce evangelical critics of government policy in India recognized, a policy of even-handedness in
matters of religion worked to the great benefit of Hinduism and
eventually Islam. Even while withdrawing from direct subsidies of
non-Christian religious practices, the government was reorganizing
the laws governing endowments of religious sites in a way that
greatly benefited certain aspects of Hinduism.[27] Evangelicals lost
a bitter battle over attempts to provide Bible teaching in government
schools. What they accepted instead was a system of government
grants to religious schools which initially benefited mission schools
disproportionately, but opened the door ultimately for remarkably effective competition from Hindu and later Islamic competitors.[28]

The Queen represented the point of view of those who hoped that British rule itself would serve to promote Christianity in India by the sheer, non-coercive example of good government by a Christian power. Her own support for private, non-missionary medical care for women in India reflected her embarrassment that Christianity was represented in India by missionaries, including women doctors. But she was doomed to disappointment at the hands of her own principles. The necessities of British rule in India, and the peculiarities of the religious settlement in Great Britain, dictated a religious policy that taught a different lesson, one that was very congenial to voluntarist Protestants. That lesson was: imperial rule is about power; religion is about liberty. If religion was to be a private matter, then the Christian presence in India had to be left in private hands, the responsibility of voluntary societies. Christian institutions were to be built by missionaries and Indian Christians, embarrassing and marginal though they were to Sydney Smith and the queen alike.

The distinction between religion and power has provided the basis for the celebratory tradition of Protestant mission historiography, including recent books by Brian Stanley and Stephen Neill that draw a sharp distinction between missionaries on the one hand and imperialism on the other.[29] Missionaries had entirely different motives, Stanley suggests, from merchants, entrepreneurs, explorers, administrators, military officers in the imperial establishment, and cannot therefore be held responsible for imperialism. Acknowledging that both Indian Christians and missionaries had been associated with imperial rule, and many of them killed in the military revolt of 1857 known to the British as the The Mutiny, Stephen Neill explains why the missionaries returned to their work: "The missionaries had come to India to preach the Gospel of Christ. They stayed on because they had come to love India and its peoples. When peace came they redoubled their efforts."[30]

≺ II ≻

The Imperial Limits of Liberty

It may be conceded that a fundamental characteristic of the modern religious settlement is formal state neutrality, whatever the various historical origins of that principle and however compromised it may be in practice. In an Indian imperial setting the forcible conversion of Hindus and Muslims was unthinkable in the nineteenth century, but it had not been unthinkable to the Portuguese or even the Dutch in earlier centuries. Certainly it can be conceded to Protestant voluntarists that, even if missionaries were imperialists (which most scholars take for granted), they were very different from other kinds of imperialists, and that the British approach to religion in India shows fundamental contrasts with earlier forms of imperial rule.

But however important formal neutrality was in shaping the modern religious settlement, and however important the imagery of conscientious choice in religion was in shaping the actions of religious men and women, in an imperial setting a simple statement declaring freedom of choice in religion raised a number of problems for missionaries. The confusion between religion and imperialism is not a creation of the twentieth century. Missionaries were after all entering non-western countries in the wake of foreign military and commercial intrusion, and promoting a religion that was undoubtedly in this context a European religion. Persistent efforts by missionaries to claim Christianity as an "oriental" religion failed to address the essential point.

Shortly after Carey entered Bengal, another voluntarist western Protestant, Dr. Van der Kemp, moved beyond the limits of European settlement in South Africa. One of his biographers, Robert Moffat, reports a conversation held with an African named Gaika in 1799 which might represent a genuine conversation, but certainly reflects genuine tensions in the voluntarist Protestant missionary presence. Moffat writes:

Under all these untoward circumstances it was impossible that the Kafirs could view Dr. V's sojourn among them in any other light than as a precursor of deeply laid strategems to get possession of their country and cattle, by the people from whom he had come, and to whom he belonged . . . Many questions were put to him respecting his object, and political connexions, and they were especially anxious to know if he were sent by the English.

In this account Van der Kemp, with Careyesque naivete, appears to be taken aback by the question, and refers to the permission he had received from the governor to travel inland. But this is not the issue from the point of view attributed to Gaika. "Did then," continued Gaika, "this plan spring forth only out of your own heart?" "This very question," says the doctor, "upbraided me of my unfaithfulness, and put this answer into my mouth: that this my plan was indeed formed only in my own heart, though it never was formed by it; but that the God of heaven and earth, in whose hands were their hearts, and my heart, had put it into it, to go to this people, and to communicate in his name, things with which their temporal and eternal happiness were connected."[31]

This "simple and honest reply" is reported to have somewhat pacified those Africans who regarded missionaries as assassins or spies, but it has hardly settled the issue of the motives and "political connexions" of the missionary. A simple disclaimer of the right and the desire to impose our convictions on any imperial subjects has been met, throughout the history of the missionary/imperial enterprise, with considerable skepticism. In 1808 Sydney Smith pointed out that "It is in vain to say, that these attempts to diffuse Christianity, do not originate from the government in India."[32] He went further: "[I]t appears to us hardly possible to push the business of proselytism in India to any length, without incurring the utmost risk of losing our empire."[33] The Indian revolutionaries of 1857 who killed Indian Christians on the presumption that they were collaborators with British imperial rule shared Smith's presuppositions about the relationship between religious choice and imperial power, not Stephen Neill's.

It is important to remember that at about the time Queen Victoria issued her disclaimer of any right or desire to impose her convictions on any of her subjects, Indian freedom fighters were being strapped to the front of cannons and blown away in front of assemblies of Europeans. In some cases a missionary was given one last chance to persuade the victim to embrace Christianity.[34] A confusion of religion and imperial power was understandable under those circumstances. The identity of religion and imperialism lies behind an historiographical tradition that stands in sharp contrast to the celebratory tradition of missionary studies: the "unmasking" of missionaries as witting or unwitting agents of imperial rule.[35]

Missionaries further confused the issue, first by getting involved in "liberal imperialist" schemes of social reform, and second by their own ongoing confusion about the relationship between Christianity and civilization, which included but was not limited to government. If men and women were free to be religious or irreligious, and free to be good or evil, imperialists were not exempt from that choice. Missionaries themselves could be good or bad. During his stay in Bombay, Anthony Norris Groves recorded that "I ventured to suggest to some of the missionaries privately that certain expensive and apparently self-indulgent habits might be avoided, but all resisted the idea."[36]

If missionaries could be good or bad, so could imperialists, privately or publicly. Imperial rule could be beneficial or harmful. Even before traveling to India, Carey was well aware that "the vices of Europeans have been communicated wherever they themselves have been,"[37] corrupting non-Europeans and giving Christianity a terrible reputation. On board ship in 1834 on his way home from India, Groves stopped off briefly in South Africa:

> I have been reading Mr. Pringle's account of a few years residence at the Cape, and it has much interested me. O, what national sins have we to answer for, if God regard the cry of the poor and destitute! As I was riding out with a dear friend of mine, at the Cape, he said every inch of the ground is soaked with the blood of its aborigines; but till I read Pringle's work, I could not have conceived that such deep cruelty dwelt in the heart of man. These poor defenceless wanderers have had their Krauls burned, their men murdered, their wives and children taken captives, and their flocks and herds driven away to enrich their merciless oppressors. O, when will the time come that our Prince shall unfurl His banner, and introduce the reign of righteousness.[38]

But other missionaries were less willing than Groves to leave the work entirely to the Prince of Peace. The missionary struggle was in that sense against "bad" imperialists, which led missionaries in the direction of trying to influence the imperial enterprise for good. This impulse was strongest in the abolitionist movement and the related humanitarian defense of "native races" in New Zealand, South Africa, and elsewhere.[39] The association of missionaries with "humanitarianism" in Africa and the South Pacific led to steady criticism of missionaries from open and often bitterly racist critics like Richard Burton. Missionary involvement with government policy might come through private voluntary persuasion, the exposure of private abuses, the exposure of public abuses, or, most commonly, what we would now call lobbying, which led to another round of entanglement with the state. "Influence" was appropriate for a private voluntary organization, which is how the missionaries and mission societies saw themselves. And it was that self-conception that compelled voluntarist Protestants like Henry Venn, secretary of the Church Missionary Society, to approach Whitehall to encourage gov-

ernment officials to maintain the naval squadron off the coast of
West Africa.

This reformist liberal imperialism, with its occasional advocacy
of military force in a good cause, created confusion about the relationship between religion and state power. Missionaries themselves
found criticism of their involvement with state power very irritating,
and they had an answer for their critics. We have nothing to do with
government directly, they argued. We are simply attempting as private Christian citizens to be an external force for good. But that answer was not persuasive to everyone, particularly when it involved
the advocacy of military force in what was asserted to be the interests of (passive, defenseless) native races.

Entanglement with state power by missionaries who rejected
state power as a means of conversion led to one set of contradictions. Another came from missionary confusion about the distinction between Christianity and Western culture. From the time of Carey to the present, missionaries have been hopelessly confused about
which aspects of Western culture are to be associated with Christian
faith, and which aspects are purely western and may therefore be
considered optional for non-Western Christians. Every generation of
missionaries has accused the previous generation of westernizing
non-Western peoples rather than merely christianizing them.

On a conceptual level, the primacy of "christianizing" over "civilizing" usually carried the day in missionary circles, although not
without contest. The debate over whether men and women must
be "polished and refined" before becoming Christian showed that
some British Christians had serious doubts about whether uncivi-
lized peoples could be christianized. That those doubts survived well
into the nineteenth century is evident from the controversy surrounding Canon Isaac Taylor's 1887 address to the Wolverhampton
Church Congress, where he suggested that (from a religious point of
view) Islam was more suitable than Christianity for Africans in their
present state of civilization.[40]

Even more vigorous controversy surrounded schemes by David
Livingstone and many others to promote commercial development
in Africa as a means of fostering Christianity, programs that constituted a related attempt to sort out the relationship between Christianity and civilization. But in the end schemes to see that men were
polished and refined in the techniques of cotton cultivation faded

away along with other schemes to elevate men and women to a suitable level of civilization for Christianity.[41]

The confusion at the conceptual level degenerated into a riot of contradictions at the practical level, as missionaries attempted to decide exactly what was involved when a non-Western, non-Christian adopted Christianity. At the most obvious, or at least the most visible, level came clothing. What should a Christian wear? Thus Livingstone's father-in-law, Robert Moffat, in his widely read defense of pioneer missions in South Africa, took it for granted that Christian faith brought in its train the wearing of civilized clothing. He even criticized his predecessor, Dr. Van der Kemp, for a clumsy early effort to go native: [F]requently at home and abroad, he would dispense with hat, shirt, and shoes, while the patron and advocate of civilization. These were anomalies and shades of character, which of course added nothing to his usefulness."[42]

Moffat believed that decent Victorian clothing was evidence of the civilizing consequences of Christianity, but there was no doubt in his mind which came first. He argued that "Much has been said about civilizing savages, before attempting to evangelize them. This is a theory which has obtained an extensive prevalence among the wise men of this world; but we have never yet seen a practical demonstration of its truth." Yet in the very same paragraph he observed that it is the gospel which teaches them "to adorn the Gospel they profess, in their attire as well as in their spirit and actions. It would appear a strange anomaly, to see a Christian professor lying at full length on the ground covered with filth and dirt, and in a state of comparative nudity, talking about christian diligence, circumspection, purification, and white robes! The Gospel teaches that all things should be done decently and in order."[43]

At the time Moffat was confidently promoting western dress as the outward and visible sign of prior inward transformation, a missionary of the evangelical Church Missionary Society (CMS), the Rev. Thomas Valpy French, arrived to set up a college in Agra, "determined to like everything native that is not positively harmful." There, and with even more determination later at the Anglican Divinity School in Lahore, he urged or forced Indian Christian students to abandon the western dress they preferred for Indian dress in order to teach them "to appreciate the fact that the gospel of Christ has only an accidental, not essential connexion with the English."[44]

This apparent contradiction can be explained in part by a system of racial hierarchy in which Africans are associated with savagery and Indians with civilization, although one that has fallen from past glories. What the incidents have in common is the exercise of power by the missionary over non-Western Christians, a variety of imperial power that attracted the attention of Victorian theorists. But for our purposes now the point is the sheer level of confusion and eccentricity at work at the local level, all obscured by the self-confidence of missionary pronouncements on the subject of Christianity and civilization.

It is important when examining missionary rhetoric on this subject to recall that missionaries were professionals, promoting the institutional interests of a new profession. Even if "civilization" was a secondary effect of a more important change, it nonetheless remained an important tool in the appeal to a broader public to send money. Almost any useful argument will sound reasonable to someone with a school budget to protect. Furthermore, "civilization" was a useful product to sell to skeptical government officials, or government officials who might be in a position to offer practical assistance. This leads once again back to a relationship between religion and imperial power in its most transparent form, government power.

There can be no doubt whatsoever that missionaries believed the civilizing influences of Christianity, extremely important though they were, to be secondary effects. But in their opportunism, when addressing the government or a skeptical public, the civilizing effects were put first for rhetorical purposes. Thus Robert Moffat brandished the fearsome prospect of an Islamic Africa, the tri-colored flag waving on her bosom, bearing the ensigns of the mystery of Babylon, the crescent of the false prophet, and the emblems of pagan darkness, from the shores of the Mediterranean to the colony of the Cape of Good Hope, and so on.[45] Missionaries to Africa frequently called for the extension of government power or influence in order to suppress the slave trade or slavery or disorders of various kinds. From the mid-nineteenth century, missionaries devoted a large and growing share of their attention to competing for government grants for mission schools.

It is easy to mistake the self-interested arguments of missionaries as inadvertent exposures of the secular, imperialist, material base of the missionary movement, when in fact they are limited rhetorical strategies attempting to extract grants from the government of favors that were useful, but not essential, to the overall enterprise. Or they represented an attempt to stir up broad public support that was essential to religion in a world of contested terrain. Such rhetorical strategies were in fact *less* important in an imperial than in a domestic context, at least in England and Scotland, where nineteenth-century ecclesiastical expansion was driven by a highly successful attempt to frighten the public with the prospect that society would fall apart without the leavening influence of churches and chapels. As that strategy ceased to work in the early twentieth century, it was the churches rather than society that fell apart.

But however important formal neutrality was in shaping the modern religious settlement, and however important the imagery of conscientious choice in religion was in shaping the actions of religious men and women, in an imperial setting a simple statement declaring freedom of choice in religion did little to erase doubts about the relationship of missionaries and government agents. With humanitarian agitation, and education grants, once again the wheel turned back to an entanglement between religion and imperial power, to the meddling magistrate abjured by early Baptists. Even when missionaries refrained from exposing themselves to the charge of being government agents, the perception that they were hand-in-glove with other imperialists was omnipresent. Missionaries complained to each other that they were constantly required to rebut this silly confusion, but it was really their own fault. If missionary rhetoric led them into contradictions which further confused their already confused critics and contemporaries, it is not surprising that twentieth-century historians are confused about the relationship between religion and empire. Power was not in the end something that missionaries could ignore, resting content with Groves in "the joy of having nothing to do with these things." Missionaries found that the imperial context set limits to their assumption that men and women are free to choose.

≺ III ≻

A Religious Critique of Imperial Power

A number of nineteenth-century missionaries and mission theorists devoted a considerable amount of relatively sophisticated thought to the relationship between imperial power and religious persuasion.

One of the most eminent mid-nineteenth-century missionary theorists was Henry Venn (1796–1873).[46] Born three years after Carey sailed for India, Venn was from 1846 until his death the secretary (that is primary administrator) of the Church Missionary Society, the largest and most influential of the missionary societies of the Church of England.

Venn was a clergyman, but more important than that, he was an administrator, and his thoughts on religion and imperial power grew out of attempts to solve problems that were simultaneously imperial, theological, and administrative. One problem concerned the relationship between western missionaries and non-western Christians, a relationship that appeared in an ecclesiastical setting as one of dependence. Yet Venn, a voluntarist Protestant at heart, believed that the relationship should be transformed into one of equality, of independent non-western Christians dealing with independent western Christians, all equally subject of course to the sovereignty of Christ. This transformation was his administrative responsibility, since he was in charge of religious institutions encompassing "a few scattered converts . . . in an artificial state of dependence upon Christian Europeans."[47] His administrative problem was also an imperial problem, as Venn acknowledged, because at the heart of imperialism is unequal power between westerners and non-westerners.

Venn's attempt to grapple with the problems of imperialism appears from a late twentieth-century point of view to be self-interested. It was also clumsy and blind. He had no means of anticipating the challenges of the anti-imperial political and military struggles of the late nineteenth and twentieth centuries. But there can be little doubt that Venn was groping toward some solution to a problem familiar to twentieth century scholars: unequal power in an imperial setting. Venn viewed western missionaries, his employees, with the same skepticism as an American university dean might look upon faculty members in subordinate departments: simultaneously self-aggrandizing and lazy. He once wrote to an American counterpart, Rufus Anderson, that, in his dealings with missionaries, he had "an increasing conviction that Missionaries are too backward to trust their Native Agents of all classes . . . I have observed in numerous instances that a pressure from home has put the native forward; and that subsequently the Missionary has expressed his surprise and satisfaction at the result."[48] This is not an analysis

of state power, which would have left Venn mired in the same contradictions as other voluntarist missionaries. It is an analysis of other
forms of imperial power: the power of western wealth and prestige;
the power of the employer, the educator, and the clergyman.

Venn shared with other Victorian voluntarists the contradictions
and confusions over state power and the relationship between Christianity and civilization. Although accepting the missionary distinction between state power on the one hand and religious and civil liberty on the other, Venn failed to recognize, as we do now almost
automatically, the full extent and significance of the informal entanglement of the missionary movement with state power. As a loyal
Anglican he supported a state church, considering it consistent with
religious liberty if not religious equality, and he dealt at length with
the relationship between his mission and the Indian ecclesiastical
establishment.

In the long struggle over government educational policy in India,
Venn failed to recognize the entanglement with state power involved
in promoting "non-denominational" Bible teaching in government
schools in India. The contortions, contradictions, and sometimes
outright hypocrisy of CMS policy statements in India represent the
last bastions of confessional religion, if confessional religion is defined as encompassing compulsory religion, sustained by the imperial relationship of missionaries to the people of India. Even Venn's
admirers conceded that the CMS under his guidance never developed
a policy that would consistently allow it to receive major government funding for educational institutions without compromising its
principles.[49]

Plaintive CMS directives explaining the great anxiety over the entanglement of the mission with government in educational policy
were followed by a capitulation to the enticements of government
grants. As early as 1855 the CMS, under Venn's guidance, recognized
the imperial trap into which they were falling in this statement on
educational policy, which must be quoted at some length in order to
follow its twists and turns:

The Government of India profess to have the real welfare of the country at
heart, and one instrument by which they believe that will be effectually promoted is education . . . Their assistance, however, being offered to missionary agents, as teachers generally, and not as Christian Teachers, it is clear
that the state of the case renders it unavoidable to proffer the same aid to all

teachers in common, without respect to their faith, and Hindus, Mahomedans, or Roman Catholics, if good secular teachers, will have an equal claim upon Government grants.

The committee wished to make it clear, however, that

They are anxious, as a general principle, to point out that their educational work is still *Missionary*. The Society are willing to accept the aid of Government, so far as they will give it. But they consider themselves as doing their own work, and not as standing in the position of Schoolmasters to the Government; and in reference to the fear expressed as to the secularizing tendency of the system, they feel every confidence that their Missionaries will be alive to the paramount importance of maintaining the Missionary principle intact, and that they will watch unto prayer, lest any injurious influence, arising from the encouragement given to the secular branch of their teaching, obtain any advantage over them. The Committee are alive to the difficulty, but cannot abandon the line of operation opening before them without a trial. It is one which admits of no remedy but that which is derived from on high; and they are unwilling to believe that it will be withheld.[50]

Tracing the workings of Providence, which appeared so transparent to Carey and Groves, proved beyond the grasp of the CMS committee. We are seeing a state church accommodate itself to the voluntary principle in its relationship to a state—in this case to a state that, far from promoting Christianity as state policy, was giving grants to Hindus and Muslims and shoring up "temple endowments" in a sweeping legal settlement with consequences felt to this day.

Just as he became entangled with state power through the back door of education grants, so did Venn become involved through his "humanitarian" defense of black rights in Africa and the West Indies. In a letter of 1863 to H. S. Freeman, governor of Lagos, Venn asserted a special relationship between missionaries and colonized peoples, one which was distinct from the providential messengers of God's grace: "Missionaries stand in a very different relation to the Government of a Colony from all other settlers or merchants. They are not only the representatives of a Christian Society at home, which has always been allowed confidential access to the Home Government; but they have also a recognized relation to the native races as their confidential advisers, and in some sort their protectors and representatives with the British authorities."[51]

This point of view led Venn in more than one instance to direct advocacy of military presence. The CMS intervened periodically to urge the government against any retrenchment in the naval squadron off the west coast of Africa, designed to suppress the slave trade. In 1849 Venn met for an hour with Lord Palmerston: "I pointed out on the map the situation of Abeokuta, and the importance of securing the present opening for legitimate commerce by a British Resident at Abeokuta, an armed boat on the lagoon, or a fort at Badagry."[52] By "legitimate commerce," Venn meant commerce by Africans for Africans, or if necessary commerce conducted for the benefits of Africans by British "friends of Africa."

Venn's policies led into contradictions even more profound than the advocacy of a naval squadron, for the CMS was at least not directly involved in outfitting military vessels. Under Venn's leadership, however, they became involved in schemes for promoting "healthy" commerce in West Africa, under the direction of African Christians. Venn was a major promoter of the link between commerce and Christianity, a commitment that led directly to major compromises with his own conception of the spiritual purity of the missionary bureaucracy that he headed. It is easy to misunderstand his position, because it was a compromising and compromised one. He regarded the missionary movement as being involved in a major struggle, not in this case with African savagery or Indian idolatry, but with western traders. As he continued in his letter to the Governor of Lagos, "all experience proves that a British Colony on the Coast of Africa, where European traders have the chief consideration, instead of promoting, retards the civilization of the surrounding tribes."[53]

"Healthy" commerce, for Venn, was commerce controlled by Africans, preferably African Christians. Venn became involved in the 1850s in attempts to set up agricultural and commercial institutions in Sierra Leone and Nigeria, including cotton wholesaling under the care of an African clergyman, the Rev. Samuel Crowther, Jr. The problems caused by the scheme are made clear in a letter to the Rev. Mr. Crowther and an African associate, Mr. H. Robbins:

It must be ever borne in mind and made manifest to others, especially to European merchants engaged in the Africa trade, that the sole object of the Institution is to encourage native industry, and to teach Christian converts to support themselves when by their Christianity they will be cut off from former associations and employments, either by their connexion with idolatry, or through the jealousy and opposition of the heathen or Mahomedans. Especially it must be constantly shown that the funds of the Church Missionary Society do not support the Institution, and are not in any way implicated in its commercial character; that the Society is only in the position of landlord of the workshops and warehouse, and the owner of the "plant" employed in the trades, which are let out to the managers; so that the Society incurs no risk whatever, while it receives remuneration for the use of its property.[54]

Venn's West African policy of promoting commerce led into the same contradictions and protestations of innocence as the Indian policy of involvement with government education. The contradictions were evident to Venn at the time, but ways to avoid the contradictions were not so clear. He struggled to make it clear to everyone that the CMS was not *directly* involved in trading, only seeking to foster healthy trade by Africans for the benefit of Africans. In 1851 he traveled to Manchester to meet with Mr. Clegg, a wealthy cotton merchant and CMS supporter who was involved in promoting the cotton trade in West Africa, according to Venn, "from a pure desire of encouraging native industry." They went to the cotton factory, loaded all the African account books in Mr. Clegg's carriage, and hauled them to his home. "We then set to work upon Mr. Clegg's ledgers, to ascertain the state of his African trade. Sixty-three native correspondents had done business with him . . . He had entered upon the business from a pure desire of encouraging native industry. We spent six hours upon these books in order to disentangle the accounts, and show that the Church Missionary Society was in no way involved in any commercial responsibilities."[55] Venn was attempting in those six hours, not only to disentangle the accounts, but to disentangle religion from imperialism.

Venn was extremely enthusiastic about the benefits of trade, if it were conducted by Africans for the benefit of Africans. We take for granted the links between various forms of imperial power: commerce, gunboats, religion. But even at the height of enthusiasm for a link between commerce and Christianity, Venn himself was attempting to disentangle religion from what we characteristically see as another form of imperial power, commerce. His frequent protestations of misunderstanding—"we are not government schoolteachers"; "we are not African traders"—show that he understood the dilemma he faced.

Venn's genuine commitment to religious liberty comes out more clearly in his biography of St. Francis Xavier, although it is very difficult for twentieth-century readers to focus on his analysis of religion and imperial power.[56] The book is full of anti-Catholic commentary that if written now would be regarded as pure bigotry. The voluntarist Protestant missions regarded themselves as locked into a global geo-political struggle, not only with Hinduism and Islam and African fetishism, but with Roman Catholicism as well. Venn would have agreed in principle with Carey's judgment that "Papists are in general ignorant of divine things," although he would have certainly demurred from the further judgment that "Nor do the bulk of the Church of England much exceed them, either in knowledge or holiness."[57] For someone in Venn's position to write a biography of Xavier was itself extraordinary, particularly since Venn displayed a considerable amount of admiration for aspects of Xavier's character.

Venn's primary point in writing the book was not further to discredit Roman Catholicism, which needed no discrediting in the minds of his audience. It was to persuade his Protestant audience that it was neither institution-building, nor clerical authority, nor state power that would spread Christianity, but a genuine and entirely voluntary change of heart by non-European non-Christians. It was a defense of conscientious choice as the central principle of religion. The book was directed to rebutting Protestant errors, notably "a craving for the romance of Missions; the notion that an autocratic power is wanted in a Mission, such as a Missionary Bishop might exercise; a demand for a degree of self-denial in a Missionary bordering upon asceticism."[58]

Furthermore, the fatal error for a missionary was to become involved with the state. Venn singled out "the great fault of Xavier's character, viewed from a Missionary point of view, namely, his trust in an arm of flesh, rather than in the power of divine truth. Had he been a mere Missionary he might have been led to a blessed discovery of the truth of the Gospel, and that it is the power of God unto salvation. The arm of flesh on which he leaned was a snare and a weakness to all his Missionary enterprises."[59] In his mission to Japan "Xavier erected a Mission upon the treacherous foundations of secular support. With the honest intention of promoting Christianity, he introduced into the work the elements of political intrigue and complications . . . Thus the Mission planted by Xavier was extinguished in blood, after existing for nearly ninety years; and this *through the political power on which Xavier had leaned in all his Missionary enterprises.*"[60] Venn warned Protestant voluntarists, deeply implicated in the imperial enterprise, that Catholic missions "have not contained within themselves the principle of permanent vitality. Where they are not upheld by the sword, they are overborne by opposition. Their apparent success for a time has been the result of favourable worldly circumstances; and when those circumstances have changed, the Mission has come to nothing."[61]

In context, this biography was an anti-imperial text. In order to make that point entirely clear, Venn threw in an apparently gratuitous attack on a recent (1862) speech on Indochina in the French Senate where the minister of state declared that we "shed the blood of France there, to represent the spirit of religion, and plant that cross which is the symbol of the empire and of civilization."[62]

Venn's goal was to establish a mission independent of civil power, and conceptually distinct from Western civilization. His involvement with the state in Indian religious education, and in the promotion of western commercial expansion in Africa, obscures that goal. His attack on institutional expansion contradicted the essential fact about missionaries: everywhere they went, they were first and foremost institution builders. His own judgment on Xavier could be applied to his own contradictory roles: "It is impossible also to reconcile, on Christian principles, the various offices which he attempted to sustain. At one time he was a preacher of love and peace; at another the agent of the cruel and accursed Inquisition; at another the instigator of a crusade."[63]

But when all such qualifications are made, it remains the case that Venn recognized, in a way that Xavier could hardly have been expected to recognize, that the rules governing religion had changed fundamentally. It is not possible to find in Venn the kind of critique of imperial power that can be found in some post-1880s missionary circles, notably in the work of C. F. Andrews.[64] But his understanding of imperialism went beyond a commitment to a separation of religion from government, and voluntary consent in matters of religion. The voluntary consent had to be more than formal, and genuinely uncoerced. Of Xavier, he observed, "All his hopes of success rested upon the incessant inculcation of dry formularies, and in the strictness and severity of external religion . . . such nominal and deficient Christianity can never bring men out of heathenism, or, at least, enable them to stand in the day of trial."[65]

This was not merely an attack on Catholicism, but a warning to

Protestants. Consent must be genuine if it is to be self-sustaining, and it must be self-sustaining if it is to be permanent. Unlike the work of the missionary societies, empires are ephemeral. Venn's analysis of voluntary consent extended to a recognition of the nature of power in an institutional and cultural setting, a recognition, as Edward Said has argued with such force, that power does not flow merely from the barrel of a cannon, but from books and technology and scholarship and (Venn would add although Said ignores it) religion. Venn for the most part ignored the question of unequal power between men and women, except for occasional and predictable rhetorical flourishes about the victimization of Indian women by Indian men. Missionary wives carried out their own partly autonomous professional responsibilities to a far greater extent than clergymen's wives at home. But the status of women as missionaries in their own right was only addressed explicitly in the 30 years after Venn's death, when the missionary movement was flooded with single women who demanded recognition of their own professional status.[66] For Venn, missionaries were men and women were wives, a formulation that allowed him to evade questions of the relationship between men and women under his administration. But in his arguments about dependency he faced squarely the question of unequal power between western Christians and non-western Christians in an imperial setting.

Venn was not of course the first or only person to recognize the contingent, temporary, and ephemeral character of the Western imperial presence. As early as 1791 the editor of the annual report of the SPCK commented on a sermon by a "native priest," Sattianaden: "How long it may be in the power of the Society to maintain Missionaries; how long the fluctuations in the affairs of this world will afford duration to the Mission itself, is beyond our calculation; but if we wish to establish the Gospel in India, we ought to look beyond the casualties of war, or the revolutions of empires; we ought in time to give the native a Church of their own, independent of our support."[67] "Beyond the revolutions of empires" is a decisive phrase. The British Empire, like the Roman Empire, was doomed to disappear, while God's work on earth would continue much longer. But how should the churches proceed? How do you create a permanent church in an ephemeral empire?

For high-church Anglicans in the tradition of the SPCK and (later) the SPG, this became a matter of providing missionary bishops, bishops who would precede the church and provide the nucleus for the organization of a "native" church. The first missionary bishop, so designated, was an American, Jackson Kemper, Episcopal missionary bishop to Missouri and Indiana. At his consecration in 1835 George Washington Doane, bishop of New Jersey, outlined the high concept of a missionary bishop:

And if there be, in Indiana or Missouri, in Louisiana, Florida or Arkansas, some scattered handfuls here and there of Churchmen—or, if obedient to the Saviour's mandate, to preach the Gospel unto every creature, we send out heralds of the Cross to China, Texas, Persia, Georgia or Armenia—upon what principle can we neglect, or on what ground can we refuse,—since from their feebleness and poverty they cannot have a Bishop of their own, or in their ignorant blindness, they do not desire it,—to send to them, at our own cost and charge, and in the Saviour's name, a Missionary Bishop?[68]

Despite his own almost exclusively clerical social background, Venn's Protestant principles prohibited any dependence on missionary bishops for church extension. Even if he had not feared the authority of bishops on theological grounds, his theory of missionary extension was based on a recognition of the centrality of voluntary recruitment for the future of Christianity (or for that matter, any religion in the modern world).

He recognized the unique problems faced by an established church when the key to success in the modern religious settlement is self-sustaining recruitment, and contrasted Anglican missions unfavorably with the missions of other denominations unencumbered with a confessional legacy:

The unfavourable contrast may be explained by the fact that other denominations are accustomed to take part in the elementary organization of their Churches at home, and therefore more readily carry out that organization in the Missions. Whereas in our Church the Clergy find everything relating to elementary organisation settled by the Law of the Land:—as in the provision of tithes, of church-rates, of other customary payments, in the constitution of parishes, and in parish officers, our Clergy are not prepared for the question of Church organisation.[69]

This is a succinct and perceptive recognition of the disadvantages faced by the Church of England, then and now, in a competitive religious environment. Venn's ability to step outside his insular ecclesiastical world and see its deficiencies was a consequence of his thought about religion in an imperial setting.

Although Venn accepted the authority of bishops, subject to hard bargaining about their proper sphere of authority, he certainly did not regard the provision of a bishopric as the essential point in maintaining continuity beyond the revolutions of empires. The church should come before the bishop. The church should be a native church. A native church should have, ideally, a native bishop. Such a church would presumably be, among other things, capable of defending itself against episcopal tyranny if necessary. Venn was searching for a formula for a non-western Christian church in a new world of contested religious terrain. He struggled to develop a missionary strategy that would generate a native church that was, in the famous three-fold formula, a non-western church based on the principles of self-support, self-government, and self-extension.

Elements of this formula can be found scattered throughout his writing, although the phrase was put forward in a systematic way by Venn in a set of instructions to missionaries in 1855, and the subsequent papers of 1861 and 1866 which were reissued in 1866 as a statement of official CMS policy.[70] A further goal of the mission was to be the "euthanasia of the mission."[71] Euthanasia was to be achieved by the creation of a non-western pastorate supported by the funds of the non-western church. Only such a church could survive beyond the revolutions of empires.

By the euthanasia of the mission, Venn did not mean the euthanasia of the missionary society, the organization that he headed. The profession of missionary was a new one, developed along with other new professions in the nineteenth century. Missionaries were characteristically organized geographically into specific missions, with distinct and variable provision for women as they took over the movement in the late nineteenth century. The mission, in Venn's sense, was a bureaucratic unit, resembling an academic department, within which missionaries carried out their professional lives. It is a serious and common error to think of missionaries as evangelists in pith helmets rather than professional institution-builders. They too were committed to building an indigenous church. But in the process they were to be the subjects of the euthanasia, which gave them a rather different point of view from the remote missionary administrator in London.

I have already alluded to Venn's suspicion of missionary paternalism, and his habit of taking the side of non-western Christians in their frequent controversies with missionaries. The result was chronic conflict between Venn and missionaries. After his death, there was ongoing conflict between his successor bureaucrats in London and CMS missionaries around the world over issues of the authority to be given to non-western Christians; of progress toward the establishment of a self-supporting, self-governing church; of visible signs of preparation for the euthanasia of the mission, as opposed to pious statements of good intentions.[72]

Inevitably they clashed over issues of race. Venn's timetable for an independent non-European church was far more ambitious than Macaulay's vague hopes for a self-governing India at some undetermined but never-to-arrive future. Venn intended to see self-governing, non-western churches in his lifetime, and he worked hard to cultivate, groom, and encourage non-western leadership, especially in West Africa. The progress of the church in Sierra Leone he considered proof of the feasibility of his schemes for fostering a church prepared to survive beyond the revolutions of empires. The history of Sierra Leone, he argued in 1865, "bespeak[s] a people of some energy and wealth. Undoubtedly; the Negro has a head for business and a heart for religion; and let the facts which the West-African Mission discloses answer the speculations of the present day as to his position in the intelligent creation."[73] "But the crowning success of the native ministry," he continued, "is the appointment of a negro minister to be a Bishop of the United Church of England and Ireland, consecrated under the royal licence."[74]

For many years Venn had groomed Samuel Crowther for a position as first black African bishop and had become a friend as well as ecclesiastical patron. In 1851 he recorded in his diary: "Then to the Foreign Office, where Lord Palmerston had appointed a meeting with S. Crowther. Went to Lord P's private residence, had an interview of nearly an hour. Lord P. Thoroughly investigated the circumstances of Abeokuta and the late Dahomian War; showed great interest in the subject, and listened with much kindness to all our remarks . . . Then went with S. Crowther and his son to Kew Gardens . . . [M]et in the Gardens the family of Chevalier Bunsen."[75]

Venn regarded himself as a friend of the African people, standing in sharp contrast to the open racists like Richard Burton who constantly denigrated Sierra Leone. After encountering Samuel Crowther in a coastal steamship, Burton dismissed him as "our Gorilla, or Missing Link."[76] Running throughout Venn's own arguments on race is a strain of paternalistic condescension characteristic of the abolitionists and their humanitarian successors, as well as the characteristic confusion of Christianity and civilization. But Venn was clear on one point: western Christians were not fit to be the leaders of a healthy, non-western church. They were rendered unfit by their status as Europeans. Why had Anglican missions succeeded in Sierra Leone but failed in Jamaica? The failure to provide "Negro teachers for the Negro race." Missionaries had acted as pastors in Jamaica, and under those conditions black Christians "will not form a vigorous Native Church, but as a general rule they will remain in a dependent condition, and make but little progress in spiritual attainments. The same congregation, under competent native Pastors, would become more self-reliant, and their religion would be of a more manly, home character."[77]

This commitment explains Venn's jubilation over Crowther's appointment as bishop of the Niger Delta:

The first year of Bishop Crowther's Episcopate has not yet closed; but it is not too soon to speak of the admirable humility, wise forethought and large-minded spirit in which he had laid out his plans, and won golden opinions from all who have had the opportunity of judging of his administrative powers. The effect of this appointment upon the whole of the native ministry throughout our Missions has been remarkable. It has given them a lively demonstration of the truth that a native Church is not to be kept too long in a state of dependence, but that the mother Church will commit the superintendence to a native Bishop as soon as the native church is ripe for such a measure. By this a great impulse has been given to native ministers to cultivate a manly independence of mind, and to recognise the responsibilities of their position.

Crowther remained bishop of the Niger Delta until his death in 1891, when he was replaced by a white Englishman. Venn did not live to see the failure of his aspirations. Much of value has been written about this episode, which is usually taken to be evidence that a new wave of racism overwhelmed the missionary movement in the 1890s.[78] This argument fails to do justice to the complexity of Victorian racism, which infected absolutely everything done in relationship to Africa, whether in mid century or later. There was a divisive fight on the CMS home committee on this issue in 1891, when defenders of Venn's Afrophile views were defeated on the grounds that Venn's ideas were racist because segregationist. Anti-racism was used in this context as a tool for promoting European interests in a multi-racial church, anticipating the Western liberal condescension of the ecumenical movement.

This is not a simple question of enlightened metropolitan bureaucrats thwarted by self-seeking, narrow-minded professional missionaries in the field. Many missionaries were as committed as Venn to promoting a self-governing church, and promoting it quickly. Good-faith efforts failed, not only because of missionary self-interest, but also because of the deficiencies of Venn's ideas in an imperial setting. It is possible to see in these debates the pervasive and inescapable nineteenth-century Western sense of racial hierarchy. But there is also evidence of the extraordinary complexity of racism, the shifting rhetorical uses of racist ideas, and the way in which the questions—missionaries, imperialists or not? missionaries, racist or not?—drive out of the discussion different theological points of view which do not fit well into those categories all the time.

Venn regarded himself in the abolitionist tradition as a friend of Africa, and a friend of Africans in both Africa and the West Indies. He would have preferred to see develop in the empire autonomous racially based churches, with overlapping separate episcopates for different races and cultures. He was a segregationist because, in theological terms, he was anti-imperialist. Venn recognized that a multi-racial church in a colonial setting would inevitably be dominated by the Europeans with superior academic training and financial resources. In the 1890s defenders of white bishops for black Africans argued their policy on anti-racist grounds. The doctrine of separate churches for separate races was unacceptable, they argued, for Christians committed to a universal, united, world-wide church. The doctrine of the unity of the church was another mask of conquest, anti-racism being used in the service of white domination.

It would be simple and perhaps helpful for some purposes to pour Venn into a mold labeled "racist" and pour him out for our inspection, for in important ways, despite Venn's differences with hostile enemies of black people like Richard Burton, all Europeans were racists in the nineteenth century. For other purposes, Venn could be poured into a mold labeled "anti-imperialist." His defenders working in the celebratory tradition of missionary history have done just that.

In the wake of an explicit twentieth-century condemnation of the missionary movement as an imperialist enterprise, and the emergence of missionary anti-imperialism of a recognizable twentieth-century variety in the writings of C. F. Andrews and others, missionaries began to look for anti-imperialist forefathers and found one in Venn. After Venn's death, it is asserted in a preface to a recent biography of Venn, missionary policy was entirely reversed. "Ecclesiastical colonialism characterized by disdain of indigenous abilities became the new order. A sense of intellectual and spiritual superiority along with rigorous paternalism infected all British mission."[79]

But this point of view thoroughly misrepresents both Venn and the essential continuity of missionary history in the nineteenth century. Rather than seeing Venn as "imperialist or anti-imperialist," or as "racist or anti-racist," it makes more sense to think of him as exploring the limits posed to voluntary religion by the imperial setting, riddled as it was with racism. Racism was a complex set of attitudes influenced in this case by a theology of missions, or in more general terms, ecclesiology: the definition of a church as a voluntary society, without the oversight of meddling magistrates or East India Company secretaries. Venn's was a theology of conscientious choice in matters of religion, and how that freedom might be implemented in what Venn recognized as an imperialist and racist context, even if he would not have used the words in the same way.

Imperialist though as he was, Venn identified and confronted some of the corrupting effects of imperialism. He recognized that if you claim an exemption from the burdens of political power, you simultaneously assume an obligation to avoid the use of state power to promote religion. Furthermore, Venn recognized the informal nature of imperialism as inequality. That is what the Victorian debate about the dangers of dependency in the church is all about.

But it can hardly be said that Venn's prescriptions for overcoming the internal imperialism of the Christian church were a success. Missionaries in many parts of the world made extensive efforts to promote such a church, efforts which generally failed, not only because of missionary paternalism, and not only because of racism, but because of the inadequacy of Venn's own diagnosis of imperialism. There is obviously not time here to examine them all, but surveying the history of missions in an imperial setting, it appears fair to say that a genuine self-supporting, self-governing, and self-extending church could develop only after the missionaries went home, or after the non-western church grew so large as to escape the control of the missionary.[80]

The origins of the failure of the Victorians to develop, outside the apparatus of the state, a self-governing, self-supporting, and self-extending church, whether in the Niger Delta or in Punjab, can be found scattered throughout the memoranda and minutes of Henry Venn himself. He failed to grasp the extent to which the voluntarist religion of the nineteenth century had been caught in a giant imperialist trap, undercutting the voluntarist premises of their entire mission and leaving the missionary enterprise labeled in the twentieth century, not incorrectly, as among other things a massive exercise in cultural imperialism. He diagnosed the disease, which was inequality, but never succeeded in prescribing a workable cure.

If Venn's efforts to transcend the revolutions of empires met with little success in their day, they are nonetheless instructive today. It is quite likely that there was no way out of the imperialist trap in the nineteenth century, but there were better and worse attempts to escape it. Venn was part of the attempt to create a new religious settlement in the modern world, one based on religion as conscientious choice. That story can best be understood in the light of that master narrative, as a story of competing values in contested terrain rather than as part of an inexorable decline and marginalization of Venn's values by the invisible hand of secularization. Furthermore, Venn was examining the limits of voluntary religion in an imperialist context. Some of his successors in the missionary world recognized far more clearly that their movement was caught in an imperialist trap, one that they partly constructed themselves, and some of them struggled to develop new ways out of it.

With our great advantages of hindsight, we can see the limits placed on voluntarist religion by imperialism itself. Voluntarist Protestants, encountering the problems of cultural imperialism within the church itself, found them to be insoluble. Venn never fully recognized the extent to which his missionary enterprise was caught in the imperialist trap, but at some point historians must recognize that people cannot be expected to question the credentials of their own society all the time. Venn himself once wrote an article on how the church appeared to be flourishing in Madagascar after missionaries were thrown out. But the logic of that argument, for someone at the head of a major missionary society, led in directions that were unacceptable, involving as they did the euthanasia, not of particular missions, but of the entire nineteenth-century missionary enterprise.

<>

REFERENCE MATTER

≺ ≻

Abbreviations

AMPiWP	Archiwum Miasta Poznania i Województwa Poznańskiego
BHStA	Bayerisches Hauptstaatsarchiv
CMS	Church Missionary Society
EHR	*English Historical Review*
FBA	Fürstlich von Bismarck'sches Archiv
GStAPrKB	Geheimes Staatsarchiv Preußischer Kulturbesitz
HStAD	Hauptstaatsarchiv Düsseldorf
JMH	*Journal of Modern History*
PD	Hansard's *Parliamentary Debates*, third series
SBVLHA	*Stenographische Berichte über die Verhandlungen des Land-tages, Haus der Abgeordneten*

≺ ≻

Notes

CHAPTER I

1. Edwin S. Gaustad, *Liberty of Conscience: Roger Williams in America* (Grand Rapids, MI, 1991); Richard S. Dunn and Mary Maples Dunn, *The World of William Penn* (Philadelphia, 1986).

2. Herbert Butterfield, *The Whig Interpretation of History* (London, 1931).

3. Sidney E. Mead, "From Coercion to Persuasion: Another Look at the Rise of Religious Liberty and the Emergence of Denominationalism," *Church History* 25 (1953): 317–37. Perry G. E. Miller, "The Contribution of the Protestant Churches to Religious Liberty in Colonial America," *Church History* 4 (1935): 57–66.

4. John B. Frantz, "The Awakening of Religion among the German Settlers in the Middle Colonies," *William and Mary Quarterly* 33 (1976): 273.

5. Claudio Veliz, *The New World of the Gothic Fox: Culture and Economy in English and Spanish America* (Berkeley, 1994); see also chapter 10, this volume.

6. Bernard Bailyn, *The Peopling of British North America* (New York, 1986).

7. Jon Butler, *The Huguenots in America: A Refugee People in New World Society* (Cambridge, MA, 1983); James Lockhart and Stuart B. Schwartz, *Early Latin America: A History of Colonial Spanish America and Brazil* (Cambridge, 1983).

8. Richard Hofstadter, *America at 1750: A Social Portrait* (New York, 1971), 199.

9. Richard J. Hooker, ed., *The Carolina Backcountry on the Eve of the Revolution* (Chapel Hill, NC, 1953), 103.

10. David Martin, *Tongues of Fire: The Explosion of Protestantism in Latin America* (Oxford, 1990), 31.

11. The best discussion of how different the English colonies were from each other and from England itself is John M. Murrin, "A Roof Without Walls: The Dilemma of American National Identity," in Richard Beeman et al., eds., *Beyond Confederation: Origins of the Constitution and American National Identity* (Chapel Hill, NC, 1987), 333–48.

12. Claudio Veliz, *The Centralist Tradition of Latin America* (Princeton, NJ, 1980); see also chapter 10, this volume.

13. Jon Butler, *Awash in a Sea of Faith: Christianizing the American People* (Cambridge, MA, 1990).

14. Rhys Isaac, *The Transformation of Virginia, 1740–1790* (Chapel Hill, NC, 1982), 143–57.

15. Albert J. Raboteau, *Slave Religion: The "Invisible Institution" in the Antebellum South* (New York, 1978), 105–6.

16. Carl Bridenbaugh, *Myths and Realities of the Colonial South* (New York, 1969), 319.

17. For the plight of the Episcopal Church in Virginia, see David Lynn Holmes, Jr., "William Meade and the Church of Virginia, 1789–1829" (Ph.D. diss., Princeton Univ., 1971), 166–90.

18. Perry Miller, *Orthodoxy in Massachusetts, 1630–1650* (Cambridge, MA, 1933).

19. William Ames, *The Marrow of Theology*, trans. John Dykstra Eusden (Durham, NC, 1968).

20. Stephen A. Marini, *Radical Sects of Revolutionary New England* (Cambridge, MA, 1982).

21. Kenneth A. Lockridge, *Literacy in Colonial New England: An Enquiry into the Social Context of Literacy in the Early Modern West* (New York, 1974).

22. On Manning, see Michael Merrill and Sean Wilentz, eds., *The Key of Liberty: The Life and Democratic Writings of William Manning, "A Laborer," 1747–1814* (Cambridge, MA, 1993).

23. Randall Balmer, *A Perfect Babel of Confusion: Dutch Religion and English Culture in the Middle Colonies* (New York, 1989), 86.

24. Gary Nash, *Quakers and Politics: Pennsylvania, 1681–1726* (Princeton, NJ, 1968).

25. Richard W. Pointer, *Protestant Pluralism and the New York Experience: A Study of Eighteenth-Century Religious Diversity* (Bloomington, IN, 1988), 11.

26. Ibid., 39.

27. Ibid., 38.

28. James T. Lemon, *The Best Poor Man's Country: A Geographical Study of Early Southeastern Pennsylvania* (Baltimore, 1972).

29. W. R. Ward, *The Protestant Evangelical Awakening* (Cambridge, 1992), 61–63, 241–60.

30. Henry Melchior Muhlenberg, *The Journals*, trans. Theodore G. Tappert and John W. Doberstein (Philadelphia, 1942), 1:67.

31. Kenneth D. McRae, "The Structure of Canadian History," in Louis Hartz, *The Founding of New Societies* (New York, 1964), 219–33.

32. Charles Francis Adams, ed., *The Works of John Adams, Second President of the United States*, 10 vols. (Boston, 1850–56), 9:375.

33. Gordon S. Wood, *The Radicalism of the American Revolution* (New York, 1992), 365–69.

34. Sean Wilentz, *The Kingdom of Mathias* (New York, 1994).

35. Richard Carwardine, *Evangelicals and Politics in Antebellum America* (New Haven, CT, 1993).

36. Martin, *Tongues of Fire*, 21.

37. See Peter Cartwright, *Autobiography of Peter Cartwright, the Backwoods Preacher* (New York, 1856), 123.

38. Roger Finke and Rodney Stark, *The Churching of America, 1776–1990* (New Brunswick, NJ, 1992), 54–57.

39. Rowland Berthoff, "Writing a History of Things Left Out," *Reviews in American History* 14 (1986): 1–16.

40. See Alan Taylor, *Liberty Men and Great Proprietors: The Revolutionary Settlement on the Maine Frontier, 1760–1820* (Chapel Hill, NC, 1990), 123–53; D. Michael Quinn, *Early Mormonism and the Magic World View* (Salt Lake City, 1987).

41. Quoted in Andrew R. L. Cayton, *The Frontier Republic: Ideology and Politics in the Ohio Country, 1780–1825* (Kent, OH, 1986), 59.

42. For Campbell, see Robert Richardson, *Memoirs of Alexander Campbell*, 2 vols. (Cincinnati, 1913); John C. Nerone, "The Press and Popular Culture in the Early Republic: Cincinnati, 1793–1843," (Ph.D. diss., Univ. of Notre Dame, 1982), 316–18; Frank J. Heinl, "Newspapers and Periodicals in the Lincoln-Douglas Country, 1831–1832," *Journal of the Illinois Historical Society* 23 (1930–31): 411.

43. On these developments, see David L. Rowe, *Thunder and Trumpets: Millerites and Dissenting Religion in Upstate New York, 1800–1850* (Chico, CA, 1985).

44. Lockhart and Schwartz, *Early Latin America*, 160.

45. Richard D. Altick, *The English Common Reader: A Social History of the Mass Reading Public, 1800–1900* (Chicago, 1957).

46. See the very interesting historical and theoretical overview in Martin, *Tongues of Fire*, 1–26.

47. Three recent works that illuminate Mormonism as popular religion are John L. Brooke, *The Refiner's Fire: The Making of Mormon Cosmology, 1644–1844* (Cambridge, 1994); Marvin S. Hill, *Quest for Refuge: The Mormon Flight from American Pluralism* (Salt Lake City, 1989); and D. Michael Quinn, *Early Mormonism and the Magic World View* (Salt Lake City, 1987).

48. Adam Smith, *The Wealth of Nations* (New York, 1933), 746.

49. See John Wigger, "Taking Heaven by Storm: Enthusiasm and Early American Methodism, 1770–1820," *Journal of the Early Republic* 14(1994): 167–94; and Dee Andrews, *Popular Religion and the Revolution in the Middle Atlantic Ports: The Rise of the Methodists, 1770–1800* (Princeton, NJ, forthcoming).

50. Dow quotes the Snethan letter in Lorenzo Dow, *History of the Cosmopolite* (New York, 1814), 353–55. For Dow's reputation as a holy man with unusual powers, see Charles Coleman Sellers, *Lorenzo Dow: The Bearer of the Word* (New York, 1928), 148–51.

51. Reports of this enthusiasm and ecstacy in Nathan Bangs's manuscript journal were later deleted from the printed version. See also Wigger, "Taking Heaven by Storm."

52. For discussions of the two trips of Lorenzo Dow to Great Britain and his problems with Methodist authorities, see Richard Carwardine, *Trans-*

Atlantic Revivalism: Popular Evangelicalism in Britain and America, 1790–1865 (Westport, CT, 1978), 103–7; and Julia Stewart Werner, *The Primitive Methodist Connexion: Its Background and Early History* (Madison, WI, 1984), 45–47.

53. Dow's significant role in stimulating interest in camp meetings in England is explored in ibid., 45–47; and in Deborah Valenze, *Prophetic Sons and Daughters: Female Preaching and Popular Religion in Industrial England* (Princeton, NJ, 1985), 78–79.

54. David Hempton has commented that although Methodism had earlier mounted a successful challenge to one religious establishment, at the turn of the century it was well on the way to creating another. See Hempton, *Methodism and Politics in British Society 1750–1850* (Stanford, 1984), 80. The work of W. R. Ward is also excellent on the external pressures upon the Methodists and their internal quest for order. See Ward, "The Religion of the People and the Problem of Control, 1790–1830," in *Popular Belief and Practice*, ed. G. J. Cuming and Derek Baker (Cambridge, 1972), 237–57; and Ward, *Religion and Society in England 1790–1850* (New York, 1973), 21–53.

55. Catherine Brekus, "Female Evangelism in the Early Methodist Movement, 1784–1845," in Nathan O. Hatch, ed., *Methodism and the Shaping of American Culture* (forthcoming).

56. Daniel Coker, *Dialogue Between a Virginian and an African Minister* (Baltimore, 1810), 40–41.

57. Gary B. Nash, *Forging Freedom: The Formation of Philadelphia's Black Community, 1720–1840* (Cambridge, MA, 1988).

58. Parley Pratt, *A Voice of Warning* (New York, 1837), 29–30.

59. *The Book of Mormon* (Palmyra, NY, 1830), 111. See also *Evening and Morning Star* 2, 20 (May 1834): 305–7.

60. Hill, *Quest for Refuge*, 33.

61. Hill, "The Rise of Mormonism in the Burned-over District: Another View," *New York History* 61 (1980): 411–30. Hill derives his figures from Davis Bitton, *Guide to Mormon Diaries and Autobiographies* (Provo, UT, 1977).

62. W. R. Ward, "The Legacy of John Wesley: The Pastoral Office in Britain and America," in Anne Whiteman et al., *Statesmen, Scholars and Merchants* (Oxford, 1973), 346–48.

63. John F. Schermerhorn and Samuel J. Mills, *A Correct View of That Part of the United States Which Lies West of the Allegany Mountains with Regard to Religion and Morals* (Hartford, 1814), 41.

64. Barbara McFarlane Higdon, "Role of Preaching in the Early Latter Day Saint Church" (Ph.D. diss., Univ. of Missouri, 1961), 35, 56–57, 72–73; Oliver Olney, *The Absurdities of Mormonism Portrayed* (Hancock Country, IL, 1843), 28.

65. See Steven L. Shields, *Divergent Paths of the Restoration* (Bountiful, UT, 1975).

66. Ibid., 113.

67. *Doctrine and Covenants*, 2ᵈ ed. (Nauvoo, IL, 1844), 132:7.

68. For a helpful discussion on this increasing emphasis by Joseph Smith on unquestioning loyalty, see Lawrence Foster, *Religion and Sexuality: Three American Communal Experiments of the Nineteenth Century* (New York, 1981), 140–43.

69. Hill, *Quest for Refuge*, 143.

70. Alexis de Tocqueville, *Democracy in America*, trans. Henry Reeve, 2 vols. (New York, 1945), 1:274.

71. Ray Allen Billington, *The Protestant Crusade, 1800–1860: A Study of the Origins of American Nativism* (New York, 1938).

72. Richard J. Carwardine, *Evangelicals and Politics in Antebellum America* (New Haven, CT, 1993), 288–91.

73. Butler, *Awash in a Sea of Faith*.

74. R. Laurence Moore, *Selling God: American Religion in the Marketplace of Culture* (New York, 1994).

75. This theme is argued powerfully in Carwardine, *Evangelicals and Politics*.

CHAPTER 2

1. David A. Hollinger, *Science, Jews, and Secular Culture: Studies in Mid-Twentieth-Century American Intellectual History* (Princeton, NJ, 1996), 80–96, 155–74.

2. For an earlier example of this outlook, see Frank M. Turner, *Contesting Cultural Authority: Essays in Victorian Intellectual Life* (Cambridge, 1993), 210–17.

3. C. P. Snow, *The Two Cultures: and a Second Look* (Cambridge, 1963), 48, 87–93. I owe this reference to Professor David Hollinger.

4. F. B. Smith, *The People's Health, 1830–1910* (New York, 1979); Anthony S. Wohl, *Endangered Lives: Public Health in Victorian Britain* (Cambridge, MA, 1983); Gerald L. Geison, *The Private Science of Louis Pasteur* (Princeton, NJ, 1995); Stephen Kern, *The Culture of Time and Space, 1880–1918* (Cambridge, MA, 1983).

5. Voltaire, *Letters on the English*, Leonard Tancock, trans. (London, 1980), 37.

6. Ibid., 41.

7. David Bien, *The Calas Affair: Persecution, Toleration, and Heresy in Eighteenth-Century Toulouse* (Princeton, NJ, 1960).

8. Voltaire, *Letters on the English*, 70.

9. Jack Fruchtman, *The Apocalyptic Politics of Richard Price and Joseph Priestley: A Study in Late Eighteenth-Century Republican Millennialism* (Philadelphia, 1983).

10. David Spadafora, *The Idea of Progress in Eighteenth-Century Britain* (New Haven, CT, 1990), 363–75.

11. Adam Smith, *An Inquiry into the Nature and Causes of the Wealth of Nations* (Indianapolis, 1981), 2:796.

12. Maurice Crosland, "The Image of Science as a Threat: Burke versus

Priestley and the 'Philosophic Revolution'," *British Journal for the History of Science* 20 (1987): 277–307.

13. Quoted in H. T. Dickinson, *Liberty and Property: Political Ideology in Eighteenth-Century Britain* (London, 1977), 202.

14. Adrian Desmond, *The Politics of Evolution: Morphology, Medicine, and Reform in Radical London* (Chicago, 1989), 101–52.

15. Jack Morrell and Arnold Thackray, *Gentlemen of Science: Early Years of the British Association for the Advancement of Science* (Oxford, 1831), 29–34, 224–56.

16. For an important discussion of the manner in which denominational rivalries could adversely affect public life, see Neil J. Smelser, *Social Paralysis and Social Change: British Working-Class Education in the Nineteenth Century* (Berkeley, 1991).

17. See Robert Bruce Mullin, *Episcopal Vision/American Reality: High Church Theology and Social Thought in Evangelical America* (New Haven, CT, 1986); and Nathan O. Hatch, *The Democratization of American Christianity* (New Haven, CT, 1989).

18. Deryck W. Lovegrove, *Established Church, Sectarian People: Itinerancy and the Transformation of English Dissent, 1780–1830* (Cambridge, 1988).

19. Robert Young, *Darwin's Metaphor: Nature's Place in Victorian Culture* (Cambridge, 1985), 126–63; Turner, *Contesting Cultural Authority*, 101–27; Larry Stewart, *The Rise of Public Science: Rhetoric, Technology, and Natural Philosophy in Newtonian Britain, 1660–1750* (Cambridge, 1992), 3–6, 143–82. On the German scene, see Frederick Gregory, *Nature Lost? Natural Science and the German Theological Traditions of the Nineteenth Century* (Cambridge, MA, 1992).

20. John Hedley Brooke, *Science and Religion: Some Historical Perspectives* (Cambridge, 1991), 117–51, 192–225.

21. Benjamin Schwartz, *In Search of Wealth and Power: Yen Fu and the West* (Cambridge, MA, 1964).

22. Joseph Hamburger, "Religion and *On Liberty*," in Michael Laine, ed., *A Cultivated Mind: Essays on J. S. Mill Presented to John W. Robson* (Toronto, 1991), 139–81.

23. James R. Moore, *The Post-Darwinian Controversies: A Study of the Protestant Struggle to Come to Terms with Darwin in Great Britain and America, 1870–1900* (Cambridge, 1979), 19–100.

24. *Times*, May 25, 1864, 8–9.

25. T. H. Huxley, *Methods and Results* (New York, 1896), 284.

26. Turner, *Contesting Cultural Authority*, 171–200.

27. Charles D. Cashdollar, *The Transformation of Theology, 1830–1890: Positivism and Protestant Thought in Britain and America* (Princeton, NJ, 1989); Frank M. Turner, "Religion," in Brian Harrison, ed., *The History of the University of Oxford* 8 (Oxford, 1994): 293–316.

28. Bernard Lightman, *The Origins of Agnosticism: Victorian Unbelief and the Limits of Knowledge* (Baltimore, 1987), 116–76.

29. H. Floris Cohen, *The Scientific Revolution: A Historiographical Inquiry* (Chicago, 1994); Richard Yeo, *Defining Science: William Whewell, Natural Knowledge and Public Debate in Early Victorian Britain* (Cambridge, 1993).

30. Pietro Redondi, *Galileo: Heretic*, Raymond Rosenthal, trans. (Princeton, NJ, 1987).

31. Mario Biagioli, *Galileo, Courtier: The Practice of Science in the Culture of Absolutism* (Chicago, 1993).

32. Jean Le Rond D'Alembert, *Preliminary Discourse to the Encyclopedia of Diderot*, Richard N. Schwab, trans. (Indianapolis, 1963), 74–85. D'Alembert also includes Descartes among the liberators of human thought despite reservations about his scientific ideas. He associates Descartes's achievement with his having been able to pursue his thought in Holland (77).

33. Julian Martin, *Francis Bacon, the State, and the Reform of Natural Philosophy* (Cambridge, 1992), 175.

34. James R. Jacob and Margaret C. Jacob, "The Anglican Origins of Modern Science: The Metaphysical Foundations of the Whig Constitution," *Isis* 71 (1980): 251–67; Margaret C. Jacob, *The Newtonians and the English Revolution, 1689–1720* (Ithaca, NY, 1976); Larry Stewart, *The Rise of Public Science: Rhetoric, Technology, and Natural Philosophy in Newtonian Britain, 1660–1750* (Cambridge, 1992), 3–182.

35. John Spurr, *The Restoration Church of England, 1646–1689* (New Haven, CT, 1991).

36. Frank E. Manuel, *The Religion of Isaac Newton* (Oxford, 1974), 51–80.

37. Ian Harris, *The Mind of John Locke: A Study of Political Theory in Its Intellectual Setting* (Cambridge, 1994), 185–91; W. M. Spellman, *The Latitudinarians and the Church of England* (Athens, GA, 1993), 132–54; Robert E. Sullivan, *John Toland and the Deist Controversy: A Study in Adaptations* (Cambridge, MA, 1982), 51–141.

38. Thackray and Morrell, *Gentlemen of Science*, 267–96; Roger Cooter, *The Cultural Meaning of Popular Science: Phrenology and the Organization of Consent in Nineteenth-Century Britain* (Cambridge, 1984).

39. Janet Oppenheim, *The Other World: Spiritualism and Psychical Research in England, 1850–1914* (Cambridge, 1985); Frank M. Turner, *Between Science and Religion: The Reaction to Scientific Naturalism in Late Victorian England* (New Haven, CT, 1974), 68–133.

40. Turner, *Between Science and Religion*, 8–37; Turner, *Contesting Cultural Authority*, 151–200.

41. Hollinger, *Science, Jews, and Secular Culture*, 155–74.

42. Max Weber, "Science as a Vocation," in H. H. Gerth and C. Wright Mills, eds., *From Max Weber: Essays in Sociology* (New York, 1946), 142.

43. Nancy Stepan, *The Idea of Race in Science: Great Britain, 1800–1960* (London, 1982); George Stocking, *Race, Culture, and Evolution: Essays in the History of Anthropology* (New York, 1968); id., *Victorian Anthropology* (New York, 1987); George L. Mosse, *Toward the Final Solution: A History of European Racism* (Madison, WI, 1985); John M. Efron, *Defenders of the*

Race: Jewish Doctors and Race Science in Fin-de-Siècle Europe (New Haven, CT, 1994).

44. Michael K. Burleigh and Wolfgang Wippermann, *The Racial State: Germany 1933–1945* (Cambridge, 1991), 89–92.

45. Paul Weindling, *Health, Race and German Politics between National Unification and Nazism, 1870–1945* (Cambridge, 1989), 97.

46. Michael Burleigh, *Death and Deliverance: 'Euthanasia' in Germany 1900–1945* (Cambridge, 1994).

47. Philip Curtin, *The Image of Africa: British Ideas and Action 1750–1850* (Madison, WI, 1964); T. F. Gossett, *Race: The History of an Idea in America* (New York, 1968); Michael D. Biddiss, *Father of Racist Ideology: The Social and Political Thought of Count Gobineau* (London, 1970); Daniel Gasman, *The Scientific Origins of National Socialism* (London, 1971).

48. Jon Butler, *Awash in a Sea of Faith: Christianizing the American People* (Cambridge, MA, 1990), 129–63.

49. Michael Adas, *Machines as the Measure of Man: Science, Technology, and Ideologies of Western Dominance* (Ithaca, NY, 1989), 199–342.

50. "Religion," *Encyclopaedia Britannica*, 11th ed. (1911); John Burrow, *Evolution and Society: A Study in Victorian Social Theory* (Cambridge, 1968), passim; Stocking, *Victorian Anthropology*, 188–97; id., *After Tylor: British Social Anthropology 1888–1951* (Madison, WI, 1995), 3–178.

51. See Annie E. Combes, *Reinventing Africa: Museums, Material Culture and Popular Imagination* (New Haven, CT, 1994) for a discussion of some exceptions to this generalization.

52. Woodruff D. Smith, *Politics and the Sciences of Culture in Germany, 1840–1920* (New York, 1991); Weindling, *Health, Race and German Politics*; William H. Schneider, *Quality and Quantity: The Quest for Biological Regeneration in Twentieth-Century France* (Cambridge, 1990); see also Turner, *Contesting Cultural Authority*, 201–30 for the English case.

53. Frederick Gregory, *Scientific Materialism in Nineteenth-Century Germany* (Dodrecht, 1977), 189–90.

54. Jeffrey Allan Johnson, *The Kaiser's Chemists: Science and Modernization in Imperial Germany* (Chapel Hill, NC, 1990); Alan D. Beyerchen, *Scientists Under Hitler: Politics and the Physics Community in the Third Reich* (New Haven, CT, 1977); Weindling, *Health, Race and German Politics*, 449–565; Mark Walker, *German National Socialism and the Quest for Nuclear Power, 1939–1949* (Cambridge, 1989).

55. David Joravsky, *The Lysenko Affair* (Cambridge, MA, 1970); V. Soifer, *Lysenko and the Tragedy of Soviet Science* (New Brunswick, NJ, 1994).

56. Paul Mojzes, *Religious Liberty in Eastern Europe and the USSR Before and After the Great Transformation* (Boulder, CO, 1992).

57. Harry W. Paul, *From Knowledge to Power: The Rise of the Science Empire in France, 1860–1939* (Cambridge, 1985), 243–50, 288–353.

58. Ronald Numbers, *The Creationists* (New York, 1992).

CHAPTER 3

1. Leo XIII, *Encyclical Letter on Human Liberty (Libertas Praestantissimum)* (London and New York, 1888), 7.

2. George Parkin Grant, *Technology and Empire: Perspectives on North America* (Toronto, 1969), 114 n.3; C. B. Macpherson, *The Political Theory of Possessive Individualism: Hobbes to Locke* (Oxford, 1962), 142–43.

3. The transition from the belief in "the objective right of divinely revealed and natural laws" to "the subjective rights of individuals" is described in J. L. O'Donovan, "Historical Prolegomena to a Theological Review of 'Human Rights'," *Studies in Christian Ethics* 9 (1996).

4. Isaiah Berlin, "Two Concepts Of Liberty," in *Four Essays On Liberty* (London, 1969), 122 and 131; I am indebted to Mark A. Noll for a reminder to remember Berlin.

5. Quoted in Antony Black, *Political Thought In Europe 1250–1450* (Cambridge, 1992); for discussion see Peter N. Miller, *Defining The Common Good: Empire, Religion and Philosophy in Eighteenth-Century Britain* (Cambridge, 1994), 2.

6. See M. R. D. Foot and H. C. G. Matthew, eds., *The Gladstone Diaries* 1–14 (Oxford, 1968–94).

7. The development of voluntaryism as the vehicle through which Protestant Dissenters adopted liberalism, and were incorporated into Gladstone's Liberal party, is described more fully in J. P. Ellens, *Religious Routes to Gladstonian Liberalism: The Church Rate Conflict in England and Wales, 1832–1868* (University Park, PA, 1994).

8. Ernst Lee Tuveson, *Millennium and Utopia* (New York, 1949).

9. G. F. A. Best, "The Constitutional Revolution, 1828–1832, and its Consequences for the Established Church," *Theology* 62, no. 468 (June 1959): 226–34.

10. John Keble, ed., *The Works of That Learned and Judicious Divine Mr. Richard Hooker*, 7th ed., rev. by R. W. Church and F. Paget (New York, 1887), 8:330.

11. *PD* (HL) 24, col. 654 (June 20, 1834).

12. Ibid. 22, cols. 577–78 (Mar. 24, 1834).

13. W. E. Gladstone, *Speech on the Commission of Inquiry into the State of the Universities of Oxford and Cambridge* (Oxford, 1850).

14. Samuel Wilberforce to Gladstone, Apr. 20, 1838, Bishop Samuel Wilberforce MS., e.2, "copy," fols. 4 and 6.

15. The Rev. John Hill's Diary, June 24, 1835, MS. St. Edmund Hall, 67/9, Bodleian Library, fol. 9.

16. A Priest of the Church of England, *A Few Words Upon the Admission of Dissenters to the University of Oxford* (Oxford and London, 1854).

17. Ibid., 16.

18. Hebdomadal Register, 1833–41 (Apr. 28, 1834), Oxford University Archives MS. WPX/24/5, fol. 25.

19. *PD* (HC) 22, col. 591 (Mar. 24, 1834).

20. Ibid., col. 16.

21. Leo XIII, *Encyclical Letter*, 7.

22. *PD* (HC) 22, col. 909 (Apr. 17, 1834); S. M. Waddams, *Law, Politics and the Church of England: The Career of Stephen Lushington 1782–1873* (Cambridge, 1992).

23. *PD* (HC) 24, col. 654 (June 20, 1834).

24. Ibid. 22, cols. 631–32 (Mar. 25, 1834).

25. A. H. Clough to Edward Hawkins, Jan. 23, 1848, Oriel College Library, *Letters* 8, no. 727.

26. Edward Hawkins to A. H. Clough, Jan. 24, [1848], ibid., no. 728.

27. Frederick Oakeley, *A Letter to His Grace the Duke of Wellington* (Oxford, 1835), 12.

28. Ibid., 15.

29. Ibid., 15–16; a diversity of approaches to tying religious tests to church authority is noted by W. R. Ward, *Victorian Oxford* (London, 1965), 90.

30. John Frederick Maurice—Rusticus [Frederick Denison Maurice], *Subscription No Bondage, or the Practical Advantages Afforded by the Thirty-nine Articles as Guides in all the Branches of Academical Education* (Oxford, 1835), v and 13. By 1853 Maurice came to oppose religious tests in the universities, having concluded that they were not generally used in the way he believed appropriate; see *Dictionary of National Biography* 13 (Oxford, 1894): 97–105.

31. Clericus [Charles P. Eden], *Self-Protection. The Case of the Articles* (Oxford, 1835), 4.

32. Ibid., 22.

33. Ward, *Victorian Oxford*, chap. 9; D. A. Winstanley, *Later Victorian Cambridge* (Cambridge, 1947), chap. 3; the transmogrification of American confessional universities is described in George M. Marsden, *The Soul of the American University: From Protestant Establishment to Established Nonbelief* (Oxford, 1994); for a recent discussion of developments in Canada see Michael Gauvreau, *The Evangelical Century: College and Creed in English Canada from the Great Revival to the Great Depression* (Montreal, 1991).

34. Ordinance framed by the Commissioners appointed for the purpose of the Statute 17th and 18th Vict. c.81, in relation to Merton College. Published in Supplement to *The London Gazette*, May 11, 1857, Pembroke College, Oxford Archives, 60/12/171, 1667.

35. "Copy of Regulations and Ordinances for the Amendment of the Statutes of Lincoln College, Oxford . . . approved by the Commissioners," ordered to be printed by the House of Commons, Feb. 21, 1856, Pembroke College, Oxford Archives, 60/12/159.

36. The history of the mid-Victorian church rate conflict is given in J. P. Ellens, *Religious Routes*.

37. W. E. Gladstone, *The State in its Relations with the Church* (London,

1838), 39; H. C. G. Matthew, ed., *The Gladstone Diaries* 3 (Oxford, 1974): xxvi–xxvii; Deryck Schreuder, "Gladstone and the Conscience of the State," in P. Marsh, ed., *The Conscience of the Victorian State* (London, 1979); R. J. Helmstadter, "Conscience and Politics: Gladstone's First Book," in B. L. Kinzer, ed., *The Gladstonian Turn of Mind* (Toronto, 1985). A. M. C. Waterman has shown that Tory organicism rested on theology and the language of the Book of Common Prayer which encouraged perceiving "social and political relations in terms of a sacramental unity in the Body of Christ"; see his "'The Grand Scheme of Subordination': the Intellectual Foundation of Tory Doctrine," in *The Australian Journal of Politics and History* 40, Special Issue, 1994: "Ideas and Ideology: Essays in Memory of Eugene Kamenka," ed. N. A. Rupke and D. W. Lovell.

38. *Standard*, Jan. 13, 1834; Ellens, *Religious Routes*, 38. The argument that England existed as a traditional Christian state and society until 1832 has been made by J. C. D. Clark in *English Society, 1688–1832: Ideology, Social Structure, and Political Practice during the Ancien Regime* (Cambridge, 1985). A revised version of Clark's argument is made by Robert Hole in *Pulpits, Politics, and Public Order in England, 1760–1832* (Cambridge, 1989).

39. *PD* (HC) 152, col. 648 (Feb. 21, 1859); J. P. Ellens, "Lord John Russell and the Church Rate Conflict: The Struggle for a Broad Church, 1834–1868," *Journal of British Studies* 26 (Apr. 1987): 232–57; Richard Brent, "The Whigs and Protestant Dissent in the Decade of Reform: The Case of Church Rates, 1833–1841," *EHR* 102, no. 405 (Oct. 1987): 887–910.

40. James E. Bradley, *Religion, Revolution, and English Radicalism: Nonconformity in Eighteenth-Century Politics and Society* (Cambridge, 1990); H. S. Skeats and C. S. Miall, *History of the Free Churches of England 1688– 1891* (London, 1894), 443, 444; Roger H. Martin, "The Place of the London Missionary Society in the Ecumenical Movement," *Journal of Ecclesiastical History* 31, no. 3 (July 1980): 283–300; *Eclectic Review* 11 (Apr. 1834): 320; R. K. Webb, *Modern England From the 18th Century to the Present* (New York, 1980), 37; Ellens, *Religious Routes*, 44–45.

41. R. K. Webb, "From Toleration to Religious Liberty," in J. R. Jones, ed., *Liberty Secured? Britain Before And After 1688* (Stanford, 1992); David M. Thompson, *Nonconformity in the Nineteenth Century* (London, 1972), 1– 22; R. W. Davis, *Dissent in Politics, 1780-1830: The Political Life of William Smith, M.P.* (London, 1971), 50.

42. *Patriot*, June 27, 1832, 185.

43. *PD* (HC) 22, cols. 1012–63 (Mar. 21, 1834).

44. *Patriot*, May 7, 1834, 149–52; G. I. T. Machin, *Politics and the Churches in Great Britain, 1832–1868* (Oxford, 1977), 45; Ellens, *Religious Routes*, 40-42.

45. *Patriot*, May 10, 1834, 157.

46. *Leicestershire Mercury*, Dec. 17, 1836 and Jan. 28, 1837; Machin, *Politics and the Churches*, 54–55; Ellens, *Religious Routes*, 58.

47. E. Tottenham, *A Speech on the Subject of the Established Church and Church Rates* (London, Feb. 14, 1837), 2.

48. *Standard*, Feb. 2, 1837; *John Bull*, Feb. 19, 1837, 92; Ellens, *Religious Routes*, 60-61.

49. *PD* (HC) 36, cols. 1255, 1267 (Mar. 3, 1837).

50. Ibid. 38, col. 1073 (May 23, 1837); Brent, "The Whigs and Protestant Dissent"; Norman Gash, *Reaction and Reconstruction in English Politics, 1832–1868* (Oxford, 1965), 73; Ellens, *Religious Routes*, 61–68.

51. Eustace R. Conder, *Josiah Conder: A Memoir* (London, 1857), 284–86; *Patriot*, Apr. 15, 1839, 237 and May 16, 1839, 237.

52. *PD* (HC) 53, col. 97 (Feb. 11, 1840); Ellens, "Lord John Russell," 244–45; id., *Religious Routes*, 79–80.

53. *PD* (HC) 53, col. 97 (Feb. 11, 1840); *Patriot*, Feb. 13, 1840, 100 and Jan. 25, 1841; Minutes of the Dissenting Deputies, May 29, 1840, Guildhall MS. 3083, 9, 449–50.

54. Arthur Miall, *Life of Edward Miall* (London, 1884), 28–33; C. Binfield, *So Down to Prayers: Studies in English Nonconformity, 1780-1920* (London, 1970), chap. 5.

55. *Nonconformist*, Apr. 14, 1841, 1.

56. D. W. Bebbington, *Evangelicalism in Modern Britain: A History From the 1730s to the 1980s* (London, 1989), chaps. 2 and 3; see also Bradley, *Religion, Revolution, and English Radicalism*, chap. 4.

57. A. J. Morris, *The Anti-State-Church Catechism Adapted for Popular Use* (London, 1845), 191.

58. *Congregational Magazine*, n.s. 2 (1834), 358.

59. Machin, *Politics and the Churches*, 228; *Nonconformist*, Mar. 3, 1852, 166; *Record*, Mar. 1, 1852.

60. Lord Stanley to Disraeli, July 19, 1852, Hughenden Papers B\20\,5\5 54, LSE microfilm, film 131; Blomfield to Derby, July 19, 1852, "private," Derby Papers 127\6; Blomfield to Derby, "Church Rates" (printed), Derby Papers 127\6; Ellens, *Religious Routes*, 107.

61. Minutes of the Dissenting Deputies, Dec. 7, 1852, Guildhall MS. 3083, 12, 290; Mar. 9, 1853, fols. 329–30; Minutes of the ASCA, Apr. 13, 1853, GLRO A\LIB\ 1, 2, 489; *PD* (HC) 127, cols. 607–23 (May 26, 1853); Ellens, *Religious Routes*, 109–11.

62. *PD* (HC) 138, cols. 692–94 (May 16, 1855).

63. *Parliament and the Church-Rate Question: An Historical Sketch* (London, 1861), 15.

64. *The Times*, Feb. 19, 1856; E. D. Steele, *Palmerston and Liberalism, 1855–1865* (Cambridge, 1991), 70.

65. *PD* (HC) 140, cols. 1896–1903 (Mar. 5, 1856).

66. Ibid., 1919–27; Ellens, *Religious Routes*, 131–32.

67. *Patriot*, May 9, 1856, 230.

68. *Liberator*, Aug. 1, 1856, 179.

69. *PD* (HL) 151, cols. 799–839 (July 2, 1858); Ellens, *Religious Routes*, 144–51.

70. *PD* (HC) 152, cols. 610–29 (Feb. 21, 1859); Ellens, *Religious Routes,* 153.

71. *PD* (HC) 152, col. 648 (Feb. 21, 1859); Ellens, "Lord John Russell," 252; id., *Religious Routes,* 154.

72. *PD* (HC) 152, col. 658 (Feb. 21, 1859).

73. Bradley, *Religion, Revolution, and English Radicalism,* 139.

74. Ibid., 418.

75. Bebbington, *Evangelicalism,* 74 and discussion on 42–74.

76. Henry Dunckley, *The Charter of the Nations; or, Free Trade and its Results* (London, 1854). I am indebted to Dr. John Walsh of Jesus College, Oxford, for pointing me to this essay.

77. See a discussion by Eugenio F. Biagini in *Liberty, Retrenchment and Reform: Popular Liberalism in the Age of Gladstone, 1860–1880* (Cambridge, 1992), 50–59; for a review of changing views of wealth and commerce see Boyd Hilton, *The Age of Atonement: The Influence of Evangelicalism on Social and Economic Thought, 1795–1865* (Oxford, 1988), 120–25.

78. Dunckley, *Charter of the Nations,* 360–62; Naomi Churgin Miller, ed., *The Political Writings of Richard Cobden* 1 (New York, 1973): 150.

79. 1 Timothy 6:10 (RSV).

80. Dunckley, *Charter of the Nations,* 400 and X.

81. Ibid., 403.

82. Bebbington, *Evangelicalism in Modern Britain,* 54–55, 74; Bradley, *Religion, Revolution, and English Radicalism,* 417–19.

83. Dunckley, *Charter of the Nations,* 402.

84. Ibid., pt. 3, chap. 2, sec. 3.

85. Ibid., 413; Bebbington, *Evangelicalism in Modern Britain,* 81–86; see also Hilton, *The Age of Atonement,* 10.

86. Dunckley, *Charter of the Nations,* 417–20.

87. Ibid., 420.

88. Ibid., 421.

89. Miller, *Defining The Common Good,* 1–2, and 420.

90. Thomas Aquinas quoted in Black, *Political Thought In Europe 1250–1450* (Cambridge, 1992), 32 and discussed in Miller, *Defining The Common Good,* 2.

91. Bradley, *Religion, Revolution, and English Radicalism;* Miller, *Defining The Common Good,* chaps. 5 and 6.

92. Bebbington, *Evangelicalism in Modern Britain,* 54–74; Bradley, *Religion, Revolution, and English Radicalism;* Miller, *Defining The Common Good,* chaps. 5–6; J. C. D. Clark, *The Language of Liberty 1660–1832: Political Discourse and Social Dynamics in the Anglo-American World* (Cambridge, 1994); Alan P. F. Sell, *Dissenting Thought And The Life of The Churches* (Lewiston, NY, 1990).

93. Ellens, *Religious Routes,* 158.

94. Miller, *Defining The Common Good,* 348; Clark, *English Society, 1688–1832.*

CHAPTER 4

1. Priestley, *Essay on the First Principles of Government* (1768) and other works cited in R. K. Webb, "From Toleration to Religious Liberty," in J. R. Jones, ed., *Liberty Secured? Britain Before and After 1688* (Stanford, 1992), 158–98.

2. William Enfield, *An Apology for the Clergy, and particularly for the Protestant Dissenting Ministers: A Sermon preached at the Ordination of the Rev. John Yates and the Rev. Hugh Anderson, in Liverpool, October 1, 1777* (Warrington, 1777). Although Enfield stressed the freedom to choose orthodox or heterodox paths, he suggested that liberal colleagues would look more kindly on the latter option.

3. John Seed, "'A Set of Men Powerful Enough in Many Things': Rational Dissent and Political Opposition in England, 1770–1790," in Knud Haakonssen, ed., *Enlightenment and Religion: Rational Dissent in Eighteenth Century Britain* (Cambridge, 1996), 140–68.

4. To Sara Sophia Hennell, Sept. 24, 1831, in her *Memoirs of Charles Christian Hennell* (London, 1899), xxx. More generally, Ian Bradley, *The Call to Seriousness: The Evangelical Impact on the Victorians* (London, 1976), especially chap. 1, "Vital Religion"; and Martin Fitzpatrick, "Varieties of Candour: English and Scottish Style," *Enlightenment and Dissent* 7 (1988): 35–56.

5. David Newsome, *The Parting of Friends: A Study of the Wilberforces and Henry Manning* (London, 1966), 52–53, 128, 212. On the Manchester invitation, Howard M. Wach, "Culture and the Middle Classes: Popular Knowledge in Industrial Manchester," *Journal of British Studies* 27 (1988): 398, citing Athenaeum Directors' Minute Book 3:338–39, Manchester Central Reference Library M2/1/3. Professor Wach generously supplied fuller information from that source than he was able to include in the article.

6. William Wilberforce, *A Practical View of the Prevailing Religious System of Professed Christians* (London, 1798); and Thomas Belsham, *A Review of Mr. Wilberforce's Treatise, entitled* A Practical View . . . &c. *in Letters to a Lady* (London, 1798).

7. Peter B. Nockles, *The Oxford Movement in Context: Anglican High Churchmanship, 1760–1857* (Cambridge, 1994). See also F. C. Mather, *High Church Prophet: Bishop Samuel Horsley (1733–1806) and the Caroline Tradition in the Later Georgian Church* (Oxford, 1992); and Nigel Aston, "Horne and Heterodoxy: The Defence of Anglican Beliefs in the Late Enlightenment," *EHR* 108 (1993): 895–919.

8. R. K. Webb, "A Crisis of Authority: Early Nineteenth-Century British Thought," *Albion* 24 (Spring 1992): 1–16.

9. A central, now forgotten document of the time was Augustus and Julius Hare, *Guesses at Truth* (1827). See Merrill Distad, "Julius Charles Hare and the 'Broad Church' Ideal," in P. T. Phillips, ed., *The View from the Pulpit: Victorian Ministers and Society* (Toronto, 1978), 45–65; and Robert Preyer,

"Victorian Wisdom Literature: Fragments and Maxims," *Victorian Studies* 6 (1963): 245–62.

10. A recent important discussion of the problem of atheism is Joseph Hamburger, "Religion and *On Liberty*," in Michael Laine, ed., *A Cultivated Mind: Essays on J. S. Mill presented to John M. Robson* (Toronto, 1991), 139–81, the notes to which contain extensive citations to the literature. See also the *ex parte* survey by Leonard W. Levy, *Blasphemy: Verbal Offense against the Sacred, from Moses to Salman Rushdie* (New York, 1993), in which chaps. 13–17 and 19–23 deal with the English situation relevant to this chapter.

11. Richard J. Helmstadter and Bernard Lightman, eds., *Victorian Faith in Crisis: Essays on Continuity and Change in Nineteenth-Century Religious Belief* (Stanford, 1990).

12. Peter Nockles (*Oxford Movement in Context*, 69) argues that this rebellion has a better claim as the beginning of the Oxford Movement than John Keble's sermon on "National Apostasy" to which J. H. Newman, in his *Apologia*, gave canonical status.

13. This doctrine held that the sacrament of baptism fully regenerated the infant into a holy life, making any post-baptismal sin worse. Like all Evangelicals, Gorham emphasized the possibility of redemption and so challenged both traditionally orthodox High Churchmen and the new Tractarians who took an exalted view of the sacraments and of the priestly function of administering them. Even a sympathetic study like G. C. B. Davies, *Henry Phillpotts, Bishop of Exeter, 1778–1869* (London, 1954) recognizes Phillpotts's truculent narrowness.

14. The two archbishops, who later were added to the Committee's membership, were asked to participate in the deliberations on *Gorham* but had no part in the decision. On the Committee, P. A. Howell, *The Judicial Committee of the Privy Council, 1833–1876: Its Origins, Structure and Development* (Cambridge, 1979).

15. Ieuan Ellis, *Seven against Christ: A Study of "Essays and Reviews"* (*Studies in the History of Christian Thought*) (Leiden, 1980); Josef L. Altholz, *Anatomy of a Controversy: The Debate over "Essays and Reviews"* (Aldershot, U.K., 1994).

16. Pietro Corsi, *Science and Religion: Baden Powell and the Anglican Debate, 1800–1860* (Cambridge, 1988).

17. Warren R. Dawson, *Charles Wycliffe Goodwin, 1817–1878: A Pioneer in Egyptology* (Oxford, 1934), traces his remarkable subsequent career as lawyer, colonial judge, and a founder of British Egyptology.

18. The most relevant of many books on Jowett is Peter Hinchliff, *Benjamin Jowett and the Christian Religion* (Oxford, 1987).

19. *The "Essays and Reviews" and the People of England: A Popular Refutation of the Principal Propositions of the Essayists* (London, 1861), 3–4.

20. S. M. Waddams, *Law, Politics and the Church of England: The Career of Stephen Lushington, 1782–1873* (Cambridge, 1992).

21. Lushington continued as a member of the Committee but did not sit on the appeal, though he was consulted on a point of interpretation.

22. Thirlwall's remark was reported in *The Times*, Apr. 22, 1864, quoted in *The Life and Letters of Rowland Williams, D.D., with Extracts from his Note Books, edited by his Wife* (London, 1874), 2:155. For Unitarian reactions to the decisions and reporting of views in other journals, *Unitarian Herald*, July 5, 1862, Feb. 20, 1864, and Mar. 24, 1865; *Inquirer*, June 28 and July 5, 1862, Feb. 13 and 20 and July 23, 1864.

23. As an undergraduate, Williams had burst forth with a paean to truth and some time later was delighted to find that an elderly, unknown clergyman he heard preach in Cambridge was indeed Julius Hare. *Life and Letters* 1:243–44 on truth; 1:49 on Hare; 1:241–43, 274–77, 2:86–89 on reading; 2:184 on Quakers.

24. Rowland Williams, *Hints to my Counsel in the Court of Arches, November-June-1861-1862* (privately printed, 1861–62), 1, 3–4, 12, 17–18.

25. Id., *Persecution for the Word, with a Postscript on the Interlocutory Judgment and the Present State of the Case* (London, 1862).

26. *Essays and Reviews: A Protest to the Right Reverend the Lord Bishop of Salisbury* (London, 1861).

27. James Fitzjames Stephen, *Defence of the Rev. Rowland Williams, D. D. in the Arches' Court of Canterbury* (London, 1862). See the entertaining, clear, though hardly unbiased account in Leslie Stephen, *The Life of Sir James Fitzjames Stephen* (London, 1895, repr. South Hackensack, NJ, 1972), 184–203.

28. James Parker Deane, *Considerations on the Exercise of Private Judgment, by Ministers of the United Church of England and Ireland, in Matters connected with the Doctrine and Discipline of the Church* (London, 1845).

29. Court of Arches, Westminster . . . before the Right Honorable S. Lushington, Dean of the Arches, MS transcript of the speeches of counsel in the British Library 1:103–5.

30. K. J. M. Smith, *James Fitzjames Stephen: Portrait of a Victorian Rationalist* (Cambridge, 1988), 168–77, argues that Stephen was closer to John Stuart Mill than he appears. See also Hamburger, "Religion and 'On Liberty'."

31. These arguments are put directly on pp. 24–25, 44–46, 282–83, 330–31 of Court of Arches transcript.

32. "Unpublished Papers of Bishop Warburton," *British Critic* 29 (Apr. 1841): 427, quoted in Nockles, *Oxford Movement*, 71. See more generally Robert Pattison, *The Great Dissent: John Henry Newman and the Liberal Heresy* (1991). On the evolution of Bishop Warburton's language of liberty, see Webb, "From Toleration to Religious Liberty," 168–71.

33. David Newsome, *Parting of Friends*, 333, where Wilberforce is also quoted as telling another clergyman that he preferred an earnest preacher of Christ and the Cross to a perfunctory preacher with whom he was in dogmatic agreement.

34. Wilberforce to Bishop of London, Oct. 26, 1853, *Life and Letters* 2: 214–15; to Jelf, Aug. 27, 1853, 2:209. These balanced scruples bring to mind the nickname "Soapy Sam," unfairly given Wilberforce by contemporaries. On eternal punishment generally, relevant also to the Wilson case, Geoffrey Rowell, *Hell and the Victorians: A Study of the Nineteenth-Century Theological Controversies concerning Eternal Punishment and Eternal Life* (New York, 1974).

35. For general background, Walter P. Metzger, *Academic Freedom in the Age of the University* (New York, 1955); on the long-continued ideological purpose of the English university in the ancillary field of history, Reba N. Soffer, *Discipline and Power: The University, History, and the Making of an English Elite, 1870–1930* (Stanford, 1994).

36. To J. H. Newman, May 13, 1836, quoted in Nockles, *Oxford Movement*, 117.

37. Samuel Hinds, *Inquiry into the Proofs, Nature, and Extent of Inspiration, and into the Authority of Scripture* (Oxford, 1831), 3–6.

38. See n. 6 above.

39. John C[ale] Miller, *Bible Inspiration Vindicated: An Essay on "Essays and Reviews"* (Oxford, 1861). Miller was the Evangelical rector of St. Martin's, Birmingham, a fellow of Lincoln College, Oxford, and honorary canon of Worcester.

40. Hamilton thought that the essayists wanted to go to law, a guess borne out by a letter from Rowland Williams to the Unitarian minister John Relly Beard, May 27, 1861 (Unitarian College MSS): "As to the mere result of the trial, I can see no room for doubt. I greatly prefer retaining within the church that portion of modified freedom, which I have deliberately adopted, but if the law will not sustain so much, it is as well that we should know it."

41. This paragraph and the preceding are based on Hamilton's charges (*A Charge to the Clergy and Churchwardens of the Diocese of Salisbury*) for 1861, 1864, and 1867, all published in Salisbury, though the last also carried a London imprint.

42. John Octavius Johnson, *Life and Letters of Henry Parry Liddon* (London, 1904), 72–77.

43. On the translation and its background, Luther A. Weigle, "English Versions after 1611," *Cambridge History of the Bible* 3 (Cambridge, 1963): 368–73; Ashwell, *Life of Wilberforce*, 504–6.

44. Peter Hinchliff, *God and History: Aspects of British Theology, 1875–1914* (Oxford, 1992). On the Congregationalists and Mansfield College, Mark D. Johnson, *The Dissolution of Dissent, 1850–1918* (New York, 1987), chaps. 3–4; on the Unitarians and Manchester College, R. K. Webb, "Transplanting the Vine: Manchester College in London and Oxford," *Faith and Freedom* 44 (Autumn 1991): 78–97.

45. E. R. Norman, *Church and Society in England, 1770–1970* (New York, 1976), chaps. 5–6, places this departure in context.

46. On *Lux Mundi*, Peter Hinchliff, "Jowett and Gore: Two Balliol Essay-

ists," *Theology* 87 (1984): 251–59, and, more generally, *God in History,* especially chap. 5; Johnston, *Liddon,* 360–82. The Jowett quotation is taken from Hinchliff, *Jowett,* 67.

47. H. S. Perris, *Inquirer,* Dec. 19, 1903.

48. The best account of modern Unitarianism, brief but brilliant, is H. L. Short, "Presbyterians under a New Name," in C. G. Bolam et al., *The English Presbyterians, from Elizabethan Puritanism to Modern Unitarianism* (Boston, 1968), 219–86.

49. See the rumors of disaffection with Martineau and his friends eagerly retailed by Robert Brook Aspland to John Gordon (Sept. 7, 1851, Unitarian College MSS B 1.15) about "*deep complaints* amongst the Hope St. people of the chops & changes which their minister is perpetually giving them." The most important lay supporter of the new views was Richard Holt Hutton, who as a young and brash co-editor of the transformed *Inquirer* and later from more exalted journalistic reaches never ceased to defend Martineau. The Unitarian College MSS mentioned above are in the John Rylands University Library of Manchester, a location that will not be repeated in subsequent citations.

50. Aspland to John Gordon, Sept. 7 [1859], Unitarian College MSS B 1.15.

51. Crabb Robinson Diary, Nov. 19, 1840, Dr. Williams's Library.

52. *Inquirer,* Dec. 28, 1844.

53. Bache to John Gordon, Mar. 6, 1847, Unitarian College MSS, B 1.19.

54. Ibid., Sept. 22, 1851, Unitarian College MSS, B 1.19. The Martineau sermon is in *Essays, Reviews, and Addresses* 4:470–82.

55. Tagart to John Gordon, Aug. 21, 1848, Feb. 11, 1857. Unitarian College MSS, C 1.28 and B 1.11; Tagart, *Locke's Writings and Philosophy . . . vindicated from . . . Contribution to the Scepticism of Hume;* Beard to Gordon, Feb. 11, 1857, Unitarian College MSS B 1.11.

56. Martineau to Helen Bourn Martineau, Sept. 22, 1826, Speck Collection, Bancroft Library, University of California, Berkeley.

57. Ibid., Jan. 17 and Oct. 8, 1859, Unitarian College MSS B 1.19.

58. Bache to Gordon, Jan. 21, 1864, Unitarian College MSS B 1.19. For instances of Aspland's contempt, an undated letter, probably in 1858, to Gordon and again, Feb. 9 and 28, 1860, Unitarian College MSS B 1.15.

59. *Inquirer,* May 26, 1866; throughout most of the 1860s that paper and the *Unitarian Herald* contain much discussion of the issues, in which the theme of religious liberty occupies the central place.

60. For Rees, Crabb Robinson Diary, Mar. 22, 1848, Dr. Williams's Library. On the third professorship, Aspland to Crabb Robinson, Sept. 8, 1853, Dr. Williams's Library. Edward to Lucy Tagart, Oct. 1, 1856, Speck Collection, Bancroft Library, University of California Berkeley. Martineau replaced Tagart at Little Portland Street chapel after Tagart's untimely death in 1857.

61. Martineau to John Gordon, Dec. 28, 1872, Unitarian College MSS B 1.22.

62. *Memorials of Robert Spears, 1825–1899* (Belfast, 1903).

63. J. H. Muirhead, *Reflections of a Journeyman in Philosophy*, ed. John W. Harvey (London, 1942), 67.

64. Arthur J. Long, "The Life and Work of J. Estlin Carpenter," in Smith, *Truth, Liberty, Religion*, 283; Muirhead, *Reflections*, 65.

65. R. K. Webb, "John Hamilton Thom: Intellect and Conscience in Liverpool," in Paul T. Phillips, ed., *The View from the Pulpit: Victorian Ministers and Society* (Toronto, 1978), 237–41. Charles Beard, *The Kingdom of God . . . preached . . . during the Twentieth Annual Congress of the National Association for the Promotion of Social Science* (London, 1876).

66. "The Task of Liberal Religion," *Inquirer*, July 3, 1909. Wicksteed in *Inquirer*, Sept. 7, 1912. Jacks in *Inquirer*, Apr. 24, 1920.

67. Leonard Smith, *Religion and the Rise of Labour: Nonconformity and Politics in Lancashire and the West Riding, 1880–1914* (Keele, 1993) is an account of the diversion of political loyalty.

68. The English schism is detailed in Edwin B. Bronner, *"The Other Branch": London Yearly Meeting and the Hicksites, 1827–1912* (London, 1975). The discussion here and following is deeply indebted to Elizabeth Isichei, *Victorian Quakers* (Oxford, 1970); Edwin B. Bronner, "Moderates in the London Yearly Meeting, 1857–1873: Precursors to the Quaker Liberals," *Quaker History* 54 (1990): 356–71; Thomas C. Kennedy, "Heresy-Hunting among Victorian Quakers: The Manchester Difficulty, 1861–73," *Victorian Studies* 30 (1990–91): 227–53; Roger C. Wilson, "The Road to Manchester, 1895," in J. William Frost and John M. Moore, eds., *Seeking the Light: Essays in Quaker History in Honor of Edwin B. Bronner* (Wallingford, PA, 1986), 145–62; and id., *Manchester, Manchester, and Manchester Again: From "Sound Doctrine" to "A Free Ministry"*, Friends Historical Society, Occasional Series No. 1 (London, 1990).

69. Rowntree, *Quakerism* (London, 1860), 184–85. Rowntree's question was asked, and answered, more brutally by a Nottingham clergyman, the Rev. Thomas Hancock, whose essay *The Peculium* (London, 1860) won second prize in the competition. Hancock argued that, having long since done its work, Quakerism had no choice but to be absorbed into the universal church whose triumph was now certain. This "Puseyite" tract brought down the wrath of the reviewer in the traditionalist *British Friend* (Jan. 1860) and of a correspondent the next month in the same journal.

70. *"Essays and Reviews"; A Lecture delivered to the Manchester Friends' Institute*, 3d ed. (Manchester, 1860).

71. *British Friend*, May 1861; *Friend*, June 1861.

72. A new reformation was also a central concern for the Rev. Charles Beard, the New-School Unitarian who was minister of Renshaw Street chapel in Liverpool. It forms the main purpose of his influential Hibbert Lectures, *The Reformation of the Sixteenth Century in its Relation to Modern Thought and Knowledge* (London, 1883) and is foreshadowed in his *Port Royal: A Contribution to the History of Religion and Literature in France* (London, 1861).

73. [Anna Lloyd Thomas,] *J. Bevan Braithwaite: A Friend of the Nineteenth Century. By his Children* (London, 1909), 88.

74. The motto of the evangelical *Friend* also suggested an order of priority: "In essentials unity, in non-essentials liberty, in all things charity."

75. Recently in the withdrawal by the bishop of Chichester of the license of a clergyman who denies a personal God. *Church Times,* July 29 and Aug. 5, 1994.

CHAPTER 5

The research for this essay was supported by grants from the Lucius N. Littauer Foundation and by the DeWitt Wallace Fund of Macalester College. I would like to acknowledge the cooperation of the Board of Deputies of British Jews in giving me access to their Minute Books, which are kept at the office of the Board. These books are cited in the notes as Board of Deputies, *Minute Books.* The published reports of the Board, which were issued half-yearly until 1874 and yearly thereafter, are cited as Board of Deputies, *Reports.*

1. Jacob Katz, ed., *The Role of Religion in Modern Jewish History* (Cambridge, MA, 1975).

2. Whether this increased ability to ignore religion is the result of increasing secularism in European society is a matter of lively debate among historians and sociologists. The dissolving of orthodox strictures on all facets of life makes the term *secularization* an appropriate one in referring to the Jewish experience. For further discussion of this issue, see chapter 11 in this volume and Steve Bruce, ed., *Religion and Modernization: Sociologists and Historians Debate the Secularization Thesis* (Oxford, 1992).

3. Among others, see David Sorkin, *The Transformation of German Jewry, 1780–1840* (New York, 1987); Marion A. Kaplan, *The Making of the Jewish Middle Class: Women, Family, and Identity in Imperial Germany* (New York, 1991); Paula E. Hyman, *Gender and Assimilation in Modern Jewish History: The Roles and Representation of Women* (Seattle, WA, 1995); Phyllis Cohen Albert, *The Modernization of French Jewry: Consistory and Community in the Nineteenth Century* (Hanover, NH, 1977); Jonathan Frankel and Steven J. Zipperstein, eds., *Assimilation and Community: The Jews in Nineteenth-Century Europe* (Cambridge, 1992); Paula E. Hyman, *The Emancipation of the Jews of Alsace: Acculturation and Tradition in the Nineteenth Century* (New Haven, CT, 1991); David Cesarani, ed., *The Making of Modern Anglo-Jewry* (Oxford, 1990); Todd M. Endelman, *The Jews of Georgian England, 1714–1830: Tradition and Change in a Liberal Society* (Philadelphia, 1979); David Feldman, *Englishmen and Jews: Social Relations and Political Culture, 1840–1914* (New Haven, CT, 1994).

4. Katz, *Role of Religion,* vii.

5. Michael Meyer, *Response to Modernity: A History of the Reform Movement in Judaism* (New York, 1988), 18.

6. Quoted in Michael R. Marrus, *The Politics of Assimilation: A Study of the French Jewish Community at the Time of the Dreyfus Affair* (Oxford, 1971), 52. Michael Meyer has described Mendelssohn as a "reformer of Jewish life, but . . . not a reformer of Judaism," a distinction that is particularly relevant for our purposes. Meyer, *Response to Modernity*, 13.

7. H. H. Ben-Sasson, "The Middle Ages," in H. H. Ben-Sasson, ed., *A History of the Jewish People* (Cambridge, MA, 1976), 480.

8. Ben-Sasson, "Middle Ages," 486.

9. Jewish emancipation is central to most accounts of nineteenth-century Jewish history. For a brief account of the progress of Jewish legal equality, see S. Ettinger, "The Modern Period," chaps. 45, 49, and 50, in Ben-Sasson, *History of the Jewish People*.

10. Hyman, *Gender and Assimilation*, 53. For the attitudes of German rabbis, see Sorkin, *Transformation of German Jewry*, 137.

11. Quoted by Isaiah Friedman, "Dissensions Over Jewish Identity in West European Jewry," in Katz, *Role of Religion*, 128–29.

12. See, for example, Meyer, *Response to Modernity*, 143–44, for a discussion of why reform made the most headway in Germany. See, too, Albert, *Modernization of French Jewry*, 125–26, 232–33, for some French examples.

13. The following discussion is based on Kaplan, *Making of the Jewish Middle Class*, 69–84, and Hyman, *Gender and Assimilation*, 10–49.

14. Marrus, *Politics of Assimilation*, 60.

15. Katz, *Role of Religion*, 3.

16. For conversion, see Todd M. Endelman, ed., *Jewish Apostasy in the Modern World* (New York, 1987).

17. Todd M. Endelman, "German Jews in Victorian England: A Study in Drift and Defection," in Frankel and Zipperstein, *Assimilation and Community*, 64.

18. Ben-Sasson, "Middle Ages," 720.

19. Hyman, *Alsace*, 157.

20. Ibid., 142–43.

21. Ibid., 151.

22. Ibid., 79.

23. For some examples, see Meyer, *Response to Modernity*, 57–58, 110; and William O. McCagg, Jr., *A History of Habsburg Jews, 1670–1918* (Bloomington, IN, 1989), 136–37, 150–51.

24. Charles H. L. Emanuel, *A Century and a Half of Jewish History Extracted from the Minute Books of the London Committee of Deputies of the British Jews* (London, 1910), 26.

25. Ibid., 44.

26. For "fashionable religiosity," see Israel Finestein, "Jewish Emancipationists in Victorian England: Self-imposed Limits to Assimilation," in Frankel and Zipperstein, *Assimilation and Community*, 41. For the orthodoxy of the Anglo-Jewish elite, see Todd M. Endelman, "The Englishness of Jewish Modernity in England," in Jacob Katz, ed., *Toward Modernity: The European*

Jewish Model (New Brunswick, NJ, 1987), 22; and id., "Communal Solidarity Among the Jewish Elite of Victorian London," *Victorian Studies*, Spring 1985, 497–505.

27. Meyer, *Response to Modernity*, 109–110.

28. Ibid., 52.

29. Ibid., 109.

30. Ibid., 125–26.

31. For the Kulturkampf, see chapter 6 in this volume. For a fuller discussion of the impact of the Kulturkampf on the Jewish community, see Uriel Tal, *Christians and Jews in Germany: Religion, Politics, and Ideology in the Second Reich, 1870–1914* (Ithaca, NY, 1975), 81–120.

32. Tal, *Christians and Jews in Germany*, 112–17.

33. David Landes, "Two Cheers for Emancipation," in Frances Malino and Bernard Wasserstein, eds., *The Jews in Modern France* (Hanover, NH, 1985), 291.

34. Landes, "Two Cheers," 291.

35. For religious struggles in France, see chapters 8 and 9 in this volume.

36. David C. Itzkowitz, "Cultural Pluralism and the Board of Deputies of British Jews," in R. W. Davis and R. J. Helmstadter, eds., *Religion and Irreligion in Victorian Society: Essays in Honor of R. K. Webb* (London, 1992), 85–101.

37. The concept of cultural pluralism is derived from the American rather than the European experience. See Bernard Wasserstein, "'As individuals everything . . . as a group nothing': The Flawed Emancipation of the Jews in Europe," *European Studies Review* 12 (1982): 201, for criticism of Paula Hyman for using this American model in a European context. I am, of course, arguing that it is applicable to the English experience.

38. Endelman, "Communal Solidarity," 497–505.

39. Zosa Szajkowski, "Secular Versus Religious Jewish Life in France," in Katz, *Role of Religion*, 109. But for a somewhat different view, see Phyllis Cohen Albert, "Israelite and Jew: How did Nineteenth-century French Jews Understand Assimilation," in Frankel and Zipperstein, *Assimilation and Community*, 88–109.

40. Marrus, *Politics of Assimilation*, 130.

41. *Jewish Chronicle*, London, May 3, 1867.

42. Albert, *Modernization of French Jewry*, 153.

43. Ibid., 155.

44. Ibid., 157.

45. It is worth recalling, in full, the famous words of the deputy Clermont-Tonnere during the debate over the emancipation of the Jews during the French Revolution. "The Jews should be denied everything as a nation, but granted everything as individuals; they must disown their judges, they must have only ours; they must be refused legal protection for the maintenance of the supposed laws of their Jewish corporation; they must constitute neither a state, nor a political corps, nor an order; they must individually become citizens; if they do not want this, they must inform us

and we shall then be compelled to expel them. The existence of a nation within a nation is unacceptable to our country." Quoted in Jay R. Berkovitz, *The Shaping of Jewish Identity in Nineteenth-century France* (Detroit, 1989), 71.

46. Albert, *Modernization of French Jewry*, 234–35.

47. For a full discussion of this issue, see Israel Finestein, "An Aspect of the Jews and English Marriage Law During the Emancipation: The Prohibited Degrees," *Jewish Journal of Sociology* 7, 1 (June 1965): 3–21.

48. Board of Deputies of British Jews, *Report*, Aug. 1869, 14; Mar. 1871, 16–17. *Minute Book* 10, 348. See also chapter 3, this volume.

49. For a fuller discussion of the campaign to amend the Factory Act, see Itzkowitz, "Cultural Pluralism and the Board of Deputies of British Jews."

50. Board of Deputies of British Jews, *Report*, Apr. 1880, 17.

51. Feldman, *Englishmen and Jews*, 298.

52. Ibid., 366–68.

CHAPTER 6

1. For a comprehensive picture of this literary sub-category and its audience, see Josef Schmidt, *Quo vadis? — woher kommst du? Unterhaltungsliterarische konfessionelle Apologetik im Viktorianischen und Wilhelminischen Zeitalter* (Bern, 1990).

2. Standard accounts include Johannes B. Kißling, *Geschichte des Kulturkampfes im Deutschen Reiche*, 3 vols. (Freiburg, 1911–16); Georges Goyau, *Bismarck et l'Eglise. Le Culturkampf (1870–1887)*, 4 vols. (Paris, 1911–13); and Erich Schmidt-Volkmar, *Der Kulturkampf in Deutschland 1871–1890* (Göttingen, 1962). For the most recent account, see Ronald J. Ross, *The Failure of Bismarck's Kulturkampf: Catholicism and State Power in Imperial Germany, 1871–1887* (Washington, DC, forthcoming).

3. The best discussion is David Blackbourn, "Progress and Piety: Liberals, Catholics and the State in Bismarck's Germany," in David Blackbourn, *Populists and Patricians: Essays in Modern German History* (London, 1987), 143–67.

4. Despite its age and obvious bias, the standard account of the Old Catholic movement remains Johann Friedrich von Schulte's, *Der Altkatholizismus. Geschichte seiner Entwicklung, inneren Gestaltung und rechtlichen Stellung in Deutschland* (Giessen, 1887); for an interesting, if not always convincing, recent assessment, see Thomas Mergel, *Zwischen Klasse und Konfession. Katholisches Bürgertum im Rheinland 1794–1914* (Göttingen, 1994), 282–305.

5. See Richard Blanke, "The Polish Role in the Origin of the *Kulturkampf* in Prussia," *Canadian Slavonic Papers/Revue Canadienne des Slavistes* 25, 2 (June 1983): 253–62.

6. Helmut Walser Smith, *German Nationalism and Religious Conflict: Culture, Ideology, Politics, 1870–1914* (Princeton, NJ, 1995), 20.

7. Heinrich Bornkamm, "Die Staatsidee im Kulturkampf," *Historische*

Zeitschrift 170 (1950): 276–94, 301. For a traditional restatement of the Kulturkampf's origins, see Otto Pflanze, *Bismarck and the Development of Modern Germany*, 3 vols. (Princeton, NJ, 1990), 2:106–14, 179–202. Cf. Ernst Engelberg, *Bismarck. Das Reich in der Mitte Europas* (Berlin, 1990), 104–52.

8. Report from Anton Freiherr von Cetto, Nov. 28, 1873; BHStA München, Abteilung Allgemeines Staatsarchiv, Bayer. Gesandtschaft, Päpstl. Stuhl 819, no. 50/xxxv. Germany's Catholics concurred. Julius Bachem, a prominent Catholic politician and member of the well-known Cologne publishing clan, described the Kulturkampf as a "Diocletian persecution." Jul. Bachem, *Erinnerungen eines alten Publizisten und Politiker* (Cologne, 1913), 133.

9. Georg von Hertling, *Erinnerungen aus meinem Leben*, 2 vols. (Kempten, 1920), 1:261–62; Kißling, *Geschichte des Kulturkampfes* 2:299, 3:131. Harassed and humiliated again and again, the Hertlings even considered emigration from Germany. "I would rather not live in a country where such injustices take place," Hertling wrote to his wife in 1872. Quoted in Margaret Lavinia Anderson, *Windthorst: A Political Biography* (Oxford, 1981), 179.

10. Ross, *Failure of Bismarck's Kulturkampf*, chap. 4.

11. *Staat und Kirche im 19. und 20. Jahrhundert. Dokumente zur Geschichte des deutschen Staatskirchenrechts*, Ernst Rudolf Huber and Wolfgang Huber, eds., 4 vols. (Berlin, 1973–88), 2:598.

12. *Trierer Kulturkampfpriester. Auswahl einiger markanten Priester-Gestalten aus den Zeiten des preußischen Kulturkampfes*, ed. Karl Kammer (Trier, 1926), 92; Adolph Rösch, "Der Kulturkampf in Hohenzollern," *Freiburger Diözesan-Archiv* 16 (1915): 47.

13. Ronald J. Ross, "The *Kulturkampf* and the Limitations of Power in Bismarck's Germany," *The Journal of Ecclesiastical History* 46, 4 (Oct. 1995): 676.

14. Karl Bachem, *Vorgeschichte, Geschichte und Politik der Deutschen Zentrumspartei*, 9 vols. (Cologne, 1927–32), 3:308–9. Governmental records put the figure somewhat higher. According to an official tally, some 340 religious houses among a total of 955 were said to have been closed. See report entitled "Nachweisungen von denjenigen Orden und ordensähnlichen Kongregationen, welche zur Zeit des Erlasses des Gesetzes vom 31. Mai 1875 bestanden haben," n.d.; Staatsarchiv Königsberg i. Pr., Oberpräsidium, Rep. 2, II, No. 2187, Bd. 2, Bl. 58. See also W. Hankamer, *Das Zentrum, die politische Vertretung des katholischen Volksteils. Die Geschichte seiner Entstehung und seiner Tätigkeit unter besonderer Berücksichtigung des kirchenpolitischen Konflikts* (Essen, 1927), 70.

15. Herbert Lepper, "Die kirchenpolitische Gesetzgebung der Jahre 1872 bis 1875 und ihre Ausführung im Regierungsbezirk Aachen. Ein Beitrag zur Geschichte des 'Kulturkampfes' in der Erzdiözese Köln," in *Annalen des Historischen Vereins für den Niederrhein, insbesondere das alte Erzbistum Köln* 171 (1969): 251.

16. *SBVLHA*, Dec. 11, 1878, 1:279.

17. See *The Poems of Gerard Manley Hopkins*, W. H. Gardner and N. H. MacKenzie, eds., 4th ed. (London, 1967), 51–63; Ronald J. Ross, "Enforcing the Kulturkampf: The Bismarckian State and the Limits of Coercion in Imperial Germany," *JMH* 56, 3 (Sept. 1984): 469.

18. Ludwig Ficker, *Der Kulturkampf in Münster*, ed. Otto Hellinghaus (Münster, 1928), 101–2; Manfred Scholle, *Die preußische Strafjustiz im Kulturkampf 1873–1880* (Marburg, 1974), 269–70.

19. Kißling, *Geschichte des Kulturkampfes* 3:126.

20. Lech Trzeciakowski, *The Kulturkampf in Prussian Poland*, trans. Katarzyna Kretkowska (Vol. 283, East European Monographs) (New York, 1990), 93–94.

21. Ibid., 93.

22. Ibid., 94.

23. Jentzsch [Landrat] to Königliche Regierung in Münster, Aug. 4, 1875; GStAPrKB (Merseburg), Geheimes Zivilkabinett, 2.2.1., No. 23762, Bl. 211v[erso]; Friedrich Albrecht Graf zu Eulenburg and [signature illegible] to Wilhelm I, Aug. 12, 1875; *ibid.*, Bl. 207v.

24. Heinrich Schiffers, *Der Kulturkampf in Stadt und Regierungsbezirk Aachen* (Aachen, 1929), 138.

25. J. Schürmann, *Johann Bernard Brinkmann, Bischof von Münster im Kulturkampf. Erinnerungen von J. Schürmann*, 8th-10th ed. (Münster i. Westf., 1925), 111.

26. For the most comprehensive account, see David Blackbourn, *Marpingen: Apparitions of the Virgin Mary in Nineteenth-Century Germany* (New York, 1994).

27. J. Bachem, *Erinnerungen*, 141.

28. Quoted in Hans-Ulrich Wehler, *The German Empire, 1871–1918*, trans. Kim Traynor (Leamington Spa, U.K., 1985), 91.

29. See Ross, *Failure of Bismarck's Kulturkampf*, chap. 8.

30. Hans Joachim Reiber, *Die katholische deutsche Tagespresse unter dem Einfluß des Kulturkampfes* (Görlitz, 1930), 126–27; Ulrich Fohrmann, *Trierer Kulturkampfpublizistik im Bismarckreich. Leben und Werk des Preßkaplans Georg Friedrich Dasbach* (Trier, 1977), 74; Ross, "Enforcing the Kulturkampf," 473.

31. Ross, "Enforcing the Kulturkampf," 473.

32. Reiber, *Die katholische deutsche Tagespresse*, 12.

33. Hans Goldschmidt, "Bismarcks Stellung zur Justiz," *Deutsche Juristen-Zeitung* 37, 7 (Apr. 1, 1932): 400.

34. Arthur von Brauer, *Im Dienste Bismarcks. Persönliche Erinnerungen* (Berlin, 1936), 31; Robert H. Keyserlingk, *Media Manipulation: A Study of the Press and Bismarck in Imperial Germany* (Montreal, 1977), 74; Pflanze, *Bismarck* 2:235.

35. Ross, "Enforcing the Kulturkampf," 473.

36. Ibid.; Reiber, *Die katholische deutsche Tagespresse*, 131.

37. Kißling, *Geschichte des Kulturkampfes* 2:300. For the political context of the Majunke case, see Pflanze, *Bismarck* 2:236–39.

38. See Philipp Wasserburg, *Zwei Monate auf der Festung Darmstadt* (Mainz, 1874).

39. Hans-Wolfgang Wetzel, *Presseinnenpolitik im Bismarckreich (1874–1890). Das Problem der Repression oppositioneller Zeitungen* (Bern, 1975), 137. For a description of a police search of the premises of the *Kuryer Poznański*, a Polish Catholic newspaper in Posen, see police report of Mar. 16, 1876; AMPiWP (Poznań), 4911, Bl. 1. Abschrift.

40. Franz Emil Heitjan, *Die Saar-Zeitung und die Entwicklung des politischen Katholizismus an der Saar von 1872 bis 1888* (Saarlouis, 1931), 36.

41. Ibid., 35.

42. Ibid., 51; Fritz Hellwig, *Carl Ferdinand Freiherr von Stumm-Halberg 1836–1901* (Heidelberg, 1936), 103.

43. See Margaret Lavinia Anderson and Kenneth Barkin, "The Myth of the Puttkamer Purge and the Reality of the *Kulturkampf*: Some Reflections on the Historiography of Imperial Germany," *JMH* 54, 4 (1982): 350–78.

44. Der Ober-Staatsanwalt in Paderborn to Adolf Leonhardt, Apr. 18, 1874; GStAPrKB (Merseburg), Ministerium des Innern, Rep. 77, Tit. 413, No. 35, Bd. 4, Bl. 47v. Emphasis added.

45. Ibid., Bl. 47v–48.

46. Der Staatsanwalt in Borken to Ober-Staatsanwalt in Münster, Sept. 9, 1872; GStAPrKB (Merseburg), Rep. 77, Tit. 413, No. 35, Bd. 3, Bl. 37v.

47. See Reich Chancellor to Eulenburg, Mar. 18, 1873; GStAPrKB (Merseburg), Rep. 77, Tit. 413, No. 35, Bd. 3, Bl. 52–54v.

48. Schmidt-Volkmar, *Der Kulturkampf*, 170; Ross, "Enforcing the Kulturkampf," 463.

49. *SBVLHA*, Apr. 19, 1875, 2:1342. Quoted in Ed. Hüsgen, *Ludwig Windthorst. Sein Leben, sein Wirken* (Cologne, 1911), 180; Anderson and Barkin, "Myth of the Puttkamer Purge," 659; and Ross, "Enforcing the Kulturkampf," 464.

50. Hermann Oncken, *Rudolf von Bennigsen*, 2 vols. (Stuttgart, 1910), 2:281.

51. *Frankfurter Zeitung*, no. 3 (Jan. 3, 1875): 1; Ross, "Enforcing the Kulturkampf," 464.

52. Jonathan Sperber, *Popular Catholicism in Nineteenth-Century Germany* (Princeton, NJ, 1984), 243.

53. Schiffers, *Der Kulturkampf*, 122; for the experience of Catholic judges, on the other hand, see Thomas Ormond, *Richterwürde und Regierungstreue. Dienstrecht, politische Betätigung und Disziplinierung der Richter in Preußen, Baden und Hessen 1866–1918* (Frankfurt am Main, 1994), 391–94.

54. The above discussion is based on Franz Kaufmann, *Leopold Kaufmann, Oberbürgermeister von Bonn (1821–1898). Ein Zeit- und Lebensbild* (Cologne, 1903), 177–91; Goyau, *Bismarck et l'Eglise* 2:285–87; Heinrich Brück, *Geschichte der katholischen Kirche in Deutschland im 19. Jahrhundert*, 4 vols. (Mainz, 1901), 4:373; and Julius Bachem, *Die Parität in Preußen* (Cologne, 1897), 9.

55. Kaufmann, *Leopold Kaufmann*, 187.

56. Robert Bosse, "Erinnerungen," in *Die Grenzboten* 2 (1904): 404; Erich Foerster, *Adalbert Falk. Sein Leben und Wirken als Preußischer Kultusminister* (Gotha, 1927), 94–95; Otto Pfülf, *Der Wirkliche Geh. Ober-Regierungsrat Josef Linhoff, der letzte Veteran der "Katholischen Abteilung"* (Freiburg im Breisgau, 1901), 59–61.

57. Bosse, "Erinnerungen," 31; Foerster, *Adalbert Falk*, 95–96.

58. Dietrich Wegmann, *Die leitenden staatlichen Verwaltungsbeamten der Provinz Westfalen 1815–1918* (Münster in Westfalen, 1969), 186.

59. Staatsministerium to Wilhelm I, Dec. 1875; GStAPrKB (Merseburg), *Nachlaß* Falk, Rep. 92, No. 12c, Bl. 25–25v. Abschrift.

60. Clipping from *Norddeutsche Allgemeine Zeitung*, Jul. 22, 1874; HStAD, Reg. Düssseldorf 287, Bl. 203.

61. Sperber, *Popular Catholicism*, 211.

62. Ibid., 212.

63. Blackbourn, *Marpingen*, 30.

64. Königliche Regierung, Abtheilung des Innern [in Cassel] to Eulenburg, Sept. 29, 1874; GStAPrKB (Merseburg), Preussisches Kultusministerium, Rep. 76IV, Sekt. 12, Abt. XII, No. 4, Bd. I.

65. Wegmann, *Verwaltungsbeamten*, 184.

66. Quoted in Blackbourn, *Marpingen*, 232.

67. Quoted in ibid.

68. William N. Medlicott, *Bismarck and Modern Germany* (London, 1965), 112; Winfred Taffs, *Ambassador to Bismarck: Lord Odo Russell, First Baron Ampthill* (London, 1938), 14.

69. *SBVLHA*, Jan. 17, 1873, 1:631.

70. See, for example, Dagmar Herzog, *Intimacy and Exclusion: Religious Politics in Pre-Revolutionary Baden* (Princeton, NJ, 1996).

71. See Marjorie Lamberti, "State, Church, and the Politics of School Reform during the Kulturkampf," *Central European History* 19, 1 (Mar. 1986): 63–81, esp. 80.

72. Clipping from *Magdeburgische Zeitung*, no. 151, n.d. (c. Mar. 1874); GStAPrKB (Merseburg), Rep. 77, Tit. 413, No. 35, Bd. 4, Bl. 31; Ross, "The *Kulturkampf*," 683–84. Regarding Catholics as fanatics and extremists undoubtedly helped to erode the liberals' moral and legal inhibitions against the use of harsh and ruthless measures.

73. See Blackbourn, "Progress and Piety," 143–67.

74. Blackbourn, *Marpingen*, 264–65.

75. Smith, *German Nationalism and Religious Conflict*, 29–30.

76. Ibid., 29.

77. Stanley Zucker, *Ludwig Bamberger: German Liberal Politician and Social Critic, 1823–1899* (Pittsburgh, PA, 1975), 93–95.

78. Blackbourn, *Marpingen*, 266.

79. See Francis A. Arlinghaus, "British Public Opinion and the Kulturkampf in Germany, 1871–75," *The Catholic Historical Review* 34, 4 (Jan. 1949): 385–413. These scruples, however, were not always in evidence. Soon after the May Laws were introduced in 1873, Benjamin Jowett, Master of

Balliol College, wished Bismarck every success in his campaign against the Roman Church. Benjamin Jowett to Sir Robert Morier, July 21, 1873; Jowett Papers, Balliol College, Oxford. For this information I am grateful to Prof. Jacob P. Ellens, letter of Dec. 6, 1995.

80. Quoted in Walter Reichle, *Zwischen Staat und Kirche. Das Leben und Wirken des preußischen Kultusministers Heinrich v. Mühler* (Berlin, 1938), 467–68. A recent account makes much the same point. The Reformation of the sixteenth century and the ensuing religious wars created not a united Protestant Germany but a deeply divided German Reich. Even with national unification after 1870–71 Germany's "confessional division meant that a cultural rift ran straight through the empire" with "the historical consciousness of" both Catholics and Protestants "burdened by enduring memories of mutual intolerance." See Smith, *German Nationalism and Religious Conflict*, 10.

81. Bornkamm, "Die Staatsidee im Kulturkampf," 61.

82. Willibald Beyschlag, *Aus meinem Leben*, 2 vols. (Halle, 1896–99), 2: 359–60.

83. Quoted in Gordon A. Craig, *Germany, 1866–1945* (New York, 1978), 75; see also *Geist und Gesellschaft der Bismarckzeit 1870–1890*, ed. Karl Heinrich Hoefele (Göttingen, 1967), 382.

84. Quoted in Reichle, *Zwischen Staat und Kirche*, 462.

85. Ellen Lovell Evans, *The German Center Party, 1870–1933: A Study in Political Catholicism* (Carbondale, IL, 1981), 68; Karl Kuppisch, *Die deutschen Landeskirchen im 19. und 20. Jahrhundert* (Göttingen, 1966), 77. See also Reichle, *Zwischen Staat und Kirche*, 494, 494 n. 27.

86. Gottfried Kögel, *Rudolf Kögel. Sein Werden und Wirken*, 3 vols. (Berlin, 1901–4), 3 : 111. Quoted in Evans, *Center Party*, 68.

87. See Ross, *Failure of Bismarck's Kulturkampf*, chaps. 7 and 8.

88. Sperber, *Popular Catholicism*, 230; Ross, "The *Kulturkampf*," 684.

89. Court transcript, Mar. 8, 1876; Staatsarchiv Münster, Oberpräsidium No. 2133, 38 [*Abschrift*]; Königliche Regierung, Abtheilung des Innern [in Münster] to Eulenburg, Mar. 2, 1874; GStAPrKB (Merseburg), Rep. 77, Tit. 413, No. 35, Bd. 3, Bl. 165–66; Thümmel to Leonhardt, Mar. 1, 1874; GStAPrKB (Merseburg), Rep. 77, Tit. 413, No. 35, Bd. 4, Bl. 95; Ross, "The *Kulturkampf*," 684.

90. Clipping from *Magdeburgische Zeitung*, no. 151, n.d. (c. Mar. 1874); GStAPrKB (Merseburg), Rep. 77, Tit. 413, No. 35, Bd. 4, Bl. 31; Ross, "The *Kulturkampf*," 684–85.

91. Anderson, *Windthorst*, 175; Lech Trzeciakowski, "The Prussian State and the Catholic Church in Prussian Poland, 1871–1915," *Slavic Review* 26, 4 (1967): 625; Ross, "The *Kulturkampf*," 685.

92. Ross, "The *Kulturkampf*," 685.

93. Clipping from *Elberfelder Zeitung*, no. 116, n.d. in Acta betreffend Begräbnisse von Altkatholiken und dabei verübte Excesse; HStAD, Regierung Düsseldorf 132, Bl. 1.

94. Foerster, *Adalbert Falk*, 282.

95. Johanna von Bismarck to Herbert von Bismarck, Jan. 16, 1875; FBA, *Nachlaß* Bismarck, Best. C, Box 6, Frame 0964.

96. For details, see H. Wiermann [Hermann Robolsky], *Geschichte des Kulturkampfes. Ursprung, Verlauf und heutiger Stand* (Leipzig, 1885), 128.

97. Ross, "The *Kulturkampf*," 685.

98. Blackbourn, *Marpingen*, xxxiv.

99. See, for example, Anderson, *Windthorst*, 402.

100. Ibid.

101. See Ronald J. Ross, "Critic of the Bismarckian Constitution: Ludwig Windthorst and the Relationship between Church and State in Imperial Germany," *Journal of Church and State* 21, 3 (Autumn 1979): 483–506.

102. Ibid. For a competing opinion, see chapter 7 in this volume.

103. For details, see Ernst Heinen, "Antisemitische Strömungen im politischen Katholizismus während des Kulturkampfes," in *Geschichte in der Gegenwart. Festschrift für Kurt Kluxen*, Ernst Heinen and Hans Julius Schoeps, eds. (Paderborn, 1972), 259–99; and Rudolf Lill, "Die deutschen Katholiken und die Juden in der Zeit von 1850 bis zur Machtübernahme Hitlers," in *Kirche und Synagoge. Handbuch zur Geschichte von Christen und Juden*, Karl Heinrich Rengstorf and Siegfried von Kortzfleisch, eds., 2 vols. (Stuttgart, 1968–72), 2:377–94. The view that Catholic anti-Semitism was chiefly a response to the Kulturkampf and a means to attract Protestant conservative support against Bismarck and the liberals has been subjected to close scrutiny in Helmut Walser Smith, "Religion and Conflict: Protestants, Catholics, and Anti-Semitism in the State of Baden in the Era of Wilhelm II," *Central European History* 27, 3 (1994): 283–314; and Helmut Walser Smith, "The Learned and the Popular Discourse of Anti-Semitism in the Catholic Milieu of the Kaiserreich," *Central European History* 27, 3 (1994): 315–28.

104. The nature and character of this dispute is described in Foerster, *Adalbert Falk*, 114–21; Erwin Gatz, "Bischof Philippus Krementz und die Rezeption des I. Vatikanischen Konzils im Bistum Ermland," *Annuarium Historiae Conciliorum* 4 (1972): 149–58; and Bernard Maria Rosenberg et al., "Aus der Geschichte des Gymnasiums zu Braunsberg," *Zeitschrift für Geschichte und Altertumskunde des Ermlandes (Braunsberg)* 30 (1966): 576 80.

105. Excommunication decree from Philippus Krementz against Paul Wollmann, July 4, 1871; GSAPrKB (Berlin), Preussisches Justizministerium, Rep. 84a, No. 10831, Bd. 2, Bl. 4 (p. 1); Pastoral letter from Krementz to members of Ermland diocese, July 22, 1871, ibid., Bl. 4v–11 (pp. 2–15); and Foerster, *Adalbert Falk*, 115.

106. For the discussion of this legal issue, see Heinrich von Mühler to Staatsministerium, Dec. 20, 1871, in *Die Vorgeschichte des Kulturkampfes. Quellenveröffentlichungen aus dem Deutschen Zentralarchiv*, ed. Adelheid Constabel ([East] Berlin, 1956), no. 126, 160–63.

107. Sperber, *Popular Catholicism*, 244.

108. Ibid.

109. Ibid.

110. By 1870 German liberalism had acquired a genuinely patriotic imperative and even messianic image of its own and Germany's mission in the world. This mission was cultural, idealistic, self-righteous, and moral. This ideology, moreover, proceeded in a haze of rhetoric and self-congratulation toward frankly repressive policies. For a typical example, see [Ferdinand Gregorovius], *The Roman Journals of Ferdinand Gregorovius, 1852–1874*, ed. Friedrich Althaus, trans. Mrs. Gustavus W. Hamilton (London, 1907), entry of Aug. 15, 1870, 375.

111. Ross, "Enforcing the Kulturkampf," 460.

112. See Ross, *Failure of Bismarck's Kulturkampf*, chaps. 2 and 9.

113. Fritz Nova, "The Motivations in Bismarck's Kulturkampf," *Duquesne Review* 10 (Spring 1965): 23.

114. Craig, *Germany*, 71.

115. Ibid.

116. Heinrich von Treitschke, "Die Maigesetze und ihre Folgen," in *Zehn Jahre Deutscher Kämpfe. Schriften zur Tagespolitik*, 3d ed. (Berlin, 1897), 90–92. Emphasis in English in original.

117. Bornkamm, "Die Staatsidee im Kulturkampf," 276–83.

118. Karl Buchheim, *Ultramontanismus und Demokratie. Der Weg der deutschen Katholiken im 19. Jahrhundert* (Munich, 1963), 284.

119. Bornkamm, "Die Staatsidee im Kulturkampf," 45–46.

120. Blackbourn, *Marpingen*, 86.

121. Ross, "Enforcing the Kulturkampf," 477.

122. Calculations based on figures provided in K. Bachem, *Zentrumspartei* 3:308–9.

123. Siegfried von Kardorff, *Bismarck im Kampf um sein Werk* (Berlin, 1943), 59; Ficker, *Der Kulturkampf in Münster*, 369; Fr. Dittrich, *Der Kulturkampf im Ermlande* (Berlin, 1913), 218; Kißling, *Geschichte des Kulturkampfes* 3:112–15; Julius Falter, *Der preußische Kulturkampf von 1873 bis 1880 mit besonderer Berücksichtigung der Diözese Paderborn* (Paderborn, 1909), 127, 135–36; and Dettmer, *Verwaltungsbehörden*, 115.

124. For the former see Lothar Gall, "Die partei- und sozialgeschichtliche Problematik des badischen Kulturkampfs," in Alfons Schäfer, ed., *Oberrheinische Studien. Neue Forschungen zu Grundproblemen der badischen Geschichte im 19. und 20. Jahrhundert* 2 (Bretten, 1973): 93–132; for the latter, Winfried Becker, "Der Kulturkampf als Europäisches und als Deutscher Phänomen," *Historisches Jahrbuch* 101, 2 (1981): 422–46.

125. John McManners, *Church and State in France, 1870–1914* (London, 1972), 51.

126. Michael A. Gordon, *The Orange Riots: Irish Political Violence in New York City, 1870–1871* (Ithaca, NY, 1993), 139.

127. I have found no reports at all of Catholics who lost their lives as a direct consequence of Kulturkampf repression. If there had been loss of life, there is every likelihood that Catholic publicists would have broadcast the charge to denigrate their oppressors. Any assessment of the Kulturkampf's

harshness, of course, must also take into account the obvious fact that the experience of imprisonment—or even the prospect of confinement—indirectly led to the death of at least two of Prussia's bishops. For details, see Ross, "The *Kulturkampf*," 675 n. 25.

128. For the description of injuries sustained in the Marpingen dispute, see Blackbourn, *Marpingen*, 205. "No soldiers were reported injured," he writes, "against more than sixty victims of blows received from rifle-butts or (in a few cases) of cuts from bayonets."

129. For the discussion of these issues, see Ross, *Failure of Bismarck's Kulturkampf*, chap. 9.

CHAPTER 7

For their valuable comments, I wish to thank all the participants in the conferences that led to this volume, and particularly Stephen Tonsor; I am also indebted to Thomas Kselman for wise and helpful criticisms on an earlier draft of this essay.

1. On the importance (and intellectual seriousness) of that tradition and the efforts to break away from it, Hans Maier, *Revolution and Church: The Early History of Christian Democracy, 1789–1901* (South Bend, IN, 1969).

2. Chapter 3 in this volume, which includes a discussion of traditional Christian conceptions of liberty, is helpful here.

3. Kenneth Scott Latourette, *Christianity in a Revolutionary Age* 1, *The Nineteenth Century in Europe: Background and the Roman Catholic Phase* (New York, 1958), remains a useful encyclopedic account.

4. Austin Gough, *Paris and Rome: The Gallican Church and the Ultramontane Campaign, 1848–1853* (Oxford, 1986).

5. A process that began from necessity as a result of the effects of the French Revolution; see Susanne Desan, *Reclaiming the Sacred: Lay Religion and Popular Politics in Revolutionary France* (Ithaca, NY, 1990), 219–25. Often viewed with concern by the hierarchy, it nevertheless continued through devotional associations, mutual aid societies, and recreational activities to blossom in Catholic Action and Catholic subcultures late in the century.

6. Alexis de Tocqueville, *Democracy in America*, Phillips Bradley, ed. (New York, 1959), 1:311.

7. Measures to remove the remaining restrictions on the Church, priests, and Catholic orders continued to be needed from 1829 to the 1880s, with the last passed in 1926; Walter J. Arnstein, *Protestant Versus Catholic: Mr. Newdegate and the Nuns* (Columbia, MO, 1982), 217–19. Looking primarily at Ireland, Fergus O'Ferrall, *Catholic Emancipation: Daniel O'Connell and the Birth of the Irish Democracy, 1820–30* (Dublin, 1985), 273, considers the measures of 1829–30 as having "inaugurated the liberal democratic era."

8. Ventura, a well-known liberal theologian who had suffered great disfavor during the papacy of Gregory XVI, became a prominent figure under

Pius IX and subsequently preacher to Napoleon III. See Sheridan Gilley, "The Catholic Church and Revolution," in D. G. Boyce, ed., *The Revolution in Ireland, 1879–1923* (London, 1988), 157–88.

9. See the correspondence in *Tre liberali e un Papa: Giuseppe Pasolini, Luigi Carlo Farini, Marcho Minghetti nelle memorie di Giuseppe Pasolini, raccolte da suo figlio* (Bologna, 1991).

10. A collection of the bishops' letters and statements from this period is in the Paris Archives Nationales, F⁹ 5604. See also Paul Christophe, *Les choix des clergés dans les révolutions de 1789, 1830 et 1848* (Lille, 1976), 143–76.

11. Alan J. Reinerman, *Austria and the Papacy in the Age of Metternich* 2 (Washington, DC, 1989): 257–58.

12. Renato Mori, *Il Tramonto del Potere Temporale, 1866–1870* (Rome, 1967), 540.

13. M. Baudry d'Asson, Oct. 22, 1904, *Annales de la Chambre des Deputés, Débats parlementaires, 1904* (Paris, 1905), 80.

14. Robert Aubert, *Le pontificat de Pie IX (1846–1878)* (Paris, 1962?), 224–62.

15. And they remained clearer even at the end of the century on what Christian liberty was not, for example the freedom to choose what to believe or whether to worship (*Libertas Praestantissimus*, 1890).

16. A modern awareness of the importance of public opinion thus stimulated Rome's extraordinary narrowing of acceptable theological discussion, silencing many of those most interested in exploring the religious values inherent in political freedom and allowing the threat of condemnation to pervade the internal life of the clergy and greatly increase the role of the Holy Office. See Gerald McCool, *Catholic Theology in the Nineteenth Century: The Quest for a Unitary Method* (New York, 1977), 132–33.

17. Frances Lannon, *Privilege, Persecution, and Prophecy: The Catholic Church in Spain, 1875–1975* (Oxford, 1987), 126–29 and passim; a more sympathetic case can be made for such attitudes in the previous decade, Vincente Carcel Orti, *Iglesia y revolución en España, 1864–1874* (Pamplona, 1979).

18. Robert E. Sullivan, "Modernizing Tradition: Some Catholic Scholastics and the Genealogy of Natural Rights," in Tony Siebers, ed., *Religion and the Authority of the Past* (Ann Arbor, MI, 1993), 188–90.

19. Pierre Pierrard, *Du prêtre français au XIXᵉ siècle* (Paris, 1986), 216–18.

20. Jean-Marie Donegani, *La Liberté de choisir: pluralisme religieux et pluralisme politique dans le catholicisme français contemporain* (Paris, 1993), 469. Of course, it is much easier to speak of a Catholic politics in a non-Catholic country; see Dermont Quinn, *Patronage and Piety: The Politics of English Roman Catholicism, 1850–1900* (Stanford, 1993).

21. See Michela Nacci, "La civiltà non cattolica: Una certa immagine dell'America," *Il Mulino* 340 (Mar.-Apr. 1992): 192–203.

22. "The Church in the Modern World," published in *The Rambler*, Jan.

1860, reprinted in J. Rufus Fears, ed., *Selected Writings of Lord Acton* 3, *Essays in Religion, Politics, and Morality* (Indianapolis, 1985), 613.

23. Secession appealed to Acton more than slavery worried him; he wrote Robert E. Lee in November 1866, "I saw in State Rights the only available check upon the absolutism of the sovereign will, and secession filled me with hope," George Watson, *Lord Acton's History of Liberty* (Cambridge, 1994), 46. On how little Christianity had to say on politics, see Acton's note cited in ibid., 74. Hugh A. MacDougall considers the tension between Acton's Catholicism and his liberalism to have led to his intellectual stalemate; MacDougall, *The Acton Newman Relations: The Dilemma of Christian Liberalism* (New York, 1962), 184–85.

24. Sullivan, "Modernizing Tradition," 200.

25. Thomas J. Johnston, John L. Robinson, and Robert Wyse Jackson, *The History of the Church of Ireland* (Dublin, 1953), 243.

26. And much more fully described in chapters 8 and 9 in this volume.

27. The denunciation of the *Sillon*, like the failure of the *Jeune Ligue de la République*, had international repercussions in Catholic circles.

28. Edward Berenson, *Populist Religion and Left-Wing Politics in France, 1830–1985* (Princeton, NJ, 1984), esp. 36–73, 97–126.

29. Thomas Nipperdey, *Religion im Umbruch: Deutschland, 1870–1918* (Munich, 1988), 124–53; Jean-Baptiste Duroselle, *L'Action sociale des catholiques en France* (Paris, 1951).

30. For a recent summary see Paul Misner, *Social Catholicism in Europe from the Onset of Industrialization to the First World War* (New York, 1991).

31. Although there were comparable examples in most Catholic countries, none was relatively more impressive than the response in poverty-stricken Ireland, preoccupied with its own political issues. Emmet Larkin, *The Consolidation of the Roman Catholic Church in Ireland, 1860–1870* (Chapel Hill, NC, 1987), xvi.

32. The subject of chapter 6 in this volume.

33. Margaret Lavinia Anderson, "Piety and Politics: Recent Work on German Catholicism," *JMH* 63, 4 (Dec. 1991): 692.

34. William J. Callahan, *Church, Politics, and Society in Spain, 1750–1874* (Cambridge, MA, 1984), 174–75.

35. Emmet Larkin, *The Historical Dimensions of Irish Catholicism* (Washington, DC, 1984), 10–11.

36. Philippe Levillain, *Albert de Mun: Catholicisme français et Catholicisme romain du syllabus au raillement* (Paris, 1983), 1005–7.

37. Caroline Ford, "Religion and Popular Culture in Modern Europe," *JMH* 65, 1 (Mar. 1993): 152–75; David Blackbourn, *Marpingen: Apparitions of the Virgin Mary in Nineteenth-Century Germany* (New York, 1994); William Christian, *Moving Crucifixes in Modern Spain* (Princeton, NJ, 1992); James Donnelly, "The Marian Shrine of Knock: The First Decade," *Eire-Ireland* 28 (1993): 55–99; Thomas A. Kselman, *Miracles & Prophecies in Nineteenth-Century France* (New Brunswick, NJ, 1983); Jonathan Sperber, *Popular Catholicism in Nineteenth-Century Germany* (Princeton, NJ, 1984);

Mary Lee Nolan and Sidney Nolan, *Christian Pilgrimage in Modern Western Europe* (Chapel Hill, NC, 1989).

38. Margaret Lavinia Anderson, "Interdenominationalism, Clericalism, Pluralism: *Zentrumsstreit* and the Dilemma of Catholicism in Wilhelmine Germany," *Central European History* 21 (1938): 350-78.

39. Pierre Pierrard, *Histoire des curés de campagne de 1789 à nos jours* (Paris, 1986), 205-35.

40. Raymond Grew, "Catholicism in a Changing Italy," in Edward R. Tannenbaum and Emiliana P. Noether, eds., *Modern Italy: A Topical History Since 1861* (New York, 1974), 254-73.

41. Callahan, *Church, Politics, and Society in Spain*, 199.

42. Gilley, "The Catholic Church and Revolution," 163-69. Christine Alix, *Le Saint-Siège et les nationalismes en Europe, 1870-1960* (Paris, 1962) is, surprisingly, one of the few comparative treatments.

43. Larkin, *Irish Catholicism*, 101-2.

44. Dagmar Herzog, "Anticlericalism and the Formation of German Liberal Thought," unpubl. paper, cited with permission; a related argument is made in Ralph Gibson, *A Social History of French Catholicism, 1789-1914* (New York, 1989). The classic statement of this concern is Jules Michelet, *Le Prêtre, la femme, et la famille* (Paris, 1845, and frequently republished through the century).

45. On the similar attitude of Spanish anticlericals, Callahan, *Church, Politics, and Society in Spain*, 256; Crispi took that position in Italy.

46. In France's Fifth Republic it has been the Church that keeps citing the separation of Church and state; Donegani, *La Liberté de choisir*, 45-76.

47. Lannon, *Privilege, Persecution, and Prophecy*, 120, notes that the dictatorships of Primo de Rivera and Francisco Franco, "met with a general approval denied the republic of 1931-36 and never fully accorded the constitutional monarchy of 1876-1923." The Spanish Church, he adds, "found it hard to come to terms with parliamentary democracy and pluralism."

48. See Larkin, *Consolidation of the Church in Ireland*, 275-340; Alexander Sedgwick, *The Raillement in French Politics, 1890-1898* (Cambridge, MA, 1965), 102-17.

49. Larkin, *Irish Catholicism*, 1-5. On the Church's determination to engage in Irish politics, see David W. Miller, *Church, State, and Nation in Ireland, 1898-1921* (Pittsburgh, PA, 1973), 44-112.

50. Klaus Epstein, *Matthias Erzberger and the Dilemma of German Democracy* (Princeton, NJ, 1957).

51. John W. Boyer, "Catholic Priests in Lower Austria: Anti-Liberalism, Occupational Anxiety, and Radical Political Action in Late Nineteenth-Century Vienna," *Proceedings of the American Philosophical Society* 118, 4 (Aug. 1974): 337-69.

52. The new criticism stimulated frightened intolerance among Protestants, too; see chapter 4 in this volume.

53. Alcide de Gasperi, "Intorno all'Enciclica 'Pascendi'," *Il Trentino,*

Sept. 19, 1907, repr. in *I Cattolici trentini sotto l'Austria* 1, 1902–1908 (Rome, 1964), 255.

54. Paul Roulers, *Politique sociale et christianisme* (Paris, 1968).

55. Lester R. Kurtz, *The Politics of Heresy: The Modernist Crisis in Roman Catholicism* (Berkeley, 1986), 24, 46–47, 81–89, 153–63, 168.

56. Emile Poulat, *Catholicisme, démocratie et socialisme* (Paris, 1977) and *Histoire, dogme et critique dans le crise moderniste* (Paris, 1962).

57. *El Kulturkampf Internacional por Cardinal Sancha* (Toledo, 1901) provides a striking example.

58. Geoffrey Cubitt, *The Jesuit Myth: Conspiracy Theory and Politics in Nineteenth-Century France* (Oxford, 1993).

59. The great cause-célèbre illustrating conflicting conceptions of what that meant was the Mortara case of 1858. In the Romagna in the papal states a young Jewish boy who was thought to be dying was secretly taken to be baptized by the family's Catholic servant. He lived however; and when his baptism became known, the authorities took him to Rome to be raised as a Catholic. He became a priest.

60. The distinguished Catholic historian René Rémond recently so characterized the tension at a Catholic conference, cited in Gilley, "The Catholic Church and Revolution," 271–72.

CHAPTER 8

1. The story of the struggle between *les deux France* emerged during the debates in and around the Estates General and the National Assembly in 1789, and in the first polemical accounts of the French Revolution. It has continued to the present day, told in the churches, the press, the schools, the legislature, the political groups, and the history books. I mention as illustrations just a few books leading up to the bicentennial in 1989: Anne-Marie Maudite and Jean Maudite, *La France contra la France: La séparation de l'église et de l'état, 1902–1906* (Paris, 1984); Émile Poulat, *Liberté, Laïcité: la guerre des deux France et le principe de la modernité* (Paris, 1988); Pierre Pierrard, *L'église et la révolution, 1789–1889* (Paris, 1988); Michel Vovelle, *La révolution contre l'église: de la raison a l'être suprême* (Paris, 1988). See Robert Gildea, *The Past in French History* (New Haven, CT, 1994); Steven Laurence Kaplan, *Farewell, Revolution: Disputed Legacies, France, 1789–1989* (Ithaca, NY, 1995); and id., *Farewell, Revolution: Historians' Feud* (Ithaca, NY, 1995).

2. Pamela H. Pilbeam, *Republicanism in Nineteenth Century France, 1814–1871* (London, 1995).

3. Gérard Cholvy, *La religion en France de la fin du XVIIIe à nos jours* (Paris, 1991); Adrien Dansette, *Religious History of Modern France*, trans. John Dingle, 2 vols. (New York, 1961).

4. *La France ecclésiastique pour l'année 1787* (Paris, 1786); *The Statesman's Yearbook, 1869* (London, 1869), 90.

5. *La France ecclésiastique: almanach-annuaire du clergé pour l'an de grace 1900* (Paris, 1900); *The Statesman's Yearbook, 1928*, 860; David Barrett, *World Christian Encyclopedia* (New York, 1982), 295.

6. Timothy Tackett, *Religion, Revolution, and Regional Culture in Eighteenth Century France: the Ecclesiastical Oath of 1791* (Princeton, NJ, 1986).

7. Gérard Dagon, *Petites églises de France* (Annéville, France, 1971); id., *Petites églises et grandes sectes* (Paris, 1951, 1963); I. D. de la Thibauderie, *Églises et évêques catholiques non romains* (Paris, 1962); Dansette, *Religious History* 1:129-32; Barrett, *Enclyclopedia*, 300-301.

8. The progress of the Roman Catholic revival is displayed in the succession of Catholic almanacks and yearbooks that appeared over the century, most notably *Almanach ecclésiastique de France; Almanach du clergé de France;* and *La France ecclésiastique, Almanach du clergé.*

9. Claude Langlois, *Le Catholicisme au féminin: les congrégations françaises à supérieure générale au XIXe siècle* (Paris, 1984); O. Arnold, *Le corps et l'âme: la vie religieuse au XIXe siècle* (Paris, 1984); Ralph Gibson, *A Social History of French Catholicism* (London, 1989).

10. J. Devlin, *The Superstitious Mind: French Peasants and the Supernatural in the Nineteenth Century* (New Haven, CT, 1987); T. A. Kselman, *Miracles and Prophecies in Nineteenth Century France* (New Brunswick, NJ, 1983); Gibson, *Social History*, passim; C. T. McIntire, *England against the Papacy, 1858-1861* (Cambridge, 1983).

11. Edward Berenson, *Populist Religion and Left-Wing Politics in France, 1830-1852* (Princeton, NJ, 1984); Michael Fogarty, *Christian Democracy in Western Europe, 1820-1953* (Notre Dame, IN, 1957).

12. Michel Darbon, *Le conflit entre la droite et la gauche dans le Catholicisme français, 1830-1953* (Toulouse, 1953); René Raymond, *La droite en France de 1815 à nos jours* (Paris, 1954).

13. Armand Lods, "Population Protestante," in Edmond Davaine, *Annuaire du Protestantisme français* (Paris, 1893), 149-51; *Statesman's Yearbook for 1928* (London, 1928); Th. De Prat, *Annuaire Protestant 1865-67* (Paris, 1865); Burdette C. Poland, *Protestantism and the French Revolution* (Princeton, NJ, 1957), 283-86; Samuel Mours and Daniel Robert, *Le protestantisme en France de la XVIIIème siècle à nos jours, 1685-1970* (Paris, 1972), 428.

14. See the yearbooks throughout the century: *Nouvel annuaire Protestant; Annuaire Protestant; Tablettes historiques du Protestantisme français; Annuaire du Protestantisme français.* See also André Encrevé, *Protestants français au milieu du XIXe siècle: les Reformées de 1848 à 1870* (Geneva, 1986).

15. See the annual yearbooks; A. Jundt, *Histoire résumée de l'église Luthérienne de France* (Paris, 1935); Marcel Scheidhauer, *Les Églises Luthérienne en France, 1800-1815: Alsace-Montbéliard-Paris* (Strasbourg, 1975); Mours and Robert, *Le protestantisme en France.*

16. The Protestant yearbooks attempted to include all Protestants in their compilations. Barrett, *Encyclopedia*, 295, 300-301; André Encrevé, *Les Pro-*

testants en France de 1800 à nos jours: histoire d'une réintégration (Paris, 1985).

17. See the series of the *Annuaire israélite*; Erwin Schnurmann, *La population juive en Alsace* (Paris, 1936), 6–8; Roger Berg, *Histoire du rabbinat français: XVIe–XXe siècle* (Paris, 1992); Patrick Girard, *Les Juifs de France* (Paris, 1983); Jay R. Berkowitz, *The Shaping of the Jewish Identity in Nineteenth Century France* (Detroit, 1989).

18. *Gouvernement Général Civil de l'Algérie, État de l'Algérie au 31 décembre 1882 publié d'après les documents officiels* (Alger, 1883); Barrett, *Encyclopedia*, 295. Charles-Robert Ageron, *Les Algériens musulmans et la France, 1871–1919*, 2 vols. (Paris, 1968); Victor Piquet, *L'Algérie française: un siècle de colonisation, 1830–1930* (Paris, 1930), 240–49; Jocelyne Cesari, *Être musulman en France: associations, militants, et mosquées* (Paris, 1994); Édouard Petit, *Organisation des colonies françaises et des pays de protectorat*, 2 vols. (Paris, 1894–95).

19. Phyllis Stock-Morton, *Moral Education for a Secular Society: the Development of Morale Laïque in Nineteenth Century France* (Albany, NY, 1988); Michel Vovelle, *Religion et révolution: la déchristianisation de l'an II* (Paris, 1976); Barrett, *Encyclopedia*, 295.

20. Edict of Nov. 19, 1787, in *Receuil général des anciennes lois françaises depuis l'an 420 jusqu'à la Révolution de 1789*, 29 vols. (Paris, 1822–33), 28:472–82.

21. Gallican Articles, Mar. 19, 1682, in Debidour, *1789–1870*, 651–52; Geoffrey Adams, *The Huguenots and French Opinion, 1685–1787: the Enlightenment Debate on Toleration* (Waterloo, ON, 1991); Poland, *Protestantism*, 71–82.

22. Catherine Bergeal, *Protestantisme et tolerance en France au XVIIIe siècle: de la revocation à la révolution, 1685–1789* (Carrières-sous-Poissy, 1988); Poland, *Protestantism*, 20–26.

23. See Jean Marie Dargaud, *Histoire de la liberté religieuse en France et de ses fondateurs*, 5 vols. (Paris, 1859), 1:i–ii.

24. See, for example, the commemorative calendar in *Nouvel Annuaire Protestant 1821* (Paris, 1821).

25. Poland, *Protestantism*, 158.

26. Decrees of Jan. 28, 1790, and Sept. 28, 1791, in Achille Edmond Halphen, *Recueil des lois, décrets, ordonnances, avis du Conseil d'état, arrêtes et réglements concernant les Israelites, depuis la révolution de 1789* (Paris, 1851), 1–2, 9–10; and Patrick Girard, *Les juifs de France de 1789 à 1860* (Paris, 1976), 275–76.

27. Declaration of Aug. 28, 1789, in Zaccaria Giacometti, *Quellen zur Geschichte der Trennung von Staat und Kirche* (Tübingen, 1926; repr. ed., Aalen, 1974), 1–2; Dale Van Kley, ed., *The French Idea of Freedom: the Old Regime and the Declaration of Rights of 1789* (Stanford, 1994).

28. Poland, *Protestantism*, 153–58; Jean Bauberot, "Liberté religieuse et Laïcité," in *Les catholiques français et l'héritage de 1789* (Paris, 1990), 94–98.

29. Texts in Giacometti, *Geschichte*, 3–14; and Debidour, *1789–1870*, 652–63.

30. Civil Constitution of the Clergy, July 12/Aug. 24, 1790, in Giacometti, *Geschichte*, 3–12.

31. Decree of Nov. 27/Dec. 26, 1790, in ibid., 12–14.

32. Tackett, *Religion*, 40–44.

33. Constitution of Sept. 3, 1791, in Giacometti, *Geschichte*, 14.

34. Texts in Laura Governatori Renzoni, *La separazione tra stato e chiese in Francia e la tutela degli interessi religiosi* (Milan, 1977), 12–13; and Giacometti, *Geschichte*, 14–24.

35. Michel Vovelle, *Religion et révolution: la déchristianization de l'an II* (Paris, 1976); id., *La révolution contre l'église*, passim.

36. Decree of Dec. 19, 1793, and law of Nov. 17, 1794, in Charles Fourrier, *L'enseignement français de 1789 à 1945* (Paris, 1965), 48–52.

37. Marquis de Condorcet, *Écrits sur l'instruction publique*, 2 vols. (Paris, 1989); Fourrier, *L'enseignement*, 24–26.

38. Decrees of Feb. 21, May 30, Sept. 29, 1795, and Constitutional Act of Aug. 22, 1795, in Giacometti, *Geschichte*, 24–31.

39. Law of Oct. 25, 1795, in Fourrier, *L'enseignement*, 52–55.

40. Poland, *Protestantism*, 260–63.

41. Law of Apr. 8, 1802/18 germinal an X, containing the Concordat/Convention and the Organic Articles, in Giacometti, *Geschichte*, 31–39; Renzoni, *La separazione*, 16–23.

42. Law of May 10, 1806, and decree of Mar. 17, 1808, in Fourrier, *L'enseignement*, 92–100; Maurice Gontard, *L'enseignement primaire en France de la Révolution à la loi Guizot, 1789–1833* (Paris, 1959), 212–64.

43. Protestant Organic Articles of 1802, in Giacometti, *Geschichte*, 39–43; Armand Lods, *Étude sur les origines des articles organiques des cultes protestants d'après des documents inédits* (Paris, 1895); Poland, *Protestantism*, 264–72.

44. Three decrees of Mar. 17, 1808, in Girard, *Juifs 1789–1860*, 277–84; Poujol, *Quelques observations concernant les Juifs en général et plus particulièrement ceux d'Alsace* (Paris, 1806); Phyllis Cohen Albert, *The Modernization of French Jewry: Consistory and Community in the Nineteenth Century* (Hanover, NH, 1977), 56–60.

45. Law of Feb. 8, 1831, in Giacometti, *Geschichte*, 66.

46. Poland, *Protestantism*, 263.

47. Penal Code of 1810, in Giacometti, *Geschichte*, 61–63.

48. Jean-Michel Leniaud, *L'administration des cultes pendant la périod concordataire* (Paris, 1988); "Ministère et Administration des cultes, liste des lois, décrets, ordonnances et réglements organiques," in *La France ecclésiastique 1900* (Paris, 1900), 848–64.

49. Law of Apr. 10, 1834, in Giacometti, *Geschichte*, 70–71.

50. "Notice historique sur le Baptisme en France et statistique des Églises Baptistes," in A. Racine-Braud, *Tablettes historiques du Protestantisme français* (Paris, 1872), 92–104.

51. Decree of Mar. 19, 1859, in Giacometti, *Geschichte*, 233–34.

52. Articles 4, 32, and 52 of the Organic Articles of the Catholic Religion, and article 2 of the Organic Articles of the Protestant Religions, in ibid., 34, 37–39.

53. Ministère de l'instruction publique et des beaux-arts, *Statistique comparée de l'enseignement primaire, 1829–1877* (Paris, 1880), 371–72; Ageron, *Algériens* 1:292–96.

54. Ageron, *Algériens* 1:296–97; Piquet, *L'Algérie française*, 241–42.

55. Constitutional Charter of 1830, in Giacometti, *Geschichte*, 65.

56. Maurice Gontard, *L'enseignement primaire en France de la Révolution à la loi Guizot, 1789–1833* (Paris, 1959), 451–62.

57. Ibid., 462–65.

58. Fourrier, *L'enseignement*, 71, 83–84, 89–91; Gontard, *1789–1833*, 445–51; Langlois, *Catholicisme*; Raymond Grew and Patrick J. Harrigan, *School, State, and Society: the Growth of Elementary Schooling in Nineteenth Century France: a Quantitative Analysis* (Ann Arbor, MI, 1991), 251.

59. Fourrier, *L'enseignement*, 123–24; Gontard, *1789–1833*, 462–65, 475–76.

60. Dansette, *Religious History*, 216–20; Gontard, *1789–1833*, 475–78.

61. Ordinance of Feb. 29, 1816, in Octave Gréard, *La législation de l'instruction primaire en France depuis 1789 jusqu'à nos jours*, 2 vols. (Paris, 1874), 1:84–95; J. L. S. Vincent, "État actuel de l'instruction publique, pour les Protestans français," in *Vues sur le Protestantisme en France*, 2 vols. (Nîmes, 1829), 2:21–36; Charles Rodney Day, *Freedom of Conscience and Protestant Education in France, 1815–1885* (Ph.D. diss., Harvard Univ., 1964), 1, 16, 21, 26, 205–6.

62. Gréard, *Législation de l'instruction primaire* 1:96, 192–93; Berkovitz, *Jewish Identity*, 152–59; Fourrier, *L'enseignement*, 71.

63. Laws of June 28, 1833, and June 23, 1836, in Giacometti, *Geschichte*, 66–70; and Gréard, *Législation de l'instruction primaire* 1:392–99.

64. Gontard, *1789–1833*, 523–36; id., *Les écoles primaires de la France bourgeoise, 1833–1875* (Toulouse, 1964), 3–6, 12–14; Grew and Harrigan, *School, State, and Society*, 31–53, 251.

65. Statutes of Apr. 25, 1834, in Gréard, *Législation de l'instruction primaire* 1:317–23.

66. Ministère de l'instruction publique et des cultes, *Statistique de l'enseignement primaire, 1901–1902* (Paris, 1904), xxxv–xxxvi; Day, *Freedom of Conscience*, 207–8; Ministère de l'instruction publique, des cultes, et des beaux-arts, *Statistique de l'enseignement primaire, 1876–1877*, 2 vols. (Paris, 1878), 1:214–25.

67. Octave Gréard, *Éducation et instruction*, 3, *Enseignement secondaire*, 2d ed. (Paris, 1889), 284–99.

68. The laws and ordinances of Oct. 5, 1814, and June 16, 1828, in Debidour, *1789–1870*, 695–96, 699–701; Fourrier, *L'enseignement*, 67–69, 74–75, 83, 89–91, 127–29; Antoine Prost, *Histoire de l'enseignement en France, 1800–1967* (Paris, 1968), 28–31.

69. Law of Mar. 15, 1850, in Giacometti, *Geschichte*, 79–94.

70. Gréard, *Éducation et instruction*, 1, *Enseignement primaire*, 3d ed. (Paris, 1895), 72.

71. Regulation of Aug. 17, 1851, in Gréard, *Législation de l'instruction primaire* 1:257–65; Gontard, *1833–1875*, 119–20.

72. Edgar Quinet, *L'enseignement du peuple* (Paris, 1850); Ferdinand Buisson and Frederic Ernest Farrington, eds., *French Educational Ideals of Today: an Anthology of the Molders of French Educational Thought of the Present* (Yonkers-on-Hudson, NY, 1919), 1–4.

73. Ministère de l'instruction publique, *Statistique de l'enseignement sécondaire en 1865* (Paris, 1868), 240; Fourrier, *L'enseignement*, 132; Prost, *Histoire de l'enseignement*, 45; William V. Bangert, *A History of the Society of Jesus*, rev. ed. (St. Louis, MO, 1986), 454–55.

74. Grew and Harrigan, *School, State, and Society*, 279–83; Gontard, *1833–1875*, 135–43.

75. Day, *Freedom of Conscience*, 207–8; Berkovitz, *Jewish Identity*, 150–91.

76. *Annuaire Protestant 1865–1867*; Day, *Freedom of Conscience*, chap. 7.

77. Gontard, *1833–1875*, 227–30.

78. Law of July 12, 1875, in Giacometti, *Geschichte*, 98–103.

CHAPTER 9

1. Jean-Michel Gaillard, *Jules Ferry* (Paris, 1989), 477–81.

2. *Annuaire statistique de la France, 1878* (Paris, 1878), 52–55. Official actions pertaining to the religions were published in the *Journal Officiel*, which also published the *budget des cultes* and reports of the debates in the legislature about religion.

3. See Zaccaria Giacometti, *Quellen zur Geschichte der Trennung von Staat und Kirche* (Tübingen, 1926; repr. ed., Aalen, 1974), 116–17; Laura Governatori Renzoni, *La separazione tra stato e chiese in Francia e la tutela degli interessi religiosi* (Milan, 1977), 53–58; Antonin Debidour, *L'Église Catholique et l'état sous la Troisième République, 1870–1906*, 2 vols. (Paris, 1906–9), 1:passim.

4. *Moniteur universel*, Oct. 11, 1845; *Journal Officiel*, Sept. 6, 1881; Charles-Robert Ageron, *Les Algériens musulmans et la France, 1871–1919*, 2 vols. (Paris, 1968), 1:297–98, 307–15. The Muslim attendance percentages are calculated from figures given in various tables in Gouvernement Général Civil de l'Algérie, *État de l'algérie au 31 décembre 1882* (Alger, 1883).

5. Decree of Aug. 26, 1881, in *Journal Officiel*, Sept. 6 and 22, 1881.

6. Édouard Petit, *Organisation des colonies françaises et des pays de protectorat*, 2 vols. (Paris, 1894–95) 2:16.

7. See, for example, the *budget des cultes* for 1887, in *Journal Officiel*, Feb. 27, 1887.

8. Maurice Gontard, *L'oeuvre scolaire de la Troisième République: l'enseignement primaire en France de 1876 à 1914* (Toulouse, 1967), 26–28.

9. Ferry, speech at the Masonic Lodge Clémente-amitié, 1876, quoted in Antoine Prost, *Histoire de l'enseignement en France, 1800–1967* (Paris, 1968), 212.

10. Ferdinand Buisson, "L'intuition morale," Aug. 31, 1878, in id., *La foi laïque: extraits de discours et d'écrits, 1878–1911* (Paris, 1912), 3–7; id., *La religion, la morale et la science: leurs conflit dans l'education contemporaine* (Paris, 1904), 178–83; Jean-Marie Mayeur, "Ferdinand Buisson," *Dictionnaire du Monde Religieux dans la France Contemporaine, 5, Les Protestants*, ed. André Encrevé (Paris, 1988), 106–8.

11. Ferry, quoted in Gontard, *1876–1914*, 30.

12. Ferry, quoted in Gaillard, *Jules Ferry*, 493.

13. Ibid., 424–25, 434–35.

14. Ferry, quoted in ibid., 429–30.

15. Ferry, "Letter to the Primary Teachers of France," Nov. 17, 1883, in Ferdinand Buisson and Frederic Ernest Farrington, eds., *French Educational Ideals of Today: an Anthology of the Molders of French Educational Thought of the Present* (Yonkers-on-Hudson, NY, 1919), 6.

16. Law of Mar. 28, 1882, in Giacometti, *Geschichte*, 113–16; Gaillard, *Jules Ferry*, 428–32.

17. Law of Mar. 18, 1880, in Giacometti, *Geschichte*, 106.

18. Ferry, Apr. 23, 1879, in Gaillard, *Jules Ferry*, 434–35; Edouard Lockroy, speech in the Chamber of Deputies, Dec. 17, 1880, in Prost, *Histoire de l'enseignement*, 212–13; Geoffrey Cubitt, *The Jesuit Myth: Conspiracy Theory and Politics in Nineteenth Century France* (Oxford, 1993).

19. Louis Gobron, *Législation et jurisprudence de l'enseignement public et de l'enseignement privé en France* (Paris, 1896), 422–27; *Statistique de l'enseignement primaire, 1876–1877*, 21; Charles Fourrier, *L'enseignement français de 1789 à 1945* (Paris, 1965), 208.

20. Decree of Mar. 28, 1880, in Giacometti, *Geschichte*, 108–10.

21. Debidour, *1870–1906* 1:233–50; decree of Mar. 29, 1880, in Giacometti, *Geschichte*, 107–8.

22. Ferry, speech in the Chamber of Deputies, Nov. 9, 1880, in Gaillard, *Jules Ferry*, 444–45; Debidour, *1870–1906* 1:240–50.

23. Raymond Grew and Patrick J. Harrigan, *School, State, and Society: the Growth of Elementary Schooling in Nineteenth Century France: a Quantitative Analysis* (Ann Arbor, MI, 1991), 299; Ozouf, *L'École*, 272–73.

24. Gontard, *1876–1914*, 29–30; Prost, *Histoire de l'enseignement*, 376–80.

25. Buisson, "An Experiment in Moral Teaching at Fontenay-aux-Roses," Apr. 1900, in Buisson and Farrington, eds., *French Educational Ideals*, 43–58.

26. Law of June 17, 1881, in Giacometti, *Geschichte*, 110–11.

27. Pierre Chevallier, *La séparation de l'Église et de l'École: Jules Ferry et Léon XIII* (Paris, 1981), 274–81; Grew and Harrigan, *School, State, and Society*, 299; Prost, *Histoire de l'enseignement*, 377.

28. Law of Mar. 28, 1882, in Giacometti, *Geschichte*, 113.

29. Law of Oct. 30, 1886, in ibid., 117–29; decree and *arrêté* of Jan. 18, 1887, in *Lois et règlements organiques de l'enseignement primaire en France, 1881–1898* (Paris, 1898), 28–36.

30. *Journal Officiel*, Apr. 6, 1888; Gobron, *Legislation*, 424; Fourrier, *L'enseignement*, 208.

31. Grew and Harrigan, *School, State, and Society*, 291.

32. Law of June 17, 1881, in Giacometti, *Geschichte*, 111–12; Fourrier, *L'enseignement*, 188–93; Grew and Harrigan, *School, State, and Society*, 216–19.

33. Prost, *Histoire de l'enseignement*, 95, 273–74; Grew and Harrigan, *School, State, and Society*, 291; Fourrier, *L'enseignement*, 179.

34. Law of Mar. 28, 1882, in *Lois et règlements*, 5–9; Debidour, *1870–1906* 2:280–87, 301–314; Chevallier, *La séparation*, 283–341; Grew and Harrigan, *School, State, and Society*, 55–60.

35. Debidour, *1870–1906* 2:280–87.

36. Phyllis Stock-Morton, *Moral Education for a Secular Society* (Albany, NY, 1988), 101–4; Buisson and Farrington, eds., *French Educational Ideals*, 17–31; P.-H. Gay and O. Montreux, eds., I. L. Kandel, trans., *French Elementary Schools: Official Courses of Study* (New York, 1926), 31–34.

37. Gontard, *1876–1914*, 104–9.

38. Ferry to the primary teachers of France, Nov. 17, 1883, in Fourrier, *L'enseignement*, 237–42, and in Buisson and Farrington, eds., *French Educational Ideals*, 5–15; Grew and Harrigan, *School, State, and Society*, 291.

39. Edmond Blanguernon, "A Morning Prayer," and Buisson, "An Experiment in Moral Teaching at Fontenay-aux-Roses," in Buisson and Farrington, eds., *French Educational Ideals*, 50–51, 54–55, 173–75.

40. Félix Pécaut, "The Woman Normal School Principal," and Buisson, "Education of the Will," in ibid., 84–86, 160–62.

41. Louis Capéran, *Histoire contemporaine de la laïcité française*, 3 vols. (Paris, 1957–61).

42. *Statistique de l'enseignement primaire, 1901–1902* (Paris, 1904); Grew and Harrigan, *School, State, and Society*, 280.

43. Charles Rodney Day, *Freedom of Conscience and Protestant Education in France, 1815–1885* (Ph.D. diss., Harvard Univ., 1964), 210–11.

44. Decree of Feb. 13, 1883, in *État de l'Algérie . . . 1882*, 192–207; decree of Nov. 8, 1887, in *Journal Officiel*, Nov. 9, 1887; Ageron, *Algériens* 1:336–42, 2:923–28.

45. Law of July 1, 1901, in Giacometti, *Geschichte*, 131–35.

46. Leo XIII to President Emile Loubet, Mar. 23, 1900, and Cardinal Rampolla, note annexed to M. Nisard to M. Delcassé, July 6, 1901, in Giacometti, *Geschichte*, 147–49.

47. *The Statesman's Yearbook, 1906* (London, 1906), 836–40.

48. Laws of July 7, 1904, and Jan. 2, 1905, in Giacometti, *Geschichte*, 198–200, 205–9.

49. Pius X to President Loubet, Dec. 2, 1903, and Pius X, Consistorial Allocution, Nov. 14, 1904, in Giacometti, *Geschichte*, 157–59, 200–203; Buis-

son, "La liberté des congrégations et la liberté de l'enseignement," Sept. 10, 1902, in id., *La foi laïque*, 101–17.

50. Fourrier, *L'enseignement*, 208; Gontard, *1876–1914*, 136, 142, 145, 148, 150; Grew and Harrigan, *School, State, and Society*, 280; Prost, *Histoire de l'enseignement*, 218.

51. Gontard, *1870–1914*, 141–50, 172–79; Prost, *Histoire de l'enseignement*, 218.

52. The texts of the bills, laws, and main decrees and circulars up to 1908 are in Giacometti, *Geschichte*, 209–94, 302–14, 319–28, 338–54.

53. Law of Dec. 9, 1905, in ibid., 272–86.

54. Armands Lods, *La nouvelle législation des cultes protestants en France, 1905–1913: recueil complet des lois, décrets, arrêtés ministériels, statuts régissant les associations cultuelles protestantes* (Paris, 1914).

55. Encyclicals of Feb. 11 and Aug. 10, 1906, in Debidour, *1870–1906* 2: 588–601; letter of the archbishops and bishops of France, Sept. 7, 1906, in Giacometti, *Geschichte*, 316–19.

56. Circulars from the minister of public instruction and religions, Dec. 1 and 10, 1906, and laws of Jan. 2, 1907, and Apr. 8, 1908, in Giacometti, *Geschichte*, 319–28, 349–54.

57. Jean-Michel Leniaud, *L'administration des cultes pendant la périod concordataire* (Paris, 1988), 11–12, 211–16.

58. Encyclical of Jan. 6, 1907, and Allocution of Apr. 15, 1907, in Giacometti, *Geschichte*, 329–33, 345–46.

59. Ageron, *Algériens* 2: 893–97, 1234.

60. For the same language on opposite sides, see Declaration by François-Alphonse Aulard, Ferdinand Buisson, Charles Langlois, Charles Seignebos, and other members of the Comité pour défendre à l'étranger la politique religieuse de la France, *Les Texts de la Politique Française en Matière Ecclésiastique, 1905–1908* (Paris, 1909); and letter of the archbishops and bishops of France, Sept. 7, 1906, in Giacometti, *Geschichte*, 316.

61. G. Bonet-Maury, *La liberté de conscience depuis l'édict de Nantes jusqu'à la séparation, 1598–1905* (Paris, 1909).

62. Buisson, *La foi laïque*, xiii–xiv. During the ideological polemics of these years, the clarity and conviction of Buisson's *La foi laïque* in 1912 was matched among Catholic thinkers by Joseph Vaujany, *L'école primaire en France sous la Troisième République* (Paris, 1912). Their statements and rhetoric oppose each other, but both indicate the religious character and meaning of the *écoles laïques*.

63. Gay and Mortreux, eds., *French Elementary Schools*, 56–64.

CHAPTER 10

I wish to thank the Institute of History, Catholic University of Valparaiso, Chile, for its generous hospitality during the Spring (southern hemisphere) semester of 1994 which enabled me to advance and largely complete my work on this chapter.

1. The best general account remains J. Lloyd Mecham, *Church and State in Latin America*, rev. ed. (Chapel Hill, NC, 1966).

2. Technically the *patronato* was only one such power, but it has come to refer to the whole set.

3. The most serious such effort was made in the late 1840s: see Carlos Oviedo Cavada, *La misión Irarrázaval en Roma, 1847–1850* (Santiago, 1962). Unless otherwise indicated, all books cited in these notes were published in Santiago, Chile.

4. See Simon Collier, *Ideas and Politics of Chilean Independence, 1808–1833* (Cambridge, 1967), 163–64.

5. *Memoria política sobre si conviene en Chile la libertad de cultos* (Lima, 1827), 4.

6. *El Telégrafo*, no. 72, Santiago, Mar. 24, 1820. Unless otherwise indicated all newspapers or journals cited in notes were published in Santiago, Chile.

7. Javier González E., "Portales y la Iglesia," in Bernardino Bravo Lira, ed., *Portales y la consolidación del gobierno civil* (1989), 235–40.

8. Sergio Vergara Q., "Iglesia y Estado en Chile, 1750–1850," *Historia* 20 (1985): 347–52.

9. See Simon Collier, "Conservatismo chileno 1830–1860: temas e imágenes," *Nueva Historia* 2:7 (London, 1983): 143–63.

10. Edward Gibbon, *The History of the Decline and Fall of the Roman Empire*, ed. David Womersley, 3 vols. (London, 1994), 3:1004.

11. "St Thomas of Canterbury shone in the Church of God . . . and lifted it out of the slavery into which it had been condemned by the odious despotism of the kings of England": sermon by Fr. José Manuel Orrego, printed in *Revista Católica*, no. 480, Jan. 5, 1857, 2131.

12. Ibid., no. 1032, Nov. 7, 1868, 326.

13. Anon., *La tumba de Errázuriz* (1868), 17.

14. Abdón Cifuentes, *Memorias*, 2 vols. (1936), 1:165–67.

15. See Manuel Antonio Tocornal's remarks in SCN(D), July 22, 1865. The congressional record was printed continuously from 1846, and bound up annually, though without volume numbers. Sessions are referred to here by their date: sittings of the Chamber of Deputies are indicated as SCN(D), those of the Senate as SCN(S).

16. Trumbull deserves a biography. See the sketch of his life in Margarette Daniels, *Makers of South America* (New York, 1916), 185–202. Trumbull eventually became a Chilean citizen.

17. The Intendant of Valparaiso, in a striking demonstration of masterly inactivity, ruled on this occasion that only churches which had bells (the Anglican church obviously did not) could be deemed to be public: see the indignant articles in *Revista Católica*, no. 535, Mar. 22, 1858 and no. 536, Mar. 27, 1858.

18. David Trumbull, *The Constitutional History of Chile. A lecture delivered before the Young Men's Christian Association* (Valparaiso, 1883), 13.

19. See for instance, the exchanges (on the Bible) between Trumbull and

Fr. Francisco Martínez Garfías printed in *Revista Católica*, no. 539, Apr. 24, 1858, 2618–21; no. 545, May 29, 1858, 2657–61 and 2662–64; and no. 546, June 1, 1858, 2666–71. Trumbull's most famous polemic (1863) was with Fr. Mariano Casanova, on the veneration of saints.

20. Diego Barros Arana, *Un decenio de la historia de Chile, 1841–1851*, 2 vols. (1905–6), 2:552–68.

21. John Mayo, *British Merchants and Chilean Development, 1851–1886* (Boulder, CO, 1987), 23–28.

22. No. 189, Sept. 7, 1849, 151.

23. No. 281, Oct. 30, 1852.

24. *Revista Católica*, no. 213, July 24, 1850, 348. Italics in the original.

25. Ibid., no. 216, Aug. 14, 1850, 373.

26. Ricardo Donoso, *Las ideas políticas en Chile*, 3d ed. (Buenos Aires, 1975), 174–75.

27. *Revista Católica*, no. 360, May 18, 1854.

28. "¿Porqué odia al clero el Monttvarismo?" ibid., no. 1034, Nov. 21, 1868 and no. 1035, Nov. 28, 1868.

29. See Justo Arteaga Alemparte, *El desquite de un prelado* (1868).

30. For a recent discussion of the Radicals and the Freemasons, see Cristián Gazmuri, *El "48" chileno: igualitarios, reformistas, radicales, masones y bomberos* (1992), 129–48 and 172–85.

31. Benjamín Oviedo, *La masonería en Chile* (1929), 155.

32. SCN(S), Nov. 28, 1873.

33. Domingo Santa María to José Victorino Lastarria, July 30, 1865: Patricio Estellé, "El debate de 1865 sobre la libertad de cultos y de conciencia," *Estudios de Historia de las Instituciones Políticas y Sociales* 2 (1967): 219.

34. Ricardo Krebs, "El pensamiento de la Iglesia frente a la laicización del Estado en Chile, 1875–1885," in Ricardo Krebs et al., *Catolicismo y laicismo. Las bases doctrinarias del conflicto entre la Iglesia y el Estado, 1875–1885* (1981), 29–31.

35. SCN(D), June 12, 1865.
36. Ibid., June 19, 1865.
37. Ibid.
38. Ibid., June 16, 1865.
39. Ibid., June 30, 1865.
40. Ibid., June 16, 1865.
41. Ibid., June 23, 1865.
42. Ibid., June 12, 1865.
43. Ibid., June 16, 1865.
44. Ibid.
45. Ibid., June 23, 1865.
46. Ibid., Aug. 1, 1865.
47. Ibid., June 12, 1865.
48. Ibid., June 30, 1865.
49. Ibid., Aug. 5, 1865.
50. Ibid., June 16, 1865.
51. Ibid., June 23, 1865.
52. Ibid.
53. Ibid., June 16, 1865.
54. Ibid., July 3, 1865.
55. Ibid., July 8, 1865.

56. This in fact is the interpretation of the most recent student of the debates, the late Patricio Estellé, in his "El debate de 1865," 223–24.

57. "Estatuto del Club de la Reforma," Sept. 1868; as repr. in Patricio Estellé, "El Club de la Reforma de 1868–1871," *Historia* 9 (1970): 134.

58. SCN(D), Aug. 3, 1867.

59. Pastoral, Dec. 1884, quoted in Krebs, "El pensamiento de la Iglesia," 26.

60. Quoted in ibid., 56.

61. *Revista Católica*, no. 978, Sept. 28, 1867, 287–88.

62. Quoted in Sofía Correa, "El partido conservador ante las leyes laicas, 1881–1884," in Krebs et al., *Catolicismo y laicismo*, 81.

63. See Sol Serrano, *Universidad y nación. Chile en el siglo XIX* (1994), 81–89.

64. Letter of Feb. 18, 1873: *Revista Chilena de Historia y Geografía* 70 (1930): 70.

65. SCN(S), Dec. 15, 1873.

66. For a full account, see Agustín Edwards, *Cuatro presidentes de Chile*, 2 vols. (Valparaiso, 1932), 2:195–242.

67. Letter of Dec. 15, 1872: *Revista Chilena de Historia y Geografía* 76 (1932): 54–55.

68. SCN(D), Nov. 19, 1873.   69. Ibid., Nov. 14, 1873.

70. Ibid., June 19, 1873.   71. Ibid., Nov. 12, 1873.

72. Ibid., Nov. 30, 1875.

73. Ibid., Oct. 10, 1872. The congressional record does not make clear whether it was Pedro León Gallo or his brother Angel Custodio (both in the Chamber at the time) who staged the interruption.

74. SCN(S), Dec. 10, 1873.   75. Ibid., Dec. 15, 1873.

76. Ibid., Oct. 26, 1874.   77. SCN(D), Nov. 19, 1873.

78. Ibid., June 21, 1873.   79. Ibid., Oct. 29, 1877.

80. Ibid., Aug. 21, 1877.   81. Ibid., Aug. 16, 1869.

82. Ibid., Sept. 9, 1874.   83. SCN(S), June 12, 1874.

84. SCN(D), Nov. 11, 1873.   85. Ibid., Nov. 20, 1873.

86. Letter to Guillermo Matta, Sept. 11, 1882. *Revista Chilena de Historia y Geografía* 38 (1920): 334.

87. Abdón Cifuentes, *Discursos*, 2 vols. (1897–98), 2:43.

88. Domingo Santa María to Pedro Pablo Figueroa, Sept. 8, 1885: F. A. Encina and Leopoldo Castedo, *Resumen de la historia de Chile*, 8th ed., 3 vols. (1970), 3:1987.

89. For the archiepiscopal question, see Miguel Guzmán Rosales and Octavio Vio Henríquez, *Don Francisco de Paula Taforó y la vacancia arzobispal de Santiago, 1878–1887* (1964).

90. Carlos Walker Martinez, *Historia de la administración Santa María* (1889), 241.

91. Many such incidents are documented in *Las reformas teolójicas de 1883 ante el país i la historia* (1884), 403–515, and in Walker M., *Historia*, 195–227.

92. Letter to Alberto Blest Gana, Aug. 20, 1883; in Alfredo Santa María, ed., *De Taforó a Casanova* (1947), 162.

93. SCN(D), Aug. 25, 1883.   94. Ibid., July 3, 1883.

95. Ibid., Aug. 30, 1883.   96. Ibid., July 3, 1883.

97. Ibid., July 10, 1883.   98. Ibid., July 3, 1883.

99. Ibid., July 31, 1883.   100. Ibid., Aug. 23, 1883.

101. Ibid., Aug. 11, 1883.   102. Ibid., Jan. 5, 1884.

103. Ibid., Aug. 11, 1883.

104. Ibid., Jan. 5, 1884.

105. Ibid., July 10, 1883.

106. Ibid.

107. Ibid., Aug. 11, 1883.

108. Ibid., Aug. 16, 1883.

109. *Las reformas teolójicas de 1883 ante el país*, 100.

110. SCN(D), Aug. 25, 1883.

111. Walker M., *Historia*, 238, 267.

112. SCN(D), Aug. 9, 1883.

113. Ibid., Aug. 11, 1883.

114. Ibid., Aug. 21, 1883.

115. Ibid., Aug. 23, 1883.

116. Ibid., Aug. 30, 1883.

117. Ibid., July 31, 1883.

118. Ibid., Sept. 9, 1874.

119. Letter to Guillermo Matta, Aug. 18, 1884, repr. in *Revista Chilena de Historia y Geografía* 38 (1920): 341.

120. SCN(D), July 14, 1883.

121. *Las reformas teolójicas de 1883 ante el país*, vi.

122. Walker M., *Historia*, 261.

123. Crescente Errázuriz, *Algo de lo que he visto* (1934), 435–67.

124. The Church tried to remain neutral, but individual priests supported the Congress. See Carlos Oviedo Cavada, "La Iglesia en la Revolución de 1891," *Historia* 14 (1979): 275–314.

125. SCN(D), Aug. 3, 6, and 7, 1897.

126. Ibid., Aug. 6, 1897.

127. *Revista Católica* (3d ser.), 24 (1913): 1065.

128. Ibid., 216.

129. *Sinceridad. Chile íntimo en 1910*, by Dr. J. Valdés Cange (1910), 351. Italics in the original.

130. Fernando Pinto Lagarrigue, *Crónica política del siglo XX* (1970), 62–68.

131. Speech during President Balmaceda's visit to Copiapó, Mar. 1889, in Arturo Lois Fraga and Mario Vergara Gallardo, *Librepensadores y laicos en Atacama* (1956), 118.

132. *Historia de Chile 1891–1973* 1 (1981): 99–102.

133. Lois and Vergara, *Librepensadores y laicos*, 134.

134. María Eugenia Pinto P., "El positivismo chileno y la laicización de la sociedad, 1874–1884," in Krebs et al., *Catolicismo y laicismo*, 211–55.

135. SCN(D), Oct. 26, 1877.

136. To Francisco Ugarte Zenteño, July 16, 1883. *Revista Chilena de Historia y Geografía* 119 (1952): 106.

137. SCN(D), Aug. 16, 1883. (Juan Serapio Lois's wife, Raquel, was certainly an exception.)

138. Voltaire Lois, Radical, born 1919, and Renan Fuentealba, Christian Democrat, born 1917.

139. *Revista Católica*, 3d ser., 24 (1913): 213–14.

140. Lois and Vergara, *Librepensadores y laicos*, 256–58.

141. See Peter deShazo, *Urban Workers and Labor Unions in Chile, 1902–1927* (Madison, WI, 1983).

142. Pastoral of Aug. 30, 1906. *Revista Católica*, 3d ser., 11 (1906): 242.

143. Krebs, "El pensamiento de la Iglesia," 68.

144. The canonization of Chile's first saint (St. Teresa of Los Andes, a Car-

melite nun who died in 1920 at the age of nineteen) took place in March 1993. The Chilean Jesuit Fr. Alberto Hurtado was beatified in October 1994, with an attendance of several thousand Chileans (including the president of the republic) in St. Peter's Square. The timing of these events would have aroused suspicion among early twentieth-century anticlericals, but occasioned no unfavorable comment whatever in the 1990s.

CHAPTER 11

1. Elizabeth G. K. Hewat, *Vision and Achievement 1796–1956. A History of the Foreign Missions of the Churches United in the Church of Scotland* (Edinburgh, 1960), 1. The issue of liberty was also deployed as a rhetorical tool in a factional struggle within the Church of Scotland.

2. This is my own definition for purposes of this chapter. For the large literature on "confessionalism," see the useful recent summary in Benjamin J. Kaplan, *Calvinists and Libertines. Confession and Community in Utrecht 1578–1620* (Oxford, 1995), intro.

3. I am using the word "voluntarist" in a different sense from two related meanings. One is the philosophical term which denotes a commitment to the primacy of will. The other is a variant of the nineteenth-century term "voluntaryist," implying a commitment to the separation of church and state. For this use of the term see J. P. Ellens, *Religious Routes to Gladstonian Liberalism* (University Park, PA, 1994), and chapter 3 in this volume.

4. Cited in Clive Field, "A Godly People? Aspects of Religious Practice in the Diocese of Oxford, 1738–1936," *Southern History. A Review of the History of Southern England* 14 (1992): 50.

5. Cited in A. C. Underwood, *A History of the English Baptists* (London, 1947), 42.

6. Especially as it emerged outside the state churches. Enlightenment thought might in some cases strengthen "confessional" attitudes insofar as it stressed the instrumental character of religion as a method of maintaining social cohesion.

7. A notable case is the Church of England. There are cases of confessional attitudes working to a denomination's advantage in some circumstances, usually by strengthening internal cohesion.

8. I used the metaphor myself in Jeffrey Cox, *The English Churches in a Secular Society. Lambeth, 1870–1930* (New York, 1982), chap. 8; and in "The Missionary Movement," in Dennis Paz, ed., *Nineteenth Century English Religious Traditions* (Westport, CT, 1995), 197–220.

9. Although voluntarist religion, unlike confessional religion, legitimizes the decision to change religions in some contexts.

10. I am using the term master narrative in the useful sense deployed by Allan Megill in "'Grand Narrative' and the Discipline of History," in Frank Ankersmit and Hans Kellner, eds., *A New Philosophy of History* (Chicago, 1995), 151–73. In his formulation, a master narrative is a big story that makes smaller stories intelligible. Because it is a master narrative, it is often

partly hidden, lying in the background to be deployed selectively by the historian. Dorothy Ross uses the phrase "grand narrative" instead of "master narrative" in her "Grand Narrative in American Historical Writing: From Romance to Uncertainty," *American Historical Review* 100, 3 (1995): 651–77.

11. See Cox, *The English Churches*, chaps. 1 and 8; cf. further discussion in Steve Bruce, ed., *Religion and Modernization: Sociologists and Historians Debate the Secularization Thesis* (Oxford, 1992). See the closing chapter of Sheridan Gilley and W. J. Shiels, eds., *A History of Religion in Britain: Practice and Belief from Pre-Roman Times to the Present* (Oxford, 1994), for the centrality of secularization as an organizing story for modern religious history. In the secularization story, those who hold a religious point of view are doomed to marginalization by the secular forces of reason and science or, in later formulations, of technology and the rational bureaucratic organization of society. On the downward slope, men and women in the modern world who choose to be religious may do so, but only at the cost of consignment to the margins of modern society. Religious men and women appear in the modern world as sectarians, and therefore marginal, or as liberal, and therefore not really religious at all, or as "fundamentalist," anti-modern, reactionary, and a threat to all the values we hold dear.

12. On the latter group see chapters 8 and 9 in this volume.

13. It is important to keep in mind that not all evangelicals were voluntarists.

14. *Enquiry*, 79. The full title is *An Enquiry into the Obligations of Christians, to use means for the conversion of the Heathens in which the religious state of the different nations of the world, the success of former undertakings, and the practicability of further undertakings, are considered* (Leicester, 1792).

15. See Andrew Porter, "'Commerce and Christianity': the Rise and Fall of a Nineteenth-Century Missionary Slogan," *Historical Journal* 28 (1985): 597–621.

16. Sydney Smith, "Indian Missions," *Edinburgh Review* 12 (Apr. 1808): 179.

17. On Carey's work see E. D. Potts, *British Baptist Missionaries in India, 1793–1837. The History of Serampore and its Missions* (Cambridge, 1956); Kenneth Ingham, *Reformers in India, 1793–1837. An Account of the Work of Christian Missionaries on Behalf of Social Reform* (Cambridge, 1956).

18. See *Times Literary Supplement*, Mar. 19, 1993, 15.

19. See Edward W. Said, *Culture and Imperialism* (New York, 1993), 39–40, for his sketchy acknowledgment of the complicated consequences of mission work.

20. *Memoir of Anthony Norris Groves, Compiled Chiefly from his Journals and Letters*, 3d ed., by his widow (London, 1869), 99.

21. Groves, *Memoir*, 293.

22. Hans Cnattingius, *Bishops and societies. A study of Anglican colonial and missionary expansion 1698–1850* (London, 1952), 75.

23. Max Warren, ed., *To Apply the Gospel. Selections from the Writing of*

Henry Venn (Grand Rapids, MI, 1971), 20. This is Warren's description of Henry Venn.

24. Cited in Ainslie T. Embree, "Christianity and the State in Victorian India: Confrontation and Collaboration," in R. W. Davis and R. J. Helmstadter, eds., *Religion and Irreligion in Victorian Society: Essays in Honor of R. K. Webb* (London, 1992), 151.

25. Ibid., 151–65.

26. Ibid., 163.

27. On these issues see Arjun Appadurai, *Worship and Conflict under Colonial Rule: A South Indian Case* (Cambridge, 1981); Robert Frykenburg, "The Construction of Hinduism at the Nexus of History and Religion," *Journal of Interdisciplinary History* 23, 3 (1993): 523–50; Kenneth W. Jones, *The New Cambridge History of India 3, 1: Socio-Religious Reform Movements in British India* (Cambridge, 1989).

28. See Kenneth Jones, *Arya Dharm. Hindu Consciousness in 19th Century Punjab* (Berkeley, 1976).

29. Brian Stanley, *The Bible and the Flag: Protestant Missions and British Imperialism in the Nineteenth and Twentieth Centuries* (Leicester, 1990); Stephen Neill, *A History of Christianity in India, 1707–1858* (Cambridge, 1985).

30. Neill, *History of Christianity*, 431.

31. Robert Moffat, *Missionary Labours and Scenes in Southern Africa*, 11th ed. (New York, 1852), 29. On Van der Kemp see Elizabeth Elbourne, "Review Article: Concerning Missionaries: The Case of Van der Kemp," *Journal of Southern African Studies* 17, 1 (Mar. 1991): 153–64.

32. Smith, "Indian Missions," 172.

33. Ibid., 173.

34. For an example see Andrew Gordon, *Our India Missions. A Thirty Years' History of the India Mission of the United Presbyterian Church of North America* (Philadelphia, 1886), 157.

35. I have dealt with these issues in "Audience and Exclusion at the Margins of Imperial History," *Women's History Review* 3, 4 (1994).

36. Groves, *Memoir*, 230.

37. Carey, *Enquiry*, 64.

38. Groves, *Memoir*, 350.

39. For an introduction to the large literature on abolitionism, see the bibliography in Robin Blackburn, *The Overthrow of Colonial Slavery, 1776–1848* (London, 1988); on Indian missionaries and "social reform" see Ingham, *Reformers in India*; G. A. Oddie, *Social Protest in India. British Protestant Missionaries and Social Reform, 1850–1900* (New Delhi, 1979).

40. For a discussion of this and related controversies, see Andrew Porter, "Late Nineteenth Century Anglican Missionary Expansion. A Consideration of some Non-Anglican Sources," in Keith Baker, ed., *Studies in Church History* (Oxford, 1978), 355–56.

41. See Porter, "'Commerce and Christianity'," 597–621.

42. Moffat, *Missionary Labours*, 39.

43. Ibid., 332.

44. The Rev. Herbert Alfred Birks, *The Life and Correspondence of Thomas Valpy French, First Bishop of Lahore* (London, 1895), 43, 251.

45. Moffatt, *Missionary Labours*, 13–14.

46. Venn's career and ideas had some very interesting parallels with an American counterpart, Rufus Anderson (1796–1880). From 1832 until his retirement in 1866, Anderson was foreign secretary of the (mainly Congregationalist) American Board of Commissioners for Foreign Missions, the best-known and most prestigious American missionary society at mid century. On the parallels see the useful article by Wilbert R. Shenk, "Rufus Anderson and Henry Venn: A Special Relationship?" *International Bulletin of Missionary Research*, Oct. 1981, 168–72.

47. Venn, *To Apply the Gospel*, extract from a letter to a missionary in North India, the Rev. R. M. Lamb, 63.

48. CMS archives, file CM/L4, Mediterranean, 1854–64, Mar. 2, 1858, cited in Wilbert Shenk, *Henry Venn, Missionary Statesman* (Maryknoll, NY, 1983), 169.

49. See the comments by Max Warren in Warren, ed., *To Apply the Gospel*, 184.

50. Committee of Correspondence, Dec. 4, 1855, G/AZI/1, no. 89, cited in Warren, ed., *To Apply the Gospel*, 218.

51. CMS Archives, CA2/L3, Oct. 23, 1863, cited in Warren, ed., *To Apply the Gospel*, 213.

52. William Knight, *The Missionary Secretariat of Henry Venn, B. D. . . . with an introductory biographical chapter and a notice of West African commerce by his sons, the Rev. John Venn, and the Rev. Henry Venn* (London, 1880), 109. These are extracts from his private journal for Tuesday, Dec. 4, 1849.

53. Warren, ed., *To Apply the Gospel*, 213.

54. CMS Archives, CA2/L2, Oct. 21, 1856, cited in Warren, ed., *To Apply the Gospel*, 192.

55. Knight, *Missionary Secretariat*, 135.

56. Henry Venn, *The Missionary Life and Labours of Francis Xavier, taken from his own correspondence, with a sketch of the general results of Roman Catholic missions among the heathen* (London, 1862).

57. Carey, *Enquiry*, 65.

58. Venn, *Missionary Life and Labours*, iii.

59. Ibid., 155.

60. Ibid., 210 (emphasis his).

61. Ibid., 319.

62. Ibid., 79, quoting a speech of M. Bilault cited in *The Times*, Feb. 27, 1862.

63. Venn, *Missionary Life and Labours*, 79.

64. See Daniel O'Connor, *Gospel, Raj and Swaraj. The Missionary Years of C. F. Andrews 1904–14* (Frankfurt, 1990); cf. Jeffrey Cox, "C. F. Andrews and the Failure of the Modern Missionary Movement," in Stuart Mews, ed., *Modern Religious Rebels* (London, 1993), 226–44.

65. Venn, *Missionary Life and Labours*, 38.

66. In his famous pamphlet of 1792, Carey mentioned women only once, as part of the necessary impedimenta of a married Protestant missionary about to embark, "necessary for domestic purposes" he suggested, along with "[a] cow or two, and a bull." Carey, *Enquiry*, 74; cf. Jeffrey Cox, "Independent English Women in Delhi and Lahore," in Davis and Helmstadter, eds., *Religion and Irreligion in Victorian Society*, 166–84.

67. Cnattingius, *Bishops and Societies*, 52, citing SPCK Report, 1791 (London, 1792), 110.

68. George Washington Doane, *The Missionary Bishop* (New Jersey, 1835), cited in Cnattingius, *Bishops and Societies*, 201.

69. CMS Minute of 1861 on the Organization of Native Churches, CMS Archives, G/AZI/1, no. 116, July 9, 1861, cited in Warren, ed., *To Apply the Gospel*, 66–68.

70. Shenk, "Rufus Anderson and Henry Venn," 171. An American Congregationalist, Rufus Anderson, used the "three-self" triad as the basis for a major work, *Foreign Missions, Their Relations and Claims* (New York, 1869).

71. Warren, ed., *To Apply the Gospel*, passages cited on 28 and 63. Venn was using the phrase in internal minutes and letters in the early 1850s.

72. See C. Peter Williams, *The Ideal of the Self-Governing Church. A Study in Victorian Missionary Strategy* (Leiden, 1990), who tells a story of Venn's enlightened ideals defeated by narrow missionary professionalism. I have dealt with one case in "On Re-defining Crisis: The Victorian Crisis of Faith in the Punjab, 1880–1900," in Richard J. Helmstadter and Bernard Lightman, eds., *Victorian Faith in Crisis: Essays on Continuity and Change in Nineteenth Century Religious Belief* (Stanford, 1990).

73. Warren, ed., *To Apply the Gospel*, 124, citing Address to Islington Clerical Meeting, Jan. 10, 1865.

74. Ibid., 126.

75. Knight, *Missionary Secretariat*, 122, Mar. 22, 1851.

76. Richard Burton, *Wanderings in West Africa* (New York, 1991), 207.

77. Warren, ed., *To Apply the Gospel*, 78, citing a letter of Henry Venn to the bishop of Kingston on the state of the negroes of Jamaica, quoting from G/AZI/1, no. 152, Jan. 1867.

78. For a start, see Ayandele E. A., *The Missionary Impact on Modern Nigeria, 1842–1914. A Political and Social Analysis* (London, 1966); Andrew Porter, "Cambridge, Keswick, and Late Nineteenth-Century Attitudes to Africa," *Journal of Imperial and Commonwealth History* 5, 1 (1976): 5–34; Williams, *The Ideal of the Self Governing Church*.

79. Shenk, *Henry Venn*, xii (from the foreword by R. Pierce Beaver).

80. This is, I suspect, what happened in Tinnevelly, which along with Sierra Leone was treated in CMS literature as evidence of Vennite success.

Index

In this index an "f" after a number indicates a separate reference on the next page, and an "ff" indicates separate references on the next two pages. A continuous discussion over two or more pages is indicated by a span of page numbers, e.g., "57–59." *Passim* is used for a cluster of references in close but not consecutive sequence.

Library of Congress Cataloging-in-Publication Data

Freedom and religion in the nineteenth century / edited by
  Richard Helmstadter.
     p.   cm. — (The making of modern freedom)
  Includes bibliographical references and index.
  ISBN 0-8047-3087-3 (cloth : alk. paper)
  1. Freedom of religion—History—19th cen-
  tury.   I. Helmstadter, Richard J., 1934–   . II. Series.
  BV741.F79   1997
  323.44'2'09034—dc21   96-54045
                                                           CIP

ⓧ This book is printed on acid-free, recycled paper.

Original printing 1997
Last figure below indicates year of this printing:
06 05 04 03 02 01 00 99 98 97